FRANKIE AND JOHNNY

D1594034

Frankie and Johnny

Race, Gender, and the Work of
African American Folklore in 1930s America

STACY I. MORGAN

UNIVERSITY OF TEXAS PRESS ⬥ Austin

Requests for permission to reproduce material from this work should be sent to:
    Permissions
    University of Texas Press
    P.O. Box 7819
    Austin, TX 78713-7819
    http://utpress.utexas.edu/index.php/rp-form

♾ The paper used in this book meets the minimum requirements of ANSI/NISO
Z39.48-1992 (R1997) (Permanence of Paper).

LIBRARY OF CONGRESS CATALOGING-IN-PUBLICATION DATA

Names: Morgan, Stacy I., 1970–, author.
Title: Frankie and Johnny : race, gender, and the work of African American folklore
in 1930s America / Stacy I. Morgan.
Description: First edition. | Austin : University of Texas Press, 2017. | Includes
bibliographical references and index.
Identifiers: LCCN 2016035709
    ISBN 978-1-4773-1207-0 (cloth : alk. paper)
    ISBN 978-1-4773-1208-7 (pbk. : alk. paper)
    ISBN 978-1-4773-1209-4 (library e-book)
    ISBN 978-1-4773-1210-0 (non-library e-book)
Subjects: LCSH: African Americans—Folklore. | African Americans—Race identity. |
Sex roles—United States. | Popular music—United States—History and criticism. |
Music—Social aspects—United States—History and criticism. | Popular music—
United States—African influences. | Folk songs, English—United States.
Classification: LCC GR111.A47 M67 2017 | DDC 398.2089/96073—dc23
LC record available at https://lccn.loc.gov/2016035709

doi:10.7560/312070

As our American culture advances, it may be that classes will take up the Frankie song as seriously as a play by Molière or a Restoration comedy or the Provençal ballads of France.
CARL SANDBURG, *THE AMERICAN SONGBAG* (1927)

CONTENTS

ACKNOWLEDGMENTS

THIS BOOK WOULD not have been possible without the work of archivists who helped to connect me with the wealth of materials referred to in these pages. Five, in particular, who went above and beyond the call of duty in aiding my research were Todd Harvey of the American Folklife Center (Library of Congress), Marisa Bourgoin of the Archives of American Art (Smithsonian Institution), Barbara Hall and Jenny Romero of the Margaret Herrick Library (Academy of Motion Pictures Arts and Sciences, Beverly Hills), and Joellen ElBashir of Howard University's Moorland-Spingarn Research Center.

Terika Dean of the Lead Belly Estate, Brad Olsen of the New Britain Museum of American Art, and Emma Cormack of the University of Kansas's Spencer Art Museum helped supply high-quality copies of some of the images reproduced herein. My University of Alabama colleague Jeremy Butler shared technical advice on working with still images from movies.

Funding for books and for travel to conduct the archival research for this project came from the University of Alabama's College of Arts & Sciences Leadership Board and the Department of American Studies. My department chair, Lynne Adrian, provided tireless support in securing funding and whatever else was needed at every stage of the project.

Funding for expenses related to the book's images and copyright permissions was generously supplied by the Carla and Cleo Thomas Fund. The financial support that Carla and Cleo provide for our research endeavors in the Department of American Studies is truly extraordinary. I am further indebted to Cleo for his many years of rigorous correspondence, in which he has consistently offered candor, original insights, and more new kernels of knowledge than I could number.

The publishing consultant George Thompson has given of his time abundantly and provided sage advice on matters including the book's structure, negotiating the terrain of academic publishing, and revising the text. I am grateful to have had George in my corner throughout the process.

Robert Devens at the University of Texas Press latched onto this book in the making with infectious enthusiasm and exceeded what I thought possible in the quality of an editor. Whether helping conceptualize big-picture issues or thinking through minutiae of the book, Robert was exceptionally attentive to this project at every turn. Likewise, Sarah Rosen McGavick at UT Press patiently and efficiently responded to an abundance of scattered e-mails in working through the business aspects of preparing the book for publication. Kip Keller provided stellar contributions on the copyediting front. Lynne Chapman oversaw all revisions to the manuscript with remarkable promptness and professionalism.

Several friends have given abundantly of their time to help sharpen this book. My Department of American Studies colleagues Jolene Hubbs and Eric Weisbard each read a chapter from the manuscript and provided remarkably detailed, essential feedback on both the content of my arguments and the quality of my prose. Naomi Eu-jin Shadix offered her expertise on dance movements, history, and terminology to help refine my analysis of Ruth Page and Bentley Stone's *Frankie and Johnny* ballet. Steve Bunker provided useful input on my discussion of the Mexican mural movement and its influence on the United States. Quintin Slovek kindly allowed me to cite from his unpublished essay on Thomas Hart Benton. Harrison Wallace gamely fielded a series of questions pertaining to the musical aesthetics of Mississippi John Hurt and Huddie Ledbetter. Edward Tang has weathered more miscellaneous conversation fragments about this project than anyone else over the past several years and, amazingly, has not once said, "Enough about Frankie and Johnny already."

I am indebted to my parents, Jerry and Betty Jo Morgan, for their example of living with open minds and kind hearts, and to Steve and Brenda Wynn, who have welcomed me so readily into their family. A fellow could not ask for better kinfolk. Above all, my thanks to Anne Wynn, for the gifts of love, laughter, and a passion for travel adventures. I am over the moon to be spending my life with you.

This book is dedicated to the memory of Zooey the Wonder Dog.

FRANKIE AND JOHNNY TAKE CENTER STAGE: AFRICAN AMERICAN FOLK CULTURE IN 1930S AMERICA

ON THE EVENING OF June 19, 1938, the choreographers Ruth Page and Bentley Stone debuted a one-act ballet entitled *Frankie and Johnny* at Chicago's Great Northern Theatre, with an orchestrated score by Jerome Moross and a libretto by Moross and Michael Blankfort.[1] The central features of Paul du Pont's set design consisted of a saloon and an adjacent walk-up apartment building that Page described as a "red-light house."[2] As the curtain lifted, three female Salvation Army musicians—listed in the playbill as "Saving Susies"—took up positions by a lamppost downstage left and subsequently served as a Greek chorus of sorts for the events to follow. In the introduction, they sang:

> *Frankie and Johnny were lovers,*
> *Oh Lord, and how they could love,*
> *Swore they'd be true to each other,*
> *True as the stars up above.*
> *He was her man,*
> *But he done her wrong.*

One of the most oft-repeated stanzas of one of the decade's most ubiquitous ballads, this refrain encapsulated the dramatic tension at the heart of both the song and its dance adaptation: true love betrayed, with tragic consequences looming. Frankie and Johnny were not high-born Greek or Shakespearean protagonists, however; this was a tale of love gone awry on the wrong side of the tracks, which was signaled immediately by the ballet's sets, costuming, and narrative. Frankie (Page) and Johnny (Stone) lounged on the front steps of the set's brothel before Frankie retreated to her ground-floor apartment; meanwhile another woman, Nellie Bly (Ann Devine), looked down onto the street from her first-floor window. Three sharply dressed men in long coats and top hats struck up a dance, but it was not long before Johnny coaxed one of them up the steps to Nellie's apartment; as the man entered, Nellie pulled down the blind, indicating none too subtly that vice was afoot, with Johnny in the role of pimp. A series of men entered and left Nellie and Frankie's quarters, handing payments to Johnny before exiting stage right.[3] Even more surprising, a policeman stationed at a nearby lamppost came over and joined Johnny and the other male cast members in lively steps that blended elements of ballet, tap, and popular dance, and then went to Frankie's room as yet another apparent client of her sexual services.

In keeping with Frankie's profession, her costume included heels, a light shoulder wrap, and a racy dress that rested off of her shoulders and was cut nearly up to the hip on her right side. Curiously, Page also wore a cross necklace for the role, despite the fact that the ballet featured no other overt religious references except for the Salvation Army singers. Johnny was clad smartly in a crisp shirt, vest, slacks, and shoes topped by spats. As the stage cleared and the action continued, Johnny removed Frankie's shoulder wrap and the couple joined on the banister of the brothel to initiate a daring pas de deux in which Frankie languidly intertwined with Johnny's frame in an assortment of intimate poses adapted from both classical ballet and modern dance. The duo then moved about the stage in tandem, evoking a romance far more licentious than genteel in flavor (figure 1.1). Evaluating the performance some four decades later, the dance scholar Marcia Siegel aptly described it as "raw, raunchy, and proud of it."[4]

Subsequently, the front of the saloon lifted to release a series of flashily dressed male and female dancers. After engaging briefly with two of these women, Johnny's attention was captured by the show's third principal character, Nellie Bly, as she emerged from her apartment with a male client in tow. Johnny and Nellie then flamboyantly merged ballet with steps from the Charleston. When Frankie reentered, the remaining dancers promptly formed a line of bodies to shield her line of sight from Johnny's dalliance with Nellie. Before Frankie could spy the errant couple, they absconded to Nellie's room. At this stage, Moross and Blankfort's libretto offered a variation on one of the most common verses of the "Frankie and Johnny" ballad tradition:

Frankie went down to the corner saloon,
To buy her a large glass of beer,
She said to the big fat bartender,
Has my lovin'est man been here?
He was her man,
But he done her wrong.

FIGURE 1.1. Ruth Page and Bentley Stone in the Federal Dance Project production of *Frankie and Johnny*, 1938.

As this verse unfolded, an aproned bartender emerged from the saloon and engaged Frankie in a spirited, earthy dance before whispering in her ear the truth of Johnny's infidelity. Again, Moross and Blankfort placed a stock ballad verse in the mouths of their chorus:

I ain't gonna tell you no fable,
I ain't gonna tell you no lie,
Your lovin'est man just left this place,
And with him went Nellie Bly.

As in the ballad, the bartender anchors the story in a red-light district and serves as a catalyst for Frankie's discovery of the betrayal and the ensuing tragic action.

Whereas ballad renditions of the popular tale typically moved on rapidly to Frankie's revenge, the ballet paused to allow Page room to express through dance the full range of Frankie's aggrieved response to betrayal. Although Frankie briskly danced to the steps of Nellie's apartment, initially she could not bring herself to enter. Instead, returning to center stage, she executed a double *en dedans pirouette*, followed by a rapid series of chaînés and stylish "lame ducks" (*piqué* turns *en dehors*), before falling to her knees and pantomiming vigorously with her arms over her head in a manner expressive of her emotional distress. Then, in the throes of heartbreak, she rolled back and forth unceremoniously in the street. Returning to the brothel, the hysterical Frankie stomped up the steps and pounded on Nellie's door with both fists. After reluctantly witnessing Johnny and Nellie's heated embrace, Frankie retrieved a gun from her apartment and then climbed a ladder to Nellie's window, now sporting an extraordinarily long scarlet kimono, of which Hallie Flanagan, the director of the Federal Theatre Project, wrote, "the train . . . unfurls like a great blot of blood."[5] The Saving Susies narrated this action in song:

> *Frankie went back to the crib,*
> *This time it wasn't for fun,*
> *'Cause under her old red kimono*
> *She toted a Forty-Four gun.*
> *Frankie went down to the Parlor house,*
> *She looked through the transom so high,*
> *And there she saw her lovin'est man,*
> *A-lovin' up Nellie Bly.*
>
> *Frankie threw open the Parlor house door,*
> *Johnny yelled, "Frankie don't shoot."*
> *Frankie she whipped out her Forty-Four,*
> *And with it went,*
> *Root-a-toot toot,*
> *Root-a-toot toot,*
> *Root-a-toot toot,*
> *Toot.*

In the accompanying dance, despite Johnny's pleas for his life and a brief, cowardly attempt to shield himself behind Nellie, Frankie shot her unfaithful lover multiple times, and he tumbled melodramatically down the brothel steps; in an absurdly comic gesture, he landed directly on his head with his feet upright in the air until Frankie brought him fully to rest on the ground.[6] As in many versions of the ballad, Johnny then was permitted a final plea for the audience's sympathy, voiced by the Saving Susies: "Roll me over easy, / Roll me over slow, / Roll me on my right side, / 'Cause my left side hurts me so."

In the ballet's final sequence, a crowd gathered around Johnny's corpse and a group of men carried in a coffin while Frankie began to use her erstwhile lover's shroud to hang herself from a nearby lamppost. At the last moment, though, Nellie intervened and the two former rivals for Johnny's affections then mourned together over his coffin, dancing a short routine in which they jointly held a large wreath of lilies. In the Saving Susies' parting lines, they sang:

Get out your rubber-tired carriages,
Get out your rubber-tired hacks,
'Cause they're gonna bury her Johnny,
And they ain't gonna never bring him back.

Frankie and Johnny were lovers,
Oh Lord, and how they could love,
Swore they'd be true to each other,
True as the stars up above
He was her man,
But he done her wrong.

In keeping with the spirit of the ballet as a whole, the concluding action pushed elements of overwrought melodrama to the point of comedy: Nellie returned to her apartment with the policeman, Frankie stretched herself out upon Johnny's coffin in a histrionic gesture of remorse, and the Saving Susies raised glasses of beer in a toast to the fallen protagonist.

In many respects, Page and Stone's *Frankie and Johnny* might have appeared an unlikely candidate for the high-culture stage of Chicago's Great Northern Theatre. Specifically, the production's open portrayal of prostitution, bawdy dance elements, and hybrid comic-melodramatic handling of the story's central tragedy might have seemed more naturally at home in a vaudeville revue. Several critics at the time certainly seemed to think so. Describing the production as "travesty in the name of art . . . purposely conceived to give a sordid impression of a lowly strata in American life," Janet Gunn lamented in the *Chicago Herald and Examiner*: "Burlesque has moved to the Great Northern Theatre. What we've heard to be classified as classy 'art' among strip-tease dancers and their like has been dolled up under the guise of smart, satirical sophistication and presented in a torrid version of the bar-room classic of 'Frankie and Johnny.'"[7] Likewise, during subsequent revivals, Page and Stone's ballet initially was banned in Boston in 1945 and was deemed scandalous by the Paris press in 1950.[8] Still, in 1938 Page and Stone managed not simply to give *Frankie and Johnny* a high-culture treatment, but also to do so with federal government sponsorship as one of the first headliners produced for the Chicago unit of the Federal Dance Theatre, a division of the Works Progress Administration's Federal Theatre Project. Given the pervasiveness of the ballad that inspired this production, neither audience nor sponsors could have been taken wholly by surprise by the risqué nature of Page and Stone's work. After all, scarcely anyone in 1930s America could have been unfamiliar with at least some iteration of the song "Frankie and Johnny."

Perhaps owing to the combination of the story's familiarity, its comic touches, and its sexual titillation, Ruth Page and Bentley Stone's *Frankie and Johnny* ballet proved extremely popular with audiences in 1938. The *Chicago Daily Tribune*'s Cecil Smith titled his review "Frankie-Johnny Ballet a Wow with Audience" and lauded Page and Stone for having "mimed their roles with great fidelity to the facts of the case, and with a wanton lack of inhibition that stayed within the bounds of taste by maintaining an unfailing touch of humor."[9] Even reviewers such as Claudia Cassidy, who penned scathing reviews of Page and Stone's *Frankie and Johnny* in 1938 and again in response to its 1945 revival in New York City, acknowledged, "But mind you, there are a lot of people on the other side of the fence. The theater rang with applause last night."[10] Similarly, despite noting that "it would be difficult to imagine a more unpromising basis for a ballet," Cyril Beaumont called *Frankie and Johnny* "definitely the biggest success of American ballet productions in 1938" and the most popular work of the Chicago Federal Dance Project's relatively short-lived existence, enjoying an impressive six-week run; even then, the production ended only because of prior commitments by the lead dancers to tour with other projects.[11]

In the context of 1930s cultural expression, Page and Stone's turn to "Frankie and Johnny" as subject matter was far from anomalous. "In this decade," observes Jane Becker, "the public encountered folk culture on festival and theater stages, over the radio and in recordings, at country fairs and museum exhibitions, in popular magazines and published fiction, and through department stores and mail-order catalogs."[12] In contexts both academic and commercial, African American folk culture became an especially popular source of inspiration for the work of creative artists in varied media and at many levels of cultural production. The emergence of this phenomenon is best understood through two sets of historical contexts: the broad history of efforts to document and creatively adapt US folk songs, which were initiated in the late nineteenth century and flourished as a full-fledged folk culture boom during the 1930s; and the specific history and traits of "Frankie and Johnny" that caused this song, in particular, to pique the interest of widely divergent audiences.[13]

DOCUMENTING AND ADAPTING US FOLK SONGS: ROOTS OF THE 1930S FOLK CULTURE BOOM

Few descriptors of cultural expression have proved as malleable as "folk." Conventional definitions equate folk culture with rural and traditional lifeways, passed down through generations in a local, face-to-face manner. Scholars use such a framework to distinguish folk culture from high culture and popular culture, which ostensibly operate by way of intensive formal training for an elite, cosmopolitan group of practitioners and appreciators (high culture) or by means of broadly accessible forms of expression and mass market commodities (popular culture). Yet from the earliest days of US folk song collecting, folklorists ascribed the appellation "folk" to songs of unknown authorship that were being passed down in traditional fashion within rural communities. Thus, in practice, published anthologies of US folk songs from the early decades of the twentieth century included a number of tunes of urban, commercial, and relatively recent origin that had migrated into everyday use in the hinterlands. As I will detail subsequently, "Frankie and Johnny" was one such song.

Moreover, the boundaries between folk, high, and popular culture categories were and are inevitably porous. For example, "Froggie Went A-Courting," a ballad dating at least to sixteenth-century England and circulated for generations by way of both oral and written traditions, finds modern adaptations by US artists as dissimilar as the classical composer Gregory Short (as part of his American Bicentennial Sonata no. 4, from 1976) and the top 40 recording star Bruce Springsteen (on the 2006 album *We Shall Overcome: The Seeger Sessions*).[14] Far from a recent phenomenon, high- and popular-culture adaptations like Short's and Springsteen's have a long history of following closely on the heels of the collecting of folk music of the rural, oral, and traditional sort. Generally speaking, the documentation of "traditional" folk music has been the domain of folklorists (ranging from amateur enthusiasts to academically credentialed scholars), and adaptation has been the purview of creative artists. Yet the history of folk music's documentation and adaptation is best understood as parallel and, very often, deeply intertwined enterprises. In fact, the appropriation of folk culture as raw material for the work of cosmopolitan creative artists dates to the very foundations of folklore as an enterprise of formal study.

In the latter half of the eighteenth century, Johann Gottfried von Herder remarked on the degree to which the German people had readily adopted the French language and French culture as their own—or more precisely, the extent to which Herder's formally educated countrymen were doing so. While such adaptation might seem natural enough, given the prominence of Versailles and the piecemeal division of German lands at the time, this turn of events dismayed Herder to no end. The fawning over all things French struck Herder as unnatural; he had developed a worldview predicated on the advance of distinctive national cultures, wherein each nation meaningfully advanced and contributed to a pluralist world culture only by building organically upon its own native traditions. Hence, Herder turned his attention to the German peasantry, or *Volk* (folk), because they had retained orally transmitted traditions of ballads in the German tongue, much more so than Herder's bourgeois peers. Herder vigorously set about collecting folk ballads, publishing a volume of them entitled *Stimmen der Völker in ihren Liedern* (Voices of the people in their songs) in 1773. He was motivated to preserve and celebrate these folk traditions not simply for their own sake, but also in the hope that they might serve as an archive of the German "national soul" from which formally educated writers, artists, and musicians might fashion a reinvigorated German high culture. Beginning with the publication of the first edition of *Kinder- und Hausmärchen* (*Children's and Household Tales*) by the brothers Wilhelm and Jacob Grimm in 1812, Herder's vision was put into concrete practice.[15]

Roughly half a century later, folklore emerged as a dedicated field of study in Great Britain, but with a somewhat different motive and premise. For nineteenth-century British scholars like William Thoms, Edward Tylor, and Andrew Lang, folklore embodied cultural relics of the British past, or "the surviving superstitions and stories, the ideas which are in our time but not of it," in Lang's phrasing.[16] Perceiving the culture of the folk as "a lively fossil that refuses to die," most early British folklorists collected ballads and other folklore items principally as a means of better understanding the roots of their own "elite, literate, civilized European cultures."[17] To be sure, this project was inflected with its own brand of nationalism, since folklore documentation was believed to delineate the gradual advance of "civilized" peoples from the ranks of barbarism by way of an intermediary folk stage, in keeping with the prevailing Enlightenment worldview. In short, the British folklore project was more antiquarian in focus than Herder's, with a greater emphasis on documenting historical roots than on directly recasting contemporary British high culture.

As exemplified by the American Folklore Society and its *Journal of American Folklore*, both founded in 1888, the early decades of folklore collecting and commentary in the United States hewed closely to the paradigm established by British scholars, but with the crucial difference of confronting the country's greater ethnic diversity. In a mission statement in the first issue of the

Journal of American Folklore, William Wells Newell urged his peers to collect what he described as the rapidly disappearing traditions of fragile folk groups such as Scotch-Irish Appalachians, American Negroes, French and German immigrants, and Indian tribes.[18] Hobbyists and formally trained academics alike submitted materials to the *Journal of American Folklore* in the ensuing decades, almost invariably following Newell's lead in looking to what they presumed to be the most rustic and isolated pockets of the national populace (including African Americans in the US South, quite often) for evidence of folk songs, legends, and superstitions that the authors framed as throwbacks to earlier stages of civilization. The frequent assertion that white Appalachian and southern Negro dialects embodied ossified forms of English dating back to the Middle Ages is but one case in point.

In the field of folk song, the early decades of formal study were dominated by the example of Francis James Child, who sought to document the carryover of English and Scottish ballads of storied pedigree, such as "Barbara Allen," to the United States. For Child, folk songs could only degrade from pristine "originals," which were ostensibly lost in the ether of (European, English-speaking) generations past. In the spirit of scholars like Lang, Child hunted for ballads as remnants of archaic British culture, allegedly preserved via folk culture among the rural, isolated descendants of immigrants in the United States.[19] Child was not interested in the study of songs indigenous to the Western Hemisphere or in the broader spectrum of folk groups outlined by Newell. Nor did Child have any real interest in folk singers per se. Since Child believed the folk to be unselfconscious bearers of tradition, his paradigm cast the performers of folk song as essentially interchangeable ciphers. Further, Child conceived of ballads exclusively as texts and, thus, largely dispensed with the musical aesthetics of folk song traditions and said nothing of how individual performers might innovatively reshape a given ballad. After all, Child saw himself as archiving cultural survivals and not, like Herder, as gathering raw material to spur on a new, living school of contemporary national expression.

Child's protégé George Lyman Kittredge helped ensure that Child's paradigm continued to exert a strong influence through his work as a faculty member at Harvard University from 1888 until 1936. Yet the grip of Child's paradigm on the field of US folk music began to loosen with emergence of alternative approaches in the early twentieth century. For example, despite being a student of Kittredge, John Lomax, in *Cowboy Songs and Other Frontier Ballads* (1910), documented a brand of vernacular music indigenous to the United States in form and subject matter. Lomax's study was groundbreaking in two other, related ways: first, he sought folk songs from living sources rather than in printed archives alone, and he included details about the singers who served as his informants; second, Lomax made a convincing case that his collected folk songs related to the contexts of the singers' everyday lives in contemporary US settings, providing the attentive listener with abundant evidence of the "conditions of pioneer life" and "that unique and romantic figure of modern civilization, the American cowboy."[20] In short, folk music offered a valuable window onto US social history. Although less innovative than Lomax, scholars such as Olive Dame Campbell and Cecil Sharp made important advances with respect to folk music of the Appalachians; while still concerned with ballads traceable to British or Scottish origins (a legacy of Child's influence), they went further than Child in recognizing that balladry remained a thriving folk tradition adaptable to new US contexts.[21]

These varying impulses coexisted in folk music studies of the 1910s and 1920s, a period when hobbyists and scholars were busy collecting an extraordinary quantity of US folk songs, which were published in numerous anthologies. Increasingly, too, folk music enthusiasts sought distinctive US vernacular traditions, branching out beyond ballads to examine genres such as dance music, blues, work songs, and spirituals. Equally significant, African American folk music—especially that associated with the South—featured prominently in this new corpus of folk songs, as exemplified by publications such as Howard Odum and Guy B. Johnson's *The Negro and His Songs* (1925), Dorothy Scarborough's *On the Trail of Negro Folk-Songs* (1925), and Newman I. White's *American Negro Folk-Songs* (1928). In addition, folklorists now frequently included African American songs in general surveys of US folk music, including titles such as John Harrington Cox's *Folk-Songs of the South* (1925), Carl Sandburg's *The American Songbag* (1927), and John Lomax and Alan Lomax's *American Ballads and Folk Songs* (1934).

Although broadening the canon of US folk songs in important ways, such studies are frequently shot through with the kind of racist assertions characteristic of much of white America during the period, including occasional racial epithets and pervasive assumptions of Negro backwardness. Even a text such as Sandburg's *American Songbag*, which generally steers clear of such demeaning discourse, seems at cross-purposes in its appraisal of "Frankie and Albert," the earliest known title for the ballad that eventually became better known as "Frankie and Johnny." On the one hand, Sandburg terms it America's "classical gutter song." Yet in a manner that echoes Herder, within the same paragraph the poet muses, "Some day, perhaps, we may arrive at a common understanding of our own art resources and how to use them. While the Frankie story deals with crime, violence, murder, adultery, its percentage in these respects is a good deal less than in the average grand opera."[22]

Along these lines, Sandburg worked avidly to popularize folk songs for a wide audience. *The American Songbag* came with piano arrangements so that readers could play the songs themselves, and the poet made public appearances in which he performed an array of the songs from the anthology to his own guitar accompaniment.[23] "Frankie and Albert" was among the songs in regular rotation as part of his repertoire. Even if the praise of authors like Sandburg for black musical expression all too often smacked of condescension, a significant number of the generation's folk music aficionados nonetheless portrayed African American contributions as a central wellspring of the vernacular culture that they wished to document, celebrate, and adapt in order to reinvigorate US cultural expression more broadly.

Although academic folklorists took scant notice of it at the time, the commercial music industry surpassed the likes of the Lomaxes and Sandburg in enhancing the visibility of US vernacular expression during the 1920s and 1930s. Put simply, far more Americans of the 1930s would have been acquainted with the song "Frankie and Johnny" (or "Frankie and Albert") through a phonograph record, the radio, or film than through the pages of a folk song anthology. Similarly, Depression-era creative artists like Ruth Page and Bentley Stone were able to turn to the folk song "Frankie and Johnny" as the basis for their ballet not only because of the academic folklore contexts described above, but also because of a combination of advances in recording technology and the marketing strategies of record business entrepreneurs. Driven primarily by profit, entrepreneurs in companies such as Columbia, Decca, Okeh, and RCA Victor exponentially advanced the circulation of vernacular music from far-flung regions of the country by performers both black and white, helping make folk songs a pervasive part of the US soundscape.

As chronicled by the recent work of scholars such as Elijah Wald, Karl Hagstrom Miller, and Edward Comentale, the US music business developed during the 1920s in a manner that blurred divisions between "folk" and "popular" culture while simultaneously tending to regiment categories of race to a striking degree through distinct "old-time" (white) and "race" (black) marketing categories.[24] The desire to reach consumers beyond established metropolitan markets led industry personnel to travel into regions of the country beyond the northeastern seaboard in order to identify musicians with local followings who might be pitched, in niche fashion, to audiences in those same regions. In the most widely recounted of these early ventures, Okeh's Ralph Peer traveled to Atlanta and produced phonographs by Fiddlin' John Carson in 1923. Peer already had recorded artists such as the early blues stars Mamie Smith and Sara Martin and the early jazz pianists Thomas "Fats" Waller and James P. Johnson for Okeh in New York City; after the surprising success with Carson, Peer traveled extensively and recorded an astonishing number of musicians, black and white, including Jimmie Rodgers, the Carter Family, and Blind Willie McTell, in a wide range of musical genres.[25]

As rival companies followed suit, records by these and scores of other artists brought the sounds of vernacular music—blues (urban and rural), string band music, dance tunes, ballads, and more—from the margins to the center of US popular music. Styles and specific performers previously associated with a particular local or regional context reached a much wider national (and even international) audience in ways that would have been impossible even a decade earlier. Hence, argues Barry Mazor, by the 1930s, "People down South were as likely to learn a folk ballad like 'Frankie and Johnny' from Jimmie [Rodgers] as from anyone else you might name, unless it was that noted cultural preservationist Mae West."[26] So too, as Zora Neale Hurston remarked during her work for the Federal Writers' Project in Florida, by the 1930s phonograph recordings could give rise to localized adaptations within juke joints and on work crews in a blending of commercial and folk music traditions.[27] After listening extensively to "old-time" and "race" music from the Bluebird label archives in the spring of 1939, even the previously skeptical folklorist Alan Lomax declared, "My opinion is that the commercial recording companies have done a broader and more interesting job of recording American folk music than the folklorists," and he compiled a "List of American Folk Songs on Commercial Records" (350 of them!) for the Library of Congress in 1940.[28] His new perspective also was reflected in his recording sessions of the late 1930s and the 1940s with musicians such as McTell and "Jelly Roll" Morton, who gained exposure through the commercial music industry before their work with folklorists like Lomax.[29]

For their part, musicians like Carson, McTell, Rodgers, and the Carters were hardly as isolated from cosmopolitan culture as early twentieth-century scholars sometimes imagined the "folk" to be. On the contrary, their musical influences included sheet music, early records, radio, and performances by other aspiring professional musicians on the southern tent show and vaudeville circuits, as well as informal, face-to-face transmissions of the sort assumed in conventional folklore paradigms.[30] Likewise, these musicians were driven by a desire for professional self-advancement much more than by any feeling for cultural preservation of the sort that consumed academic folklorists. Even before the record business boom, W. C. Handy, esteemed as the "Father of the Blues," began to explore folk music as inspiration for his compositions after his own orchestra ceded a stage in Cleveland, Mississippi, circa 1905, to a local string band: "A rain of silver dollars began to fall around the outlandish, stomping feet. The dancers went wild. . . . There before the boys

lay more money than my nine musicians were being paid for the entire engagement. Then I saw the beauty of primitive music. They had the stuff the
people wanted. . . . Folks would pay money for it." Handy was thus drawn
to the blues not by preservationist motives, but rather by "the sight of that
silver money cascading around the splay feet of a Mississippi string band."[31]
Likewise, as detailed later in this chapter, the St. Louis songwriter Bill Dooley
seems to have penned "Frankie and Albert" in 1899 in search of commercial
success rather than in the service of communitarian ideals or any sense of a
"folk tradition."[32]

While largely unconcerned about distinctions of folkloric purity, record
company executives generally assumed that their potential audiences were divided along lines of race and region. They therefore requested particular types
of songs from particular types of singers, with an eye toward selling those records to particular types of audiences. Specifically, the offerings of many white
artists from Appalachia and the Deep South were marketed as "hill country"
or "old-time" music, while the vast majority of African American musicians
who recorded with industry leaders in the 1920s found their output pigeonholed as "race records."[33] Even so, some songs possessed broad enough appeal to pass back and forth across the color line imposed by early record company practices. "John Henry," one such song, told the legend of an African
American steel driver who defeated a mechanical steam drill in a contest to
tunnel through a mountain, only to lose his life in the process. As detailed
by Scott Nelson in *Steel Drivin' Man* (2006), Fiddlin' John Carson, Big Bill
Broonzy, and Mississippi John Hurt were only a few of the early artists to
record variations of this song. Nelson aptly notes that the lyrics to "John
Henry" only occasionally marked the racial identity of the protagonist explicitly, likely allowing some consumers of records by white artists like Carson to
imagine the folk hero as white. What is more, the song circulated in ways both
conventionally "folk" (local, informal, face-to-face) and inarguably commercial (professional musicians, records, radios), muddying distinctions between
folk and popular culture.[34] "Frankie and Johnny" operated comparably to
"John Henry" in the breadth of musical artists who recorded the song, in its
capacity to capture imaginations across racial lines, and in the diverse adaptations of the ballad's narrative to forms of creative expression other than music
alone. Indeed, Ruth Page and Bentley Stone's *Frankie and Johnny* ballet was
only one among numerous examples of this phenomenon.

IN THE SAME DECADES when the documentation of US folk songs got
underway in earnest, classically trained composers from the realm of high culture increasingly began to draw from the wellspring of American vernacular

music traditions. For example, during his late nineteenth-century residence in the United States, the Czech composer Antonín Dvořák developed an interest in spirituals by way of his student, the African American baritone singer Harry T. Burleigh.[35] Compositions such as Dvořák's famous Symphony no. 9 (1893), also known as the "From the New World," found inspiration in Native American music and African American spirituals, even if he included relatively few direct quotations from specific examples of these bodies of music. In a statement strikingly similar to the vision of Johann Herder in Germany from more than a century prior, Dvořák asserted:

> I am now satisfied . . . that the future music of this country must be founded on what are called the negro melodies. This must be the real foundation of any serious and original school of composition, to be developed in the United States. . . . These beautiful and varied themes are the product of the soil. They are American. . . . These are the folk songs of America and your composers must turn to them. All of the great musicians have borrowed from the songs of the common people. . . . Only in this way can a musician express the true sentiment of his people.[36]

One significant difference between Herder's project involving German folk ballads and Dvořák's work is that the latter cast the United States as a pluralist tapestry of ethnic cultures from which the cosmopolitan artist might draw, rather than as a singular national folk tradition.

Also paralleling Herder's sentiments were the meditations on African American music offered in W. E. B. Du Bois's *The Souls of Black Folk*, first published in 1903 and tremendously influential on the subsequent New Negro Renaissance of the 1920s. While pursuing graduate studies in Berlin in the early 1890s, Du Bois became deeply impressed by the work of Herder. In fact, the "souls" in Du Bois's title is a direct nod to the German scholar, and Du Bois's focus on spirituals (or "sorrow songs") as one of Afro-America's foremost "racial gifts" to US culture closely parallels Herder's quest to recapture the German "national soul" through the documentation of ballads from the German folk. In addition, Du Bois pointedly couples lines from Western poetry with bars of music excerpted from African American spirituals as joint epigraphs for each chapter in *Souls*. In this way, he implies the parity of Alfred Lord Tennyson and "Swing Low, Sweet Chariot," for example, as paragons of cultural expression.[37] Yet Du Bois was Victorian enough in his sensibilities to call for creative artists among the formally educated "talented tenth" to become "co-worker[s] in the kingdom of culture" by *adapting* folk culture material to the media of high culture: musical works for the formal concert hall;

poetry for literary publication in magazines and books; drama and dance for the theatrical stage. Of particular significance in Du Bois's estimation, the Fisk Jubilee Singers in 1871 inaugurated a tradition of reworking spirituals from the vernacular tradition into smoothly polished choral arrangements deemed suitable for the ears of refined audiences—a tradition joined in the 1920s by renowned vocalists such as Roland Hayes and Paul Robeson.[38]

Du Bois's focus on high-culture adaptations was not the entire story, however, even in the early twentieth century. As chronicled by David Gilbert, several African American composers of the ragtime era (1890s–1920) drew upon African American folk music to forge new brands of American popular music for the commercial marketplace. The most successful musical impresario of this generation was James Reese Europe, a bandleader and composer who successfully organized the majority of New York City's African American musicians into the Chef Club, Inc., and regularly placed them in venues such as private soirees for wealthy white families, upscale "lobster palaces" along Fifth Avenue that catered to decadent young white socialites, and even the first documented performance of African American musicians at Carnegie Hall. In their Carnegie Hall debut in 1912, Europe's Chef Club Symphony Orchestra blended elements of high and folk culture by adding banjos, guitars, and mandolins to traditional symphonic instrumentation and interweaving elements of spirituals and ragtime with classical music.[39] Europe was able to corner much of the market for high-society dance bands for his Chef Club Orchestra and allied groups through a combination of skilled musicianship, entrepreneurial energy, and savvy publicity that trumpeted the allegedly "natural" affinity of African American musicians for the rhythmic dance tunes popular with white (and black) audiences during the 1910s. In a particularly telling detail, Europe reportedly drilled Chef Club musicians to memorize their repertoire of folk and ragtime-inspired music so that they could play it before white audiences without sheet music, thus making it appear that their rigorously trained music was the product of instinctual African American talent.[40]

As the Great Migration brought thousands of African American "folk" from the rural South to the urban North by the 1920s, participants in the New Negro Renaissance continued to use folk culture as the basis for the development of a new racial and national culture. This movement, also known as the Harlem Renaissance, marked a flourishing of African American political campaigns for social equality through organizations such as the NAACP, the Urban League, and Marcus Garvey's United Negro Improvement Association, as well as a dramatically heightened level of visibility for African American creative expression in the arts that lasted from the end of World War I to the mid-1930s. Prominent guiding lights of the movement such as Du Bois (editor of the NAACP's *Crisis* magazine), Alain Locke (editor of the important anthology *The New Negro*), and Charles S. Johnson (editor of the Urban League's *Opportunity* magazine) argued for the importance of creative expression as an important catalyst for African American political advancement and helped spread such artistic work through their publications. Locke, a Howard University professor, inextricably linked African American "folk-expression" and "self-expression" in his foreword to *The New Negro* (1925). Still, he described folk culture as a kind of "cultural adolescence" rather than the desired finished products of "folk *interpretation*" marking the New Negro's full arrival on the stage of global culture. Instead, Locke offered the materials from his own anthology—by the likes of Rudolph Fisher, Jean Toomer, Aaron Douglas, James Weldon Johnson, Langston Hughes, and Zora Neale Hurston—as the ripening "first fruits of the Negro Renaissance."[41]

Among the New Negro Renaissance cohort celebrated by Locke, projects of adapting folk material regularly crossed traditional disciplinary lines of expressive media. For example, James Weldon Johnson and Aaron Douglas's collaboration *God's Trombones* (1927) sought to evoke the content and aesthetic style of African American folk sermons through Johnson's poems—with titles such as "The Creation," "The Prodigal Son," and "The Judgment Day"—and an accompanying image for each poem by Douglas. As Johnson explained his motives in the book's preface, he sought to distill the oral performances of "the old-time Negro preacher," writing admiringly: "His imagination was bold and unfettered . . . His language was not prose but poetry."[42] Notably, though, Johnson joined many of his contemporaries in his conviction that "the old-time Negro preacher is rapidly passing," like most manifestations of folk culture brought into contact with the modern, industrialized world. Hence, the author's compulsion to set down a likeness of the folk-culture original in high-culture verse for posterity. Like Du Bois, Johnson believed that for the artistry of the folk original—here, a preacher—to be fully appreciated, the oral form necessarily had to be translated (and elevated) to the kind of literary verse and artistic representations seen in the book. While some subsequent critics bemoaned that Johnson's verse stifled the inherent dynamism and spontaneity of the vernacular sermon by fixing it on the page, Johnson's goals were to reach a broader audience, make apparent the artistry of the folk sermon, and grant the folk preacher's craft some measure of permanence.

New Negro projects like those of Du Bois, Locke, and Johnson were concerned with uplift of two sorts: transmuting the raw ore of folk material, as it was commonly understood, into gems of fine art; and by so doing, raising the standing of African American culture in the estimation of the broader (white) society. As Johnson framed the matter, "The final measure of the greatness of all people is the amount and standard of the literature and the art they have produced . . . No people that has produced a great literature and art has ever been looked upon by the world distinctly as inferior."[43] These New Negro luminaries turned to folk culture because it offered a sense of grounding for articulations of collective African American identity. For one, there was a shared sense of nostalgia for the rural communitarian ethos that folk culture seemed to offer as a tonic for the stresses of life in rapidly urbanizing, industrializing city centers. Second, New Negro adaptations of traditions such as spirituals and sermons anchored contemporary African American identity in a historically rooted folk source and demonstrated a capacity for high-culture expression, displacing demeaning racial stereotypes of black menace and buffoonery with images of dignity and divine grace. Third, in much the same way that folk songs had seemed to Herder to provide a means of organically maintaining German roots in the face of a perceived onslaught of French culture, Du Bois perceived in vernacular expression evidence that the African American need not "bleach his Negro soul in a flood of white Americanism, for he knows that Negro blood has a message for the world."[44] For Du Bois, Locke, Johnson, and many of their New Negro Renaissance peers, folk culture and its adaptations thus embodied a means of demonstrating cultural *distinctiveness* even as such works also demonstrated cultural *parity* and, hence, grounds for social equality between the races.

Obviously, African American migrants from the southern United States knew more than just spirituals and folk sermons; many arrived already embracing secular forms of expression such as blues, ragtime, and jazz. But these vernacular expressions were not welcomed equally in the erudite circles of New Negro Renaissance, nor in the pages of African American newspapers. Du Bois, for example, sharply contrasted "vulgar music with the soul of the sorrow songs," hoping that the latter (spirituals) might displace the former (blues, ragtime, and secular ballads) as the foremost expressions of African American culture.[45] In a similar vein, editorial commentaries and political cartoons in prominent publications like the *Chicago Defender* chastised recent African American migrants to the urban North for indulging in rent parties, blues music, secular dance, and the like.[46] Notwithstanding such scolding from moralistic African American critics, jazz, blues, and ballads were performed more often, recorded and sold as phonographs in much greater quantity, and enjoyed by vastly larger audiences than the spirituals of Roland Hayes, Paul Robeson, or the Fisk Jubilee Singers.

Moreover, adaptation of folk culture into refined, high-culture forms was hardly the only mode through which creative artists engaged with vernacular expression in the New Negro Renaissance. As a case in point, Langston Hughes embraced the "low down folk" and their expressive culture in his influential manifesto "The Negro Artist and the Racial Mountain" (1926). Adopting a resolutely modernist position that directly defied Victorian dictates of "appropriate" subject matter, as well as Du Bois's insistence on the uplift mission of art, Hughes famously wrote: "We younger Negro artists who create now intend to express our individual dark-skinned selves without fear or shame. If white people are pleased we are glad. If they are not, it doesn't matter. We know we are beautiful. And ugly too. The tom-tom cries and the tom-tom laughs. If colored people are pleased we are glad. If they are not, their displeasure doesn't matter either. We build our temples for tomorrow, strong as we know how, and we stand on top of the mountain, free within ourselves."[47] Hughes put this credo into practice, beginning with his first two poetry collections, *The Weary Blues* (1926) and *Fine Clothes to the Jew* (1927), in which he not only wrote about the folk, but also adopted the vernacular forms of blues verse and ballads. In "The Weary Blues," for instance, Hughes's recounting of a blues musician's performance assumes the rhythm and diction of a blues song, and even weaves two lyrical verses from the piano player into the poem. This approach suggested that the vernacular expression of the blues did not need to be elevated by the learned poet in order to attain merit as art; rather, the blues was already art in its own right, on par with the verse of literary poets like Hughes. Further, the type of blues music upon which Hughes most often drew was not the rural, "down-home" music associated with the Mississippi Delta or other regions of the South, but rather the blues of African American migrants to the urban North.[48] Hughes's folk-culture source material was itself urban and cosmopolitan, an example of what the scholar Edward Comentale terms "vernacular modernism."[49] Hughes's operative definition of African American folk culture was therefore much more broadly inclusive than that of New Negro contemporaries like Du Bois or James Weldon Johnson.

Arguably, the most sophisticated engagement with folk culture among New Negro Renaissance participants was provided by Zora Neale Hurston. As has been well documented in Hurston scholarship, her corpus represents a rich interweaving of literature and ethnography, wherein ethnographic studies such as *Mules and Men* (1935) are imbued with literary qualities, and novels such as *Jonah's Gourd Vine* (1934) and *Their Eyes Were Watching God* (1937) contain folkloric elements borrowed nearly wholesale from the author's field research. Having grown up in the relatively independent black town of Eatonville, Florida, Hurston stressed the vitality and artistic merits of African American vernacular expression even more vigorously than did her friend and onetime field research companion Langston Hughes. Equally important, she situated forms of expression like music and storytelling in the contexts of everyday southern black lives, thus positioning fellow African Americans, rather than the white patrons of Harlem cabarets and theatrical stages, as the primary audience of folk expression.[50] Put another way, whereas Du Bois offered "the veil" as a central trope for African American consciousness—"The Negro is a sort of seventh son, born with a veil, and gifted with second-sight in this American world,—a world which yields him no true self-consciousness, but always lets him see himself through the revelation of the other world"—Hurston instead described a strategy of "feather bed resistance," in which the folk might offer some semblance of their selves to whites or other outsiders, while concealing their authentic expressive culture from appropriation by the outside world.[51] For Hurston, the true nature of African American folk culture was destined to remain opaque except to the expert eye of someone like herself, who was at once a cultural insider, by birth and raising, and an objective ethnographer, by dint of her training with Franz Boas and other scholars at Columbia University.

White contemporaries, too, fell under the spell of African American folk culture during these years, including some staunch exponents of modernist high culture. For example, a scene in the second act of e. e. cummings's experimental play *HIM* (1927) begins with the appearance of "two coalblack figures, one MALE and one FEMALE," who engage in a dialogue about Johnie "in de arms of de ground" in which the female identifies herself as the ground and "a large boydoll" in her arms as symbolic of Johnie. This action soon yields to a semicircle group of "SIX COALBLACK FIGURES, three male and three female" and a rendition of "Frankie and Johnny" performed by a backstage jazz band and chorus. Cummings credited the literary critic Edmund Wilson with the play's extremely ribald version of the song, which openly refers to Frankie's prostitution on Johnie's behalf and glosses Johnie's side gal, Fanny Fry, as "a parlorhouse whore." Cummings even brings a Freudian interpretation to bear on the ballad, with Frankie poised to threaten Johnie's castration in profane terms at the song's climax before being interrupted at the last moment by the appearance of "John Rutter, President pro tem. of the Society for the Contraception of Vice"—a clear jab at the censors who rigorously policed US theaters during the 1920s, targeting the likes of Mae West. Rutter's blathering is disrupted by Frankie, who causes the esteemed personage to scream and flee the stage by brandishing "something which suggests a banana in size and shape and which is carefully wrapped in a bloody napkin," that is, Johnie's severed member, or as the chorus terms it, the "BEST PART OF THE MAN / WHO DONE ME WRONG."[52]

Less obvious is the case of cummings's contemporary T. S. Eliot, who was enthralled by African American music both folk and popular. While growing up in St. Louis, Eliot was captivated by music that spanned Beethoven symphonies, Tom Turpin and Scott Joplin ragtime numbers, and raucous ballads of local origin like "Stagolee" and "Frankie and Johnny." Eliot's biographer Robert Crawford observes, "Growing up in the soundscape of St. Louis meant inhabiting a city where the highbrow European music of Wagner was performed not far from sophisticated ragtime. . . . To live at the confluence of all these musics was part of St. Louis's gift to Tom: it helped shape the lilt of his poetry, and contributed to his love of dancing."[53] Even more specifically, notes Eric Sigg, "his family home lay only a short walk from the Chestnut Valley 'sporting district,' where inside the saloons and whorehouses along Chestnut and Market Streets St. Louis became the world's ragtime capital during the ten years before 1906."[54] For example, Babe Connors's Castle Club in Chestnut Valley featured the local legend Mama Lou, who memorably performed songs such as "Bully of the Town" and "A Hot Time in the Old Town" for the parlor house's mixed-race clientele. As I will elaborate subsequently, this same district appears to have been where real-life events from Eliot's childhood years helped birth and popularize the ballad "Frankie and Johnny." Little wonder, then, that Eliot scholars have remarked on allusions to everything from minstrel shows and ragtime to balladry and jazz in the poet's early writings.[55] At least well into the 1930s, Eliot occasionally was known to express his affinity for "negro rag-time" dancing and to belt out his own lively rendition of "Frankie and Johnny."[56] Erudite expatriate though he might have become, Eliot's early exposure to African American vernacular expression seems to have remained an abiding influence, as was the case for many of his fellow modernists.

In high-culture forms as well, several US composers followed in the steps of Dvořák during the 1930s and 1940s. Most famously, Aaron Copland tapped into vernacular music with compositions such as *Rodeo* (1942) and *Appalachian Spring* (1944). Even earlier, Copland had drawn substantially on jazz in his score for Ruth Page's *Hear Ye! Hear Ye!* (1934), composed a ballet score for *Billy the Kid* (1938) that drew heavily on cowboy songs, and crafted a brief, four-minute score based the African American folk ballad "John Henry," commissioned by Alan Lomax for the CBS radio program *American School of the Air: Folk-Music of America* (1939).[57] Ruth Page and Bentley Stone's collaborator Jerome Moross had been a part of the Young Composers Group with the likes of Copland and Bernard Herrmann in the early 1930s. Like several of his peers, Moross initially worked in a dissonant, modernist style before turning to projects that sought to blend elements of high art and vernacular music in compositions that were distinctively American in character and possessed wider appeal than his purely avant-garde efforts. As early as 1933, Moross vowed to compose a "Frankie and Johnny"–based work for high-culture audiences, explaining in an interview, "What I plan to do is to take the elements that make a good Broadway Show interesting, and add them to opera. I will take Jazz and use it as the basis for true American Music."[58] Before Ruth Page's commission provided him with the opportunity to pursue his goal with *Frankie and Johnny*, Moross adapted "Negro popular song" to accompany a vocalist's rendition of poetry by Alfred Kreymborg in *Those Everlasting Blues* (1932), composed *Paul Bunyan: An American Saga* (1934) for a ballet by the Charles Weidman Dance Group, and served as vocal coach and pianist for a touring production of *Porgy and Bess* in 1937 at the invitation of George Gershwin.[59]

Porgy and Bess first hit the Broadway stage in 1935, with an African American cast, music by George Gershwin, and a libretto by Ira Gershwin and DuBose Heyward. Widely celebrated as the first native US opera, *Porgy and Bess* originated with Heyward's 1925 novel *Porgy*, a text that he and his wife, Dorothy, had adapted as a "folk play" for the stage in 1927. In all three versions — novel, play, and Broadway musical — the story is set in a poor black community of Charleston, South Carolina, known as Catfish Row. In this setting, Porgy, a disabled but noble beggar, attempts to win the love of Bess from Crown, a brutish stevedore whom Porgy eventually kills in a fight. Unfortunately for Porgy, he is released from prison only to discover that Bess has left town with Sportin' Life, a drug peddler.[60] Both DuBose Heyward and George Gershwin were adamant in framing their production as a "folk opera," deliberately blurring the folk-culture, high-culture divide. A native Charlestonian, Heyward sounded like an ethnographer when describing his brief residence with Gershwin on James Island, South Carolina, in 1934 as having "furnished us with a laboratory in which to test our theories, as well as an inexhaustible source of folk material." In short, it was a production promoted at every turn for the "earthy authenticity" of its translated folk performance, which was due to the ostensible cultural expertise of its authors and to the production's African American cast. Its success, notes Ellen Noonan, was predicated on "the assumption that authentic African American musical sound was central to American music."[61] Like "Frankie and Johnny," the *Porgy and Bess* narrative was rooted in a version of African American folk culture characterized by vice, violence, and bleak lives on the margins of mainstream society, yet was full of emotional vitality, which cultural consumers craved. Further, like Ruth Page and Bentley Stone's *Frankie and Johnny* ballet, all three iterations of the *Porgy and Bess* story met with enviable commercial and critical success, collectively representing a pinnacle of the broad fascination with African American folk culture that characterized the 1920s and 1930s.

The documentation and adaptation of US folk cultures were given new patronage and concrete structure by way of the cultural wing of President Franklin Roosevelt's New Deal programs during the 1930s. Over the course of Roosevelt's first two terms in office, as the New Deal gradually expanded to sponsor programs for artists, writers, musicians, dancers, and thespians, as well as a copious amount of photography via the Farm Security Administration, one of the overarching imperatives of the cultural work thus undertaken was to "document America." This mission involved not simply documenting US history and contemporary life, but doing so in particular ways: emphasizing the nation's "common man," or folk, much more so than the elite; extending its efforts to far-flung regional corners, rather than focusing exclusively on metropolitan centers; and embracing the nation's ethnic and racial diversity instead of chronicling only the lifeways of white Anglo-Saxon Protestants. To an unprecedented extent, New Deal culture posited an American essence that was pluralistic in socioeconomic class, geography, and ethnicity. While the exact form and focus varied by genre of expression, government agency, and individual creators' sensibilities, African Americans and the folk featured prominently in New Deal creative expression.[62]

Indeed, one of the defining features of New Deal culture was the breadth and variety of "folk" materials assembled under its auspices. For instance, government-sponsored murals displayed the exploits of legendary historical figures such as Daniel Boone and Annie Oakley and fictional folk heroes such as Paul Bunyan and Babe his blue ox, alongside a cast of anonymous industrial laborers and hearty farmers by the score. While FSA photographers captured the hardships facing sharecroppers and displaced farmers, members of the Federal Writers' Project chronicled phenomena such as the African American folk crafts and conjure practices of the Georgia Sea Islands. The publications of the Federal Writers' Project included oral histories of those born into slavery as well as substantial troves of vernacular legends, humor, and accounts of community traditions both sacred and secular. The Federal Theatre Project and Federal Dance Project staged works such as Lew Payton's *Did Adam Sin?* (1936), a musical revue based on African American folklore; Lilly Mehlman's *Folk Dances of All Nations* (1937); *How Long Brethren?* (1937), which dramatized African American struggles in the South through a synthesis of dances choreographed by Helen Tamaris and songs from Lawrence Gellert's collection *Negro Songs of Protest* (1936); and Theodore Browne's *Natural Man* (1937), a musical drama recounting the legend of John Henry as a proletarian hero.[63]

Program directors like the Federal Theatre Project's Hallie Flanagan hoped that New Deal cultural productions would invigorate the nation's populace through a renewed (or newly discovered) sense of pride in their own lifeways and traditions. The resulting cultural work very often aimed to make high-culture forms, such as theater and painting, more accessible to a mass audience by infusing such media with a substantial dose of already familiar folk-culture subject matter. Thus, the fact that Ruth Page and Bentley Stone's *Frankie and Johnny* ballet originated under the auspices of New Deal sponsorship was far from coincidental. Page even used the phrase "real folklore Americana" to describe her *Frankie and Johnny* ballet, and she was by no means alone in this regard.[64] Earlier that same year, for example, a young Katherine Dunham and the Negro unit of Chicago's Federal Dance Theatre debuted a ballet entitled *L'Ag'Ya*, which was based on folkloric material that Dunham had gathered in Martinique two years earlier; and E. P. Conkle's play *Prologue to Glory*, centered on a romance of the young Abraham Lincoln as a national folk hero in the making, began its widespread run on the Federal Theatre Project circuit. Put simply, it is worth remembering that 1930s cultural expression—New Deal or otherwise—consisted of more than just documentary images of impoverished agricultural landscapes, urban breadlines, and joblessness. Nor was it limited to the revolutionary images of proletarian workers on the march and campaigns against racial oppression of the sort forged by the period's social realists. Along with representations of hardscrabble poverty and labor strikes, the period's creative artists forged images of folkloric strongmen like Paul Bunyan and John Henry, as well as more flamboyant characters like Frankie and Johnny.

As seen in the foregoing examples, US cultural expression of the 1920s and 1930s was characterized by new and broader definitions for terms such as "folk" and "folklore." Specifically, a majority of folklore collectors and adaptors of this generation concurred with at least three significant shifts in the field. First, as illustrated by musical examples ranging from Jerome Moross to Theodore Browne, the definition of "folk" moved beyond earlier generations' tendency to restrict folklore studies to communities of (ostensible) rural isolates by redefining "folk" expression more broadly as pertaining to the "common man," or the nation's poor and working classes. Second, work by authors such as W. E. B. Du Bois, Carl Sandburg, John and Alan Lomax, and Zora Neale Hurston found in US folk cultures an effective means of mapping the nation's regional and ethnic pluralism, substantially expanding definitions of American identity in the process. Third, adaptations by the likes of James Weldon Johnson, Langston Hughes, and the Gershwins called attention not only to their own genius, but also to the artistry of the folk themselves. Together with important work by folklorists like the Lomaxes and

Hurston, this helped open a greater space for the celebration of individuals such as Bessie Smith and Huddie Ledbetter (Lead Belly) as "folk artists" in their own right—notwithstanding that such figures were not purely "folk" by the standards of earlier generations of scholars and that the means of disseminating their work was deeply reliant on modern mass media.[65]

"FRANKIE AND JOHNNY": ORIGINS AND PROLIFERATION

By the 1930s, cosmopolitan intellectuals from the realms of academia, government-sponsored programs, popular culture, and the fine arts were foregrounding folk music as a focus of heterogeneous projects for study, profit, racial uplift, and the advancement of a distinctly American school of creative expression. Yet the matter of why "Frankie and Johnny" in particular became the object of so many adaptations across distinct media and levels of cultural production merits elaboration. To understand the song's appeal in the 1930s, it is necessary to outline its origins and proliferation. For if Alan Lomax was correct in claiming that "Barbara Allen" and "Frankie and Johnny" were "America's two most popular ballads," then it is worth noting that the latter possessed a much more recent pedigree, one indigenous to the United States.[66] Folklorists from the first half of the twentieth century proposed an assortment of early roots for the song now best known as "Frankie and Johnny," claiming that, among other things, it was initiated by a first-person ballad chronicling Frankie Silver's 1831 murder of her husband, Charley, in Toe River, North Carolina (Phillips Barry); that it had become popular in Natchez, Mississippi, by the 1840s (Emerson Hough); that it was "chanted by Federal troops besieging Vicksburg in 1863" (Thomas Beer); that it had become a common tune among railroad men of the Midwest and along the Mississippi River by the 1880s (Carl Sandburg); and that it was a song popular at "Babe Connors' high-brown house in St. Louis" during the mid-1890s (Vance Randolph).[67] Some of these assertions simply do not hold up under careful scrutiny. For example, the Frankie Silver ballad appears to have little in common with the narrative of "Frankie and Johnny" beyond a female protagonist's name and the fact that she murders her male love interest; Beer failed to respond to challenges by his peers to produce any of his claimed Civil War–era manuscripts; and most of the other assertions of possible "Frankie and Johnny" precursors from the nineteenth century appear to be based on the tenuous evidence of twentieth-century interviewees who claimed to recall having heard the song in earlier decades.[68]

Among later scholars, John R. David (1984) and Cecil Brown (2005) proposed an alternative point of origin for "Frankie and Johnny": Frankie Baker's

FIGURE 1.2. Frankie Baker, 1890s.

murder of Allen Britt in St. Louis in October 1899, an argument advanced decades earlier by John Huston (1930) and in the pages of the *Missouri Historical Review* (1941).[69] As was chronicled by St. Louis newspapers at the time and elaborated in subsequent testimony during the 1930s and early 1940s by Baker and those in her circle, Baker and Britt were residents of the predominantly African American district of Chestnut Valley in the late nineteenth century, which possessed a reputation for being a place of lively saloons, vice, and more than occasional outbursts of violence (figure 1.2).[70] Baker, who was in her midtwenties, earned her living primarily through prostitution; Britt, although only a teenager, played piano for local saloons and private parties. Britt was Baker's lover and pimp, but his relationship with her was not exclusive, and she became aware of her partner's dalliances with a woman named Alice Pryor. On the evening of October 16, 1899, after Britt returned from a night on the town with Pryor, Baker shot Britt in the apartment they shared at 212 Targee Street. Grievously wounded, Britt managed to reach his parents' nearby home, but died in a hospital three days later. Frankie Baker stood trial for murder, but the judge followed the lead of the coroner's inquest in ruling Baker's action a justifiable case of self-defense.[71] Ira Cooper, a reporter for the city's weekly African American newspaper, the *Palladium*, at the time of the incident, later recounted for the *Missouri Historical Review* that a ballad titled "Frankie and Allen" had been penned by an itinerant African American musician named Bill Dooley in the immediate aftermath of the shooting. According to Cooper, Dooley's song was a "sorrowful dirge which was played thereafter in many Negro saloons and resorts." In keeping with songwriting practices of the time, Dooley reportedly performed the song himself on busy city streets in an effort to promote sales of the sheet music for his song, which cost ten cents.[72]

Since there are no physical copies of Dooley's sheet music, it is difficult to say more about the exact content or form of his composition. If Dooley drew on stock images, phrases, or even whole verses from other ballads when crafting "Frankie and Allen" in 1899, that would hardly be surprising, since such appropriations were common practice for songsmiths at the turn of the twentieth century. Particularly in an era before the widespread availability of audio recordings of music or devices on which to listen to such recordings in the domestic sphere, a popular song like "Frankie and Johnny" inevitably became something of a palimpsest—that is, the ballad's constituent influences, amassed over several decades, are probably not retraceable with precision. Not surprisingly, then, subsequent ballads called "Frankie and Albert" and "Frankie and Johnny" differ with regard to several details of the real life Baker-Britt murder case: for instance, Frankie in the ballad typically shoots Johnny at her rival's apartment or in the nearby street, whereas Frankie Baker shot Allen Britt in the Targee Street apartment that they shared—Alice Pryor was not present.[73]

What is clear, though, is that in the decade following Frankie Baker's murder of Allen Britt, a ballad titled "Frankie and Allen" or "Frankie and Albert" proliferated widely and was taken up by a number of performers. Music scholars generally agree that the white composer Hughie Cannon's "He Done Me Wrong" (1904) is the first known version of the ballad to be copyrighted. Further, by 1912 a popular white vaudeville duo, the Leighton Brothers, joined Ren Shields in publishing the first documented example of the ballad to be titled "Frankie and Johnny"; despite the change of name, this version was clearly derived from the earlier line of "Frankie and Albert" songs in tune and many essential narrative elements. In later years, "Frankie and Johnny" ballads were performed on stages and on records, and appeared in the pages of folk music anthologies alongside renditions of "Frankie and Albert" and analogous songs with a variety of alternate name combinations—Maggie, Lilly, Frances, and Josie, among others—that sprang from a shared lineage.[74] By the 1930s, the song had been performed by scores of artists, both vernacular and commercial, from varied regional and racial backgrounds. The early country blues phenomenon Jimmie Rodgers, the star of stage and screen Mae West, the jazz legend Thomas "Fats" Waller, and the folk balladeer Huddie Ledbetter were just a few of the prominent artists to record versions of the song in the years preceding Page and Stone's ballet. In his capacity as head of the Archive of American Folk Song for the Library of Congress, Robert Gordon had amassed over three hundred variants of the song by the early 1930s.[75]

With a song as widely disseminated as "Frankie and Johnny," any assertion of a "definitive" version is inevitably subjective. The self-styled "tune detective" Sigmund Spaeth observed in 1927, "Everybody that knows anything at all about Frankie and Johnnie is likely to have a version of his or her own, and there is nothing so rabid for righteousness, so bristling with self-defense, as the dyed-in-the-wool Frankie-and-Johnnie fan."[76] As one example of the variations prevalent within this ballad tradition, Moross and Blankfort's libretto for Page and Stone's ballet (quoted earlier in the chapter) omits a verse common to renditions by artists as distinct as Gene Autry and Mississippi John Hurt, which strongly hinted at Frankie and Johnny's roles as prostitute and pimp:

> *Frankie was a good woman,*
> *Everybody knows,*
> *Paid one hundred dollars*
> *To buy her man a new suit of clothes*

Still, Moross and Blankfort's version of the lyrics contains many of the narrative elements (and even exact phrasings) widely shared in sheet music, folk music anthology, and commercial phonograph versions of the ballad spanning from the early 1900s through the 1930s. In brief, one might outline these archetypal elements as the following:

- An opening or early verse establishing the protagonists' relationship as lovers and their oath of fidelity to one another (The singer often refers to

Frankie providing Albert or Johnny with gifts of stylish clothing, as in the Mississippi John Hurt verse quoted above.)

- A counterpoint refrain to the couple's pledge of true love that states some variation of "He was her man, / But he done her wrong"
- Frankie's search for an absent Johnny, including asking a bartender about Johnny's whereabouts[77]
- The bartender's confession, whether reluctant or willing, that Johnny is dallying with another woman (This woman is most commonly named Nellie Bly, but there are numerous variations, including Alice Pryor and Alice Fry.)
- Frankie's discovery of Johnny's infidelity with Nellie Bly, most often by finding them together at Nellie's room in a hotel or brothel
- Johnny begging for his life, but Frankie shooting him multiple times
- Before dying, Johnny begging Frankie to comfort him, which she typically does (Occasionally, Johnny apologizes to Frankie for having "done her wrong.")
- A stock verse marking Johnny's death and funeral, often with the image of a "rubber-tired carriage" to bear his body to the graveyard (This verse was most likely borrowed from an earlier ballad.)

A given ballad might alter a detail or omit one or more of these components, since individual composers or singers sought to put their own stamp on the song or to reach a particular type of audience. For instance, at least some "Frankie and Johnny" recordings after the 1930s by artists such as Guy Lombardo (1942) and Louis Armstrong (1959) aimed to "clean up" the song by relocating the action from a saloon or brothel to a drugstore ice cream parlor.[78]

Yet most fully developed versions of "Frankie and Johnny" in the decades before World War II shared some combination of the above-listed elements as a narrative scaffolding.[79] In its depiction of what Adam Gussow terms "intimate violence" between African Americans, the song shares thematic terrain with a number of early twentieth-century blues songs, and a motive of fervent romantic jealousy was a well-established trope of both ballad and blues homicides. But "Frankie and Johnny" ballads generally differ from the blues works analyzed by Gussow in eschewing a sense of "pleasurably violent retribution" and in their frequent appeal to melodramatic sentiment in the scenes of Johnny's death.[80] "Frankie and Johnny" likewise departs from most US murder ballads and blues in attributing violent revenge to a female protagonist.

The ending of the ballad showcases some of the most significant variations in the ways that audiences might be led to regard the song's central characters.

In some iterations, Johnny's mother appears to express grief over her son's murder, swinging sympathy toward her and her son despite Johnny's clear misdeeds. Other versions move from the shooting to Frankie in jail or on trial for Johnny's murder. Trials, where they occur, sometimes end with Frankie's acquittal, justified by the refrain, "He was your man, / But he was doing you wrong." More often, these versions end with Frankie being sent to prison or destined for the gallows or electric chair.[81]

At least from the 1920s onward, "Frankie and Johnny" ballads occasionally close with what one might construe as a protofeminist mantra:

This story has no moral,
This story has no end,
This story only goes to show
That there ain't no good in men.
He was her man,
And he done her wrong.[82]

Examining the ballad in 1960, Alan Lomax claimed: "[Frankie] took direct action—she cut down the predatory male with her smoking .44. Feminine listeners revenged themselves through little Frankie on a predominantly patriarchal society which treated them as second-class citizens and disapproved of their erotic life."[83] Lomax overstates the case somewhat. For one, regardless of whether "Frankie and Johnny" ballads include Johnny's mother, a trial, or a lament about the disingenuousness of men, they almost always include some distraught expression of "feminine" sentiment over Johnny's demise in the late stages of the ballad. At times, as in Page and Stone's ballet, Frankie expresses this grief directly over Johnny's coffin or grave. Typically, then, the ballad draws on the conventions of melodrama—Johnny's slow death, sentimental displays by Johnny's mother and Frankie—while also refusing to place its female protagonist in a purely passive, maudlin, or apologetic role. Rather, Frankie typically mourns for Johnny even as she or the narrator resolutely affirms the motive underlying her violent act of retribution: "He was my man, / But he done me wrong." In fact, this blend of traits—Victorian and modern, sentimental and unflinching, acquiescent and rebellious—that characterized so many renditions of "Frankie and Johnny" likely played a significant role in its seemingly inexhaustible popularity across generations and with wide-ranging audience demographics. Put simply, the song offered elements capable of appealing to listeners of varied stylistic tastes, moral codes, and gender ideologies.

Notwithstanding the messiness of debates over origins, I wish to follow the lead of the scholars John David and Cecil Brown in establishing two claims about "Frankie and Johnny" that are foundational to the arguments in this book. First, whatever elements Bill Dooley might have drawn from preexisting murder ballads, a composition whose details were at least loosely inspired by Frankie Baker's murder of Allen Britt was the root source of the song that captured the national imagination as it proliferated rapidly over the course of the first half of the twentieth century. Second, the "Frankie and Johnny" ballad tradition thus is grounded in African American history and expressive culture; more specifically, many variants of the song (including some of the earliest) explicitly feature a milieu of pimps, prostitutes, and saloons. Consequently, I have suggested that at first glance the ballad's contents hardly seem the typical stuff of polite society, mainstream popular culture, or high art. Attributes such as prostitution, the urban red-light district setting, and Johnny's violent death would have rendered the ballad an ill-suited choice for New Negro Renaissance racial uplift agendas, for example. Not surprisingly, then, some adaptations examined in the ensuing chapters drew accusations of forging demeaning images of African Americans, immoral images of women, and unflattering images for particular regions of the country.

Nonetheless, other contexts of the interwar years abetted the song's popularity. First, widespread public cynicism toward the strictures of Prohibition and its hypocrisies meant that "lawlessness had acquired a new cachet" by the dawn of the 1930s. Gangsters, who supplied a substantial portion of the nation's alcohol, became folk heroes of a sort, objects of both fear and admiration, in real life and especially in early-1930s motion pictures.[84] Second, as a generation of modernist, cosmopolitan Americans staged rebellions against Victorian conventions of female moral propriety, in forms that included daring flapper fashions and the bold lyrics of blueswomen such as Bessie Smith, Frankie's outlaw assertiveness also undoubtedly enhanced the ballad's appeal. Third, the popularity of "Frankie and Johnny" narratives in this period was part of a particularly intense spate of fetishization of the "black exotic" as artistic subject, which was given its highest-profile incarnations in the imaginative class and racial boundary crossings provided by African American musical revues and cabaret shows during the 1920s and early 1930s. Here, too, Alan Lomax surely touches on an element of truth when he suggests of "Frankie and Johnny" that "middle-class performers [and audiences] had the thrill of vicarious participation in the sexually uninhibited and violent life of the demi-monde," even if that is hardly a full explanation in and of itself.[85]

As will become clear over the course of this book, the song's roots in society's underclasses had significant implications for the kind of creative artists that took an interest in its possibilities as source material, the ways in which certain artists felt compelled to revise the conventions of the ballad tradition, and the responses of audiences—whether listeners, movie or theater spectators, readers, or viewers of fine art—to "Frankie and Johnny"–themed material. That said, the matter of who chose to embrace "Frankie and Johnny" as a muse, how they reworked the ballad, and how audiences received the resulting works of creative expression unfolded unpredictably and not at all uniformly. Mirroring the widespread appeal of "Frankie and Johnny" and the assortment of its incarnations in musical form, the ballad proved remarkably serviceable source material for creative artists in other media, who possessed a wide range of artistic and political agendas. That the resulting adaptations were often contested suggests just how deeply representations of folklore mattered in debates regarding race and gender, as well as regional and national identity, during the 1930s.

In the chapters that follow, I offer in-depth contextualization and analysis of five "Frankie and Johnny" works. Collectively, these case studies offer important insights into how works of creative expression alternately reinforced and challenged prevailing ideas of race and gender during the Depression era. While all the adaptations considered herein are idiosyncratic to some degree, I have arranged the chapters to trace an arc of increasingly sharp departures from the conventions of the ballad tradition. My purpose in adopting this structure is not so much to argue the merits of fidelity to tradition per se as to map the range of uses toward which creative artists sought to apply this particular song and, by extension, African American folklore more broadly. Chapter 2 takes up the example of Huddie Ledbetter, who first recorded the song "Frankie and Albert" in the Louisiana State Penitentiary, in Angola, for the folklorists John and Alan Lomax in 1933. After relocating to New York City, Ledbetter went on to share the song at formal gatherings of academic folklorists, on numerous university campuses, in professional recording studios, at meetings and rallies of the Popular Front political movement, and as a regular guest artist on Alan Lomax's folk music programs for CBS Radio. The form of the song and its reception shifted as Ledbetter's public persona moved from itinerant musician to "folk artist" to "folk activist."

As a central text of the 1930s folk culture boom, "Frankie and Johnny" made numerous leaps to expressive media beyond the bounds of recorded music. Chapter 3 examines Thomas Hart Benton's painting *Frankie and Johnny*, a prominent panel of his *A Social History of the State of Missouri* mural project for the Missouri State Capitol in 1935–1936. Although familiar with the song's characteristically tragic tone from his hobbyist pursuits in folklore and music, Benton aimed for a comic treatment of the ballad in a manner reflecting his views of the social instabilities inherent in the modern urban setting broadly and among African Americans in particular. Chapter 4 turns to John Huston's first play, *Frankie and Johnny*, which he wrote and directed in 1929 and published in book form the following year, with illustrations by Miguel Covarrubias and variants of the ballad. Like Benton, he aimed for a lighthearted brand of caricature. And although, thanks to careful research, Huston was well aware of the song's African American origins in St. Louis, he nonetheless opted to transform the racial identity of the characters from black to white and to depict Frankie as a woman driven by simpering fidelity and jealous hysteria, rather than as an assertive protagonist. Benton's and Huston's adaptations have much to tell us about how backward-looking race and gender ideologies permeated even the work of self-characterized artistic rebels and "freethinking" modernists of the 1920s and 1930s.

Chapters 5 and 6 showcase efforts by the author and actress Mae West and the poet Sterling Brown in developing ambitious adaptations of "Frankie and Johnny" in order to stage rebellions against prevailing gender codes and racial injustice. Mae West both performed the ballad and used it as a structuring premise of sorts for her hit movie *She Done Him Wrong* (1933), her first starring role for Paramount Pictures. West reversed the formula of portraying Frankie as tragic victim and instead cast herself as a protofeminist rebel in the part of Lady Lou, a self-reliant woman willing to embrace multiple relationships with men, less for love than for her own pleasure and self-advantage. To no small degree, it was precisely the appropriation of African American vernacular music that helped endow West's protagonist with her sense of erotic allure, gender rebellion, and modernity. By contrast, Sterling Brown's social realist poem "Frankie and Johnny" (1932) transposes the all-black urban context of the ballad into a rural southern world that crackles with Jim Crow brutality. Specifically, Brown recasts Frankie as the "halfwit" daughter of a "cracker" sawmill worker, and Johnny as a black sharecropper; following a series of sexual liaisons between the interracial duo, Frankie's father leads a mob that lynches Johnny at poem's end. Through his innovative reworking of the folk tradition, Brown thus transformed the familiar ballad into an anti-lynching critique.

I conclude the book with an epilogue that probes a telling absence at the center of the "Frankie and Johnny" phenomenon: namely, the paucity of adaptations authored by African American women during the period of the ballad's rampant popularity in the 1930s. Constraints imposed by the politics of respectability and uplift appear to factor substantially in this near absence. Even in the realm of music, Ethel Waters's 1938 recording, with orchestral accompaniment, for Bluebird seems a relative rarity. I offer a brief meditation on Waters's interpretation vis-à-vis the crossroads of racial uplift and entertainment imperatives that many New Negro creative artists confronted during the 1920s and 1930s, arguing that the song provided a vehicle for Waters to push boundaries of conventional respectability. I then turn to the testimony of Frankie Baker in her two lawsuits against motion picture studios that adapted the famous ballad: the first, in 1935, was against Paramount Studios and Mae West in response to *She Done Him Wrong*; the second was filed in 1938 against Republic Pictures for its film *Frankie and Johnnie* (1936).[86] Although unsuccessful in both cases, Baker attempted through legal testimony to reassert control over the narrative of her own life from the seeming omnipresence of the ballad and its adaptations.

A careful study of "Frankie and Johnny" adaptations from the 1930s, taken collectively, reveals an era of intense artistic interest in folk material and a widespread conviction regarding its potential to reinvigorate American cultural expression writ large. This zeal for the vernacular manifested in ways that reflect the full spectrum of the period's ideologies with respect to race and gender, aesthetics and politics, and occasional clashes of class and culture. On the one hand, 1930s interpretations of the ballad as often as not recast the protagonists as white, erasing the racial (but not class) origins of the song. Reinventions of the song in other media also sometimes reshaped Frankie in ways that dulled the more rebellious, unconventional edges of the ballad tradition—muting especially how the Frankie of ballad fame transgressed gender norms and expectations. Moreover, even as the flourishing of "Frankie and Johnny" allowed an African American female protagonist to take center stage, the near absence of projects authored by black women suggests a continued, problematic silencing of the voices of African American women as creative artists. The full potential of the Depression-era folk boom as a cultural moment remained unrealized on all of these important fronts.

Yet in other crucial respects, the consequences of the 1930s folk culture boom for US creative expression were profoundly transformational. Adaptations of folk material at times crossed significant barriers of cultural hierarchy, training a spotlight on poor and working-class Americans in works of fine art and popular culture to an unprecedented degree. Further, numerous vernacular interpretations brought African American experiences into view as an important part of the history and folk culture heritage of the nation as a whole. With the "Frankie and Johnny" phenomenon in particular, Langston Hughes's "low-down folks"—African American figures from the streets of a red-light district, no less!—entered the arenas of high culture and popular culture. Flawed though the works chronicled in this study may be, this much seems clear: Frankie and Johnny were deemed worth representing on larger-than-life canvases and silver screens, on the theatrical stage and the printed page, and on almost too many records to number. Frankie and Johnny's place in the realms of US folklore and the arts merited substantial debate. "Frankie and Johnny" stories were consumed by an avid public that mixed black and white, high and low, and that at times reached an impressively grand scale. For a generation of American creative artists, critics, and audiences, this story moved from society's margins to center stage.

CHAPTER 2

LEAD BELLY'S NINTH SYMPHONY:
HUDDIE LEDBETTER AND THE CHANGING
CONTOURS OF AMERICAN FOLK MUSIC

MORE SO THAN any other musician, Huddie Ledbetter embodies the diverse range of definitions of "folk" at play during the Great Depression. After leaving his native Louisiana for New York City in the mid-1930s, Ledbetter was reimagined—with varying degrees of success—as a "folk artist," a commercial artist, and what one might term a "folk activist." Beginning in late December 1934, the father-and-son folklore team of John and Alan Lomax famously presented "Lead Belly" to northeastern audiences as primary evidence of their then-unorthodox claim for folk music's continued vitality. Even more, the Lomaxes published a book profiling Ledbetter's life and musical repertoire, *Negro Folk Songs as Sung by Lead Belly* (1936), in which they defined him as a "folk artist."[1] Through these efforts, Ledbetter and the Lomaxes together forged a new definition of the field, one that foregrounded the importance of recording specific living folk musicians rather than merely compiling variants of canonical folk songs in the manner of earlier generations of folk music scholars.

Ledbetter was central to the field of folk music in the 1930s, but remained on the periphery of the commercial music arena. By the time he entered the studios of the American Recording Corporation in 1935, record sales generally were hampered by the economic effects of the Depression, and popular tastes had gravitated away from "rustic"-sounding music like Ledbetter's in favor of swing music, suave blues vocals à la Leroy Carr, and the smooth pop stylings of crooners like Bing Crosby and Fred Astaire.[2] Ledbetter arrived on the scene too late to participate in the growth of vernacular "race record" sales during the 1920s, and passed away too early to reap the rewards of the 1960s folk music boom.[3] Still, he was a revered figure in 1960s folk music circles—unsurprisingly, given his participation in the Popular Front of the 1930s. After all, the front's politically oriented redefinition of "folk music" as songs of, by, and for America's poor and working classes, as well as the movement's direct participants, such as Pete Seeger, did much to shape the 1960s folk scene. For Seeger, Woody Guthrie, the author Richard Wright, and other participants in the 1930s Popular Front, Ledbetter represented an authentic folk musician whose work could be wedded to social justice crusades, as exemplified by his songs in support of the interracial CIO (Congress of Industrial Organizations) labor union movement and the Scottsboro Boys, a group of nine African American youths, ages twelve to nineteen, who faced execution or life imprisonment after being tried on dubious charges of raping two white women while stowing away on a train car in Alabama in 1931.[4] While such endeavors offered only modest financial remuneration, this work as a "folk activist" did much to cement Ledbetter's legendary status. Even in this one performer, then, one can see that "Frankie and Albert"—one of Ledbetter's signature songs—*moved*: geographically, to diverse audiences; and across categories of culture, clouding distinctions between folk and popular music. As Ledbetter negotiated this series of self-reinventions, the ballad fared considerably better under the "folk artist" rubric than in the commercial or "folk activist" frameworks.

An unlabeled, undated photograph from the Alan Lomax Collection in the Library of Congress's American Folklife Center offers one window onto the matter of why Huddie Ledbetter prompted such divergent interpretations. The photo presents a study in contrasts. It depicts Ledbetter seated in a wooden chair, playing a guitar, and singing (figure 2.1).[5] His face bears a look of intense concentration. The staggered lift of his toes suggests that he is tapping out a different rhythm with each foot to accompany himself, which was a distinguishing feature of his performances. As John Lomax explained to audiences in 1935, "If you don't think that's hard, try it yourself."[6] What proves most striking, though, is the contrast between the singer's attire and his instrument. The guitar is a twelve-string Stella, a relatively unusual instrument that Ledbetter said he acquired after hearing a performer in a traveling medicine show or circus play one and admiring its rich, sonorous sound.[7] With the deep scarring of its surface, the guitar looks as if it had followed Ledbetter through his rough-and-tumble life journey from rural Louisiana to the barrelhouses of Shreveport and Dallas, through prison terms in the state penitentiaries of Texas and Louisiana and on to New York City by the mid-1930s. In contrast to the battered guitar, Ledbetter's apparel is impeccable. His dress slacks, vest, and shirt all appear neatly pressed. A bow tie tops the ensemble beneath his smoothly shaven face.

The matter of appearances, and clothing in particular, was not incidental to Ledbetter's story. From his youth as the only child of a landowning black couple in northwestern Louisiana, where he was born in 1889, he regularly

FIGURE 2.1. Huddie Ledbetter in New York City, n.d. Alan Lomax Collection, American Folklife Center; courtesy of the Lead Belly Estate, Murfreesboro, Tennessee.

donned freshly ironed and starched overalls and polished black shoes as he went to work in the fields.[8] Likewise, acquaintances from his days as a nationally known performer—from the mid-1930s until his untimely death from amyotrophic lateral sclerosis (ALS) in 1949—consistently attested to his insistence on a sharp, professional appearance. Pete Seeger, for instance, noted with irony, "There I was trying my best to shed my Harvard upbringing, scorning to waste money on clothes other than blues jeans. But Leadbelly always had a clean white shirt and starched collar, well-pressed suit and shined shoes. He didn't need to affect that he was a workingman."[9] Yet at precisely the moment he went from life in Louisiana's Angola prison to national fame between 1934 and 1936, Ledbetter was repeatedly encouraged to don a prison uniform for performances with John Lomax at prestigious venues like Harvard University, in publicity photo shoots, in a nationally syndicated *March of Time* newsreel (again with Lomax), and on the theatrical stages of Harlem. Understandably, he chafed under these demeaning self-presentations even as the novelty of the convict-turned-successful-singer narrative helped establish his fame. On the whole, the cultural memory of "Lead Belly" remains a seemingly contradictory tangle of impressions: dangerously impulsive and gentle hearted, rustic and urbane, and "a combination of ferocity and folk-talent, if you can believe what's written about him."[10]

If Ledbetter's sartorial history was a complicated affair, his musical background was downright kaleidoscopic. The songs he recorded on the occasion of John and Alan Lomax's first visit to the Louisiana State Penitentiary in July 1933 are a useful index in this regard. Told by the Lomaxes that they were interested in "sinful tunes" and older material, Ledbetter offered up a breathtaking array of music: "When I Was a Cowboy" (familiar to the elder Lomax from his pathbreaking 1910 volume *Cowboy Songs and Other Frontier Ballads*); "Take a Whiff on Me," a rollicking ode to cocaine; a field holler that the Lomaxes labeled "Angola Blues"; a version of "Match Box Blues" that features yodeling; the dance tune "You Can't Lose Me Cholly"; a badman ballad titled "Ella Speed"; "Irene," the song that later became most closely associated with Ledbetter; and "Frankie and Albert" (as detailed in the opening chapter, this was an earlier title of the ballad more often recorded as "Frankie and Johnny").[11] The Lomaxes were immediately awed by the range and number of items in Ledbetter's song bag, and when, in the following year, John Lomax arranged another tour of the South in pursuit of African American folk songs for the Library of Congress, he included a return to Angola expressly to record a fuller sampling of Ledbetter's repertoire.[12]

This breadth of musical knowledge was not as anomalous as it initially seemed to the Lomaxes. For musicians like Ledbetter, who sought audiences in venues as varied as the weekend dances of black sharecroppers, urban barrelhouses, and white bourgeois parties, versatility was essential. A successful musician could offer diverse listeners the kinds of music that they most wanted to hear and, often, dance to, of necessity developing an expansive repertoire that crossed the boundaries of what Americans in subsequent decades would learn to think of as distinct musical genres. In this vein, Ledbetter recalled that the first songs he learned to play on guitar included "Green Corn" and "Poor Howard," which were popular at white square dances and at rural African American dance parties known as "sukey jumps."[13] He added work songs, hymns, blues, ballads, and more over the ensuing two decades in order to satisfy his own voracious appetite for song and the varied predilections of audiences in the rural communities, oil-boom towns, and urban red-light districts of East Texas and Louisiana.

As the phonograph industry increasingly turned its attention to vernacular southern music during the 1920s, scores of Ledbetter's contemporaries, black and white, managed to make commercial recordings of their music. Most often, such recordings were arranged through talent scouts for the newly burgeoning phonograph companies: Paramount, Victor, Columbia, and Okeh, among others. The majority of these artists soon returned to local performance contexts if their professional musical endeavors endured at all. Only a fortunate few proved popular enough to garner multiple recording sessions over an extended time, gaining regional or even national visibility and receiving session fees to supplement whatever income they were able to generate by performing live. Blind Lemon Jefferson, Fiddlin' John Carson, and Jimmie Rodgers were among the more popular. As Karl Hagstrom Miller has recently chronicled, 1920s record companies possessed well-defined ideas about the kinds of music that they wanted to record and that they considered marketable. Namely, they entrenched a racially bifurcated marketplace in which southern white artists were channeled into "hill country," "old-time," or "old familiar" music aimed at white consumers, and the work of most southern black artists was pigeonholed as "race records" intended primarily for black consumers.

Often obscured in the process was the cross-pollination of influences and repertoires that characterized musicians like Jefferson, who had performed a wide range of blues, ballads, and dance tunes in Dallas and other Texas communities during the 1910s. According to Uel L. Davis Jr., a retired postmaster in Wortham, Texas, "He'd be singing in a church one day, singing at a house of ill repute the next."[14] Yet driven by a niche-market model based on concepts of isolated black southern communities, Paramount advertised Jefferson's music as "real old-fashioned blues by a real old-fashioned blues singer" and concentrated almost entirely on that aspect of his repertoire in a career cut short by death from an apparent heart attack under enigmatic circumstances in 1929.[15] In parallel fashion, notes Barry Mazor, "though [Fiddlin' John] Carson . . . had been an urban dweller and a working live musical professional for decades, he was portrayed as a picturesque old backwoods mountaineer just in from the hills" in Okeh's promotional materials.[16] In forging such marketing approaches, Miller argues, the commercial music industry of the 1920s and early 1930s played a prominent role in shifting the emphasis of authenticity from particular songs to performers' identities and, like the Lomaxes, did so in a manner that drew substantially on stereotypes of race and region.[17]

Jimmie Rodgers was something of an exception in being able to record more broadly than Jefferson and Carson, despite also dying young (at age thirty-five, from tuberculosis, in 1933). In collaboration with the record producer Ralph Peer, Rodgers recorded string band music, Tin Pan Alley and vaudeville tunes, jazz numbers, and several examples of his signature blues yodels, and shared recording studios with a range of musicians including the Carter Family, Louis and Lil Armstrong, and the Hawaiian steel guitar player Joe Kaipo. In the process, he recorded enough blues-inflected songs for the reviewer Abbe Niles to term him a "white man gone black."[18] Like Jefferson, Carson, and Ledbetter, Rodgers was exposed to a wide range of music before he ever entered a recording studio. As Miller points out: "[Rodgers] had a fanatical love of phonograph records. He bought them 'by the ton', according to his wife Carrie, and his collection included old sentimental songs, current New York stage hits, and novelty numbers." Rodgers learned "Frankie and Johnny," for example, via a popular 1927 recording by the vaudeville star Frank Crumit, rather than through a traditional folk process of transmission. He liked the song so much, in fact, that he even performed the off-color ballad for a gathering of the Interdenominational Men's Bible Class in Miami, Florida, in the fall of 1928.[19]

Unlike Jefferson and Rodgers, Huddie Ledbetter did not first come to wider attention through commercial recordings. And the different, undeniably peculiar route of his journey from sukey jumps in rural Harrison County, Texas, to stretches in the state penitentiaries of Texas and Louisiana to national prominence did much to shape how his music and identity were culturally constructed by the varied constituencies that laid claim to Ledbetter and his work during the 1930s—academic folklore enthusiasts, the commercial music industry, and political activists primary among them. Along the way, Ledbetter built his vast musical repertoire through diverse means. Family was one early source of material. Two uncles, Bob and Terrell, were musicians, and it was Terrell who gave Huddie his first instrument, an accordion known as a windjammer. His mother, Sallie, helped teach him lullabies, spirituals, and even a jig ("Dinah's Got a Wooden Leg"). Naturally, Ledbetter also garnered material by listening to and playing with other musicians. The aforementioned early songs "Green Corn" and "Poor Howard," for example, he learned by observing the musicians Bud Coleman and Jim Fagin at country dances in Harrison County. Later, in the early 1910s, Ledbetter played in and around Dallas–Fort Worth with a young Blind Lemon Jefferson, and the two influenced each other significantly; Ledbetter's later recordings of "Blind Lemon Blues" and "Match Box Blues" (recorded by Jefferson in 1927) suggest as much.[20] Still other tunes Ledbetter came by in more unexpected settings, such as learning "Ain't Going Down to the Well No More" from Will Darling while they picked cotton on a farm in Rockwall County, Texas, in 1910, or songs such as "Ole Rattler," "Go Down, Ol' Hannah," and "The Midnight Special" while in prison in Texas in the years 1918–1925.[21]

Even though much of Ledbetter's repertoire was obtained face-to-face, in a manner in keeping with conventional definitions of folk traditions, he was by no means isolated from the larger currents of commercial music during the first three decades of the twentieth century. Paige McGinley points out that Ledbetter had ample exposure to vaudeville performers of the African American TOBA (Theater Owners Booking Association) circuit, including the Black Patti Troubadours and Bessie Smith, during his time in Shreveport, New Orleans, Houston, and other southern locales; indeed, Ledbetter himself performed in professional variety shows after his release from prison in 1925.[22] Likewise, the years 1925–1930, the hiatus between his two stints in prison, were a period that, John Crowley notes, coincided with "the first boom in sales of 'race records,' including many songs played in styles similar to those in Leadbelly's early recorded repertoire."[23] Ledbetter explained, "I learned by listening to other singers and once in a while off phonograph records. . . . I used to look at the sheet music and learn the words of a few of the popular songs like 'Aggravatin' Papa.'"[24] Hence, by the time Ledbetter arrived in New York City in January 1935, the Lomaxes observed that he possessed an affinity for "the yodeling blues and ballads of Jimmy Rogers [sic], of recent fame, whose ardent admirer Lead Belly still remains." Put simply, like most southern musicians of his generation, he was immersed in a remarkably wide variety of songs, both "folk" and commercial.[25]

The way in which Huddie Ledbetter made his way to New York City in partnership with the Lomaxes constitutes the most well-chronicled and intensely analyzed chapter of the singer's career. Ledbetter's biographers Charles Wolfe and Kip Lornell, as well as the scholars Jerrold Hirsch and Benjamin Filene, have persuasively demonstrated that the cultural construction of "Lead Belly" for a national audience was powerfully shaped by the work of the Lomaxes as cultural brokers. They first visited Angola in July 1933. Strange as their recording equipment must have appeared in its sheer size (a 315-pound Dictaphone recorder that had been specially fitted into the back of their car, along with two seventy-five-pound batteries) and in its capacity to play back the efforts of singers on-site, Ledbetter was no stranger to playing on demand for white patrons within prison walls. Most famously, he garnered a pardon from Texas governor Pat Neff after serving six-plus years of a twenty-year sentence for the murder of Will Stafford (apparently in a dispute over a woman). With good reason, the pardon is often attributed to a song that Ledbetter crafted specifically to request that favor from the governor. In point of fact, though, after first hearing Ledbetter, in January 1924, Neff kept him on hand in the Central State Prison Farm in Sugar Land so that he could perform for social gatherings of the governor's friends and political associates. According to Ledbetter, the governor told him, "I'm going to turn you loose after a while, but I'm going to keep you here so you can pick and dance for me when I come down." (Wolfe and Lornell report that Neff was especially pleased that Ledbetter could accommodate his requests for "hillbilly tunes" like "Ole Dan Tucker.") Neff issued the pardon as one of his last acts in office in January 1925.[26]

Even before Neff entered the picture, Ledbetter had managed to gain a modicum of control over his time by being permitted to travel to other camps on the prison farm to perform on Sundays. Likewise, when imprisoned in Louisiana in 1930, on a charge of "assault with intent to murder" involving a white Shreveport resident named Dick Ellert, Ledbetter came to a similar arrangement with officials at Angola.[27] In short, music was one of the few resources available at the time to an incarcerated African American man such as Ledbetter, and he used it to the best of his ability, with genuinely remarkable results in the case of his pardon by Governor Neff.

When John and Alan Lomax arrived at Angola in July 1933, they were in the midst of a folk music collecting tour across the South. While not without precedent, their project proved tremendously influential because of its scale, thematic focus, and technological innovation. As early as 1910, when he published *Cowboy Songs and Other Frontier Ballads*, John Lomax had demonstrated his break with some of the central tenets of folklore as it had been widely practiced in the United States, most obviously by focusing on folk songs that had been created in the United States rather than passed down from European traditions. His southern sojourns in 1933 and 1934 were predicated on two additional revisions: insisting that African American folk song was a central pillar of the American tradition, and preferring as his archival method field recordings to written transcriptions.[28] African American material thus featured heavily in the Lomax anthology *American Ballads and Folk Songs* (1934), including the use of freshly collected Ledbetter material for their entries on "Bill Martin and Ella Speed" and "Frankie and Albert." The revolutionary nature of this revision is suggested by the critical response of reviewers like Carl Engels, who lamented that the Lomaxes' anthology "gives one at first the impression that America depends for its folk-song literature chiefly on 'Niggah' convicts and white 'bums.'"[29]

While the Lomaxes' willingness to grant the importance of original African American folk music played an important role in democratizing the field, their rationale for focusing on black singers in the South was based on the prevailing assumption that folk music was best preserved in isolated settings where traditions would, allegedly, be kept safe from racial or commercial hybridization via contact with modern society.[30] Specifically, the Lomaxes were in search of "sinful tunes" rather than the more widely chronicled and highly regarded spirituals from the realm of African American sacred music. For these reasons, John Lomax conducted a majority of his recordings in 1933–1934 among African Americans in southern prisons, where, he presumed, he could discover performers willing to sing secular songs "the least contaminated by white influence or by the modern Negro jazz."[31] Ironically, notes Miller, "Lomax was able to collect songs in southern prisons because black inmates, far from isolated from white influence, were under constant white supervision and control." Moreover, the Lomaxes discovered that many prisoners expressed considerable reservations about singing any songs other than religious hymns and spirituals, sometimes producing the "sinful songs" that John Lomax desired only under coercion from prison wardens or guards.[32] Ethically and conceptually muddled though the Lomaxes' methods and motives may have been, their findings proved extraordinary in quality and volume: approximately 150 songs on fifteen aluminum discs and twenty-five cylinders from their first expedition, in 1933, a total that expanded rapidly in volume to nearly seven thousand discs by the time Alan left the Library of Congress in 1942 to assume a position as a producer for the Armed Forces Radio Service. In a 1941 interview, Alan estimated that he and his father had "no less than 20,000 songs in our collection" and that "sixty percent of the tunes come from the South."[33]

The Lomaxes' field experiences with Ledbetter significantly altered their collecting methods. After being released from Angola on August 1, 1934, under a recently implemented "good time" provision, Ledbetter corresponded with the elder Lomax about the possibility of working as his assistant during his ongoing southern fieldwork; he joined Lomax in Marshall, Texas, in late September. Since Alan had fallen ill and dropped out of the recording trip, Ledbetter's service as a driver and in helping with the unwieldy recording equipment was a substantial boon. Even more importantly, Lomax quickly realized that Ledbetter could demonstrate to prison inmates and other interviewees the kinds of music that he was trying to obtain. By Alan Lomax's account, their previous method sometimes consisted of simply asking whether any of their research subjects knew "Stagolee," hoping that this famous badman ballad would lead to the revelation of other, similar material. Ledbetter's extensive repertoire expanded the possibilities exponentially in this regard, as well as providing a concrete demonstration of the unpolished style that appealed to Lomax.[34]

By no means was this a one-sided exchange. As Miller observes, "Each used the other to gather audiences and get paid, even as Lomax attempted to remain firmly in control of the relationship."[35] Beyond room, board, and the small amounts of money that John Lomax occasionally (and reluctantly) turned over to Ledbetter, the folklorist encouraged him to perform his songs in a manner that explicated the meanings and fully elaborated the verses of individual songs. In addition, Ledbetter gained valuable exposure to a wealth of folk songs, many of which he added to his repertoire, including tunes, such as "Rock Island Line," that subsequently became Lead Belly fan favorites.[36]

Meanwhile, John Lomax was laying plans to bring his folk song prodigy northward so that he might showcase Ledbetter firsthand to his peers in the academic folklore community. The convention of the Modern Language Association (MLA) in Philadelphia in 1934 provided a trial run for this new chapter in the Lomax-Ledbetter partnership. Founded in 1883, the MLA shared the culture of many similar academic organizations, including an emphasis on professional decorum and a pattern of racial segregation. The American Literature Group was not founded within the larger MLA until 1921, and the majority of members' scholarship remained fixated on works of European origin. Similarly, while the conference included a small cadre of folklore scholars, most of them still adhered to the Child-Kittredge paradigm of focusing on material inherited from antiquated English and Scottish ballads.

Thus, it constituted something genuinely new in the world of academic folklore studies when Ledbetter appeared following an evening banquet of the MLA at the Benjamin Franklin Hotel on the evening of December 28, 1934. His debut was preceded by a performance of "Elizabethan Ayres" and a group sing-along of sea chanties, both of which fell squarely within the Child-Kittredge tradition. Listed in the program only as "a Negro minstrel from Louisiana," Ledbetter offered something altogether different. Following an introduction by John Lomax, he was perched in a chair atop a banquet table, where he performed for roughly half an hour. While this audience was, in important respects, a new one to the singer, he could draw upon his extensive experience of playing at parties for well-to-do white audiences in Texas and Louisiana. As the composer Charles Seeger recognized, "Lead Belly was already an astute handler of the nonfolk by the time I met him," which was in the spring of 1935.[37] The following morning, Ledbetter appeared with Lomax as part of a panel that included some of the most prominent scholars in the field of American folklore. He served as a kind of living demonstration, being listed in the conference program as "Negro convict Leadbelly of Louisiana."[38] At the conclusion of both MLA performances, in a move owing to his earlier busking experiences, Ledbetter passed his hat around the hall and collected a sum of $47.50 for his efforts. As Wolfe and Lornell wryly note, "History is silent about what Huddie himself thought of the 'Elizabethan Ayres' or the sight of a room full of formally dressed scholars bellowing out sea chanties."[39] What is certain, however, is that Ledbetter made a striking impression on this new audience, not least on the Lomaxes themselves.

WHILE JOHN LOMAX'S racial paternalism proved regrettably tenacious, both his and Alan's viewpoints on folk music evolved significantly in the face of the evidence that they encountered in their fieldwork during the first half of the 1930s. For one, although they began with a goal of merely compiling as many "Negro sinful songs" in as many variations as possible, over the course of their southern travels they developed an interest in the personae of specific performers and began to profile a handful of these African Americans in terms that explicitly declared their status as artists. In an article published in 1934, John Lomax compared the prisoner James "Iron Head" Baker to "blind Homer," and stated that Moses "Clear Rock" Platt, another prisoner, "had a store [of song] probably equal in continuous length to the Iliad."[40] The Lomaxes' fascination with such exceptional figures, as with Huddie Ledbetter, played no small role in drawing them back on an even more extensive southern recording tour in 1934 and culminated in their 1936 book-length study of Ledbetter's life story and song repertoire, *Negro Folk Songs as Sung by Lead Belly*.[41] In that volume, the Lomaxes extended their argument for considering the best African American folk singers on a par with exemplars of Western high culture: "Certainly young Mozart was no more absorbed in music than young, black Huddie Ledbetter."[42] Confronted with the vast storehouse of material acquired by men such as Baker, Platt, and Ledbetter, the Lomaxes had to face the fact that even in the ostensibly isolated environs of southern prisons, folk singers, in fact, were *not* social isolates. Rather, the Lomaxes reluctantly retooled their focus away from "folk singers" as customarily defined in favor of a framework of "folk artists," who were rooted in particular local communities and vernacular traditions yet also adapted popular songs from "outside" sources into their repertoires.

Negro Folk Songs as Sung by Lead Belly exemplifies the Lomaxes' uneven efforts to articulate this new formulation of Ledbetter as a folk artist. As they recorded and transcribed dozens of items from Ledbetter's repertoire, they could not escape the fact that songs such as "Frankie and Albert" had circulated widely by means both oral and technological, including commercial recordings and radio. Thus, the Lomaxes could not claim folkloric purity for such songs in a conventional sense. Nonetheless, as both John and Alan Lomax often did from the mid-1930s onward, they argued for the song having achieved "folk" music status by other means. Deliberately obscuring Ledbetter's many years of work as a professional musician before the 1930s, John Lomax's introduction to the book argued that social isolation and immersion in an oral culture provided the necessary grounds for establishing Lead Belly's folk authenticity: "His eleven years of confinement had cut him off both from the phonograph and from the radio. According to his own claim he knew five hundred songs learned 'by word of mouth.' He carried in his head all these words and tunes. We saw no printed page of music in either his prison cell or in his home." Yet, on the very same page as this statement inaccurately alleging Ledbetter's sequestration from records, radios, and sheet music, John Lomax offered a more nuanced acknowledgment of the musician's hybrid repertoire:

> We present this set of songs, therefore, not as folk songs entirely, but as a cross-section of Afro-American songs that have influenced and have been influenced by popular music; and we present this singer, not as a folk singer handing on a tradition faithfully, but as a folk artist who contributes to the tradition, and as a musician of a sort important in the growth of American popular music. We give at once the colorful, personal background of Negro "sinful songs" and the "life and works" of an artist* who happened to be born with a black skin and with Negro barrel-house life, convict life, and folk-lore for his artistic material.[43]

For the time, this was a rather radical assertion, even if Lomax undercut his own argument to a degree by annotating the asterisked term "artist" with the explanation "Musicians may smile, but we will let the word stand." Breaking with the prevailing model of folk songs established by scholars like Francis Child and John Lomax's own mentor, George Lyman Kittredge, the Lomaxes emphasized the creation of new folk songs in response to the new social realities of US life, and posited African American expression as a cornerstone of this new canon of US folk song. Even more, the Lomaxes prized "Negro sinful songs" (such as "Frankie and Albert") above the already recognized body of "Negro spirituals." In fact, John Lomax originally intended to title his book on Ledbetter *Negro Sinful Songs*.[44]

Alan Lomax, too, acknowledged Ledbetter's status as a "folk artist" rather than a "folk singer" in the strict sense. Specifically, the younger Lomax argued that Ledbetter's performance of "Frankie and Albert" was aesthetically faithful to an "authentic" folk tradition, suggesting that grittiness set his work apart from popular-culture adaptations:

Of late years this Negro ballad has been sung by college students who had no true understanding of its background; Mae West, John Held, Jr., and others have helped to give it a gay-nineties setting so that "Frankie and Albert" has been snickered at along with the extravagantly sentimental popular songs of that period. But, until the ballad fell into the hands of college students and barber-shop quartets, it remained a stark account of the central facts of a murder. The mountaineers and Negroes who sang it found nothing ridiculous in "Frankie and Albert."[45]

Here, Lomax affirms the African American roots of the ballad, as well as its vibrancy among a presumably working-class cohort of "mountaineers and Negroes." He imagines the ballad to be sober and dramatic in these contexts, whereas later white and well-to-do imitators opted for a mawkish, light-hearted tone.

Further, Lomax insisted that the gravity Ledbetter accorded to this particular ballad stemmed from his personal experience with scenarios comparable to those described in the song:

For Lead Belly, who knows something about murder, the ballad is not funny or "overdone." He explains why Frankie came to shoot Albert, how she was hurt in her heart when she saw him "lovin' up" Alice Fry. When Albert falls "all in a knot," Lead Belly bawls out in the agony of a man with a 41 bullet in his guts, just as he has often heard men cry out in their death agony. Mrs. Johnson at the graveyard calls on the Lord to have mercy on her son; Lead Belly has heard Negro women at country funerals in Louisiana wail over their dead sons in just this way when the "coffin sounds."[46]

Exoticism and primitivism suffuse much Lead Belly lore, but it bears emphasizing that Lomax—albeit hyperbolic—is not entirely wrong here. This particular ballad likely appealed to Ledbetter for reasons both professional and personal. In keeping with his three-decade musical career before his encounters with the Lomaxes in the mid-1930s, Ledbetter surely recognized the wide allure of this ballad to audiences of varied racial identities and socioeconomic strata. Ballads in general had been widely popular in the early twentieth century, and murder ballads in particular proved perennial favorites, merging as they often did sensational exploits of romance and violence. Having "Frankie and Albert" in his repertoire would have served the singer well in the country dance, barrelhouse, and white planter parties that were the bread-and-butter venues of his pre-Lomax career.

Beyond the song's professional utility, the world conjured up in Ledbetter's "Frankie and Albert" was one with which he had more than a passing familiarity. Most notably, Ledbetter's first residence upon leaving his parents' house in his teenage years was on Fannin Street in Shreveport, Louisiana, a notorious red-light district set aside by city authorities in an attempt to geographically contain the trade in alcohol, gambling, and prostitution. According to Wolfe and Lornell, "[The area] had at least forty whorehouses, not counting the little shotgun houses and dens where individual girls plied their trade. There were also dozens of saloons, dance halls, gambling houses, and even an opium den run by a character named 'Ol' Bob' and a smoke house in the back of a Chinese restaurant."[47] While uplift-minded African Americans tended look askance at "sin streets" like Fannin and Atlanta's Decatur Street, Tera Hunter notes, "Despite its notoriety, Decatur Street patrons were typically not the larger-than-life pimps or mobsters but ordinary women and men in search of social diversions and alternative financial prospects denied them elsewhere in their lives."[48] Similarly, Ledbetter attested to numerous acquaintances and interviewers in later years that professional opportunity and the vices of Fannin Street were the principal factors that drew him to it as he set out to forge his adult identity. The site remained a touchstone for Ledbetter long after he had left the South for New York City; as Wolfe and Lornell put it, "He always remembered the street as if it were one of his most vital formative experiences."[49] By Ledbetter's own account, he was prone to mix the wooing of sexual partners with musical performances, and opportunities on this front abounded in his new environment. The sculptor Joe Brown, for example, recalled Ledbetter explaining his work in a Fannin Street barrelhouse thus: "They gimme fifty cents a week and all the women I could handle."[50] The jazz producer and biographer Ross Russell, a late-in-life acquaintance, claimed that Ledbetter "was kept by one of the Fanning [sic] St. 'easy riders' and spent his nights on the town."[51]

The enticements of Fannin Street were accompanied by collateral risks. Even if often treated with sensationalist and racist overtones in the Shreveport newspapers, episodes of violence were distressingly common—not least those arising from disputes over romantic entanglements. Ledbetter was no stranger to such incidents before, during, or after his days and nights on Fannin Street. The prominent scar that ringed his neck resulted from one such episode in which a knife was put to his throat while he performed at a party in Oil City, Louisiana, in 1926. Likewise, a majority of Ledbetter's run-ins with the law, including his prison sentence in Texas, seem to have arisen from conflicts with other men over proprietary claims to particular women.[52] Thus, although he was never involved in a love triangle that precisely mirrored the dramatic outcome described in the ballad, the milieu conjured up by "Frankie and Albert"—a world of prostitution, saloons, and infidelity turned explosively violent—surely was one that struck Ledbetter as intimately familiar.

"Frankie and Albert" remained a staple for Ledbetter even as he added songs to his repertoire that were more politicized ("Bourgeois Blues," most famously) or, like "Rock Island Line" and "Goodnight, Irene," brought him more fame. Although he recorded it on at least six occasions, Ledbetter's fullest iterations of "Frankie and Albert" were captured in sessions with Alan Lomax in January–March 1935. Following the deluge of media interest and contract offers that ensued from Ledbetter's debut in New York City, John Lomax wished to remove the singer from what he saw as the hazards of late-night carousing and exposure to popular music that were readily available in Harlem. Further, the Lomaxes sought a tranquil locale in which to conduct extensive interviews and recordings in service of their book on Ledbetter's life and music. Mary Elizabeth Barnicle, a New York University professor and a folk music enthusiast in her own right, and Margaret Conklin, a Macmillan editor, provided this retreat in the form of a summerhouse in Wilton, Connecticut.[53] Taking up residence there, the trio quickly settled into a routine in which Ledbetter served as chauffeur and house servant, and the Lomaxes wrote. When John Lomax arranged for Ledbetter's fiancée, Martha Promise, to arrive from Louisiana and wed the singer in mid-January (with considerable newspaper fanfare orchestrated by Lomax), she assumed a role as cook, laundress, and housekeeper.[54]

Within this regressive racial dynamic, however, Alan Lomax was busy trying to organize a narrative account of Ledbetter's life history and to record Ledbetter's "complete" body of songs. All told, Alan recorded approximately eighty songs during these sessions—several of them in multiple versions, since he aimed to compile the fullest renditions of each item that Ledbetter could offer. Admittedly, the end result proved flawed. Not least, despite Alan's prominent use of dialect in the narrative entitled "Lead Belly Tells His Story," the perspective is clearly Lomax's at least as much as it is the singer's. Even more problematically, John Lomax's lengthy account of his experiences with Ledbetter all too often portrays his subject as a kind of primitive man-child, driven by powerful impulses for sex and violence.[55] Still, such a study of an individual folk singer had never before seen print. Most folklorists of Francis Child's generation, after all, had perceived folk musicians as relatively interchangeable, passive bearers of ossified folk song traditions. The fact that the Lomaxes' book featured an African American ex-convict as its centerpiece was simultaneously revealing of the period's racial paternalism (such a person constituted the most authentic "folk" representative because he was presumed to be most removed from cosmopolitan cultural influences) *and* a noteworthy gesture toward cultural pluralism (the United States had its own vital tradition of folk song, and Lead Belly was one of its key exemplars). Despite having a prominent publisher, Macmillan, the book's sales proved extremely disappointing. Still, the volume remains a trove of valuable information and a testament to the scope of Ledbetter's vast repertoire.

It was in those sessions that the Lomaxes first chronicled Ledbetter's extensive use of spoken narratives to introduce songs and to serve as interludes between verses. Scholars continue to debate the exact origins of this device. As an experienced performer, Ledbetter surely was no stranger to patter between and in the midst of his songs. In a draft of his introduction for *Negro Folk Songs as Sung by Lead Belly*, John Lomax explained, "Lead Belly has practiced this 'talking' technique ever since he began to play the guitar." Yet Lomax included a note that spoke to his and Alan's influence: "We rather suspect that Lead Belly did more talking while playing with us than he had ever done before, since he noticed that we enjoyed it so much."[56] In front of academic audiences during their 1934–1935 travels, John Lomax frequently performed the role of introducing ("explaining") the songs by his great discovery, Ledbetter, and seemed to relish doing so. But since some audience members in New York City and elsewhere in the Northeast complained that they could not understand the dialect of Ledbetter's singing, the Lomaxes increasingly encouraged Ledbetter to talk more to audiences about the subjects of his songs, for the sake of clarity. In addition, the Lomaxes were attempting to archive the full repertoire of Ledbetter's music for posterity, another reason that led Alan to encourage the singer to elaborate his spoken prologues and interludes. Alan Lomax remained clear, though, that the fashioning of these narratives was primarily the creative labor of Ledbetter himself: "He began to try and put his songs in their context. It was one of the most amazing things I've ever seen done. He actually remade all of his songs from the time we were at MLA to the time we were at Wilton. . . . He created those *cante-fables* in a month."[57] Although the unorthodox device was omitted for purposes of most subsequent commercial recordings, it proved popular with many of Ledbetter's concert audiences and, arguably, influenced the use of similar techniques by folk musicians like Woody Guthrie and Pete Seeger.

Ledbetter employs the device of narrative interludes more substantially in "Frankie and Albert" than anywhere else in his corpus of recorded music—so much so that his first Wilton recording of the ballad (January 20, 1935) runs a full nine minutes in length (see text figure 2.1).[58] Both Lomaxes considered this extended rendition nothing less than a masterpiece: John thought that

TEXT FIGURE 2.1. (*pp. 51–55*) Huddie Ledbetter, "Frankie and Albert." Words and music by Huddie Ledbetter. Collected and adapted by John A. Lomax and Alan Lomax TRO-© Copyright 1936 (renewed) 1959 (renewed) Folkways Music Publishers, Inc., New York, NY, and Global Jukebox Publishing, Marshall, Tex. Used by permission.

Frankie was a woman
Everybody know,
Made a hundred dollars,
Buy her man a suit of clothes.
Was her man, but he done her wrong.

[spoken] Albert was out all night long. When he come on home that morning just before day, he lied down to go to sleep. Frankie was working in the white folks' kitchen, and she told him—she said, "Now listen, baby, you stay here. I'm going and cook, baby, then I'll be right back." And he had a six-shooter under his pillow. No sooner had Frankie left home than Albert got up and walked away. But Frankie didn't stay long. She felt like the rascal wasn't gonna stay there. And when she got back home he was gone. And she knowed just about where she'd find him, but she got his six-shooter and on his cold trail. And he [Albert] went down to the bartender. And he told the man, "If Frankie come and ask for me, don't tell her where I am." Frankie got his six-shooter . . .

Frankie went a-walkin',
Did not go for fun.
Had under her apron
Albert's 41—
"[Gonna] kill my man, 'cause he done me wrong."

[spoken] Frankie [went] over there to the bartender—the saloon where they got all they whiskey and beer, on a credit if they ain't got no money. The man knowed 'em. And he liked Frankie. And he liked Albert. So Albert had told the man, "If Frankie come, don't tell her where I am." But anyhow you take a white man, he ain't gonna tell no lie—if he know you. If he know you got a good woman, and he knows you're treating her wrong, he's gonna tell her exactly where you is. So she walked up to the man, and he run his hand through his hair. And here's what he said . . .

Frankie went down to the Hughes's Saloon
Called for a bottle of beer
Asked the loving bartender
"Has my loving man been here?
He's my man, but he done me wrong."

[spoken] The bartender looked at Frankie, and he walked up to her.

"I ain't gonna tell you no story
I ain't gonna tell you no lie
Albert left here an hour ago
Woman named Alice Fry
He's your man, Lawd, he done you wrong.
He's your man, Lawd, he done you wrong."

[spoken] She goes on again. After she goes on, a-walkin', she walked down to her [Alice's] house. When she got to her house, she walked by, she didn't raise no alarm. She looked through the window glass. She [Alice] didn't pull the window shade down. She looked through the window glass, and there was Albert sitting in that woman's home. And arms all around the woman, and Frankie couldn't stand it.

Frankie went by her house
Did not give no alarm
Looked through the window glass
Albert's sittin' in the woman's arms
"There's my man, and he done me wrong."

[spoken] Frankie hauled off and shot him. When she shot Albert he fell down on his knees calling to the policeman.

Frankie, she shot Albert
Fell upon his knees
"Oh, policeman
Don't let that woman kill me!
I'm her man and I done her wrong
I'm her man and I done her wrong"

[spoken] Frankie walked back again a-cryin'. And she hauled off and shot him again.

Frankie she shot Albert
Fell all in a knot
"Oh Mrs. Johnson
See where your son is shot!
I'm your son, and the only one."

[spoken] Onliest child Mrs. Johnson had in the world. And Frankie went to Mrs. Johnson, fell down on her knees, after she done shot Albert.

Frankie went to Mrs. Johnson
Fell down on her knees
Crying, "Oh, Mrs. Johnson,
Will you forgive me please?
Killed your son 'cause he done me wrong."

[spoken] Mrs. Johnson looked at Frankie and she wondered, could she forgive her?

"I'll forgive you, Frankie,
I'll forgive you not
Killed poor Albert
Only son I've got.
He's my son, and the only one.
He's my son, and the only one."

[spoken] After Frankie she shot Albert, the policemens all heard it. One truck of the policemens came down. Policemens come down and hold an inquest over Albert. And they liked Mrs. Johnson, they liked Albert, and they liked Frankie. They wanted to make everything better for poor Albert's mother, and here's what they said . . .

Rubber tired hearse
Rubber tired hack
Hearse to carry Albert to the graveyard
Hack to bring his mother back
Was her son, and the only one.

[spoken] When Mrs. Johnson got to Albert, just before he died, Albert spoke one word to his mother, and this is what he said . . .

"Turn me over, mother,
Turn me over slow
Turn me over for your last time
This bullet it hurt me so
I'm your son, and the only one.
I'm your son, and the only one."

[spoken] Mrs. Johnson went and turned him over. She commenced crying.

O boy!
O boy!
O boy!
O boy!

[spoken] She began to think about the Good Lord in the sky that might help her son . . .

O Lawd!
O Lawd!
O Lawd!
O Lawd!

[spoken] She came and sat on his knee . . .

Have mercy!
Have mercy!
Have mercy!
Have mercy!

[spoken] They taken Albert to the graveyard. When they taken Albert to the graveyard and when they let him down, Frankie run to the graveyard and here's what she said . . .

Taken Albert to the graveyard
When they let him down
Frankie was a holl'in'
With a doleful sound
"Kilt you man, 'cause you done me wrong."

[spoken] Frankie, after they done buried Albert, she goes and fell down on the headboard on her knees . . .

Frankie went to the graveyard
Fell down on her knees
"Speak one word, Albert,
Give my heart some ease.
Kilt you, babe, 'cause you done me wrong.
I kilt you, babe, 'cause you done me wrong."

[spoken] Frankie went to Mrs. Johnson, fell down on her knees again—at the graveyard . . .

Frankie went to Mrs. Johnson
Fell down on her knees
Crying, "Oh, Mrs. Johnson,
Will you forgive me please?
Killed your son 'cause he done me wrong."

[spoken] Mrs. Johnson looked at Frankie and here's what she said . . .

"I'll forgive you Frankie
I'll forgive you not
Kilt poor Albert
Only support I've got.
He's my son, and the only one."

[spoken] Frankie went to the graveyard and fell down on her knees . . .

Good-bye!
Good-bye!
Good-bye!
Good-bye!

Farewell!
Farewell!
Farewell!
Farewell!

[spoken] Mrs. Johnson walked around the graveyard alone, going . . .

Oh Lawd!
Oh Lawd!
Oh Lawd!
Oh Lawd!

Oh Lawd!
Oh Lawd!
Oh Lawd!
Oh Lawd!

My son!
My son!
My son!
My son!

the song was "magnificent" and "the crown of this book," and Alan asserted, "This ballad is Lead Belly's 'Ninth Symphony,' through him becoming a small opera with stage directions."[59] Consider the first such set of "stage directions" between the opening two verses of the song:

Frankie was a woman
Everybody know,

Made a hundred dollars,
Buy her man a suit of clothes.
Was her man, but he done her wrong.

[spoken]: Albert was out all night long. When he come on home that morning just before day, he lied down to go to sleep. Frankie was working in the white folks' kitchen, and she told him—she said, "Now listen, baby, you stay here. I'm going and cook, baby, then I'll be right back." And he had a six-shooter under his pillow. No sooner had Frankie left home then Albert got up and walked away. But Frankie didn't stay long. She felt like the rascal wasn't gonna stay there. And when she got back home he was gone. And she knowed just about where she'd find him, but she got his six-shooter and on his cold trail. And he went down to the bartender. And he [Albert] told the man, "If Frankie come and ask for me, don't tell her where I am." Frankie got his six-shooter . . .

Frankie went a-walkin',
Did not go for fun.
Had under her apron
Albert's 41—
[Gonna] kill my man, 'cause he done me wrong."

In both this version and a March recording of the song from the Wilton sessions, one can hear Ledbetter begin to move from the first verse to the second before catching himself and then launching into the first extended spoken narrative, a hesitation suggesting the relative newness of the interludes.[60] Even though the spoken interludes become gradually shorter as the song progresses, they wind up dwarfing the amount of time devoted to the lyrical verses. Spelling out details of motive (for example, Albert is clearly identified as a duplicitous "rascal") and plot (the gun used to kill Albert is his own), the spoken narrative provides a depth of backstory not present in most versions of the ballad. The vivid, theatrical imagery in such spoken passages helps the listener visualize the actions and thoughts of the central actors. If anything, Ledbetter risks "over-telling" the story by racing ahead of the sung verses in his spoken narrative.

The Wilton recordings contain many of the elements standard to the ballad tradition of "Frankie and Albert": Frankie spending her earnings on an extravagant suit for Albert; Frankie asking a bartender for information regarding Albert's whereabouts; Frankie's discovery of Albert in the arms of another woman (here named Alice Fry) and her subsequent shooting of Albert; Albert in the throes of death crying out for his mother; and Frankie's subsequent expression of grief over Albert's demise, even as she holds fast to the justness of her actions.[61] But Ledbetter introduces significant variations in the ballad, too. For one, his Frankie earns money to support Albert by working as a cook or a domestic rather than as a prostitute. By prevailing moral standards, giving Frankie this job casts her in a more virtuous light than Frankie the streetwalker. On a related point, Ledbetter's rendering of "Frankie and Albert" marks the racial identity of the characters more explicitly than do most versions of the ballad. For example, Frankie is depicted as an African American working in a white household. That she toils in such unsavory conditions would seem to make Albert's philandering rambles about town—all night long and again the next morning!—particularly galling. Intriguingly, too, Ledbetter casts the bartender as a white man who takes Frankie's part in the conflict by telling her of Albert's infidelity with Alice Fry. (In a spoken aside in the second Wilton recording, Ledbetter offers, "But you take a white man, he gonna tell you the truth. If he know you, and both of you is alright, he'll sure tell the woman over the man.") None of this is to say that Ledbetter's telling of this saga is intended as a political critique of social inequalities per se, but these features ground his characters in trenchant realities of race and gender power relations to a greater degree than any other recording of the song from this era.

A second distinguishing feature of Ledbetter's "Frankie and Albert" is the degree of attention that he devotes to the character of Albert's mother, Mrs. Johnson. As is common in other versions of the ballad, she first appears at her son's side after he has been shot by Frankie. Albert pleads, with his final utterance, "Turn me over, mother, / Turn me over slow . . . I'm your son, and the only one." Yet whereas most renditions of the ballad are nearing their end with this verse, Ledbetter's version is only at its halfway mark. As Alan Lomax astutely recognized, "He saves his pity for the survivors of the murder."[62] In an element seemingly unique to Ledbetter, he narrates, "Mrs. Johnson went and turned him over. She commenced crying." And then he wails more than sings, "Oh boy!" and "Oh Lawd!" and "Have mercy!" four times each. Her grief thus commands center stage and makes of the song at least a double tragedy: Albert's death is both her loss and Frankie's.

As the song continues, Frankie begs forgiveness from Albert's mother. Although apparently torn in her feelings, Mrs. Johnson ultimately refuses such a pardon:

Frankie went to Mrs. Johnson,
Fell down on her knees.
Crying, "Oh, Mrs. Johnson,

Will you forgive me, please?
[I] killed your son 'cause he done me wrong."

[spoken]: Mrs. Johnson looked at Frankie and she wondered, could she forgive her?

I'll forgive you Frankie,
I'll forgive you not,
Killed poor Albert,
Only son I've got.
He's my son, and the only one.
He's my son, and the only one.

These verses are not unique to Ledbetter, but they are uncommon. In his study of over two hundred versions of the ballad, Bruce Buckley identifies only eighteen variants that include Frankie's petition to Albert's or Johnny's mother; in all the items that include a reply, the mother denies Frankie's request.[63] Ledbetter's decision to eschew the more common, stock verses that place Frankie in a courtroom or in prison when she is adjudicated for her lover's murder has the important effect of placing the moral weight of the conflict within African American circles, and specifically between the two parties most immediately affected by Albert's death.

Following this encounter between lover and mother, Ledbetter describes Albert's funeral with stock verses before turning to more extended exclamations of grief, from both Frankie and Mrs. Johnson, that echo those made immediately after Albert's death. Frankie repeats an impassioned "Good-bye!" and "Farewell!" four times each, followed by Mrs. Johnson's refrains of "Oh Lawd!" and "My son!" to close the first Wilton recording of the song. In a review, Denis Preston noted the artistry at work in Ledbetter's progression from an early narrative emphasis on the lives of Frankie and Albert to a more expressly emotional handling of Frankie and Mrs. Johnson in the latter half of the song:

> With the ballad's progress these spoken interpolations become shorter and shorter, until, at last, they are swept aside altogether by the rising tide of the climax. This is not the work of any ordinary guitar-plucking wayward minstrel. From the dawdling opening—part spoken, part sung—to the reiterated cry of the mother, the heartrending "My son, my son . . ." this is an artist, fully conscious of his subject's dramatic context and his own ability to convey the mounting tension of its drama.[64]

What can't be made fully apparent on the pages of the Lomaxes' *Negro Folk Songs as Sung by Lead Belly* is the emotional resonance with which Ledbetter imbues the repeated exclamations that close the song. Delivered in a plaintive falsetto meant to emulate the voices of Frankie and Mrs. Johnson, these grief-stricken utterances accomplish at least two rather remarkable feats. For one, they place Mrs. Johnson on par with Frankie and Albert as a central character in the ballad. By song's end, Mrs. Johnson shares equal time with Frankie in expressing sorrow over Albert's death. If anything, Ledbetter's vocals enunciate Mrs. Johnson's lamentations more emphatically, and with a sharper rise in pitch, than Frankie's parallel cries.

Second, these brief refrains manage to instill sympathy for the departed Albert, a character that Ledbetter already has described as a shameless adulterer who "has done [Frankie] wrong." Consistent with some other versions of the ballad, Albert pleads for protection from a policeman after taking the first bullet from Frankie, and for comfort from his mother once he knows that his death is imminent. But nowhere does Albert expressly ask for forgiveness from Frankie for his transgressions. Ledbetter delivers Albert's last lines with a guttural inflection that conveys the pain that he suffers in his final moments. This, together with the amount of time and emotional intensity devoted to expressions of grief by Frankie and Albert's mother, makes Ledbetter's rendition of the ballad at least loosely congruent in tone with the lamentations of Mary and Martha at the feet of the crucified Jesus—particularly with Mrs. Johnson's repeated cries of "Oh, Lawd!" and "Have mercy!" and "My son!" and the singer's highly unusual reference to blood flowing from Albert's side.[65] In this way, Ledbetter configures Albert as *both* scoundrel *and* martyr, to a degree unmatched in the vast corpus of recordings of the ballad.

Nor does he choose sides between mother and romantic partner. Part of the effectiveness of Ledbetter's ballad as tragedy is that it retains a degree of moral ambiguity, maintaining empathy for both Frankie and Mrs. Johnson—and even Albert, "rascal" though he may have been. In a gesture of evenhandedness, Ledbetter's spoken narration describes the response of the policemen who arrive on the scene of Albert's death: "They like Mrs. Johnson, they like Albert, and they liked Frankie." How Ledbetter happened upon this twist is hard to say with certainty. One cannot help wondering, though, whether the stark emotional expression of a mother separated from her only son was made more meaningful for the singer by the death of his own mother while he languished in Angola prison. Whatever the case, the remarkably elaborate narrations of the spoken interludes and the raw, almost purely emotive expressions of grief by Frankie and Mrs. Johnson remain Ledbetter's two most original contributions to the "Frankie and Albert" ballad tradition.

The impact of Ledbetter's conversations with the Lomaxes and his encounters with folklore-minded audiences is illuminated by comparing this 1935 recording in Wilton with his earlier performances of "Frankie and Albert" for the Lomaxes at Angola in July 1933 and July 1934. On the occasion of the Lomaxes' first visit, Ledbetter opened "Frankie and Albert" with a verse in which Albert's mother, Mrs. Johnson, repudiates Frankie's plea for forgiveness before moving to a more conventional, chronological ordering of the next four verses:

> *I'll forgive you Frankie*
> *I'll forgive you not*
> *Killed poor Albert*
> *Only son I've got*
> *He's my son and the only one*
>
> *Frankie was a woman*
> *Everybody know*
> *Made a hundred dollars*
> *Buy her man a suit of clothes*
> *Was her man, Lawd, he done her wrong*
>
> *Frankie she shot Albert*
> *Fell upon his knees*
> *Crying, "Oh policeman!*
> *[unintelligible] that woman kill me*
> *I'm her man, Lawd, I done her wrong"*
>
> *Frankie went to Mrs. Johnson*
> *Fell down on her knees*
> *Crying, "Oh Mrs. Johnson*
> *Will you forgive me, please?*
> *I killed your son, 'cause he done me wrong"*
>
> *Taking Albert to the graveyard*
> *Laid him in the ground*
> *Frankie she was singing*
> *Oh with a doleful sound*
> *"Killed my man 'cause he done me wrong"*[66]

This 1933 rendition differs significantly in at least three respects from the 1935 recording of the ballad that Ledbetter made in Connecticut. Perhaps most obviously, the 1933 prison recording lacks the spoken narratives that distinguish so many of the Connecticut sessions, lending additional credence to the suggestion that Ledbetter elaborated this technique in collaboration with the Lomaxes. Second, the 1933 version begins in media res, not yet having described the circumstances of Albert's death or the plea for forgiveness to which Mrs. Johnson's verse is the response. Third, even leaving aside the matter of spoken narratives, the verses of Ledbetter's 1933 "Frankie and Albert" represent a radically condensed version of the ballad. Omitted are key elements such as Frankie's acquisition of a firearm, her search for Albert and Alice Fry, the confrontation between Frankie and Albert, Albert's lamentations after being shot, and the expressive wailing of Frankie and Mrs. Johnson over Albert's death.

Even with all that the Lomaxes themselves and subsequent biographers have written about their pioneering recording trips of the 1930s, it is impossible to know the exact circumstances of those sessions. The Lomaxes describe a process in which, typically, they tried out numerous would-be singers and recorded the best of them during stretches that lasted as long as twelve hours. In 1933, they seem to have worked quickly, trying to efficiently catalogue and document a repertoire of what they considered interesting material. Hence, during their first visit to Angola, Ledbetter progressed through the previously mentioned playlist in rapid-fire fashion, performing only fragments of each song. The recording of "Frankie and Albert" is typical in this regard, moving at a brisk tempo and clocking in at roughly one minute and fifteen seconds. As part of their return recording junket in the summer of 1934, the Lomaxes sought out Ledbetter for fuller treatment of his storehouse of songs. On this occasion, they attained an extended version of "Frankie and Albert," one over four minutes in length and very closely mirroring the version recorded the following year in Connecticut—except for a change in the order of some verses and the absence of spoken narrative interludes.[67] Thus, it seems safe to conclude that Ledbetter was acquainted with an especially rich, full version of "Frankie and Albert" before beginning his travels throughout the South and Northeast with the Lomaxes.

Whatever the exigencies of the initial Ledbetter recordings, it is clear that his first recording of "Frankie and Albert" in 1933 depended for its effectiveness on listeners well acquainted with its narrative; listeners lacking that familiarity would almost surely have found themselves struggling to connect the dots between the fragmented verses, especially in light of the nonchronological placement of the initial verse. Such liberties were the sort that Ledbetter presumably could have taken when performing a well-known ballad like "Frankie and Albert" in his earlier days as a professional musician, playing for sukey-jump or saloon audiences in Texas and Louisiana. In such settings, singers might offer a sampling of verses in the manner of Ledbetter's 1933 Angola recording, their precise sequencing being less crucial than hitting a ballad's highlights in a way that satisfied audiences, Likewise, Library of Congress field recordings of "Frankie and Albert" from other singers seldom approached the breadth of detail found in Ledbetter's 1934 Angola and 1935 Wilton recordings of this ballad. More typical was the version collected by John Lomax from James Wilson in the Virginia State Penitentiary in May 1936, a five-verse rendition that omitted any direct mention of Frankie's shooting of Albert. Notably, too, this version by Wilson and his unnamed guitar accompanist featured a bouncy, upbeat tempo, a nontraditional touch suggesting that they were well acquainted with commercial adaptations of the ballad.[68]

As with the spoken interludes, the distinctiveness of Ledbetter's focus on Albert's mother, Mrs. Johnson, falls into stark relief when placed alongside contemporaneous recordings of the song by other artists. Mississippi John Hurt's "Frankie" is one such work. Hurt claimed to have learned the song when he was twelve years old, and it was one of eight songs he cut in Memphis for Okeh Records in February 1928, during the heyday of the race record business. Hurt was one of scores of southern vernacular singers recruited by local phonograph company agents in search of new talent for the recently developed race record and old-time markets. In addition to performing music at local house parties and the community store, Hurt occasionally played in and around his hometown of Avalon, Mississippi, with the white fiddle player Willie Narmour, and it was Narmour who introduced Hurt to Tommy Rockwell, an Okeh recording director. Like Ledbetter, Hurt's extensive repertoire included ragtime, ballads, blues, and dance tunes. Recognizing that blues were not Hurt's forte, Rockwell originally intended to release his records in Okeh's "old-time" line, but ultimately they were included as part of the company's "race" list, and evidently did not sell particularly well. Despite Rockwell liking his initial Memphis tracks well enough to invite him to New York City to record an additional twelve sides in December 1928, Hurt was unable to make a lasting career in the music business at the time. He returned to a life of sharecropping, railroad work, and other manual jobs in his home state until being rediscovered and becoming a significant figure in the 1960s folk music revival.[69]

Hurt's "Frankie" differs both lyrically and musically from Ledbetter's 1930s renditions of the ballad. His lyrics open:

Frankie was a good girl, everybody knows.
She paid a hundred dollars for Albert one suit of clothes.
He's her man, and he done her wrong.

Frankie went down to the corner saloon, she didn't go to be gone long.
She peeked through the keyhole in the door, spied Albert in Alice's arms.
"He's my man, and he done me wrong."

Frankie called Albert. Albert says, "I don't hear."
"If you don't come to the woman you love, gonna haul you outta here.
You's my man, and you done me wrong."

Frankie shot old Albert, and she shot him three or four times.
Says, "Stroll back, out smokin' my gun. Let me see is Albert dyin'.
He's my man, and he done me wrong."

Hurt's narrative thus begins with a standard verse essentially similar to Ledbetter's opening, and proceeds in a roughly parallel vein, albeit shorter than
what Ledbetter recorded for the Lomaxes in 1934 and 1935. At this point,
however, Hurt's tale goes in another direction:

Frankie and the judge walked down the stand, and walked out side to side.
The judge says to Frankie, "You're gonna be justified.
Killin' a man, and he done you wrong."

Dark was the night, cold was on the ground.
The last word I heard Frankie say, "I done laid old Albert down.
He's my man, and he done me wrong."

"I ain't gonna tell no story, and I ain't gonna tell no lie.
Well, Albert passed 'bout an hour ago, with a girl they call Alice Frye.
He's your man, and he's done you wrong."

In a relatively standard practice for early twentieth-century musicians, Hurt
incorporates a line from another song entirely here, Blind Willie Johnson's
treatment of Christ's trial in the Garden of Gethsemane, "Dark Was the Night,
Cold Was the Ground" (1927); thus, like Ledbetter, Hurt at least obliquely
invokes the crucifixion. Also, like Ledbetter's first recordings of the ballad for
the Lomaxes at Angola in 1933 and 1934, Hurt's record offers the verses in a
way that slips out of a straightforwardly chronological recounting of events;
in this case, the final verse is a stock stanza voicing the words of the bartender
to Frankie as she searches for Albert.

Unlike Ledbetter's Wilton recordings, though, Hurt fills the space between verses with light-fingered, dulcet guitar work rather than spoken
elaborations on the action.[70] Equally significant for comparative purposes,
Hurt's "Frankie"—like many versions of the ballad—does not feature Albert's

mother at all. Nor does Hurt employ anything like Ledbetter's guttural vocal-izations or piercing falsettos to convey intensity of emotion in the characters' voices, instead delivering his trademark legato vocals unhurriedly and almost soothingly, despite the song's tumultuous content.[71] Unlike Ledbetter, Hurt joins many contemporary singers of "Frankie and Albert" in placing Frankie in front of a (presumably) white judge, who acquits her of the shooting. Even more, the judge terms Frankie "justified" and walks out of the courtroom "side to side" with her. Frankie is not without remorse, of course. Hurt next places her in a vivid nighttime scene at the graveyard, where he—as narrator—overhears her sorrowful but resolute confession at Albert's grave. Notably, Hurt's "Frankie," rather than Ledbetter's epic "Frankie and Albert," was selected for inclusion in Harry Smith's influential *Anthology of American Folk Music* (1953) and became a favorite of early 1960s folk music enthusiasts.[72] Without a doubt, the fact that Hurt was still alive to be rediscovered and cele-brated in the 1960s played a role in this discrepancy. Arguably, though, Hurt's concision (his song is less than three and a half minutes), clear vocal elocution, distinctive fingerpicking on guitar (very different from Ledbetter's intense strumming), and gentle demeanor were equally important factors in helping him find an enthusiastic reception with these later audiences.[73]

Both the correlations and the distinctiveness of "Frankie and Johnny" within Ledbetter's own repertoire are revealed by a comparison with the singer's 1935 Wilton recording of "Ella Speed." Like "Frankie and Albert," "Ella Speed" was based upon a real-life lover's quarrel over infidelity that ended in murder. Recognizing this shared thematic terrain, the Lomaxes placed "Ella Speed" immediately preceding "Frankie and Albert" in a section on ballads in *Negro Folk Songs as Sung by Lead Belly*. And just as Alan Lomax termed the latter "Lead Belly's 'Ninth Symphony,'" he found "Ella Speed" to be "perhaps the finest combination of simple ballad style, unsophisticated folk melody, and fitting accompaniment" in the singer's oeuvre. According to Lomax, Ledbetter claimed at least a share of the authorship of the latter ballad: "Lead Belly says that not long before he moved to Dallas, Bill Martin shot down Ella Speed in the street and that along with the other musicians of that area he composed this ballad."[74] In actuality, the origins of the song appear to predate even "Frankie and Albert," stemming from the 1894 murder of Ella Speed by Louis "Bull" Martin in New Orleans.[75] Hence, both ballads were probably at least a decade old and widely circulating by the time Ledbetter added them to his song bag. Nonetheless, his substantially revised adaptation might constitute grounds for claiming a kind of (re)authorship of the song.

Much as he had with "Frankie and Albert," Ledbetter recorded an abbre-viated version of this ballad as part of his initial sessions with the Lomaxes at

Angola in 1933 and then developed substantial spoken interludes to expound upon and contextualize his lyrics before recording the song with Alan Lomax in Wilton in 1935.[76] For example, the latter version of the song opens:

Ella Speed was downtown, having her loving fun,
Along come Bill Martin with his Colt 41.
Ella Speed was downtown, having her loving fun,
Along come Bill Martin with his Colt 41.

[spoken]: Bill Martin was a long and slender man. And he wasn't nothing but a professional gambler. And Ella Speed, she was one of the star women. Which everybody loved Ella Speed and everybody liked Bill Martin. But Bill Martin wouldn't hit a lick at a snake, which he was a bartender and professional gambler.[77]

As with "Frankie and Albert," Ledbetter thus uses the spoken interludes in this song to clarify the identity and motives of the central characters. Beyond their parallel origins and formal similarities, Ledbetter's "Frankie and Albert" and "Ella Speed" share a striking number of motifs: each centers on a murder committed by a lover wronged by acts of infidelity; the weapon in each case is a Colt 41; each describes both the male and female protagonists as well-liked members of their communities, whatever their flaws; and both Frankie and Bill Martin express considerable sorrow for the loved ones that they slew. Further, in Ledbetter's hands, both ballads effectively convey an air of epic tragedy. As Bill Martin laments while watching his former lover's body pass by on a train car:

She's gone, she's gone, she's gone,
And crying won't bring her back.
She's the onliest woman that I ever loved.
She's gone down some lonesome railroad track.

Parallel to Ledbetter's "Frankie and Albert," these lines are part of a longer sequence of verses that concludes the ballad with a chilling portrait of the cold finality of death in terms that are simultaneously tangible and existential.

For all their similarities, these two ballads feature important differences, some of which highlight the distinctiveness of "Frankie and Albert," not only in Ledbetter's repertoire but also in US folk balladry more broadly. In contrast to his portrayal of Frankie as a hardworking domestic, Ledbetter's description of Ella Speed as "one of the star women" seems to cast her as a stage performer, or perhaps as a professional of another sort in a barrelhouse or brothel. In either case, both she and Bill Martin ("a bartender and professional gambler") seem no strangers to the kinds of red-light districts that Ledbetter knew well in Shreveport and Dallas. An even more significant difference from "Frankie and Albert" is the reversal of gender roles: the male protagonist slays his female counterpart. While this framework places the song in terrain more typical of badman ballads featuring the likes of Stagolee and John Hardy, Ledbetter's Bill Martin goes against type in interesting ways. For one, he flees from the scene of the murder and hides out from authorities for a time (just how long is not spelled out by Ledbetter). Then, when called before the judge, "Bill Martin fell down upon his knees, / Crying, 'Judge, have mercy on me'"—an interesting gender reversal of similar imagery from "Frankie and Albert," in which the female protagonist expresses strong emotion. Likewise, as the judge prepares to render his decision, "Bill Martin wring his hands and he started to crying." The judge—notably less lenient than the one in "Frankie and Albert"—spares Martin from hanging, but sentences him to life in prison and to stand at the freight depot as his wife's body passes by on a train car. It is at this point that Martin powerfully expresses still more grief, through the verses quoted above, namely, "She's gone, she's gone, she's gone."

For her part, the character of Ella Speed remains notably voiceless. In Ledbetter's "Frankie and Albert," Albert is given two verses directly in his voice as he is shot by Frankie, and his mother in a sense speaks for him even beyond his death. By contrast, Ella receives no direct lines in Ledbetter's song. Although she is mourned by the women of the community collectively ("The womens was all singing with a doleful sound, / When Bill Martin shot de woman down"), this seems more like an invocation of a Greek chorus than the moving personal lamentations of Mrs. Johnson in the singer's "Frankie and Albert." Nor is the scene of Ella Speed's death rendered in anything like the exacting detail devoted to that of the male protagonist of Ledbetter's "Frankie and Albert."

I have argued that Ledbetter's "Frankie and Albert" features three prominent protagonists, each of whom is accorded considerable moral sentiment and empathy, as well as a kind of moral ambiguity, as when the singer presents Albert as both unfaithful scoundrel and beloved mother's son. By contrast, "Ella Speed" seems much less the title character's song than Bill Martin's. Although the murder committed by Martin is portrayed less sympathetically than Frankie's shooting of Albert, the song clearly centers on *his* "cold-blooded murder with his Colt 41," *his* plea for mercy before the judge, and, finally, *his* expression of grief. So too, just whom listeners should "take heed" of in the saga of Ella Speed's death is left somewhat ambiguous. Is it a warning not to follow in Ella Speed's footsteps ("downtown, having her fun")? Or is it a caution to avoid Bill Martin's fate by heeding Ledbetter's injunctions: "Don't kill no women. You might do around and you might kill a man; but please don't kill no women. They put you under the pen"?[78] Perhaps both messages are at work. In his personal life, Ledbetter was not above imposing a double standard, expecting a level of fidelity from his female partners that he did not observe himself. But given John Lomax's observation that the foregoing spoken interlude was the only time he saw Ledbetter give a direct word of advice to his audiences of male prisoners during their 1934 southern recording sessions, "Ella Speed" ultimately remains a ballad primarily by, about, and for men.[79] The relative uniqueness of Ledbetter's "Frankie and Albert" as a female-centered song expressing no small degree of female agency is all the more striking by way of contrast.

UNLIKELY AS THE SCENE OF Huddie Ledbetter seated atop a banquet table in a stately Philadelphia hotel and performing for a gathering of college professors might have seemed just eighteen months before the 1934 MLA conference, it was far from Ledbetter's last performance before academic audiences. While still working on *Negro Folk Songs as Sung by Leadbelly*, John Lomax arranged a tour through New York and Massachusetts campuses for March 1935 that was received warmly at virtually every stop. Audiences of folk music enthusiasts and students from privileged backgrounds felt magnetically drawn to something that many had never before seen: an African American musician direct from the South, relatively unvarnished in style and viscerally powerful in stage presence. Most famously, Harvard's Professor Kittredge remarked midperformance, "He is a demon, Lomax."[80] Dorothy Mullenneaux later recalled of the performance that she witnessed as a student at the Albany Girls' Academy as part of this tour, "We were trembling to see a 'murderer' fresh out of jail. But Lead Belly won our hearts so much that I passed my love of his music on to my six children."[81] In a similar vein, Frank Warner of the New York Folklore Society recalled, "At his best—with his guitar organically fused into himself and his wild uninhibited voice in full cry—Lead Belly brought a spine-tingling, hair-raising impact to people who had never listened to back street, rock-breaking, swamp-grown Negro singing. He translated a way of life into music. He spoke it true."[82]

Typically, these campus visits consisted of a formal concert featuring explanatory commentary by Lomax and music by Ledbetter, often followed by additional Ledbetter performances at parties hosted later the same evening by faculty members and at appearances in classrooms the following morning. Professor Louis Jones recollected one such after-party gathering at Albany

State: "[Professor Harold] Thompson put a chair up on the dining room table and Huddie sat there with a quart of gin by his side and his 12-string guitar and played us until dawn. Well, 'til the bottle was empty, which was pretty near dawn."[83] Along the way, Ledbetter experienced northern Jim Crow, requiring him to be housed in black YMCAs and with local black families. Yet his forays into black nightclubs free of Lomax's supervision were consistently met with suspicion and berating lectures from the anxious folklorist.

In the academic settings traversed by Ledbetter—with John Lomax in 1934–1935 and under other arrangements in subsequent years—ballads such as "Frankie and Albert" seem to have enjoyed an enthusiastic reception. As remarked in chapter 1, the fact that a ballad about a murder in an African American red-light district proved widely popular with predominantly white, well-educated, and well-off audiences speaks—on one level—to an appetite for black exotica. Indeed, white audiences of all social strata had long demonstrated an eagerness to consume theatrical spectacles of African American sex and violence in the form of blackface minstrelsy and so-called coon songs, even as they simultaneously condemned real-life African Americans generally for an alleged lack of self-control on these same fronts.[84] In this vein, the ballad of "Frankie and Johnny" offered Ledbetter's academic audiences a window onto titillating exploits of infidelity, violent revenge, and emotional displays of remorse and grief—all from the safe, vicarious distance of a song performed in a concert or lecture hall. Ledbetter's persona generated an aura of exoticism in its own right for academic audiences, as the aforementioned statements from Kittredge, Mullenneaux, and Warner suggest. Looking back, Alan Lomax asserted, "Without the violent past, the white audience never would have noticed him."[85]

Still, such an interpretation hardly constitutes the entirety of the song's appeal. The popularity of songs like Ledbetter's "Frankie and Albert" also reflected an antiquarian thirst for music with a pedigree lengthier than the typical popular hit gracing the radio airwaves. Adhering to academic folklore's abhorrence of commercial influences, the Lomaxes repeatedly encouraged Ledbetter to emphasize material like "Frankie and Albert" while attempting to deter the singer's impulse "to include 'That Silver-Haired Daddy of Mine' [by Gene Autry, the singing cowboy] or jazz tunes such as 'I'm in Love with You, Baby.'" The Lomaxes were adamant on this point: "He could never understand why we did not care for them. We held him to the singing of music that first attracted us to him in Louisiana."[86] They thus chose to omit such material from the catalogue of his repertoire in *Negro Folk Songs as Sung by Leadbelly*. Consequently, argues Miller, "Lomax's censorship propagated an image of a racial and market isolation that contradicted Ledbetter's musical experiences and the long history of commercial music in the South."[87]

What these points might obscure is the fact that the popularity of "Frankie and Albert" with the academic community was an excellent example of Ledbetter and the Lomaxes' success in implementing a *new* definition of folk music. After all, "Frankie and Albert" would have failed to meet the definition of folk music that prevailed in scholarly circles during the 1910s and 1920s by virtue of having origins in the relatively recent past (c. 1899), an identifiable author (Bill Dooley), and, perhaps most importantly, a history of circulation by both vernacular and commercial means via oral, written (sheet music), and phonographic means. Under the more capacious paradigm of folk emerging in the 1920s and 1930s, the trait of being "of, by, and for the common people" assumed centrality, and surging currents of nationalism meant that origins indigenous to the United States became desirable rather than suspect. In addition, aside from a few scholarly specialists, the university audiences before which Ledbetter did so much to establish his national reputation were not attuned to (or simply did not care much about) distinctions involving the precise historical pedigree of a song's origins and mode of transmission in the terms that had concerned Francis Child and George Kittredge. The idea of authenticity still mattered greatly in the 1930s, but under the new framework advocated by the Lomaxes and their peers, authenticity became located in the identity of the performer more than in the song. This was especially true for African Americans from the South, whom both folklorists and record companies (often erroneously) portrayed as being isolated from cosmopolitan and commercial influences.[88] By such criteria, Ledbetter's upbringing in the rural, hardscrabble South and his incarcerations following brushes with the law seemed, to the Lomaxes and many northern commentators, to provide him with an authentic folk identity.

The terms in which Ledbetter's public folk identity was constructed during his period of collaboration with the Lomaxes proved deeply problematic, not only through the lens offered by twenty-first-century identity politics, but also in its consequences for the singer's career during his lifetime. As the introductory lectures and interview statements provided by the Lomaxes filtered into news media coverage of Ledbetter's arrival in the Northeast, a particular narrative soon emerged that would profoundly shape subsequent public perceptions of "Lead Belly." Most notorious was a story in the *New York Herald Tribune* that bore the headline "Lomax Arrives with Leadbelly, Negro Minstrel: Sweet Singer of the Swamplands Here to Do a Few Tunes Between Homicides." Beyond its sensationalistic title, this story referred to Ledbetter as "a powerful, knife-toting Negro" who allegedly "bears an undying affection" for his "Big Boss," John Lomax—all of which helped to crystallize how Ledbetter subsequently was cast as an object of simultaneous terror and fascination for white audiences.[89] An installment of the *March of Time* newsreel series in March 1935 sounded a strikingly similar note in bringing the Ledbetter-Lomax story to the nation's motion picture houses. The film re-creates a scene of Ledbetter eagerly seeking out John Lomax following his release from Angola, which it misleadingly attributes to Lomax having de-livered the singer's recorded plea for a pardon to Louisiana governor O. K. Allen. Following Lomax's account of events, this encounter in the newsreel features Ledbetter obsequiously currying the folklorist's favor—"Please boss, take me with you. You'll never have to tie your shoestrings anymore, if you'll let me, long as you keep me with you"—even as he also produces a knife in response to Lomax's inquiry.[90] The fact that Ledbetter bore a prominent scar across his neck from a past scrape while performing in Oil City, Louisiana, enhanced this perception of his allegedly violent, dangerous nature. Another early article in the *New York Herald Tribune* explained that John Lomax's "chief fear was that the quick-tempered, knife-toting Negro would get loose in Harlem and win for himself another such scar as that which now girdles his neck from ear to ear."[91]

A feature story in the April 19, 1937, issue of *Life* magazine distills the essence of this Lead Belly lore. Subtitled, "Bad Nigger Makes Good Min-strel," the four-paragraph article focuses almost entirely on the singer's al-leged propensity for sex and violence, his criminal history, and the seemingly obligatory retelling of twice singing his way to freedom (inaccurate in the Louisiana case). Repeating the concerns of John Lomax, the article alleges, "Money and fame going to his head, Lead Belly broke with Lomax early in 1935."[92] Equally suggestive are the photographs that accompany the article. The lead image is Otto Hess's photograph of Ledbetter singing and playing his twelve-string Stella guitar while seated atop a pile of feed sacks before an array of barrels (figure 2.2).[93] The photo links the singer with the presumed rudimentary aspects of his past in rural agricultural labor through his attire: blue denim work shirt, red bandana tied about his neck, and a pair of over-alls with leg cuffs rolled up to showcase his bare feet. On the facing page, a close-up image of Ledbetter's hands at work on his guitar is captioned "These Hands Once Killed a Man" (figure 2.3). Years later, Jane Caspar, who had the opportunity to see Ledbetter perform at Cornell University in 1947, recalled *Life*'s jarring combination of text and image.[94] As in so many formulations of Ledbetter's identity, the *Life* article's nod to his status as artist was made with a condescending wink or an asterisk—framing him as both artist and primitive Negro, both "good minstrel" and "bad nigger."

Although the Lomaxes seem to have regretted the sensationalistic excesses of these mass media narratives regarding Lead Belly, they did their share to perpetuate some these narratives' details.[95] For one, the Otto Hess photo-

"Ol' Howard's dead and gone,
Lef' me here to sing this song."

THESE HANDS ONCE KILLED A MAN

FIGURE 2.2. Huddie Ledbetter. This photograph by Otto Hess served as the frontispiece for John A. Lomax and Alan Lomax, *Negro Folk Songs as Sung by Lead Belly* (New York: Macmillan, 1936), and was later reprinted in "Lead Belly: Bad Nigger Makes Good Minstrel," *Life*, April 19, 1937. Courtesy of the Lead Belly Estate, Murfreesboro, Tennessee.

FIGURE 2.3. Huddie Ledbetter's hands, 1936. This photograph, captioned "These Hands Once Killed a Man," appeared in "Lead Belly: Bad Nigger Makes Good Minstrel," *Life*, April 19, 1937. Courtesy of the Lead Belly Estate, Murfreesboro, Tennessee.

graph of Ledbetter atop feed sacks first appeared as the frontispiece to *Negro Folk Songs as Sung by Lead Belly*. John Lomax repeatedly promoted the claim that he had helped obtain Ledbetter's pardon from Angola, and he encouraged Ledbetter to perform in a convict's uniform at venues such as Harvard University and in overalls on several other occasions.[96] To be sure, many early stars of the Grand Ole Opry "played hillbilly" through elements of "poor white" costuming and affected dialect, but Ledbetter's experiences seem particularly demeaning, since the costumes were not wholly voluntary.[97] Put simply, despite his important efforts to democratize American folk music, John Lomax's thinking was shot through with racial paternalism of a sort characteristic of southern patricians of his generation. Hence, in a news story about Huddie Ledbetter's wedding to Martha Promise in January 1935, John Lomax declared, "Here in the North, you sympathize with Negroes as an oppressed race, but don't know them as individuals. In the South, though, we don't think about the race as a whole, we get to know and love the individual Negro." One could hardly find a more illustrative example of what the folklorist and occasional Alan Lomax collaborator Zora Neale Hurston lamented as the "pet Negro" problem.[98]

In reality, the relationship between the elder Lomax and Ledbetter proved relatively short-lived, fracturing after just a few short weeks of tours to academic sites, precisely because the singer chafed under Lomax's patronizing curfews and miserly allotment of Ledbetter's share of their earnings. Always distrustful of any gesture by the singer indicating a desire for independence, Lomax confessed after one such conflict on their northeastern tour that Ledbetter's face seemed to him an impenetrable "ebony mask—glum, dour, and forbidding." So too, John Lomax's vision for Huddie and Martha involved life on a farm in rural Louisiana, suggesting that Lomax felt his folk music prodigy might make for an interesting showpiece, but ultimately did not *belong* in the cosmopolitan Northeast.[99] Understandably, the Ledbetters had greater ambitions for the continued flourishing of Huddie's musical career. Hence, they went back to Louisiana following their time with the Lomaxes only briefly before returning to New York City in March 1936 to pursue opportunities in the commercial arena.

Once back in New York, Ledbetter found that his opportunities in the commercial sphere were not nearly as promising as he had hoped. One of his first jobs was a run at Harlem's Lafayette Theater, which required that Ledbetter again don prison clothes and reenact the infamous, mythologized pardon saga for which he now was best known by the general public. A short-lived gig at the Apollo Theater followed, which billed him as "Lead Belly, the pardoned killer!"[100] Not surprisingly, these scenarios were hardly what Ledbetter had in mind for his return to the big-city stage. Despite having coerced Ledbetter to don convict clothes the previous year, even John Lomax acknowledged that "he always hated to wear them."[101] For a story ostensibly about Ledbetter's liberation, the narrative of Lead Belly's pardon and collaboration with John Lomax came to operate as something of a representational prison house. As biographers Wolfe and Lornell note, it was as if he was trapped in a loop of the *March of Time* newsreel.[102] Further, although he was once again playing for predominantly African American audiences, Harlem was not Shreveport. Material such as "Frankie and Albert," "Ella Speed," and "Take a Whiff on Me," which had proved successful in the earlier, Louisiana-Texas stages of Ledbetter's career, seemed to strike Harlem audiences of the mid-1930s as hopelessly outdated, bearing too many echoes of life in the Jim Crow South—a far cry from the swing and big band jazz acts that typically headlined the Apollo. Paige

McGinley explains that while Apollo audiences indulged selective throwbacks to southern roots traditions, overall "the Apollo promoted an aspirational middle-class aesthetic."[103] Only later, in such rare stints as an extended run at the Village Vanguard in Greenwich Village during the early 1940s was Ledbetter able to comfortably revisit his full repertoire of material and fully control the staging of his own performances in a commercial club setting.[104]

Unfortunately, Ledbetter's partnerships with record companies proved mostly disappointing as well. His first sessions with the American Recording Corporation (ARC) in 1935, logged simultaneous with his residency with the Lomaxes in Wilton, Connecticut, were telling of the dilemmas he would confront vis-à-vis the commercial music business. ARC's Art Satherley, an industry veteran who previously had recorded artists like Blind Lemon Jefferson and Gertrude "Ma" Rainey for Paramount, appears to have been operating under the paradigm that had gained dominance in the music industry during the 1920s, in which record companies typically steered southern African American performers toward what was perceived as the most racially distinctive genre, blues. Hence, Satherley ignored powerful ballads such "Frankie and Albert" and "Ella Speed," as well as Ledbetter's cowboy songs and "hillbilly" tunes, and instead attempted to market him as a blues singer with releases such as "Packin' Trunk Blues" and "Fo' Day Worry Blues."[105] While certainly a part of the singer's catalogue, such blues numbers were by no means his most distinctive, memorable material. Equally important, as noted previously, by the mid-1930s popular tastes were shifting away from country blues toward swing music and crooning pop vocals. In hindsight, it is thus not surprising that Ledbetter's ARC releases met with meager sales.[106]

In one among many testimonials of the power of Ledbetter's live performances, Jane Caspar testified of a 1947 Cornell University performance that "Lead Belly shot off sparks," and many audiences seemed to agree.[107] Likewise, figures central to the history of American folk music—Alan Lomax, Woody Guthrie, and Pete Seeger among them—counted Ledbetter as nothing less than a musical giant. A memorial concert held at New York City's Town Hall in January 1950 is a useful index of Ledbetter's stature among musicians, especially those of a politically progressive persuasion. Tributes in word or song came from Guthrie, Brownie McGhee, Sonny Terry, Pete Seeger's group the Weavers, Jean Ritchie, the Reverend Gary Davis, W. C. Handy, Eubie Blake, Sidney Bechet, Count Basie, and the calypso legend Lord Invader, with Alan Lomax serving as chief organizer and master of ceremonies.[108]

Unfortunately, the timing of Ledbetter's interactions with the music industry from the time of his New York City debut in 1935 to his untimely passing from ALS in 1949 never aligned in a way that produced profits commensurate with his fame or the legendary impact of his live performances. Reflecting on his career as a pioneering producer of music by both black and white artists during the 1920s and 1930s, Ralph Peer explained, "I quickly discovered that people buying records were *not* especially interested in hearing standard or folkloric music. What they wanted was something new—built along the same lines."[109] In this light, the same qualities that made Ledbetter captivating to folklorists and folk music enthusiasts, such as the perceived "rusticness" of his vocal delivery and guitar work, may have distanced him from the broader record-buying public.

Suggestively, in 1950—the year after Ledbetter's death—the Weavers released a version of "Goodnight, Irene" with Decca Records that rose to the number one spot on the *Billboard* sales charts. Ledbetter had performed an abbreviated version of this tune in his very first recording session with the Lomaxes at Angola in 1933, and it became one of the songs most often associated with him during the 1940s. Yet, Ledbetter never enjoyed a chart-topping hit with it or any other song. Subsequently, the Weavers would also score successes with "Rock Island Line" and "The Midnight Special," more musical items linked closely with Ledbetter in the previous decade. As Robbie Lieberman puts it, "It may have meant a lot to them that they had learned 'Goodnight, Irene' from Leadbelly . . . but it meant little to the record-buying public."[110] Race certainly looms large in the contrasting market outcomes of recordings by these musical friends, as did the Weavers' subdued vocal stylings and instrumentation relative to Ledbetter's. Also important, though, were the shifting currents of the music world; by midcentury, a group whose members lacked rural or working-class authenticating bona fides could nonetheless be positioned as a "folk music" act capable of scoring crossover success with a mainstream pop music audience. The Popular Front social movement, although on the wane by the time the Weavers enjoyed mainstream success, was crucial to this transformation.

WITH HIS TIES TO John Lomax effectively severed and his commercial ventures with ARC failing to catch fire, Ledbetter found a place alongside the likes of Pete Seeger and Woody Guthrie within the emerging culture of the Popular Front during the late 1930s and early 1940s. Spurred by a shift among Communist Party members and their allies from sectarian activism in the first half of the 1930s to more broadly inclusive coalition building in the latter half of the decade, the Popular Front emphasized the role of creative expression in helping draw widespread attention to social justice issues. As Rachel Donaldson observes, folk music was a primary vehicle by which the Popular Front "solidified their pluralist view of democracy," rearticulating it

in a manner that combined "racial, ethnic, and religious pluralism with a celebration of the economically marginalized common within left-wing and lib-
eral circles."[111] In Guthrie's functionalist formulation, "Every folk song that I
know tells how to fix something in this world to make it better; tells the world
what is wrong with it, and what we've got to do to fix it better. If the song
does not do this, then it is no more of a folk song than I am a movie scout."[112]
What mattered, from this vantage, was less where a song *came from* (that is,
"tradition" in the folklorist's sense) than what a song could *do* to sway hearts
and minds. Tradition became, as Edward Comentale notes, "a tool to be used
in the present rather than a static image or ideal of the past." Hence, Guthrie
appropriated freely from Tin Pan Alley tunes and commercial records (both
blues and "hillbilly") when it suited his purposes, recasting these source materials through the prism of his own "folksy" persona and populist sense of
mission.[113]

Initially, Ledbetter's primary conduit to the Popular Front was Mary
Elizabeth Barnicle. Barnicle had helped host Ledbetter and the Lomaxes in
both New York City and Wilton, Connecticut, upon their arrival in 1935, and
she had hosted Ledbetter in her classes at New York University as early as February of that year.[114] From the Ledbetters' return to New York City in 1936
until Huddie's death in 1949, Barnicle continued to serve as one of his most
important supporters. She made numerous recordings of Ledbetter's music
and acted as his de facto manager at times. Equally important, she introduced
Ledbetter to the coalition of union members, political activists, and creative
artists that constituted the Popular Front. Barnicle acquainted Ledbetter with
musicians such as Kentucky's Tillman Cadle (Barnicle's husband, as of 1936),
Sarah Ogun Gunning, and Aunt Molly Jackson (who Guthrie once termed
"the woman Leadbelly"), and she helped arrange the first handful of Ledbetter's many performances for labor union events and other progressive social
justice causes. Among the constituencies that Ledbetter played in support of
during the second half of the 1930s and early 1940s were striking Kentucky
coal miners, California migrant workers, and the Loyalists in the Spanish
Civil War. By contemporaneous accounts, these allegiances were sincerely
felt. Woody Guthrie, who stayed with Huddie and Martha Ledbetter many
times during the early 1940s, recalled seeing the singer read the *Daily News*,
Daily Mirror, and the US Communist Party's *Daily Worker*, all in a typical
morning.[115]

In turn, Ledbetter inspired tributes from fellow "cultural workers" of the
Popular Front, such as Charles White's magisterial mural at Hampton University entitled *The Contribution of the Negro to Democracy in America* (1943)
(figure 2.4). The mural chronicles a history of African Americans' freedom

FIGURE 2.4. Charles White, *The Contribution of the Negro to Democracy in America*, 1943. Courtesy of the Hampton University Museum Collection, Hampton, Va.

struggles that includes rebellions against slavery (Nat Turner and Denmark Vesey, as well as the abolitionist work of Frederick Douglass, Harriet Tubman, and Sojourner Truth), African American participation in US military campaigns from the Revolutionary War onward, and cultural work by creative artists. White located his portrayal of Ledbetter, captured midsong with a determined visage and a guitar, in the lower-right corner of the mural, adjacent to Ferdinand Smith (leader of the National Maritime Union) and the politically radical actor-singer-orator-activist Paul Robeson. As with his place in the Popular Front movement more broadly, Ledbetter thus was recast by White as an African American folk activist.[116]

Alan Lomax, who was more politically progressive than his father and stayed in touch with Ledbetter throughout the late 1930s and 1940s, was another bridge to the Popular Front.[117] For instance, Ledbetter performed alongside the likes of Woody Guthrie and Josh White in several installments of the Alan Lomax–hosted CBS radio programs *Folk Music of America* (1939–1940), *Back Where I Come From* (1940–1941), and *Wellsprings of Music* (1941). Highly innovative in the use of folk music as a vehicle for the analysis of

US social history, each episode of these programs blended live music performances grouped around themes such as freedom (on the seventy-fifth anniversary of the ratification of the Thirteenth Amendment), death, gambling, children's rhymes, jailhouse songs, sea chanties, and Negro work songs, with historical contextualization from Lomax. Among other examples, Ledbetter performed "The Western Cowboy" on an episode devoted to western songs, the work song "Lining Track" for an installment on railroad songs, and tunes like "Gwine Dig a Hole to Put the Devil In," "C. C. Rider," and "Gallis Pole" for a special broadcast focused specifically on his own life and music. In at least some iterations, these episodes concluded with an adaptation of one of the folk songs from earlier in the show by a formally trained composer and professional orchestra.[118]

In keeping with the hallmarks of Popular Front culture, these programs focused primarily on working-class experiences through song and were remarkably interracial in composition of the performers. In an era where many state chapters of the American Federation of Musicians still enforced rigid racial segregation, the mere fact that performers like Ledbetter, Guthrie, Josh White, and Burl Ives could share studio space and airtime was significant.[119] The easy rapport among this circle extended beyond the radio studio. In the early 1940s, Ledbetter performed on several occasions by himself and in combination with some of these same performers at Café Society, an important venue in New York City's Popular Front scene.[120] Ledbetter also performed alongside Ives, White, the Almanac Singers, and a cadre of Popular Front poets at the leftist American Writers' Congress in 1941 as part of a session devoted to intersections between poetry, songwriting, and folk music.[121] These musicians regularly socialized offstage as well, and, as mentioned, Huddie and Martha opened their home to Guthrie on several occasions when he was between permanent residences.[122]

Within Popular Front circles, new definitions of "folk music" took shape that departed from both the older Francis Child model *and* the formulations of John Lomax. Building on radical precedents such as Joe Hill and the International Workers of the World's *Little Red Songbook* of the 1910s and 1920s, musicians in the Popular Front frequently appropriated familiar melodies, but repurposed the tunes with new lyrics apropos of contemporary social justice crusades.[123] Within this framework, "folk music" was defined primarily as songs that articulated the concerns of poor and working-class Americans, including migrant workers, striking miners, sharecroppers, chain gang laborers, and African Americans in the Jim Crow South. Having always expanded his musical offerings to meet the desires of new audiences and to satisfy his own creative urges, Ledbetter was more than up to this new challenge. With input from Alan Lomax, Ledbetter turned an experience of his mixed-race entourage being scorned by both white and black middle-class residents of Washington, D.C., into a Popular Front favorite titled "Bourgeois Blues."[124] While social critique was an implicit part of some of the work songs in Ledbetter's repertoire, this new brand of music possessed an unambiguously sharper edge:

Well, them white folks in Washington they know how
To call a colored man a nigger just to see him bow
Lord, it's a bourgeois town
It's a bourgeois town
I got the bourgeois blues
Gonna spread the news all around[125]

In a similar vein, he fashioned music lamenting the injustice accorded the Scottsboro Boys—perhaps the foremost cause célèbre of the Depression-era Left—and performed the songs at venues such as a fund-raiser for their legal defense sponsored by the Federal Writers' Project and attended by two of the Scottsboro mothers. Such activities clearly run counter to the "Uncle Tom" accusations that Ledbetter sometimes faced from peers during the 1930s and 1940s.[126]

Naturally, this turn in folk music sponsored by the Popular Front posed consequences for Ledbetter's repertoire. In one particularly telling example, Ledbetter was invited to the US Communist Party's Camp Unity by the composer Earl Robinson in the summer of 1936. As Robinson recalled, the resulting clash of cultural sensibilities was initially tumultuous: "After an evening of 'Frankie and Albert,' 'DeKalb Blues,' and 'Ella Speed,' songs of bad women and gun-toting Negro gamblers, . . . where the protest could barely be understood through his dialect, the camp was in an uproar. Argument [flared about] whether to censure him, or me, or both." Prompted by Robinson's explanation that the outlaw exploits of these ballads were a poor match for the Communist Party's racial justice objectives, Ledbetter adjusted his selection on the following night to feature "Bourgeois Blues" and "Scottsboro Boys," with great success; as Robinson put it, "The air was considerably changed."[127] Not everyone in the Popular Front scene was so dogmatic, of course. Burl Ives, for one, later recalled "Frankie and Albert" as his favorite Lead Belly song, terming it "tremendous."[128] But references to such ballads are few and far between in accounts of Ledbetter's Popular Front activities. This new audience preferred songs with an unambiguous moral message to ballads that spotlighted infidelity, prostitution, gambling, and murder.

Members of the Popular Front likewise attempted to reformulate Ledbetter's public identity in a manner more in keeping with their own ideological mission. Richard Wright's feature story on Ledbetter for the Communist Party's *Daily Worker* in 1937 is representative in this regard. An African American refugee from the violence of the Jim Crow South in his own right, Wright believed that he had found in Ledbetter a "folk artist" that could articulate issues of racial injustice in terms accessible to the American masses. In Wright's account, "This folk singer tells tales of dodging white mobs, of wandering at night to save his life, and of how he would snatch a few hours of companionship with his friends when the white folks weren't looking. He tells of cutting sugar cane in the rain; of picking a bale of cotton in two days; and of seeing black men drop dead from the heat of Southern suns in the cotton fields."[129] This list of themes is not inaccurate, but it is highly selective, speaking primarily to the new material that Ledbetter was developing with a Popular Front audience specifically in mind. To cite but one alternate catalogue, the jazz enthusiast Frederic Ramsey observed, "He can tell stories about houses of prostitution, bad men, gambling men, a girl 'makin' an hones' livin', boys, by the workin' of her tail,' about calamitous floods, the Hindenburg disaster, drinking beer and riding around in an automobile (Huddie's symbol for prosperity is a V-8), about little children, and especially about all women, 'who are pretty flowers.'"[130] In this regard, Ledbetter clearly had as much in common with a fabulist like the jazz legend "Jelly Roll" Morton as he did with someone like Woody Guthrie.

Willfully disregarding the apolitical and vice-themed aspects of Ledbetter's oeuvre, Wright also reconstructed Ledbetter's personal story in heroic, even mythical terms:

> When 50-year-old Huddie Ledbetter planks himself in a chair, spreads his feet and starts strumming his 12-stringed guitar and singing that rich, barrel-chested baritone, it seems that the entire folk culture of the American Negro has found its embodiment in him. . . .
>
> Down South the white landlords called him a "bad nigger" and they were afraid of his fists, his bitter, biting songs, his 12-stringed guitar, and his inability to take injustice and like it. Because they feared him and respected his hardness they called him "Lead Belly." And at the first opportunity that came their way they threw him in jail.[131]

For Wright, Ledbetter was not an exotic, dangerous ex-convict; he was a former political prisoner. In all this, Wright was consciously rewriting the racial paternalism and primitivizing impulse of the narrative fashioned by

John Lomax in *Negro Folk Songs as Sung by Lead Belly* and the accompanying news media stories on the occasion of the singer's first trip north in 1935. In fact, Wright asserts that the singer's relationship with John Lomax had been a straightforward case of racial exploitation and "one of the most amazing cultural swindles in American history."[132] The fact that Ledbetter never seems to have been quite as staunchly political as someone like Richard Wright scarcely seemed to matter. As with the Lead Belly narrative shaped collaboratively by the Lomaxes and print media coverage in the preceding years, so too did Popular Front writers build on certain observable facts (in this case, Ledbetter's critique of Jim Crow inequalities) to formulate the Lead Belly their own identities and agendas demanded. The relative prominence of "Frankie and Albert" within Ledbetter's active repertoire rose and fell accordingly.

PISTOL PACKIN' MAMA: IMPERILED MASCULINITY IN THOMAS HART BENTON'S *A SOCIAL HISTORY OF THE STATE OF MISSOURI*

THE VENERABLE FOLKLORE SCHOLAR Archie Green once admiringly referred to the artist Thomas Hart Benton as "a folklorist without an academic diploma."[1] Although known mainly as a leading painter of "American Scene" murals, Benton sustained an abiding interest in folk music from the mid-1920s until his death in 1975. And while often termed a "regionalist" by art historians, Benton hardly confined his folkloric and artistic interests to his native Missouri. Rather, the artist regularly journeyed along American byways in the West, South, Midwestern Ozarks, and Appalachia in the prime years of his career, filling numerous sketchbooks with drawings of local characters and scenery—both rural and urban—that later found their way into his panoramic paintings.[2] To say nothing of highly influential summers in Martha's Vineyard, which his biographer Justin Wolff convincingly argues did as much as Missouri to shape his ideas regarding agrarian labor, Jeffersonian ideals, and the integral relationship between environment and culture.[3] Along the way, Benton managed to collect roughly 130 folk songs as part of his far-flung US travels during the 1920s and 1930s, including "unwritten tunes and odd variants" of folk songs such as "John Hardy," "John Henry," "Casey Jones," "Cluck Old Hen," "Sourwood Mountain," and "Frankie and Johnny." The artist greatly admired the work of the folk music collector John Lomax, and when the two met in Kansas City in 1942, Benton expressed to Lomax his desire (never realized) to record Ozark fiddlers for the Library of Congress. Further, it was Benton who helped direct the modernist composer and musicologist Charles Seeger to the importance of folk music, and Benton who introduced the song "John Henry" to Seeger's son, Pete.[4]

In this vein, the art historian Leo Mazow aptly terms Benton an "anthological modernist," linking him with the broader Depression-era impulse to systematically document and represent the variety of American vernacular expressions. Whereas Benton's acquaintances such as Lomax, Carl Sandburg, and Burl Ives collated audio and literary collections of such music, the artist anthologized folk songs primarily through paintings and prints.[5] Murals in particular struck Benton as a desirable vehicle for his artwork because they offered a scale capable of rendering complex montages of American life and, often, venues capable of reaching an audience beyond typical patrons of art galleries and museums. His *Frankie and Johnny*, for instance, was part of a larger set of government-sponsored murals entitled *A Social History of the State of Missouri* (1935–1936), which chronicled, among other things, hearty pioneers settling the land, contemporary factory labor, Mark Twain characters, and the Jesse James–Cole Younger gang. Benton fashioned these paintings in an accessible narrative style within a public location, the Missouri State Capitol. As detailed in this chapter, Benton's *Social History* offered fellow Missourians a collective self-portrait that was, by turns, both flattering and self-critical, epic and touched with humor. Within the larger sweep of these murals, Benton relegated *Frankie and Johnny* to a light-hearted diversion, but it nonetheless proves revealing of the vexed race and gender ideologies that informed the artist's Depression-era artwork.

Perhaps ironically, the premium that Benton placed on the practical utility and local rootedness of artwork derived not only from his midwestern upbringing, coursework at the Art Institute of Chicago, and engagement with the pragmatist ideas of the American philosopher John Dewey, but also from transnational routes, such as his exposure to the writings of John Ruskin and Hippolyte Taine while living in Paris from 1908 to 1911 and his engagement with the work of Mexican muralist contemporaries.[6] Indeed, although the US folk boom of the 1920s and 1930s frequently manifested itself in expressions of fervent patriotism by Benton and many of his contemporaries, one of its important early catalysts was found in the political revolutions and fine arts renaissance of Mexico.

In the wake of Mexico's tumultuous military and political upheavals of the 1910s, Secretary of Popular Education José Vasconcelos initiated a program in 1921 for visual artists to adorn the walls of a number of government buildings with murals that would celebrate the nation's history and culture in a manner widely accessible even to illiterate members of the populace.[7] The most famous of these artists was Diego Rivera. By the 1920s, Rivera was looking both forward and backward for a sense of direction for his painting. On the one hand, Rivera had studied cubism in France during the 1910s, and despite being an avowed communist, in the late 1920s he expressed frustration that artists in the Soviet Union were insufficiently modern(ist) and innovative in their aesthetic ambitions.[8] On the other hand, Rivera was deeply influenced by the fresco murals of artists like Michelangelo, which he carefully studied firsthand in Italy in 1920. Upon returning to his homeland from Europe, Rivera ventured into the countryside and was so deeply impressed with the folk cultures of Mexico's peasantry that he became determined to draw upon them as a basis for a new, *mestizaje* brand of national art that blended elements of the country's indigenous and European heritages.

Rivera's *indigenismo*, or warm embrace of indigenous cultural traditions, stood in contrast with the prevailing tendency of Mexico's early twentieth-century elite to look toward France and Britain for a sense of "culture," but he found a sympathetic governmental patron in Vasconcelos. Consequently, the scores of murals that Rivera painted at sites such as Mexico's Ministry of Education combined fresco techniques and modernist montage aesthetics in scenes that consistently valorized the communitarian ethics, foodways, clothing, crafts, and ballads (including politically radical *corridos*) of Mexico's indigenous folk cultures, in counterpoint to representations of the greed and corruption of a global capitalist elite.[9] In so doing, the artist posited these valuable manifestations of folk cultural heritage as traditions around which contemporary citizens might base their sense of "Mexicanidad" at the dawn of what Rivera and Vasconcelos hoped would be a revolutionary new era.

The Mexican mural movement soon exerted substantial influence on cultural expression in the United States. For one, Rivera and fellow Mexican artists such as José Clemente Orozco and David Alfaro Siqueiros were featured in exhibits at such prominent US venues as the Museum of Modern Art and the Metropolitan Museum of Art, and they completed a number of mural commissions in the United States, to considerable fanfare and, in several instances, controversy.[10] In turn, a number of US artists and writers made the pilgrimage south of the border to witness the cultural revolution and art of Mexico firsthand. Out of these exchanges, the example of the Mexican muralists deeply impressed a whole generation of US artists, especially social realists in search of a usable blueprint for how to reach a wider audience with inspirational images of the historical past and social justice concerns in the present.[11]

After Franklin Roosevelt took office in 1933, he sought to confront the challenges of the Great Depression through a series of government-sponsored jobs programs that would provide constructive work for the unemployed, create useful infrastructure, and rekindle the nation's collective sense of morale. In addition to programs that employed Americans in fields such as engineering, surveying, and construction, Roosevelt's New Deal soon encompassed programs that put US creative artists back to work as well. Not coincidentally, the earliest of the latter efforts involved funding artists to paint murals in post offices, courthouses, housing projects, and other public buildings. While Roosevelt had little interest in sponsoring the production of Marxist social critiques in the mode of murals by Rivera and his peers, the US artist George Biddle nonetheless cited the Mexican mural movement as his primary inspiration in successfully petitioning the president to create New Deal agencies involving visual art.[12]

Much like Vasconcelos's aims in Mexico, the idea of the New Deal art programs was that if artists provided reassuring chronicles of both the history and the contemporary scene of particular places, those images would instill local communities with an enhanced sense of pride that would inspire them to tackle the challenge of national recovery. Like many other regionalist or American Scene painters of the 1930s, Benton adamantly distanced himself from what he termed the "Marxist dogmas" of Rivera's art, but he shared with the Mexican mural movement and its US offshoots an enthusiasm for the primacy of working-class persons as subjects and intended audiences. Benton commented retrospectively, "The Mexican concern with publicly significant meanings and with the pageant of Mexican national life corresponded perfectly with what I had in mind for art in the United States. I also looked with envy on the opportunities given Mexican painters for public mural work."[13] Particularly in the midst of the Great Depression, regionalist painters like Benton found in the Mexican turn to folk culture "the precise kind of usable past that cultural workers sought during a time of social instability because it consisted of traditions that had sustained generations of Americans through hard times."[14] Benton conveyed his support for the New Deal agenda through a lecture tour promoting the US government–sponsored art projects in the Midwest during the winter of 1934–1935; he undertook the tour at the behest of Audrey McMahon of the Federal Art Project, just a few months before he began preliminary work on his *Social History* murals for the Missouri State Capitol.[15]

Like many US folklore enthusiasts of the 1930s, Benton was motivated by two central convictions: folk communities possessed more authentic, natural expressions of American identity than did the rarefied circles of metropolitan high culture; and folk cultural traditions were under threat of erasure by the forces of modernity and commercialism. In his autobiography *An Artist in America* (1937), Benton reflected on his travels through the Ozarks: "The old music cannot last much longer. I count it a great privilege to have heard it in the sad twang of mountain voices before it died."[16] Thus, it fell to creative artists to rescue folk traditions and their associated values through documentation and adaptation; never lacking confidence, Benton felt himself to be supremely qualified for such an undertaking. As Mazow puts it, "For the artist, musical compositions were about quickly disappearing folkways, but as artistic subject matter they also provided a methodology with which to rehash

FIGURE 3.1. Thomas Hart Benton playing the harmonica, Martha's Vineyard, 1940s.

the values he attributed to their composers, performers, and audiences."[17] Although, as we shall see, Benton's desired idealization of rural lifeways met with numerous complications, he nonetheless held fast to the notion that such communities—and particularly their folk music—provided an essential resource for artists desiring to counteract what he saw as the US art world's deference to European influences.

Benton's interests in musical performance merit remarking on as well. He became an avid harmonica player beginning around 1931 (figure 3.1). Thereafter, in locales as varied as Greenwich Village, Martha's Vineyard, and Kansas City, he regularly played with groups comprising friends, family members, professional musicians (including Charles Seeger), fellow artists, and art students (including the young Jackson Pollock) during the 1930s and 1940s; he developed his own idiosyncratic notation system for the harmonica; when he appeared in a January 1940 broadcast of the NBC radio program *Art for Your Sake*, the script intercut interview segments with relevant excerpts from secular and sacred folk music; and he recorded a six-song album for Decca entitled *Saturday Night at Tom Benton's* in 1941.[18] Benton played the harmonica regularly on breaks from working on *A Social History of the State of Missouri*, prompting one newspaper reporter to note, "He seems far more enthusiastic about playing the harmonica . . . than over the mural."[19] Benton drew subject matter from specific songs, but, as Wolff notes, their attraction went deeper: "Folk songs appealed to Benton's sense of narrative structure. As in his murals, these songs present history anecdotally: in folk tunes, colorful characters and scenarios serve more general stories about injustice, labor, or outsider status."[20] In this sense, Benton's art of the 1930s can be seen as a "people's history" not only in its favoring of anonymous everymen over famous leaders as subjects, but also in its accessible form and flair for dramatic tableau.

All that said, it bears noting that Benton's musical tastes ran the gamut from folk songs such as "The Jealous Lover," "Pretty Polly," "Blackjack Davie," and "Froggie Went A-Courting" to classical works by the likes of Haydn, Mendelssohn, Bach, and Dvořák.[21] Recognizing this breadth of interests proves crucial for grappling with Benton's artwork. For as often as Benton disavowed the lessons of his early art experiences with abstraction in the United States and Europe (pointing instead to influences such as Tintoretto and El Greco), his American Scene aesthetic was, in truth, a synthesis of documentary impulses and modernist sensibilities. As with his wide-ranging tastes in music, Benton's artistic practice bore the imprint of diverse influences.

Benton was well versed in songs like "Frankie and Johnny" at a level beyond passive listening. In fact, during a 1935 trip to Iowa City, where he had his first meaningful meeting with the American Scene painter Grant Wood, Benton followed a talk on the University of Iowa campus with an evening at a local social club, where he and Wood donned mock Victorian whiskers for playful photos and Benton then played "Frankie and Johnny" on the harmonica.[22] This episode is instructive in several respects. For one, Benton's consistent desire not only to catalogue folk music, but also to play it speaks to the desire of many Depression-era collectors—the Lomaxes, Zora Neale Hurston, and Carl Sandburg, among others—to inhabit a folk persona, albeit only situationally and performatively. To be sure, folk enthusiasts broached these crossings in different ways and to differing degrees, but Benton shared with the likes of the Lomaxes and Hurston a participatory approach to mastering the folk material that they encountered in the field. One also can observe in Benton's Iowa City exploits a strongly felt impulse to convey American folk culture multimodally. Hence, rather than being content to paint folk subjects and let those paintings speak for themselves, Benton here—as he did repeatedly throughout the 1930s—felt compelled to join visual expression with elements of story and song. In much the same way that the Lomaxes and Ledbetter collaborated to forge interdisciplinary folk productions for nonfolk audiences, Benton delivered folk material through performative, auditory elements as well as through painting, lithography, and illustrations.

Benton often claimed a kind of authority regarding folk culture because of the time he spent in rural America, which he felt distinguished him from modernist contemporaries such as Alfred Stieglitz, but he recognized that he was not exactly one of the folk. As the campiness of the mock-Victorian whiskers in Iowa City suggests, Benton's role as traditionalist was to some degree an affected pose. In the formulation of Thomas Craven, an art critic and friend of Benton's, the artist was always "half-hobo and half-highbrow."[23] This was, after all, the same artist who had adopted a walking stick and beret during his years in France, earning himself the nickname "le petit Balzac."[24] In addition, while we do not have a recording of Benton performing "Frankie and Johnny," the solemn vocals and orchestral strings of tracks such as "Wayfaring Stranger" on his *Saturday Night at Tom Benton's* album strongly suggest that he was not simply trying to mimic the musical performances of folk musicians. Likewise, his paintings seldom attempt a simple mimesis of Depression-era realities; to the contrary, Benton's famous mural projects feature ambitious, stylized montages of locally significant reference points infused with the artist's attempted wit and social commentary. Put another way, Benton's murals are no more a transparent window onto folk realities than a composition such as Aaron Copland's *Appalachian Spring* is unvarnished folk music.

More than a mere matter of hobbyist interest, Benton took folk and popular music seriously as artistic expressions. In a November 1940 lecture at the University of Wisconsin, for example, Benton referred to the popular song "Pistol Packin' Mama" as "true art," arguing that it had significantly affected American culture and that "from a quantity of art forms like 'Mama,' a truly national brand of art will form in the post-war world."[25] The art historian Erika Doss thus asserts that, for Benton, folk arts were "a socially regenerative force."[26] Equally important, unlike many of his contemporaries, Benton did not draw an insistent line between authentic "folk" songs and popular music—at least not always. As early as his 1932 *The Arts of Life in America* mural project, for example, Benton completed a pair of paintings entitled *Folk and Popular Songs*, which blended lyrical fragments from such diverse songs as "St. Louis Blues," "Git Along, Little Dogies," and "Frankie and Johnny" ("Bring out your rubber tired hearse . . .")—all within a modernist design that evoked the wheels and exhaust pipes of a speeding automobile (figure 3.2). As Leo Mazow suggests, these murals posited folk and popular song as nothing less than "the force propelling the American machine."[27] The extent of Benton's veneration for vernacular musical expression is seen in

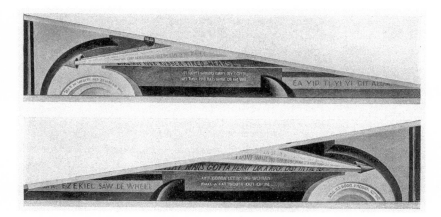

FIGURE 3.2. Thomas Hart Benton, *Folk and Popular Songs*, from *The Arts of Life in America*, 1932. Courtesy of the Whitney Museum of American Art.

the frequency with which he drew upon musical performance and particular songs as muses for his own artistic work. Vivien Green Fryd observes that by the mid-1930s, he had already completed paintings entitled *Lonesome Road* (1927) and *The Ballad of the Jealous Lover of Lone Green Valley* (1934), which illustrated well-known folk songs, as well as the country-and-western-inspired lithograph *Coming 'Round the Mountain* (1931) and scenes of folk community musical events like *Country Dance* (1928).[28] In 1961 Benton explained to a curious scholar that *Jealous Lover* was part of a "folksong series . . . part of the general plan of American myth and history at which, as you know, I'm still working."[29] Further, he completed the mural *The Sources of Country Music* for Nashville's Country Music Hall of Fame shortly before his death in 1974.

Fryd's examples are all associated with musical traditions popularly understood as "white"—traditions still in the process of being codified into the genre of "country music" during the Depression decade. With his *Frankie and Johnny* mural, Benton turned to a ballad that was African American in subject and origin, but possessed considerable crossover appeal. By this point in the mid-1930s, the artist had crafted a diverse corpus of African American representations, including enslaved workers, chain gang members, victims of racial violence, noble black proletarians laboring alongside their white peers, and minstrel-show-worthy caricatures of black musicians, dancers, gamblers, and religious worshippers. While one could scarcely confuse his paintings with those of a Marxist radical like Diego Rivera, Benton's ambitious series *The American Historical Epic* (1924–1927) included the forthright indictment of a white slaver whipping a scantily clad black man while two nude women and an unclothed child cower nearby. A subsequent work, *City Building* from Benton's *America Today* murals (1930), portrays a muscular African American with a jackhammer working alongside white peers on a construction project. By contrast, Benton's *Arts of the South*, completed for the Whitney Museum of American Art in 1932 as part of the *Arts of Life in America* project, featured craps shooters, exaggerated physiognomies, and impoverishment (without a sense of the causes or contexts contributing to poverty) as a representation of "black folk arts" (figure 3.3).[30] With good reason, the latter painting led perennial adversaries such as the artist Stuart Davis and the critic Meyer Schapiro to accuse Benton of egregious racial slander.[31] Contradictory as these modes of African American representation might appear, Benton maintained a capacity for all three types of imagery—victims of oppression, heroic proletarians, and cartoonish caricatures—in his subsequent artwork.

In 1935, Benton moved from New York City back to his native Missouri to accept both a teaching position at the Kansas City Art Institute and a major mural commission, *A Social History of the State of Missouri*, from the state legislature. For the mural, to be located in the Missouri State Capitol, Benton would be paid $16,000, inclusive of his expenses.[32] This mural project, which

FIGURE 3.3. Thomas Hart Benton, *Arts of the South*, from *The Arts of Life in America*, 1932. © T. H. Benton and R. P. Benton Testamentary Trusts/UMB Bank Trustee/ Licensed by VAGA, New York, NY. Image courtesy of the New Britain Museum of American Art, New Britain, Conn.

includes Benton's *Frankie and Johnny*, displays his three principal modes of African American representation. Benton was recruited to this task on the heels of his aforementioned midwestern lecture tour promoting the New Deal art programs and his completion of a similarly themed project entitled *A Social History of the State of Indiana*, a massive 14' by 230' expanse of murals that he completed for that state's pavilion at the 1933 World's Fair in Chicago.[33] The explanations that Benton offered for the move back to his native state were simultaneously full of bluster and revealing of the artist's ideology. In stark terms, he spoke and wrote of his desire to cast off what he deemed the insulated, overly intellectual, and effete atmosphere of the New York City art world in favor of reconnecting with what he described as the clear-headed and vigorous milieu of "plain Missouri people" in the nation's heartland—much as his fellow artist Grant Wood had urged him to do earlier that same year.[34] These imagined oppositions shaped the artist's Missouri State Capitol murals profoundly, even as the intense criticism of the finished project by state residents belied Benton's claims of easy rapport with the "common man."

Completed in 1935 and 1936, Benton's murals are located in the former House Lounge of the state capitol; the two long walls of the rectangular room measure approximately 55' × 14', and the short walls 25' × 14'. The narrative flow of the murals attempts to sketch the state's settlement and development chronologically, moving across three walls through the following subjects: *Pioneer Days* and *Early Settlers*; *Politics, Farming, and Law in Missouri*; and *St. Louis* and *Kansas City* (figures 3.4–3.7). The fourth wall consists of rather bland imagery of cornfields and power lines, interrupted by a series of windows. Throughout, as in so much of his work from the late 1920s onward, Benton depicts anonymous yeoman farmers and artisanal laborers much more so than specific, prominent leaders from the state's history. In the center of each of the three narrative walls Benton placed panels depicting what he termed "mythical" characters with ties to Missouri: Mark Twain's Huckleberry Finn and Jim admire a successful fishing catch aboard their raft on the banks of the Mississippi River between the *Pioneer Days* and *Early Settlers* panels; the Jesse James and Cole Younger gang commits two robberies—one of a bank and the other of railroad—in the middle of the long *Politics, Farming, and Law* wall; and Frankie shoots Johnny in a tumultuous barroom scene between Benton's bustling St. Louis and Kansas City murals (figures 3.8–3.9). In all three cases, Benton took for granted that the characters represented in the mythical panels would be immediately recognizable to his 1930s viewers without a need for identifying labels.

Benton's choices for the three panels depicting Missouri's mythology are curious, mixing as they do characters familiar primarily from song (Frankie and

FIGURE 3.4. Thomas Hart Benton, *Pioneer Days, Huckleberry Finn and Jim, and Early Settlers*, from *A Social History of the State of Missouri*, 1935–1936.

FIGURE 3.5. Thomas Hart Benton, detail of *Politics, Farming, and Law in Missouri*, from *A Social History of the State of Missouri*, 1935–1936.

FIGURE 3.6. Thomas Hart Benton, detail of *Politics, Farming, and Law in Missouri*, from *A Social History of the State of Missouri*, 1935–1936.

FIGURE 3.7. Thomas Hart Benton, *St. Louis*, *Frankie and Johnny*, and *Kansas City*, from *A Social History of the State of Missouri*, 1935–1936.

FIGURE 3.8. Thomas Hart Benton, *Jesse James*, from *A Social History of the State of Missouri*, 1935–1936.

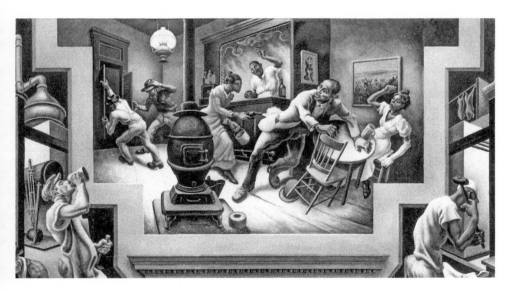

FIGURE 3.9. Thomas Hart Benton, *Frankie and Johnny*, from *A Social History of the State of Missouri*, 1935–1936.

Johnny), literature (Huck Finn and Jim), and a complex amalgam of "formal history, folksong, and oral tale" in the case of Jesse James.[35] Although derived from different realms, these mythical subjects are united by the fact that all are outlaws of a sort; Benton referred to them collectively as "our great, but somewhat disreputable, heroes." They thus remain distinct from the anonymous figures appearing elsewhere in the mural. Benton tried to heighten this difference formally, explaining, "Because of their mythical character, I did not want to introduce them into the main, and generally more prosaic, actions of the mural."[36] Hence, he set Huck Finn and Jim, the James-Younger gang, and Frankie and Johnny off from the other panels through painted architectural forms "where the actual architectural frame was prominent" in the walls of the House Lounge. Also, in contrast to the larger, adjoining panels, Benton cast all three "mythical" murals as nighttime scenes.[37]

Benton was often derided in overly simplistic terms by his more radical contemporaries as a reactionary who retreated from the modern, the political, and the multicultural with his mid-1930s move from metropolitan New York City back to the American heartland. As scholarship by the likes of Justin Wolff, Leo Mazow, and Erika Doss has helped illuminate, none of these accusations told the whole story, even if each contains a kernel of truth. Even a brief examination of *A Social History of the State of Missouri*—arguably the most representative project of the artist's signature style—complicates the claims of Benton's critics. For one, both the mythical and more strictly historical paintings include a significant African American presence. Although interracial solidarity remained far from the norm for US society in the 1930s, Benton's *Early Settlers* panel includes a prominent pair of muscular white and black male laborers toiling together on a timbering project to clear and settle the "untamed" Missouri wilderness. Elsewhere, a comparably muscular African American stockman labors in the slaughterhouse of Benton's *Kansas City*.

The accusation that Benton abandoned socially critical commentary for a simplistic rural nostalgia likewise requires substantial qualification. As in several other 1930s mural projects, Benton's *Social History* celebrates at least some aspects of the vitality of urban, contemporary St. Louis and Kansas City in ways that formally parallel the energetic builders, pioneers, and farmers of his earlier, rural Missouri epochs. For example, his two city panels include several images of manly factory labor as well as the scene of a political dinner that blends seamlessly into a bustling nightclub featuring a leggy blonde woman dancing on its stage. Further, contrary to what leftist detractors of the day sometimes alleged, Benton's outlook on US history was far from uncritical. As Wolff observes, the people's history that Benton forged in his murals refused "to be either wholly cynical or wholly optimistic about America's transformation from an agrarian republic to an industrial society."[38] In keeping with the New Deal aesthetic that defined the decade's public art, Benton's *Social History* moves chronologically through a trajectory that equates the transition from past to present with the attendant development of enhanced technology and infrastructure, and with a gradual shift from rural to urban landscapes. As elsewhere in his art, Benton seems to lament the gradual displacement of the Jeffersonian ideal of the yeoman farmer or the individual craftsman by big business over the course of his historical saga.

Yet some form of corruption is evident in virtually every era of Benton's Missouri chronicle, not just in the contemporary urban scenes, where, for example, the artist caused considerable consternation by including the likeness of Kansas City's Democratic machine power broker "Boss" Tom Pendergast at the political dinner. Many of the artist's points of critique pertain specifically to racial inequality and social intolerance: in *Pioneer Days*, a white frontiersman trades whiskey to an American Indian for animal furs, and a smaller panel below depicts the whipping of slave laborers in eighteenth-century lead mines; *Early Settlers* pointedly places a nearly naked black man on an auction block close to an outdoor white baptismal service to connote the hypocrisy of a Christian society condoning slavery; another *Early Settlers* scene depicts a slave being whipped, and a smaller panel below renders the violent displacement of an early Mormon community, complete with a burning house and one mob victim being tarred and feathered; *Politics, Farming, and Law in Missouri* incorporates the silhouette of a lynching victim in front of raging flames that represent the massive destruction of the US Civil War; and a small tableau below and to the right of *Frankie and Johnny* shows impoverished black men on a Depression-era street corner while a black woman scavenges coal next to a railroad track—in direct contrast to its mirror image of a luxurious Kansas City nightclub with a black jazz band being enjoyed by wealthy white patrons during Prohibition.[39] In addition, ominous plumes of black smoke are a strikingly consistent presence throughout Benton's Missouri history. Whether deriving from the lead mines of the 1730s, a burning house or body, the smokestacks of surging steamboats and trains, or the towers of industry, this insistent motif of black smoke announces quite explicitly that the problems of social inequality and the processes of technological expansion were far from new in the twentieth century.

Benton's *A Social History of the State of Missouri*, then, is by no means Pollyannaish in tone. The art historian Matthew Baigell observes, "Although the artist seems to have doted on homespun anecdotes, glorified democratic processes, and rejoiced over the productivity of the people and the land, the seamier aspects of Missouri's history are admitted to an exceptional degree in a set of murals designed for a state capitol."[40] Henry Adams goes so far as to argue that two central themes of the artist's Missouri murals are "the oppression of minorities and the amorality of capitalism."[41] Nor were Benton's social critiques missed by observers at the time; the murals drew a firestorm of negative commentary from the state's legislators, journalists, and other leaders. As a *Life* magazine feature pithily put the matter at the time, "Benton likes Missouri but Missouri does not like Benton's Missouri."[42] For example, Lou Holland, a former executive manager of the Kansas City Chamber of Commerce, highlighted the *Frankie and Johnny* scene as one of the murals' many inappropriate subjects, telling a reporter for the *Kansas City Star*: "They do not show Missouri in the proper light. Missouri is not proud of hangings and Negro honky-tonks. She is not proud of the whipping of slaves, the slave block and Jesse James holdups. . . . The figures, themselves, in the paintings, and the execution in general are terrible and not in taste."[43] Missouri state representative Max Asotsky pronounced, "They'd go swell in a lot of Kansas City barrooms." Benton's critics thus faulted his work both for showcasing Missouri's flaws and for focusing on déclassé subjects that did not mesh well with a high-culture model of art as an agent of uplift and a celebration of society's ideals. In response, Benton irreverently claimed, "I would rather exhibit my pictures in whore houses and saloons where normal people would see them"; and in fact, the artist subsequently hung his painting *Persephone* (1939), a nude, in Billy Rose's Diamond Horseshoe nightclub in New York City's Times Square.[44]

Such caustic comments were jarring to Benton's self-image as a populist. Wolff explains, "He was dismayed by the criticism, which was unforeseen (was this the public he'd so longed for in New York?) and struck him as stupid (since when was history supposed to be beautiful?)."[45] Still, Benton hardly took such criticisms lying down; he granted interviews to several newspapers and mounted the speaker's platform in a variety of venues to defend his work. On one such occasion, he told a Junior League audience in St. Louis in March 1937, "The space could have been filled with portraits of governors, but more people throughout the nation have heard of Frankie and Johnnie than of any of Missouri's governors. . . . Frankie and Johnnie are a rough symbol, but a good one, of what is happening all the time in a certain stratum of our society."[46] Likewise, in "The Missouri Mural and Its Critics," a systematic defense of the project written that same year, Benton again defended elements such as Frankie and Johnny on the grounds of their sociological merit: "The actions of Frankie and Johnny back on the St. Louis waterfront, although they are not of the present, illustrate better the realities of life as it is actually lived than do anybody's opinions about the Constitution."[47] And in his second autobiography, *An American in Art* (1969), Benton said of the mythical characters of his Missouri State Capitol murals, "They were the most famous characters spawned in the history of Missouri, and any realistic depiction of the State would have to take them into account."[48] Despite Benton's gestures toward isolating the mythical panels from the project's historical narrative, his peculiar phrasing about Twain's characters and folk song's Frankie and Johnny being necessary to "any realistic depiction" of Missouri suggests an equivocation regarding the line between historical actors and creatively (re)imagined characters. Specifically, in the "Missouri Mural" passage cited above, Benton curiously argues for the contemporaneous documentary value of a real event from the 1890s that had been transformed into numerous artistic ballad permutations and, from there, readapted into yet another creative iteration by Benton himself.

Benton was an artist who prided himself on the amount of planning that went into his murals, even boasting in an interview that he did not make mistakes in his murals because they were so carefully planned. "I'm a kind of half-assed historian anyhow," he claimed with pride. "I've read all my life."[49] The Missouri State Capitol project was typical in this respect. Benton spent approximately nine months researching and designing the murals, and only the final six months of 1936 completing the work on the walls. Benton's extensive research on the history of his subject is reflected in notes that contain details on such varied topics as the number and types of businesses in early nineteenth-century St. Louis, the history of steamboats, and specific Missouri skirmishes preceding and during the US Civil War.[50] As was his accustomed practice by this time, Benton also drew heavily on his voluminous collection of sketches from his years of travel across the United States—what he termed "that research I had done just by living"—as models for most of the anonymous subjects of his *Social History of the State of Missouri* murals.[51] He complemented his existing body of sketches by traveling around his home state expressly for this project:

> During the making of my Missouri mural I traveled all over the state. I met all kinds of people. I played the harmonica and wore a pink shirt to country dances. I went on hunting and fishing parties. I attended an uproarious three-day, old settler's drunk, in the depths of the Ozarks. I went to political barbecues and church picnics. I took in the honky-tonks of the country and the night clubs of Kansas City and St. Louis. I went to businessmen's parties and to meetings of art lovers' associations. I went down in the mines and out in the cornfields. I chased Missouri society up and down from the shacks of the Ozark hillbillies to the country club firesides of the ultimately respectable.

From this it would seem that I should know my Missouri—and in a sense I think I do.[52]

Benton's self-image as an artist plainly centered on the concept of himself as a champion of the "common man" who understood the heartland of the nation through extensive firsthand experience. In this, the artist was in keeping with the prevailing spirit of his times, with its emphasis on the documentation and artistic adaptation of the lives of ordinary Americans.

Given the breadth of Benton's research and the numerous gestures of social criticism regarding racial injustice found in the Missouri State Capitol murals as a whole, it seems somewhat contradictory that in the two mythology panels featuring African Americans, the artist turns to a shopworn racial iconography. The first such panel features the characters Huckleberry Finn and Jim. Twain's novel, representing a quest for freedom from societal constraints through travel on the open river, appealed to an artist like Benton, who loved the adventure of the open road. Elaborating on Twain's appeal in his auto-biography, Benton wrote, "The river waters are suggestive of release. Their currents sing of freedom to everyone," and he returned to *The Adventures of Huckleberry Finn* just a few years later by providing a series of over eighty illustrations for a new edition of the novel. In fact, Benton had expressed an interest in Huckleberry Finn as a potential mural subject at least as early as his 1934 speaking tour of the country on behalf of the Federal Art Project; and he originally intended to focus all his Missouri State Capitol artwork on characters from Twain's fiction, before discovering how much wall space he had available.[53] As in the celebrated novel, Huck and Jim appear in Benton's mural as travelers on a compelling journey. They stand aboard their raft next to a riverbank at night, Jim holding a successful catch of fish. In the background, a steamboat named the *Sam Clemens* churns along the river, trailing a long stream of black smoke, simultaneously evoking the themes of mobility and industrial advancement.

In the context of Twain's 1880s—or Benton's 1930s, for that matter—presenting Huck and Jim as allied outlaws in this way was in some respects a daring act. Benton emphasizes the duo's shared fugitive status through their similar attire of rolled up slacks and wide-brimmed hats, paired with muscled, shirtless torsos and bare feet.[54] This rendering of Jim's torso and arms finds company with much Depression-era art that uses well-developed musculature as a sign of masculine valor; in particular, his physique bears some resemblance to that of a shirtless African American laborer directly below and to his right, as well as those of two shirtless white male laborers in other panels of *A Social History of the State of Missouri*. Yet this imagery denotative of masculine strength does not gainsay the fact that Jim, an adult of towering stature, is shown as an equal of the adolescent Huck, and often follows the boy's lead. In short, Benton reproduces the muddled racial ideology at the heart of Twain's fiction, presenting Huck and Jim in a manner awash with romanticism. Overall, the mural provides a nostalgic interlude between the *Pioneer Days* and *Early Settlement* period of Missouri's history.[55]

This consideration of Benton's Huck and Jim is important for understanding the artist's representation of Frankie and Johnny in the same project. *Frankie and Johnny* is the most consciously comic scene in Benton's *A Social History of the State of Missouri*. The humor of this painting, such as it is, is driven by the symbolic unmanning of the ballad's male protagonist in ways loosely reminiscent of the artist's treatment of Jim and plainly kindred to the kind of buffoonery still prevalent in popular-culture representations of African Americans during the 1930s. Several elements combine to give Benton's *Frankie and Johnny* a cartoonish quality: Frankie fires her pistol with a facial expression of frenzied intensity, and without bothering to set aside her pail of beer; with panic on his face, Johnny anxiously flees his jealous lover, in the process toppling a stein of beer and the round table and chair at which he was recently seated; the bartender stands with open mouth and raised arm in response to the sudden, unexpected spectacle of violence; and Johnny's female companion, Nellie Bly of ballad fame, likewise cries out in alarm and raises her bare right arm in astonishment, contrasting with the decorous long glove reaching above the elbow on her left arm. Further, as Ernest Irvine observed of the background action on the left margin of the painting in a 1939 booklet about Benton's Missouri murals, "much merriment has been caused by the two gentlemen making their hurried departure—the one at the left holding frantically to his hat while the one at the right has expended so much energy in his 'get away' that one of the buttons on the rear of his trousers just couldn't 'stand the strain' and has severed its connection, thus allowing one his suspenders to fly in the breeze."[56]

Perhaps even more significantly, the shot fired from Frankie's pistol in the painting appears destined not to mortally wound her lover, but rather to strike him in the buttocks. Amid the initial flurry of commentary on the murals in 1937, one observer in the *Kansas City Star* noted of such a placement of the shot: "It's quite wrong, and would require a lot of revision in the song. . . . The artist ought to make Frankie load up and try again."[57] In fairness, Cecil Brown notes the existence of variations of the ballad that take a similar comic turn:

> *Frankie said to the Judge,*
> *"Well, let all such things pass,*
> *If I didn't shoot him in the third degree*
> *I shot him in his big brown ass."*[58]

However, this was hardly the most common version of the song; Bruce Buckley chronicled only six similar variants among over two hundred examples of "Frankie and Johnny" compiled for his study.[59] Nor does a variant verse of this sort appear in the version of the "Frankie and Johnny" lyrics that Benton selected to appear alongside the print version of his mural in the 1969 catalogue raisonné of his lithographs.[60] This represents, in any event, a highly suggestive choice on Benton's part; not least, it immediately removes the ballad from the realm of epic tragedy and positions it, instead, in the realm of racial comedy of an all-too-familiar variety.

Since Benton prided himself on the meticulous authenticity of his mural subjects and based his figures on historical research and sketched portraits of actual Missouri residents, it bears emphasizing that *Frankie and Johnny* seems to depart sharply from the artist's credo. The mural appears to be at odds with the one description of a black urban saloon that I have been able to locate in Benton's writings. In a suggestive passage from his autobiography, Benton expressed disappointment following a trip to Memphis's Beale Street: "For I had always heard of it as an uproarious place. I wandered into a poolroom but sensed that I was not welcome and moved on. The colored boys in there, giving businesslike attention to their game, were well dressed and spoke quietly. Outside, the country folks were louder, gayer, and more picturesque, but they too seemed to be bent more on business than fun. . . . For abandoned Negro gaiety it was a flop."[61] Benton's *Frankie and Johnny* mural seems to offer an antidote to such sober realities, replacing the soft-spoken, serious-minded African Americans of the artist's firsthand observations with an animated scene of black-on-black violence played for entertainment value. This was a common theme of early twentieth-century blackface minstrel theater, advertising, cartoons, and film; "coon songs" like "The Bully Song" (popularized by the white vaudeville star May Irwin) and the artwork for the genre's sheet music covers exemplify the motif.[62] Perhaps Benton's penchant for caricature should not prove surprising, since he began his career as an artist with the aim of becoming a professional cartoonist. As Benton was fond of recounting, his first paying job as an artist was as a cartoonist for the *Joplin American* while he was still a teenager.[63] In this same vein, the young artist frequently adorned the envelopes of his letters home from Joplin and Chicago with figures such as a smiling black man with missing teeth, a rakish black man with exaggerated features and a feathered hat leaning against a fence, Italian immigrants with floppy hats and hoop earrings, white hayseeds, and the like.[64]

Although the mural smacks of racial condescension, the fact that Benton selected "Frankie and Johnny" and placed the ballad on par with the esteemed literary creations of Mark Twain and the legendary Jesse James (himself celebrated in numerous works of folk and popular music) is significant. It reflects both the extent to which the artist took "folk heroes" and popular music seriously as forms of American cultural expression—"legend is a chronicle of a people's mind," said Benton—and his impulse toward racial inclusivity.[65] The latter impulse, however, was not without its complications and limitations. Benton's racial politics were vexed, at best. As noted earlier, he wove several pointed critiques of racial injustice into *A Social History of the State of Missouri*. Almost concurrently, he participated in the NAACP-sponsored *An Art Commentary on Lynching* exhibition in New York City in February 1935, contributing a large oil painting entitled *The Lynching*, which depicts its subject as one of unmistakable horror.[66] At the same time, though, Benton was a man enmeshed in the racist predilections of his era, referring to Chicago's Italian quarter as "the most dirty, slovenly, dilapidated place on earth," expressing his wariness of venturing into Jewish neighborhoods after dark, and being prone to the casual use of "nigger," "darkies," "pickaninnies," and other derogatory language in his private correspondence, interviews, public talks, and autobiographies. Strange though it might seem, he was capable of pointing out the horrors of the South's chain-gang labor system and then, in almost the same breath, offering stunningly bigoted assertions, such as, "The Negro is not stupid but, on the other hand, he is not farseeing. As a rule he is ignorant."[67]

Such preconceptions appear to have shaped Benton's Missouri State Capitol murals in important ways not heretofore remarked on. For example, Frankie's wide-eyed expression and apparently errant shooting, as well as the upturned angle and chaotic feel of the scene as a whole, all contrast markedly with the poise and balance of the outlaws in Benton's *Jesse James* mythology panel. One could in no way confuse the gunplay of Benton's *Jesse James* with that of his *Frankie and Johnny*. In their shared theme of gun violence, both paintings represent inversions of the societal status quo. Yet Benton seems to regard the James-Younger gang's holdups of a train and a bank as Robin Hood–style exploits, which was how they were sometimes recast in folk ballads. As early as 1910, John Lomax collected an example that pronounced, "Jesse was a man, a friend to the poor, / He would never see a man suffer pain," and Alan Lomax later recounted a version with the line, "He robbed from the rich and gave to the poor."[68] Regardless of the countervailing historical record, such an interpretation seems comprehensible: many Americans viewed railroad companies and banks askance, as robber baron empires, in both the 1870s heyday of the James-Younger gang and the Great Depression, when Benton painted. (Indeed, the nature of James's targets seems to have played a significant part in his perennial popularity in US folk song and legends.) With confidently wielded firearms, James and his cohort disrupt the principal engines of modernizing Missouri and the rest of the American frontier during the late nineteenth and early twentieth centuries, in a scene resonating with the artist's reservations about the occasionally rapacious tendencies of capitalist institutions of transportation and commerce. As Mazow puts it, "Benton likewise positioned himself as a 'man of the people,' a renegade against officially sanctioned injustice, and he surely saw a kindred spirit in the James folktype."[69]

Benton's *Frankie and Johnny* also ruptures the social order. In the most literal sense, Frankie obliterates the tranquility of the saloon in which the painting's action takes place, which Benton dramatizes via the awkward, forward-leaning angle of the panicked Johnny and the upended barroom table. But whereas Frankie's resorting to arms may be justified by her lover's philandering, one struggles to imagine the artist identifying with her actions in quite the same way as with Jesse James's exploits. Rather, from Benton's vantage, the scene's reversal of gender expectations has the air of an unnatural rift in the usual way of things or, at best, a subject fit more for entertainment than for serious social commentary or idealization of the sort he seems to accord to the James-Younger gang. The contrast between the description of the *Jesse James* and *Frankie and Johnny* panels in a text published by the *Missouri Social Studies Bulletin* during the 1930s is telling: "You will stand long before a virile Jesse James as he holds up the C and A [railroad]. You will smile, perhaps, at Frankie and Johnny."[70] Notwithstanding Benton's praise of the female-centered song "Pistol Packin' Mama," Jesse James is an object of admiration that provides a display of vigorous manhood, while Frankie is an object of lighthearted amusement that shows a black man menaced by his gun-toting lover. The artist's *Frankie and Johnny* panel therefore seems to play to long-standing stereotypes regarding emasculated black men and overly "mannish" black women.[71] This tone seems significantly at odds with the ballad tradition that provided the source material of Benton's mural; what is lamented as tragedy in most performances of the "Frankie and Johnny" ballad assumes a comic air in Benton's handling. To be sure, Benton included both the James gang and Frankie and Johnny in his *Social History* murals as gestures intended to deflate what he saw as the pretensions of elite Missourians' desired self-image for their state. Nonetheless, Benton accords the two real-life-incidents-cum-legends very different degrees of gravity.

Notions of gender play a role in shaping these distinctions, and they are as important as, but inseparable from, factors of race. Evidence for this point abounds in even the most cursory review of Benton's American Scene artwork. Nearly all scholarly commentators on Benton point to self-reliant labor, especially work by men, as a central and defining virtue in both his historical and contemporary-themed works. Benton prized this value so deeply that he usually rendered workers in modern factory settings in terms more consistent with the "skilled labor and worker autonomy" characteristic of an earlier age of independent craftsmen than with the automaton image of assembly-line workers. *A Social History of the State of Missouri* is no exception, featuring Missourians hard at work, from the trapping and mining enterprises of the era of colonization and settlement through the offices and industrial sites of the 1930s. As Doss surmises, "His art focused on the labors of muscular, macho, and presumably heterosexual men who were shown free of corporate *and* female restraint."[72] Seen in this light, the male characters of Benton's *Frankie and Johnny* panel—the anonymous men in "comic" flight from the impending violence, the bartender, and, especially, the male protagonist—are surely found wanting. Even the other figures of the Missouri State Capitol project's mythology panels seem more in step with the artist's ideals regarding the virtue of productive labor than do the characters of *Frankie and Johnny*: Jim holds a catch of fish, and the James-Younger gang holds up a bank and a train, part of the money from which they later will pass on to the poor, according to Missouri legend as Benton understood it.[73]

By contrast, the world of Frankie and Johnny is one of leisure, depicting a "sporting life" gone awry as the result of Johnny's reckless infidelities. In the scene painted by Benton, Johnny pursues no ends beyond his own pleasurable indulgence of alcohol and women's company—or overindulgence, as the case seems to be. Here, one also might note the artist's inclusion of a widely circulated Anheuser-Busch print of Otto Becker's *Custer's Last Fight* (1896) on the wall of the saloon behind Johnny and Nellie Bly. A popular barroom image during Benton's youth, this work was a direct model for some of his earliest amateur art endeavors.[74] More to the point, in this context the Becker print likely serves as a sly commentary on Johnny's impending fate. While at first glance this juxtaposition seems to suggest an element of continuity between the violence of settling the western frontier and Frankie's exploits, the contrasts—this violence being a domestic dispute waged in a saloon rather than on a field of battle, and with Frankie symbolically unmanning her erstwhile lover—suggest that this act of violence from a folk song lacks the heroic stature Benton accorded to the US Calvary and to Robin Hood–style outlaws such as Jesse James and his gang.

Besides rendering a scene of infidelity and relational chaos in terms that might have played to many white preconceptions of black life, Benton's *Frankie and Johnny* depicts its male protagonist as embodying a surplus of leisure time that contrasts markedly with the masculine ideals usually evident in Benton's American Scene paintings. In fact, these ideals are fully in evidence in the mural panels that flank "Frankie and Johnny" in *A Social History of the State of Missouri*. Benton aptly sites *Frankie and Johnny*, an urban tale with origins in St. Louis, between his *St. Louis* and *Kansas City* murals. Contrary to the frequent dismissal of regionalist artwork as thoroughly anti-urban and antimodern, Benton's city scenes here combine towering metallic industrial forms that would appear at home in the era's celebratory precisionist art by the likes of Charles Sheeler, Louis Lozowick, and Elsie Driggs with snapshots of individual skilled labor that project confidence and dignity. The resulting output includes products such as shoes, beer, and beef, three items for which the state's two largest cities were well known. With a savvy bit of compositional configuration, Benton leads the viewer's eye from the brewery, a location of alcohol's production, to the saloon, a site of alcohol's consumption. Through a productive combination of mechanized technology and proletarian labor, one bears witness to Benton's vision of the sustaining of heroic manly labor in modern, industrialized contexts. And while one brewer does tip back a mug of beer, Quintin Slovek usefully points out that viewers might interpret this as the brewer's rightful reward for his labor rather than as a purely decadent indulgence, in light of the surrounding production context.[75] Benton's Johnny, as a pimp and philanderer, stands firmly outside of this iconography of manly labor.

From the brewery to the saloon, in what was undoubtedly an attempt at gallows humor by the artist, the fleeing Johnny tips vertically forward in the frame as if about to fall into the slaughterhouse assembly line of the adjacent Kansas City scene. If Benton analogizes Johnny to the cattle of the urban market's slaughterhouse—butchered and strung up in visceral fashion—the ill-fated protagonist is just as surely contrasted with the African American stockman, or "knocker," whose raised hammer stands poised to strike a death blow to the waiting livestock below. The latter image of manly proletarian labor closely resembles figures such as the prominent African American wielding a jackhammer in Benton's earlier *City Building* mural for the *America Today* project (1930), and other images of the period too numerous to count.[76] As in so much artwork of the 1930s—both regionalist and social realist—characters such as the hammer-wielding stockman embody precisely the kind of masculine working-class vitality and earning power that were deeply imperiled by Depression-era joblessness. In contrast to the productive capacity of the stockman and his ilk in the art of the time, Benton's Johnny appears to be awash in the realm of consumption: of beer, women, and smartly tailored clothing. Even more, many versions of the ballad attribute the finances for this sporting life not to Johnny's own industry, but rather to Frankie's earnings on his behalf as a prostitute. He is a pimp or, in early twentieth-century slang, an

FIGURE 3.10. Thomas Hart Benton, *The Ballad of the Jealous Lover of Lone Green Valley*, 1934. © T. H. Benton and R. P. Benton Testamentary Trusts/UMB Bank Trustee/Licensed by VAGA, New York, NY. Image courtesy of Spencer Museum of Art, The University of Kansas, Museum purchase: Elizabeth M. Watkins Fund, 1958.0055.

"easy rider," not an earnest laborer. The cumulative impact of these contrasts with the kinds of masculinity most often celebrated in the period's visual culture makes Johnny's demise an ignoble one indeed.

Benton's interpretation of "Frankie and Johnny" is further illuminated by a careful comparison with the work from his oeuvre that is its closest thematic precedent, *The Ballad of the Jealous Lover of Lone Green Valley* (1934; figure 3.10). Like *Frankie and Johnny*, the latter work involves a painterly adaptation of a popular song that tells the story of a lover's envy turned to violence: Edward fatally stabs his fiancée, Lemo, over a suspected betrayal. The differences between the two paintings are significant, however. In compositional terms, *Jealous Lover* employs a device in which the ballad scene seems to flow forth from a trio of folk musicians in the lower-right ground of the canvas, whereas Benton's *Frankie and Johnny* contains no such explicit cue to the painting's ballad-derived status.[77] Particularly with its dreamlike swirled forms, *Jealous Lover* bears the obvious marks of an imaginative tale brought to life through music, while *Frankie and Johnny* appears planted on firm floorboards, like those of a theatrical stage. So too, in the earlier painting: the violence is inflicted with a knife rather than a gun; the setting is a pastoral meadow rather than an urban saloon; the figures are white rather than black; and it is a male lover who enacts his revenge upon a female partner. Not coincidentally, the tone of Benton's *Jealous Lover* is one of tragedy rather than comic farce. This is so even though the song traditions from which Benton drew his inspirations consistently validated Frankie's motivations but left those of the male killer in "Jealous Lover" vague at best. To be specific, the female victim of "Jealous Lover" protests her innocence earnestly and is wrongfully sacrificed to her fiancé's purely imagined notions of her infidelity.[78]

In this regard, the painting—like the "Jealous Lover" ballad upon which it is based—plays to well-established narrative conventions of male violence and female martyrdom. As noted in the opening chapter, the "Frankie and Johnny" ballad tradition reverses this formula by almost invariably casting Frankie as a righteous agent of vengeance, even as the very act of revenge compounds her suffering. Notwithstanding his philandering, even Johnny sometimes receives a measure of empathy from ballad singers like Huddie Ledbetter via a melodramatic death and the grief of his mother. By contrast, within Benton's conception of appropriate gender identities, the fact that Johnny would be subjected to violence from a woman, and that he would flee such an assault in a panic, both mark him as a fit subject for ridicule. Hence, the artist's comic treatment of what most singers articulated as a tragic tale.

The ideal of vigorous manhood was one that Benton felt intensely and personally. The Benton scholar Matthew Baigell observes that projecting "a personal image emphasizing physical strength and masculinity" obsessed the artist to no small degree.[79] In his youth and young adulthood, Benton's notions of masculinity shaped his interests in boxing and football, sports in which he participated actively despite his diminutive stature, and which he continued to turn to as occasional artistic subjects throughout his life.[80] As an adult, Benton infamously—and habitually—pilloried museums, galleries, and other facets of the institutionalized art world as being overrun with homosexuals. For example, in a 1941 interview, Benton described the typical museum as "a graveyard run by a pretty boy with delicate wrists and a swing in his gait."[81] He worked very hard throughout his life to shape a public persona that contrasted sharply with this demeaning stereotype of art-world effeminacy: "I go into all athletics and . . . I am generally known, by now, as an artist unlike the usual type. The popular idea of an artist is summed up by a consumptive appearance coupled with feminine habits. The fact that I do not fit that idea has given the boneheads a better opinion of the profession and consequently singled me out as a person worthwhile."[82] In one of Benton's parting salvos upon leaving New York City for his native Missouri in 1935, he claimed that the former locale "has lost all masculinity."[83]

How far the fearful Johnny stands removed from Benton's manly ideal gains additional context from considering the artist's reflections on his own father. In his published writings and unpublished manuscripts, Benton consistently expressed disappointment regarding the disparity he perceived between his father's public and private personas. To the outside world, Benton's father projected an air of authority and served as a US congressman (1897–1905), but Benton despaired that his father was routinely overruled and contradicted within the domestic sphere by Elizabeth Wise Benton, the artist's mother.[84]

Bearing all these issues in mind, one can observe that neither Jim of the *Huckleberry Finn* panel nor Johnny embodies a masculine ideal in keeping with the artist's sensibilities: Jim is presented as a peer of a white adolescent, and Johnny appears as a creature of pure consumption who is set to flight by a woman. In different ways, each of these black male figures from the artist's mythology panels is rendered as a kind of manchild: fully grown in physical stature, but not wholly a man in the ways that the artist conceived of masculinity. To be clear, Benton was capable of creating sympathetic representations of African American men, but seemingly only as proletarian laborers, such as the stockman in his *Kansas City* panel or the workers in his "John Henry"-inspired lithograph *Ten Pound Hammer* (1967), or else as the martyred victims of mob violence and systematic oppression, such as the lynching victim and impoverished Depression-era jobless men of *A Social History of the State of Missouri*.

The corollary of these observations about Johnny as an exemplar of failed masculinity pertains to the unusual status of Frankie as a female figure in *A Social History of the State of Missouri*. By Bob Priddy's calculations, the panorama of Missouri citizens in these murals includes 198 men and 32 women.[85] Although Benton later achieved some notoriety for the female nudes in *Susannah and the Elders* (1938) and *Persephone* (1938–1939), women generally were not his preferred artistic subjects. In a revealing explanation from his autobiography *An Artist in America*, Benton claims, "It will be noticed that my travels around the back roads of America have produced few drawings of women. Women are extremely touchy about being regarded as old-fashioned or outmoded, and unless they are highly convinced of their style or beauty or up-to-dateness they cannot be induced to sit the ten or fifteen minutes it takes to make a drawing. . . . The minute I get out my pencil women flee."[86] Arguably, though, the relative paucity of prominent women in Benton's oeuvre reveals more about the skittishness of the artist toward women than the inverse.

Benton's personal attitudes toward women seem to have been, at best, riddled with ambivalence. There is, for example, the story of his first sexual encounter, in a Joplin, Missouri, saloon with a prostitute, which the artist recounted as a traumatic event: "One night my virginity was taken by a black-haired young slut who wore a flaming red kimono and did her hair in curls like a girl. The experience clashed with my submerged romanticism and I looked no further into the mysteries of sex."[87] Benton's biographer Henry Adams reports that upon the young artist's arrival in Paris in 1908, he "spent much of his time getting drunk in the cafés, where he would pick fights and quarrel with the women."[88] Then, too, upon returning from France and settling in the Lincoln Square Arcade district of New York City in 1912, Benton recounts, "One of my young ladies, in a fit of pique, stuck a knife into me." This young woman, a dancer named Lysle, had served as an artistic model for Benton before the romantic falling out.[89]

Obviously, one should hesitate to read an artist's biography into his creative work in an overly literal way. Nonetheless, this series of distressing experiences in which Benton felt himself to be victimized by women creates the intriguing possibility that the artist might have conceived of the female protagonist of the Frankie and Johnny narrative as a threatening figure rather than an object of identification and empathy, as was usually the case in musical performances of the ballad. At the very least, it is curious that in Benton's rendering, Frankie wears a bright red dress, a color frequently associated with female lasciviousness in African American vernacular music traditions. More specifically, the red kimono worn by the prostitute who unceremoniously deflowered the artist in his youth mirrors exactly the attire of Frankie in many ballads when she seeks out Johnny and shoots him. The aura of sexual license in the scene is enhanced by the presence of a small framed black-and-white portrait of a female burlesque performer with revealing cleavage, bare legs, and an upraised arm that echoes the pose of the bartender and Nellie Bly.[90]

Where women do appear in *A Social History of the State of Missouri*, they typically fill roles as helpmeets. As Matthew Baigell and Allen Kaufman astutely observe of the central *Politics, Farming, and Law* wall of Benton's Missouri State Capitol project, "Women play an active role, either working alongside their husbands or in more stereotyped activities—cooking and childcare."[91] The scholar Barbara Melosh has observed that the depiction of women in this vein was characteristic of much New Deal expression in the visual arts.[92] But one of the subtle yet significant changes as Benton's *Social History* murals move to the urban scenes involves the changing roles of women. The artist's *St. Louis* panel, for instance, features a heavily mascaraed typist in an office setting with a cherry soda on her desk, and other women appear to work at some type of assembly process in the rear ground. In *Kansas City*, a blonde dancer raises her skirt tantalizingly on a cabaret stage for an audience of men in business suits. Benton's white city women in this project thus enjoy moderately expanded opportunities, but display what the artist considered signs of moral decadence. Even here, though, none of these female subjects match the crude intensity embodied by Frankie or the immorality suggested by Nellie Bly's affair with Johnny.

Women in general are a decided minority in Benton's work, and black women are scarcer still. The only African American woman of note other than Frankie and Nellie Bly is the anonymous figure who collects coal from alongside a railroad track in a small tableau at the foot of the *Kansas City* mural. Moreover, while elsewhere in *A Social History of the State of Missouri* Benton reveres the family unit, one sees no direct suggestion of African American families anywhere in the project. In a perceptive parenthetical note regarding the minimal presence of African Americans in domestic settings, Baigell and Kaufman suggest, "Benton did not know quite how to relate them to stable social settings. They remained for him symbols of economic exploitation."[93] As I have suggested, the Missouri State Capitol murals include several scenes highlighting instances of brutal racial injustice in the state's history; the murals also include black men as laborers and, in one isolated instance, as a well-dressed observer of a political speech.[94] Usually cocksure about his knowledge of his artistic subjects, Benton seems to have been on uncertain ground when it came to representing African American women or domestic groupings.

Benton remains an artist well known for elevating the lives of ordinary Americans to the ranks of important historical actors, and rightly so. The St. Louis radio commentator Harry Flannery described Benton as "a social historian, a man who sings folk tales, it might be said, to the accompaniment of swing music . . . the Carl Sandburg of the canvas, a man who looks on the common people and presents them realistically with resounding force."[95] This hallmark of Benton's work has led some scholars to read a note of populist social critique into the *Frankie and Johnny* mural. For example, Doss suggests, "Positioning Frankie and Johnnie between depression-era workers, Benton may have been suggesting that contemporary producers likewise 'take action' and seek revenge on the fat politicos and smug patronage seekers drinking whiskey in the lower right-hand corner of Kansas City."[96] Also searching for a note of social criticism in the *Frankie and Johnny* panel, Baigell and Kaufman claim that "it reflects upon urban problems" and "speaks to the horrors of oppressive slum conditions."[97] Although Baigell and Kaufman offer a richly detailed examination of Benton's Missouri murals vis-à-vis his political sensibilities, and Doss provides one of the most original and insightful analyses of Benton's artistic career in general, I find little in Benton's biography or artistic iconography to support either of those hypotheses with respect to the *Frankie and Johnny* mural. Instead, Benton here regrettably lapses into an all-too-familiar iconography of African American comic ineptitude and moral squalor. In fairness, the ballad source is not exactly a tale suited for polite Victorian society, but the song tradition usually sounds a note of genuine tragedy, which Benton eschewed in favor of a lighter touch. Given the array of ways in which the mural's Frankie and Johnny seem to diverge from gender ideals important to the artist, it is hard to read their story as one of epic drama. Rather, the artist seems to have offered this painting as a playful diversion from his *Social History*'s larger march of progress or, at most, a signpost of what Benton saw as social instabilities inherent in the modern urban milieu broadly and in African American society in particular.

CHAPTER 4

WHITEFACE MARIONETTES:
JOHN HUSTON'S COMIC MELODRAMA

WITH GOOD REASON, John Huston remains best known today in relation to the movie industry. His father, the actor Walter Huston, provided
studio contacts and a point of entry for his Hollywood career, beginning with
screenwriting opportunities in the early 1930s (figure 4.1). From there, John
Huston's work as a director, screenwriter, and actor spanned six decades and
involved such notable films as *The Maltese Falcon* (1941), *The Asphalt Jungle*
(1950), *The African Queen* (1951), *The Night of the Iguana* (1964), and *Prizzi's
Honor* (1985). Less well known is the fact that Huston's creative debut was a
theatrical adaptation of "Frankie and Johnny" penned in 1929. For reasons
detailed below, the play was never presented in a major production for stage
or screen. To the extent that Huston's *Frankie and Johnny* remains known
at all, it is primarily through the play's publication in book form by Albert
and Charles Boni in 1930, accompanied by his researched account of the ballad's origins, several variants of the ballad, and numerous illustrations by the
prominent Mexican caricaturist Miguel Covarrubias.

Despite appearing under the auspices of a respected publisher, Huston's
Frankie and Johnny receives only the briefest of comments by Huston and his
biographers. Huston explains his original motivations tersely in his autobiography: "In 1929 I met a girl who made marionettes and worked in a marionette
theater for Tony Buffano [*sic*]: Ruth Squires. Ruth's marionette shows weren't
very good, so I wrote one for her." In an interview with the *New York Telegram*
at the time of publication, Huston said he wrote the play "just for the hell of
it."[1] This leaves much unanswered, not least the question why Huston choose
the ballad "Frankie and Johnny" as the subject of his marionette play and
exactly what kind of production aesthetics he originally envisioned. Beyond
the general factors outlined in chapter 1, the appeal of "Frankie and Johnny"
to Huston in particular would seem to have much to do with his lifelong
fascination with the "sporting life." Huston said of his own mother, Rhea,

FIGURE 4.1. Walter Huston and John Huston, early 1930s. Courtesy of mptvimages.com.

that from his earliest memories, "She was crazy about playing the ponies. She taught me that money's for spending, and to hell with the odds."[2] Following her example, Huston regularly immersed himself in the world of horse tracks, card tables, and gambling halls as a young man. His acquaintances included not only celebrated film stars, writers, and modern artists, but also card sharks, prostitutes, and other underclass denizens. Further, over the course of his life Huston married five times and by all accounts (including his own) could seldom stay faithful for long to any one woman; in the recollection of at least one of these wives, Evelyn Keyes, Huston was brazenly open about his extramarital dalliances.[3] So too, Huston enjoyed playing the role of raconteur, regaling friends with tales of his lively exploits. For example, he seems to have been especially fond of recounting the story of how, upon receiving his $500 advance for *Frankie and Johnny* from Albert and Charles Boni, he headed to a Saratoga horse track and submerged himself in a craps game in which "he ran it up to $11,000 in one evening before losing it all."[4] Little surprise that a young man so well acquainted with red-light districts would feel drawn to a sensationalistic story set in this same milieu at just three decades' remove.

The brevity of Huston's published commentary on *Frankie and Johnny* downplays the extent of his personal investment in the project. By the time of the play's publication in 1930, Huston had crafted a substantive play structured in three scenes, a prologue, and an epilogue, with openings for musical material at multiple junctures; he also had gathered thirteen variants of the ballad (representing versions from at least seven states) and penned an essay entitled "On the St. Louis Version," which accurately traced the origins of the ballad back to Frankie Baker's 1899 murder of Allen Britt.[5] In compiling that document, Huston drew on newspaper accounts, hospital records, and an interview with Richard Clay, an African American movie projectionist who claimed to have known Britt well and to have been at his bedside after the shooting. Thus equipped, Huston got most of his facts correct, including the identity of the "other woman" as Alice Pryor and the fact that Frankie Baker was residing in Portland, Oregon, in 1930. Huston framed his discussion of Baker's shooting of Britt with a general history of the midwestern "sporting circuit," in which he devoted special attention to the pattern of arrangements between female prostitutes and their male managers, or "macks."[6] His interest in "Frankie and Johnny," that is to say, went beyond mere aesthetic appreciation of a compelling ballad; it was of a piece with his fascination with the larger social world that birthed the saga and its subsequent elaborations in song. In effect, like so many creative artists of the 1920s and 1930s, Huston became something of an amateur folklorist in his own right.

The extent of Huston's familiarity with the historical background and musical versions of the Frankie and Johnny saga makes the revisions and adaptations of the source material in his play particularly striking. Among these adaptations, three are significant: recasting the characters as white; rendering his play as a comic melodrama rather than a dramatic tragedy; and depicting Frankie as a prisoner of blind fidelity and jealous hysteria rather than as a self-assured woman. Huston's decision to rework the "Frankie and Johnny" narrative in whiteface seems especially puzzling, given his complete lack of direct commentary on the rationale for the decision. Granted, the lyrics to most versions of the song do not specify the racial identity of Frankie and Johnny, but the song nonetheless seems to have been widely understood as African American in 1920s America. More to the point, Huston's essay unambiguously declares the song's African American origins, which indicates that obscuring his project's roots in black source material was not a primary motive.

Most likely, Huston's purposes were commercial, an attempt to capitalize on the "lucrative nostalgia" afforded by folk subjects during the 1920s and 1930s.[7] Admittedly, the fact that Huston originally wrote the play to be performed as a puppet theater production would seem to promise limited prestige and a modest payday, at best. But Huston also had ambitions (ultimately thwarted) of staging his play in a more prestigious theatrical venue on Broadway, with prominent white actors and actresses, in the early 1930s.[8] In 1945, Huston and Robert Milton received a contract from Richard Krakeur to stage *Frankie and Johnny* as a lavish musical, but repeated delays from Huston and Milton led Krakeur to cancel the contract.[9] During the early 1960s, Huston revisited the play with hopes (once more unrealized) of adapting it into a feature film. Clearly, then, the material continued to occupy his attention at intervals throughout the remainder of his life. In each instance, he wrote Frankie and Johnny as white protagonists. The success of folklore-themed productions with African American casts, such as Marc Connelly's *The Green Pastures* (1930) and DuBose Heyward and the Gershwins' *Porgy and Bess* (1935), suggests that this may have been an aesthetic and commercial miscalculation on Huston's part.

Regardless of motive, the decision to rewrite the racial identity of the characters places Huston's *Frankie and Johnny* within what was, by 1930, already a long tradition of white American creative artists performing similar revisions to material originating from African American culture. As noted in chapter 1, the ballad-legend tradition of "John Henry" contains several such instances of a kind of crossover popularity that sometimes did not convey the African American identity of its titular character. Likewise, at least as early as 1908, commercial sheet music for "Frankie and Johnny" featured photographs of white musicians, the Leighton Brothers, in place of African American imagery. Others followed Huston on this front: John Held's *The Saga of Frankie and Johnny*, a book of woodcuts illustrating a risqué version of the song's lyrics with white characters, was published in 1930, the same year that Huston's play appeared in book form; a forgettable 1936 Republic Pictures film, *Frankie and Johnnie*, cast Helen Morgan and Chester Morris in the titular roles; and *Frankie and Johnny*, a B-movie adaptation starring Donna Douglas and Elvis Presley, followed three decades later, in 1966. As one of the first creative attempts at fashioning a white version of "Frankie and Johnny" in a medium other than music, Huston's text thus merits examination.

One corollary of Huston's whitening of the Frankie and Johnny narrative is the play's somewhat haphazard mixture of meticulous fidelity to the author's own research on the ballad's historical background and flagrant disregard of such particulars. On certain issues, it mattered very much to Huston to get the details of midwestern "sporting life" right, including instances of slang and dress as well as the general atmosphere of boisterousness that the author took as characteristic of such an environment. Huston infuses his dialogue with references to "macks" (pimps) and "clover" (money), for instance;

and he takes care to remark on details such as Frankie's "sky blue kimono" as she marches off with a gun in search of her errant lover, and Johnny's last request to be buried "in a box-back coat and hat."[10] Yet the resulting speech of the characters defies easy classification. Frankie's rival suitor Nelly, for example, opines:

> Ye never spends on me no more, does ye, Johnny? Ye dropped me like a hot spud when she [Frankie] took up with ye. I bet she's been a-tellin' lies on me to wean ye off. I hear how you're lettin' a petticoat run your engine, — how your breeches is held up with an apron string. But I stuck up for ye. Any fool, I says, could see he was sick a takin' sass. He ain't a idjit, he knows which side his bread is buttered on. First he'll get his wad, I says, then he'll have his fun.[11]

While saturated with idiomatic expression, such dialogue resembles a clumsy approximation of Old English more than any African American or specific white ethnic dialect from turn-of-the-century America. Further, Huston was at pains to identify St. Louis as the point of origin for the "Frankie and Johnny" ballad, but he shifted the action of his play from the city's Chestnut Valley neighborhood, where Frankie Baker's shooting of Allen Britt originally transpired, to a more archetypal (and apparently all-white) red-light district in an unnamed city.

That Huston broke with the conventions of the "Frankie and Johnny" ballad tradition in choosing caricature as the aesthetic mode for his play also merits attention. Although only twenty-three years old when he wrote the play, by 1929 Huston already possessed an uncommon depth of exposure to contemporary literary currents, and he admired, in particular, the plays of Eugene O'Neill and the fiction of James Joyce. Huston was able to bear witness as his father, Walter, starred in a major production of O'Neill's *Desire Under the Elms* in 1924 and 1925. Huston later stated, "The best learning experience I ever had was watching the rehearsals of Eugene O'Neill's *Desire Under the Elms*." (Interestingly, O'Neill's *All God's Chillun Got Wings* (1924) incorporates a stray verse of "Frankie and Johnny" via the white gangster Shorty, who sings while he waits on a street corner: "And sewed up in her yeller kimona, / She had a blue-barreled forty-five gun, / For to get her man / Who'd done her wrong.")[12] Huston first encountered Joyce's *Ulysses* (1922) when his mother smuggled in a copy of the banned novel from Europe in 1927, and he found it transformative, saying that as he read it, "doors fell open."[13] Nevertheless, Huston imbued his debut literary work with neither O'Neill's fusion of naturalist and symbolist elements nor the stream-of-consciousness techniques of Joyce's fiction. To the contrary, Huston's *Frankie and Johnny* bears a stronger resemblance to the lowbrow aesthetics of vaudeville comedy.

Stated succinctly, Huston renders the story of Frankie and Johnny as a comic farce. Frankie appears self-effacing and wholly obsessed with Johnny, whereas he seems utterly self-absorbed and disdainful toward Frankie. In fact, the author's treatment of Frankie seems so extreme that contemporary readers might be inclined to read the play as a protofeminist critique of a capable woman submitting herself recklessly to such a callous man, were it not for the fact that Huston also awkwardly attempts to cast his play as a tale of true love, of sorts. Whereas renditions of the traditional ballad by singers such as Huddie Ledbetter and Mississippi John Hurt effectively capture the complex cut of emotions in which love, when wronged, might shade into righteous anger, the pull between Huston's divergent modes of cartoonish humor and syrupy romantic sentiment ultimately strains the play's coherence. His whitening of characters and lightening of tone via "humorous" treatment of the play's female protagonist both seem to have been strategies aimed at fashioning a play that he deemed palatable to a broad audience. In Huston's estimation, neither a black cast nor an assertive Frankie represented bankable propositions.

The play opens with a prologue that provides a flash-forward introducing the reader to Frankie at the gallows with a noose around her neck. Huston embellishes this arresting tableau with "the sustained beats of a funeral march" and a crowd of onlookers that includes "the Sheriff, the Madam, the Bartender, and a throng of harlots and loose gentlemen."[14] He seems to presume the audience's familiarity with the basic framework of Frankie's story, for the prologue never specifies exactly what crime has led her to this dire end. As in most variants of the ballad that depict Frankie at the gallows, Huston's protagonist represents a model of composure as she awaits her fate.[15] The illustrator Miguel Covarrubias depicts her with a serene, beatific smile (figure 4.2). In a reversal of accustomed roles, it is the condemned, Frankie, who helps assuage the guilt of her executioner, the sheriff, who asks: "An' ye won't hold it agin us, Frankie?"[16] Still, for all of Frankie's calm in the face of death, Huston does not cast her as a strong or rebellious character on the whole. To the contrary, his portrayal of Frankie's misplaced and slavish devotion to Johnny over the course of the play renders her vulnerable to repeated acts of manipulation. Even more, unlike the portrayal of her in most versions of the ballad, Huston's Frankie absorbs at least part of the blame for the play's tragic outcome. Frankie explains to the crowd gathered beneath the gallows that she leaves no material possessions, only her story, as a warning to other lovers:

FIGURE 4.2. Miguel Covarrubias, Frankie at the gallows, illustration for John Huston's *Frankie and Johnny* (1930).

"Whoever shall be born to love. Let them hear my tale, —*how I loved an' done wrong*."[17] From the outset, then, Huston indicates that his *Frankie and Johnny* constitutes a kind of morality play, notwithstanding it being set among characters from the proverbial wrong side of the tracks. But Frankie's line here subtly yet significantly reverses the attribution of blame characteristic of the ballad, most renditions of which include a refrain along the lines of "He was her man, / But he was doing her wrong."[18]

Huston's revision contrasts markedly with the version of the ballad appearing in *The Saga of Frankie and Johnny*, a book adaptation published the same year by John Held Jr. Held's publication, too, concludes with an image of Frankie at the gallows (figure 4.3), but his text ends with a verse common to the ballad tradition that explicitly enjoins female listeners not to rely on male counterparts:

> *This story has no moral.*
> *This story has no end.*
> *This story only goes to show*
> *You can't trust no God-damned men.*
> *For he was her man, and he done her wrong.*[19]

SWEET GOD I'M COMING TO THEE

FIGURE 4.3. John Held Jr., *Sweet God, I'm Coming to Thee*, illustration for
The Saga of Frankie and Johnny (1930).

Although later in the play Huston quotes the ballad's familiar refrain "he done
her wrong" in reference to Johnny, the opening prologue and closing epilogue of Huston's play muddy the issue of blame by having Frankie suggest
that she, too, has "loved an' done wrong" and by stating her desire to be
buried alongside Johnny as a last request.[20] This tension proves emblematic
of the play's capriciousness as a whole with respect to how Huston conceptu-
alized his play's two central characters.

The following exchange from early in scene 1, immediately following a
stage number in which Frankie sings "The Curse of an Aching Heart," succinctly epitomizes the gulf separating the title characters:

FRANKIE: Did ye like how I sung?
JOHNNY: Aye, ye sung good. They oughtta give ye more dough.
FRANKIE: I wasn't singin' for money.
JOHNNY: What for then?
FRANKIE: For you, Johnny.
JOHNNY: Well, they oughtta give ye more dough anyway. Let's have a shot.[21]

As captured in this brief conversation, both characters leave much to be desired. While Frankie is sympathetic in that she is good-hearted and faithful, Huston constructs her naïveté as a tragic flaw. She dreams of romance in terms of "a parlor fillt with flowers, — lilacs an' calla lilies," which seems unrealistically far removed from the rough-and-tumble world of saloons, prostitution, and gambling that she inhabits. Further, she invests far too much import in a single breezily given vow from Johnny "to be true as the stars, — me to you, an' you to me, forever"; significantly, the wording of this vow was crafted by Frankie, not by Johnny of his own inspiration.[22] Consequently, Frankie not only sacrifices virtually her entire wages to an insensitive wastrel, but also effaces her dignity in the process. As Frankie puts it to Johnny, "None'll pump their veins dry for ye, Johnny, to keep ye in clover, — a-doin' that what God an' laws ferbid, for the sake a love alone."[23] If Victorians tended to count self-sacrifice as a chief womanly virtue, Huston's modernist sensibilities see it otherwise: as an indication of foolishness and gullibility. In this vein, a review of Huston's book mused, "One suspects that members of the youngest generation are beginning to consider 'Frankie and Johnny' as a trifle 'old hat.' They suspect its colors have faded and its fundamentals have become old-fashioned for Frankie was foolish and Johnny an overbearing and stupid oaf."[24]

This characterization presents Huston with a challenge: he must convert the wilting flower that is Frankie in the play's first two scenes into a woman who commits murder by the play's finale. Predictably, he renders this transformation *not* as a moment of self-actualization, but rather as the act of a woman who is temporarily driven mad by jealousy. When the reader encounters Frankie following Johnny's abrupt decision to break off their relationship, Huston describes her as melodramatically distraught:

Frankie comes out of the saloon. Her hair is loosened and her dress is torn at the shoulder.
FRANKIE: I didn't suspect to find the same world here on the outside. I thought it would all a come to ashes an' mire, an' it would all be dead save me who was dyin'.[25]

Soon, a character named Prizefighter adds to Frankie's despair by revealing that Johnny has taken up with Nelly Bly. (Taking the place of the bartender in most versions of the ballad, Prizefighter is motivated in part by his own apparent fondness for Frankie, although that thread is not well developed in the play.) Initially, Frankie responds with denial and anger—"Ye liar! I'll dig your eyes outen your head"—followed by grim resolution; she heads for the pawnshop to purchase a gun. By the time she reaches the brothel where Johnny and Nelly Bly have rendezvoused, Frankie is wild with rage. Borrowing a line from bombastic versions of the ballad, she warns fellow prostitutes who cross her path on the way to Nelly's room, "Stand back ye floozies, or I'll blow ye all to hell!"[26] Overwrought with a thirst for retribution, once Frankie reaches Johnny she can no longer be swayed by his charms; instead, she warns, "Speak to your Lord and call him good, he's let ye live so long." Yet once she has delivered a fatal third shot to Johnny's breast, Frankie immediately is overcome with grief, sobbing over his fallen body and bestowing on him a parting kiss.[27]

Subsequent to this dramatic act of revenge, Huston makes clear that Frankie has not been fundamentally transformed by Johnny's elimination from her life. Rather, she continues to place the needs of others and her affection for the deceased Johnny above any concerns for her own well-being. After a group of macks enters with a coffin to carry Johnny's body off to the graveyard, to the musical accompaniment of a recitative version of "Frankie and Johnny," a brief epilogue returns to Frankie at the gallows. Here, her chief concern is to ensure that she will be buried beside the man who financially exploited and then jilted her, and whose consequent murder has brought her own life to a premature, tragic end. In yet another bizarre twist, Frankie not only assuages the sheriff's guilt about having to conduct her hanging, but also encourages the gathered onlookers to dance along to a lively "ragtime" version of "Frankie and Johnny" as she is hanged. She even offers a strangely chipper promise: "Ye'll have to dance lively. I'll be showin' ye new steps in a minute, steps ye've never seen before." Indeed, Huston's stage directions indicate that the onlookers *do* dance enthusiastically after the rope snaps Frankie's neck.[28]

What is one to make of these abrupt shifts in tone? In part, their awkwardness surely reflects Huston's status as a young, unpolished writer. Beyond that factor, however, Huston's characterization of the play's protagonist differs markedly from the portrayal of Frankie offered by most versions of the ballad, as well as Huston's research on the ballad and his description of the historical Frankie Baker. For example, contrast the passivity of the play's Frankie with the statement Huston quotes in his essay "On the St. Louis Version": "[Frankie] was a beautiful, light brown girl, who liked to make money and spend it. She dressed very richly, sat for company in magenta lady's cloth, diamonds as big as hen's eggs in her ears. There was a long razor scar down the side of her face she got in her teens from a girl who was jealous of her. She only weighed about a hundred and fifteen pounds, but she had the eye of one you couldn't monkey with. She was a queen sport."[29] As in performances of the ballad like Huddie Ledbetter's "Frankie and Albert," this prose passage from Huston describes a woman possessing her own desires and a willingness to claim them in assertive fashion. He recognized that the real-life Frankie Baker's murder of Allen Britt was not her first scrape with violence. Baker was, frankly stated, rough around the edges in ways necessary to survival in her social world. One need not insist that the creative artist remain shackled to a literal translation of the character from historical incident to song or to stage in order to observe that the particular ways in which Huston reworked this character served to provide audiences with a very different and less self-determined protagonist than one would find in the play's musical and real-life source material. Under no circumstances would a reader describe the Frankie of Huston's play as "one you couldn't monkey with"—quite the opposite; she is Johnny's doormat for almost the entirety of the play. Even though Frankie temporarily steps out of this mode when committing Johnny's murder, the swiftness with which Huston returns her to a role of docility, submissiveness, and amorous attachment is telling.

In sum, Huston depicts Frankie as driven by emotion rather than reason throughout the play, *both* when she dotes mindlessly on an ungrateful Johnny *and* when she brings about his demise, in what Huston's Freudian contemporaries likely would have identified as a fit of hysteria. At no point does Frankie seem equipped to escape the orbit of this gender essentialism. In fact, having committed the tragic deed at the heart of the ballad tradition, Huston's Frankie calls for the onlookers to summon the sheriff for her arrest.[30] Having dispatched her male love interest to the afterlife, she apparently has no desire to continue living. Although dressed in the trappings of comic farce, Huston's reimagining of Frankie thus has much to tell us about the extent to which thoroughly backward-looking gender ideologies permeated the work of even self-characterized freethinking modernists during the 1920s and 1930s.

For his part, the play's Johnny replicates the lack of fidelity to Frankie that is a central feature of the "Frankie and Johnny" ballad tradition. In Huston's hands, though, Johnny also is a moocher, a glutton, and a dandy—in short, an all-around cad. Nor is it as if Johnny craftily disguises these flaws from Frankie. Rather, as in the dialogue passage quoted above, he openly craves money from Frankie above all else. As scene 2 opens, Johnny spends extravagantly from Frankie's earnings on his own food—"Liver pie an' calves' foot jelly, chitt'lin's with sauce Béarnaise, poached cucumbers, raw fry, prunes, soufflé with ginger, a large stein of beer"—while ordering only a simple egg sandwich for her.[31] More dramatically still, later in this same scene Johnny badgers Frankie at great length to surrender the entirety of her savings; when he finally discovers a hidden roll of bills that she was planning to give him as a gift on the anniversary of their pledge of true love to each other, Johnny not only takes the money, but also uses it as a pretense to break off the relationship:

> JOHNNY: Yer filthy money, stole, dishonorable. I could be unkind an' tell ye to keep it.
> FRANKIE: Ye'll take it, Johnny, or ye'll break my heart.
> JOHNNY [rising]: Aye, I'll take it. For money that ye'd get that way wouldn't never do ye no good. Aye, I'll take it. An' also I can wish ye a fond farewell, now that ye've broke my trust. I can see now ye've been schemin' an' connivin' from the day we first met. Ye didn't fool me. I suspicioned ye all along. Aye,—I'll take what's comin' to me, an' bid ye goodbye,—an' may ye forget as best yer conscience'll allow.[32]

Where the ballad tradition emphatically drives home the idea that "He was her man, / But he was doing her wrong" with reference to infidelity, Huston goes considerably further by offering no indication that Johnny ever possessed even an inkling of true romantic feeling for Frankie. Rather, his relationship to her appears wholly predatory, manipulative, and exploitative.

Although Frankie is blind to Johnny's lack of redeeming qualities and tends to blame herself for his callous behavior, the play's supporting characters stress Johnny's lack of worth. The Bartender, for example, bemoans with exasperation Frankie's lack of insight into Johnny's true nature: "Her a-teamin' up with tripe like him, tripe out a the waller."[33] Even the play's Madam, identified as Johnny's mother, chastises her son for recklessly spending Frankie's money and throwing her over for Nelly Bly.[34] From the spectator's vantage, Huston offers nothing to redeem Johnny's character; he is a scoundrel, through and through. His eventual infidelity with Nelly Bly serves only as further evidence of the same disdain he has displayed for Frankie's feelings throughout the play. Huston's tale thus offers viewers a tragically flawed female protagonist and a complete void of heroic male figures—so much so that one imagines the play's lack of substantive commercial appeal may have owed, in large measure, to its lack of genuinely likable or admirable characters. William Fadiman, a Hollywood script editor, offered a critique of Huston's later "Frankie and Johnny" screenplay in the 1960s that seems apropos of the original play as well: "One of its primary problems lies in the character of Johnny. . . . He is presented as stupid, loutish, unpleasant, oafish, a boaster, and a good deal of a fool. . . . It seems incomprehensible to me that a woman such as Frankie . . . should ever fall irrevocably in love with such a man."[35]

That Huston would characterize his play's male lead in such starkly irredeemable terms is, in some respects, surprising. After all, Huston possessed a genuine fascination for the lifestyle and bearing of the mack. As he expounded in his essay "On the St. Louis Version," "The advent of the mack was something new in the American scene. His dress and his gamey affectations quickened the tempo of the life around him." Similarly, there is an open air of admiration when Huston writes, "The smartest macks touted the women who could take in the most, then gambled between themselves. The play was always for high stakes and a great deal of money changed hands."[36] While promoting his play, Huston gushed about turn-of-the-century macks: "They had a code of manners and customs all their own, and what a hell of an aristocracy it was! . . . There will never be any time so good again." Indeed, Huston's interviewer slyly observed of the author's passionate identification with his subject, "This lean and lanky young man . . . wishes he was a hard-boiled he-man of the tough, rambunctious times of Frankie."[37] In contrast, the Johnny of Huston's play possesses none of the vitality that he attributed to the historical persons who populated the world of Frankie Baker and Allen Britt. Macks, of the sort that Huston describes in his essay, appear only as pallbearers and backing characters for the play's strangely timed musical numbers. This contrast might stem partly from Huston's whitening of the play's protagonists. In other words, perhaps Huston was unable or unwilling to attribute a sense of style to a white pimp comparable to what he described in writing of Johnny's historical black counterparts. In any event, Huston credits far greater glamour to real-life African American macks of turn-of-the-century St. Louis than to the white, fictionalized character of Johnny in his play.

One also might observe that the foibles of Huston's Johnny are emphatically antithetical to what the author considered the attributes of a "real man." Gail Bederman describes early twentieth-century (white) masculinity as centered on qualities such as self-control, self-reliance, and physical power.[38] As men whose primary source of income was generated through the sexual labor of women, pimps inherently walked a fine line in relation to such codes of masculinity. Yet Huston's "On the St. Louis Version" unambiguously shores up the manhood of historical African American macks by describing them as poised, stylish men of authority who competently handled their business and "their" women. The Johnny of Huston's play, by contrast, possesses none of these traits. As suggested by his elaborate food order, quoted above, Johnny appears given to gluttonous indulgence; and his speech is "impeded by a hare lip" and utterly lacking in wit. When the Bartender knocks the Prizefighter unconscious in a comic dispute over an unpaid bar tab early in the play, Johnny opportunistically slips money out of the Prizefighter's pocket and drinks the remainder of his beer to boot. Such small-time larceny, and particularly the act of stealing from another man (while he is unconscious, no less), would seem to violate the principles Huston attributed to his idealized macks.

Similarly, Johnny's treatment of Frankie is characterized by cold indifference and ingratitude instead of the suave charisma that the author associated with macks generally. Even with the standard ballad element of Frankie giving Johnny a hundred-dollar suit, he gripes that "I'd a-rather she'd a-given me the cash."[39] In the play's climactic confrontation, too, Johnny's demeanor is far from stoic resolve; rather, Huston describes Johnny's desperate pleas for his life as "frantic" and "whimpering."[40] In fairness, Johnny's fate, as prescribed by the ballad tradition, is not the sort easily reconciled with conventional early twentieth-century codes of masculinity. In response, whether consciously or not, Huston seems to have been determined to resolve this tension by rendering Johnny as the antithesis of a masculine ideal. Perhaps symbolically unmanning his male protagonist in these emphatic ways was the only way the author could rationalize placing Johnny in a scenario in which he is slain by a woman.

While the foregoing theorizations of the gender politics at work in Huston's *Frankie and Johnny* are speculative, they are lent further credence by the unpublished screenplay drafts that Huston developed from his original play in 1963 with hopes of bringing the story to the Hollywood screen.[41] In this later adaptation, Huston maintained the general framework of his earlier play, complete with the bookended prologue and epilogue featuring Frankie at the gallows, but embellished the play with three substantive additions:

1. Frankie arrives in St. Louis in the opening scene of the screenplay as a widely celebrated performer. A gradually revealed back story explains that she was an orphan who grew up under the wing of the Madam, who is also Johnny's mother, before going away to achieve fame and fortune.
2. Huston adds several detailed accounts of Johnny's failings as a gambler, in which he consistently loses his initial stake and then wheedles his fellow players for money. Subsequently, however, Johnny enjoys an improbable run of gambling luck that seems almost mystically tied to Frankie's increased suffering.
3. Huston develops a significant new character, Stack O'Lee, as an expert gambler and a rival for Frankie's affections.[42]

Although the screenplay's revisions add some measure of complexity to the character of Frankie, they serve to enhance Huston's vilification of Johnny and the extent of Frankie's degradation as a willing martyr for a man who is recognized by everyone else as a world-class chump. The characters, meanwhile, remain white, even though Huston hoped to recruit the African American jazz legend Louis Armstrong to provide the film's soundtrack.

When Huston reworked his *Frankie and Johnny* manuscript as a screenplay, he seems to have reconsidered, to a degree, his earlier characterization of Frankie as a dim-witted sap. For example, in the screenplay Huston takes much greater pains to emphasize Frankie's initial glamour as a famed stage performer upon her arrival in St. Louis. As Huston's introductory text to the screenplay explains: "This society, like any other, produced its own aristocracy. Occasionally, a sporting woman made the transition from hustler to courtesan and her fame became nation-wide. She acquired fortunes in jewels and took her own place at the gaming tables. Men vied for her favours, which were no longer available to anyone upon payment. She was a queen sport and her name became a legend."[43] In this spirit, the 1963 text adds a lengthy scene in which Frankie sits down at a poker table with a number of hard-boiled macks and card sharks, including Stack O'Lee. Not only does Frankie maintain her composure flawlessly when Stack O'Lee defends himself by shooting an embittered fellow gambler, she also ultimately walks away with the entirety of the pot after wagering her most prized diamond necklace.[44] But even thus revised, and in the face of egregious insults to her dignity that somehow manage to outdo those in the play, Frankie maintains a slavish devotion to Johnny that still proves to be her fatal weakness. Granted, Huston's film script at least attempts to base Frankie's affection for Johnny in her nostalgic recollections of a crush rooted in the pair's shared childhood. Yet this conceit remains unconvincing, since Frankie's persona swerves inexplicably from an accomplished, confident woman of the world to a state of self-effacing submissiveness as she repeatedly supplies Johnny with gambling stakes. If anything, her greater initial heights in the screenplay drafts make her voluntary, self-sacrificing fall even more pronounced than in the author's play.

The introduction of a story thread involving the character Stack O'Lee represents an equally intriguing revision. Here, Huston merges characters from two distinct bodies of folklore, both of which have their origins in real-life incidents from the red-light districts of 1890s St. Louis, as Huston notes. Also, several variants of "Frankie and Johnny" share floating verses in common with "Stagolee," such as

Bring on your rubber-tired carriages,
Bring on your rubber-tired hack;
Took poor [Albert/Billy] to the graveyard
But they did not bring him back.[45]

In African American folklore, Stagolee or Stackolee was a quintessential badman character: a man feared by fellow African Americans and white policemen alike; an adept gambler; an expert at gunplay; and at least occasionally a pimp.[46] In keeping with this characterization, Huston presents his Stack O'Lee as a legendarily skilled gambler, a deadly gunman, and someone with whom one ought not trifle. In the aforementioned poker scene, for instance, a grizzled character named Zeke Kravert (erroneously) accuses Stack O'Lee of cheating, tries to claim a pot from the center of the table, and lunges at Stack O'Lee with a knife—only to swiftly meet his maker at the hand of Stack's derringer.[47] Even though Huston's interpretation of Stack O'Lee's traits is more faithful to his African American sources than his depictions of Frankie and Johnny, he nonetheless again refashions the character as white. In Huston's rendering, Stack O'Lee even owns a sizable Louisiana plantation.

Notwithstanding the racial transformation, Huston's purposes in introducing this new character to his 1960s screenplay are clear: practically, to add further dramatic tension through a romantic triangle involving Stack O'Lee, Frankie, and Johnny; and symbolically, to provide a foil for Johnny's decidedly flawed model of masculinity. To everyone but Frankie, Stack O'Lee obviously is the more appropriate romantic match for her; this seems most apparent in the scene when Frankie wins a large sum of money from Stack O'Lee in the poker game—something that no male character had been able to do at that point. Equally important, Huston presents both Frankie and Stack O'Lee as honorable characters, despite their red-light-district environs. By contrast, Johnny arranges for Frankie to provide sexual services to Stack O'Lee as a means of securing the gambling stake that ultimately triggers his run of good fortune; Stack O'Lee, taken aback when he discovers the true circumstances of his rendezvous with Frankie, refuses to consummate the arrangement, despite Frankie's insistence.

Even in the face of such open disregard for her feelings, Huston's Frankie maintains a tragic weakness for Johnny. She remains mentally shackled and subservient to him, and her health and wealth erode in inverse proportion to his sudden good fortune at the gambling tables: "Frankie has become merely a colorless shadow in his wake, tolerated but never welcome. The sparkle is gone from her eye, the warmth from her voice. No longer does the crowd fall silent when she sings and there is no shower of money around her feet.[48] Interestingly, Huston extends the parallel between Frankie and Stack O'Lee even further when the latter endures the loss of his leg in a poker game with Johnny shortly before the screenplay's climax and closure.[49] Collectively, the revisions incorporated into the 1960s screenplay drafts serve to accentuate threads present in Huston's play: namely, the tragic dimension of Frankie's sense of unyielding attachment to Johnny, and Johnny's status as the antithesis of Huston's masculine ideal. In the parlance of gaming tables, Huston doubled down on these core elements of his narrative, even with three decades of hindsight available to him.

AS NOTED NEAR THE OUTSET of this chapter, Huston's *Frankie and Johnny* did not enjoy much in the way of commercial success. Partly for this reason, details regarding the play's initial performances, by Ruth Squires's marionette troupe, seem virtually impossible to come by. In his autobiography, Huston offers only the following self-flattering account: "*Frankie and Johnnie* [sic] turned out to be quite a success. Sam Jaffe improvised background music for the opening performance, and the damned thing went over like a house afire."[50] Never far from vice in his young adulthood, Huston had known Jaffe since 1925, when they "lived in the same apartment building, which had a honky-tonk dance hall on the first floor, where bootleg liquor was sold under the counter and hid in Huston's hall storeroom."[51] In what might have been a near miss at a chance for greater success, Huston explained, "George Gershwin had the idea of making *Frankie and Johnnie* [sic] into an opera, and we talked about it, but before we could get around to it, George died."[52] Huston's biographer Lawrence Grobel reports an informal affair, circa 1929, in which "George Gershwin gave an exclusive party, where [Huston's *Frankie and Johnny*] was performed with Gershwin himself at the piano playing the incidental music. 'It was remarkable,' Huston remembered. 'George's music was simply great.'"[53] But Gershwin was at the time quite busy with projects such as *Showgirl* (1929) and *Girl Crazy* (1930), and when he did turn to work on an African American folk opera, it was his tremendously successful adaptation of DuBose Heyward's *Porgy and Bess* (1935).[54]

Another opportunity presented itself when the impresario Billy Rose took an interest in incorporating Huston's *Frankie and Johnny* into his sprawling Americana revue *Crazy Quilt* (1931). Rose went so far as to extend a $300 advance to Huston and promised to deliver the comic star Fanny Brice for the role of Frankie. Unfortunately, a chilly meeting between Huston and Jed Harris, one of the show's producers, led to the shelving of this plan.[55]

Despite its failure to get off the ground initially, the play's publication as a book kept it in circulation and resulted in occasional, short-lived productions over the ensuing two decades. Perhaps most notably, the showman William de Lys wrote to Huston early in 1952 to secure the author's permission to bring *Frankie and Johnny* to the stage as the debut production for his newly christened Theater de Lys, a 300-seat off-Broadway venue on Christopher Street. De Lys described an ambitious vision for staging Huston's play as "a dramatic pantomime with music and lyrics" by Irwin "Buddy" Bazelon; other promotional materials for the Theatre de Lys promised a varied repertoire that the promoter hoped would include ten plays, five ballets, seven concerts, and twenty children's productions, as well as midnight jazz concerts every Saturday. Sadly, it was not to be. De Lys's production of Huston's *Frankie and Johnny* opened and closed the same night, as the reviewer Whitney Bolden lamented: "Candied up with some fake ballet costumes, it is as stylized as a gargoyle and no one in it ever talks plain or walks simply. If a man stands at the bagnio bar, he strikes an attitude. If a dame walks across the stage, it is an angular attitude." Soon after this debacle, the wealthy philanthropist Louis Schweitzer purchased the theater from de Lys for his wife, Lucille Lortel, to manage.[56]

The following year, Ronald Bennett enjoyed greater success in developing a "dance-drama" script of Huston's *Frankie and Johnny* for the Hollywood Actors, a troupe of multiethnic youth for which Bennett served as director. Although an amateur production, Bennett's adaptation enjoyed an eight-week run at the Cabaret Theater and garnered laudatory reviews from the *Los Angeles Times*, *Los Angeles Examiner*, and *Dance News*; echoing the unusual admixture of Huston's original script, the *Dance News* review dubbed the Hollywood Actors' rendition "rough and arty." Bennett's production was, then, by far the most extensive run that Huston's play enjoyed on the stage.[57]

Given the late twentieth- and twenty-first-century association of marionette productions almost exclusively with children's entertainment—whether in the form of church and community center puppet shows or Jim Henson's Muppets—Huston's original decision to turn to a story featuring gambling, alcohol, prostitution, and murder when crafting a work for this medium might seem ill considered. By the 1920s, puppet theater had become a broadly popular form of entertainment, especially for children. Writing in 1949, Paul McPharlin noted the long-term impact of traveling marionette troupes: "That generation which was in school in the 1920s grew up knowing about puppets. It is doubtful if many adults in their thirties and forties can admit not having seen them."[58] Ruth Squires, for whom Huston wrote his play, had performed *Snow White and Seven Dwarfs* in 1929, and went on to work in marionette performances of *The Elves and the Shoemaker* and *Hansel and Gretel* the following year.[59]

The world of US puppet theater during the 1920s and 1930s was not only popular, but also far more varied in form and content than what most Americans would associate with the medium later in the century. Moreover, this diversity extended to communities across the country through a widespread network of "little theaters": as early as the 1910s, Ellen Van Volkenberg helped stage marionette performances at Chicago's Little Theatre that included Shakespeare's *A Midsummer Night's Dream*, *Alice in Wonderland*, and a work based on Japanese legends entitled *The Deluded Dragon*. During the 1920s, the Cleveland Play House produced *Shadowy Waters* by William Butler Yeats and *The Death of Chopin* (a pantomime set to music by the composer). In Evanston, Illinois, and Detroit, Paul McPharlin led works such as a nativity play entitled *Noël*, a Chinese shadow theater play titled *The Drum Dance*, a farcical burlesque of eighteenth-century drama titled *Tragedy of Tragedies*, and a "jazz pantomime" adaptation of George Herriman's comic strip *Krazy Kat*. In San Francisco, Ralph Chessé crafted renditions of Shakespeare's *Macbeth* and Eugene O'Neill's *Emperor Jones*, the latter famously a vehicle for the African American actors Charles Gilpin and Paul Robeson earlier in the decade. And in New York, the Neighborhood Playhouse hosted a variety program titled *The Grand Street Follies* from 1922 through 1927, and Remo Bufano (a mentor to Huston's friend, Ruth Squires) participated in marionette performances of a Spanish opera, *El Retablo de Maese Pedro*, and an avant-garde adaptation of *Pinocchio* with puppets designed to mimic the look of machines. Still other venues in the 1920s staged productions of *Rip Van Winkle* and *Uncle Tom's Cabin*.[60]

As even this small sampling suggests, the repertoire of marionette theater at the time Huston wrote his play showcased an extraordinary range of literary, historical, and imaginative subjects that was every bit the equal of its counterpart in the theater of live actors. The genre's practitioners drew their material from wide-ranging racial and ethnic traditions, in addition to spanning the spectrum of high, popular, and folk culture sources. McPharlin, for example, believed that puppetry held the potential to encompass "highbrow and experimental, classic and modern, even poetic and tragic."[61] In this light, Huston's looking to a folk song as source material fit well within the diverse currents prevalent in puppet theater of the times. If anything, what marks *Frankie and Johnny* as most distinctive with respect to this medium is the play's vice district setting. Still, Huston's use of caricature and his vaudevillian intermingling of comic, dramatic, and musical elements had ample precedent in the arena of marionette theater.

GIVEN HUSTON'S PENCHANT for caricature in his adaptation of *Frankie and Johnny*, he found an apt illustrator for his book publication in Miguel Covarrubias. Caricature was Covarrubias's calling card as an artist, and by 1930 the young Mexican artist was firmly ensconced among both New York City's downtown circle of Greenwich Village sophisticates and the uptown cadre of "New Negro" aesthetes and performers. Such boundary crossing was hardly unusual for those working in the creative arts during the 1920s and 1930s. Though not precisely congruent in their priorities or ideologies, these two modernist circles in which Covarrubias moved overlapped considerably and influenced each other. Put simply, the stories of the Harlem Renaissance and US modernism were inextricably intertwined.[62] Huston's fascination with African American music and his turn to "Frankie and Johnny" as theatrical subject matter were representative of such interchanges. While his social circle in New York was never as diverse as that of Covarrubias, their shared acquaintances included such notable modernists as H. L. Mencken, Eugene O'Neill, and the young Orson Welles. Huston and Covarrubias became reasonably close friends, as was clear almost two decades later when Covarrubias (along with Diego Rivera) interceded with the Mexican government on Huston's behalf to allow him to continue filming *The Treasure of the Sierra Madre* (1948) on location.[63]

Covarrubias established himself as a preeminent caricaturist in the New York cultural scene through two notable collections published by Alfred A. Knopf, *The Prince of Wales and Other Famous Americans* (1925) and *Negro Drawings* (1927), as well as his regular work for *Vanity Fair*. One of the key figures in facilitating Covarrubias's connections with both Knopf and Frank Crowninshield, the editor of *Vanity Fair*, was Carl Van Vechten, a white novelist who played a central role as a facilitator of patronage and publication opportunities for many young writers of the New Negro Renaissance.[64] Aided in part by Van Vechten's introductions, Covarrubias produced illustrations for such notable Renaissance publications as Alain Locke's anthology *The New Negro* (1925), Langston Hughes's volume of poetry *The Weary Blues* (1926), W. C. Handy's *Blues: An Anthology* (1926), and the singer Taylor Gordon's autobiography, *Born to Be* (1929). Before those projects, Covarrubias fashioned a series of eight illustrations for a feature in the December 1924 issue of *Vanity Fair* entitled "Enter, the New Negro, a Distinctive Type Recently Created by the Coloured Cabaret Belt in New York."[65] Like Hughes and many other creative artists of the 1920s, Covarrubias frequented the nightclubs of Harlem as a source of both entertainment and inspiration. In fact, Huston recollected that Covarrubias was one of those who helped introduce him to this scene: "I saw [Miguel] frequently. He initiated me into a kind of life in New York I had not known before. A life full of fascinating people and forays into little prohibition clubs. We often went to Harlem together. I don't know which of us was more taken with the dancing and music."[66] Suffice it to say, by the time he prepared the illustrations for Huston's *Frankie and Johnny*, Covarrubias possessed a wealth of firsthand observations of Harlem and was an active participant in the expressive culture of the New Negro Renaissance.

SCENE: "THE LAST JUMP", CABARET ON A
SATURDAY NIGHT
Here is Nick Fie Rastus with his "teasin' brown",
getting in a word or two (I'll say he is) between dances
and sips of that red ale which is the rage of Negro
cabarets.   Note the lady's neutral attitude, expressed
by the chaste and exquisite clasping of her hands

FIGURE 4.4. Miguel Covarrubias, *Scene: 'The Last Jump,' Cabaret on a Saturday Night*, from "Enter the New Negro," *Vanity Fair*, December 1924.

Like the work of Winold Reiss, his Austrian-born contemporary, Covarrubias's New Negro Renaissance illustrations of African Americans did not escape controversy, either then or now. Like Reiss, Covarrubias straddled the fine line between celebrating a distinctive black expressive culture and falling into the conventions of racist caricature. Consider the Mexican artist's *Scene: 'The Last Jump,' Cabaret on a Saturday Night* as an example (figure 4.4). In the context of its original appearance as part of his 1924 "Enter, the New Negro" feature for *Vanity Fair*, this illustration appeared with the following caption: "Here is Nick Fie Rastus with his 'teasin' brown,' getting in a word or two (I'll say he is) between dances and sips of that red ale which is the rage of Negro cabarets. Note the lady's neutral attitude, expressed by the chaste and exquisite clasping of her hands."[67] On the one hand, this illustration owes a debt to the long history of demeaning caricatures of African Americans in US visual culture, especially in the exaggerated rendering of the man's teeth and lips, as well as the reference to him by the moniker "Rastus."[68] Six of the seven other captions in the feature employ dialect to represent black speech. Such aspects of Covarrubias's artwork led the racial-uplift-minded W. E. B. Du Bois to offer, "I am frank to say, however, that I think I could exist quite happily if Covarrubias had never been born."[69]

On the other hand, while flawed, the artist's "Enter, the New Negro" feature was intended to declare a break with past stereotypes of African Americans, as indicated by its subtitle: "Exit, the Coloured Crooner of Lullabys, the Cotton-Picker, the Mammy-Singer and the Darky Banjo-Player, for so Long Over-Exploited Figures of the American Stage." Toward this end, the artist's "Last Jump" duo is attired in a debonair style, and the female figure exudes self-composure, as seen in "the chaste and exquisite clasping of her hands." Even more, the image evokes the aura of cultural sophistication associated with cabarets during the 1920s, a cultural scene that Covarrubias enjoyed. Stylistically, too, with its flattening of the figures and the upturned angle of the cabaret table, this illustration represents a kind of populist modernism as much as it does the conventional tropes of racial caricature. Arguably, too, the highly stylized geometric features of the female cabaret goer call to mind images by Modigliani and Matisse more than the iconography of early twentieth-century blackface minstrel posters and the like.

Of course, following the lead of Huston's script, Covarrubias was not expected to draw the title characters of *Frankie and Johnny* as African American for the play's publication. Like Huston, Covarrubias was aware of the ballad's origins, but rendered its characters in ways that bore relatively little resemblance to anything from his sizable oeuvre of African American images. In general, Covarrubias's African American women of the 1920s tended to be slender, stylish sophisticates of the Roaring Twenties flapper variety (see, for example, *Flapper*, figure 4.5) or, less often, a thickly framed woman in the mold of blues singers like Ma Rainey and Bessie Smith (as in *Entertainer*, figure 4.6). In contrast to both of these archetypes of the artist's African American imagery, Covarrubias's Frankie harkens to a turn-of-the-century era of bosomy corsets, broadly drawn curves, and heavily applied cosmetics (figure 4.7). As the actress and playwright Mae West was doing contemporaneously in her play *Diamond Lil* (1928), Covarrubias here joins Huston in looking backward nostalgically to the 1890s as a period of pre-Prohibition license and rollicking high spirits. Within this reimagined setting, the level of caricature in the artist's drawings abets Huston's overall mocking indifference toward the characters and the more outlandish turns in his play, such as the extent of Frankie's mawkishness toward Johnny and the epilogue's denouement, when she promises the onlookers, "I'll be dancin' for ye in a minute" (that is, jerking on the end of the hangman's rope) and encourages them to dance with her.[70] Even in the soberest moment of Huston's drama, in which Frankie fatally wounds Johnny, Covarrubias shows the protagonist comically feigning to turn her head away from the pistol shot, but doing so with one eye open to a cartoonish width that spans more than a third of her face (figure 4.8).

Throughout his illustrations for this volume, Covarrubias demonstrates a gift for suggestive details that enhance Huston's narrative and characterizations. For instance, Covarrubias's Johnny exhibits some of the fashion finery attributed to him in the ballad tradition and in Huston's play, such as the "hundred dollar suit" purchased for him by Frankie. The book's frontispiece depicts Johnny in an embroidered vest and jewel-encrusted hat, with diamonds adorning his suspenders, armband, and horseshoe-shaped tiepin. Even outfitted in such extravagant fashion, he beckons for still more money from Frankie, which—in a subtle distinction from Huston's play—she presents, with buoyant enthusiasm and flirtatiousness, from the inside of her garter. Yet Covarrubias also seems to have grasped the unflattering essence of Huston's Johnny, giving him beady eyes, buck teeth, and a generally simpleminded demeanor (figures 4.7–4.8). It also may be telling that the artist depicts most of the other male figures in the book with stylish mustaches, while rendering Johnny as clean shaven and, hence, less definitively masculine.

The tragedy in the illustrations of *Frankie and Johnny*, as in the play's text, seems to reside solely in Frankie's broken heart and sad fate at the gallows. In the play's epilogue, as in the prologue, the Sheriff seems reluctant to conduct the hanging; and the gathered onlookers offer what seem like a series of tributes from a wake for the soon-to-be-departed Frankie, rather than an angry mob's calls for her demise. The Bartender, for example, proclaims, "We'll draw a large un for ye, an' fix ye a snack, an set it down to your place as if ye was by us. We'll toast to ye, Frankie, like we allus done."[71] Even the play's Madam, Johnny's mother, states: "I can't forgive ye, Frankie,—I dasn't, for blood's thicker'n water. But I wish ye a soft berth wherever you're goin'. An' the bed in 202'll be kept fresh an' empty, so Johnny an' you won't be castin' around for a place to lay easy when ye make your honeymoon."[72] In a similar vein, Covarrubias's final illustration for the play emphasizes the heads bowed in grief around the scaffolding and Frankie's repose, her virtue emphasized by the heart-shaped rendering of her corseted torso (figure 4.2).

Covarrubias's illustrations reinforce the tenor of Huston's *Frankie and Johnny* in one other significant respect. Perhaps shaped in part by the conventions of puppet theater at the time, Huston charted a course between the enticement of red-light district settings, on the one hand, and "family-friendly" forms of entertainment, on the other. While the play's nods to prostitution, drinking, gambling, infidelity, murder, and public execution might

FIGURE 4.5. Miguel Covarrubias, *Flapper*, from *Negro Drawings* (1927).

FIGURE 4.6. Miguel Covarrubias, *Entertainer*, from *Negro Drawings* (1927).

FIGURE 4.7. Miguel Covarrubias, frontispiece illustration for Huston's *Frankie and Johnny* (1930).

FIGURE 4.8. Miguel Covarrubias, Frankie shoots Johnny, illustration for Huston's *Frankie and Johnny* (1930).

not have been deemed suitable for child viewers, the play attempts to buffer any accompanying shocks by presenting them with touches of humor—a wink, a joke, or even a musical number.

This point is thrown into stark relief through a comparison with another work from 1929, the artist John Held's aforementioned *The Saga of Frankie and Johnny*, a book of woodcuts accompanied by a version of the ballad's lyrics. Like Covarrubias, Held depicts the characters as white and operates in the mode of caricature. Where Held's volume most distinguishes itself is in the surprisingly risqué nature of both his selected lyrics and his illustrations. For example, his rendition includes the lines: "Frankie worked down in a crib house, / Worked there without any drawers."[73] Even if readers did not recognize "crib house" as turn-of-the-century slang for "brothel," an accompanying illustration of an apparently naked Frankie with exposed breast peeking out invitingly from behind a door would have left little doubt about Held's meaning (figure 4.9). Similarly, when Held's Frankie storms the "parlor-house" in search of Johnny and Nelly Bly, she swears: "Get out of my way, all you pimps and chippies. / Or I'll blow you all to Hell," a line borrowed from some of the more flamboyant iterations of the ballad.[74] A page later, she looks in a high window to discover the pair together in bed, and sees Johnny smiling as he smokes a cigar and Nelly Bly nude except for stockings covering her legs from thigh to calf (figure 4.10).

To be sure, details such as Huston's allusions to Frankie's work as a prostitute and Covarrubias's illustrations of women in tight-fitting corsets might have offered audiences of the day some level of titillation. Further, Huston's text for the play sets the action within the world of late nineteenth-century red-light districts. Nonetheless, the Huston and Covarrubias publication is bawdy to a much more limited degree than Held's project. For example, Covarrubias's illustration of the moment in which Frankie catches Johnny cheating on her features Nelly Bly sitting on the scoundrel's lap; Nelly looks startled and afraid, but she is *not* virtually naked or presented with an overt suggestion of postcoital bliss, as in the manner of Held's corresponding illustration (figure 4.11). Huston and Covarrubias's decisions to temper their work on this front is understandable given the censorious context of the times, in which John Kirkland's play *Frankie and Johnnie* was closed by police in Chicago during the summer of 1929 and in New York City in the fall of 1930; in the latter instance, the playwright, stage managers, and ten cast members were arrested on charges of giving an indecent performance.[75] This point of distinction between Held's work and Huston's also reflects the hybrid nature of the latter's project in a broader sense. By whitening the play's characters, fashioning a fictive world marked by nostalgia and comic melodrama rather than genuine danger, and steering clear of explicit depictions of prostitution, Huston fash-

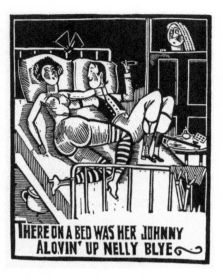

FIGURE 4.9. John Held Jr., *Frankie Worked Down in a Crib-house*, illustration for *The Saga of Frankie and Johnny* (1930).

FIGURE 4.10. John Held Jr., *There on a Bed Was Her Johnny Alovin' Up Nelly Blye*, illustration for *The Saga of Frankie and Johnny* (1930).

FIGURE 4.11. Miguel Covarrubias, Frankie discovers Johnny and Nelly Bly, illustration for Huston's *Frankie and Johnny* (1930).

ioned a truly odd play: a comic spin on a dramatic ballad, and a safe, vicarious excursion for viewers into the world of underclass vice. That the play was not wholly satisfying aesthetically because of the resulting inconsistent tone goes a long way toward explaining the play's failure to reach a major stage or movie screen in the author's lifetime.

THE FINEST WOMAN EVER TO WALK THE STREETS: MAE WEST'S OUTLAW EXPLOITS IN *SHE DONE HIM WRONG*

AS MAE WEST'S BODY lay in state at Forest Lawn's Old North Church on November 25, 1980, the organist played "Frankie and Johnny" and a handful of other tunes associated with her show business heyday of the 1920s and 1930s.[1] Although such a musical selection departed sharply from typical funeral-service fare, this song's presence could hardly have been surprising to the group of family and friends in attendance that afternoon. West began performing it as part of a touring variety show with Harry Richman in 1922, opting for a style that owed more to blues than balladry and often pairing it with a shimmy dance.[2] From its appearance in her popular stage play *Diamond Lil* (1928) onward, "Frankie and Johnny" became a signature number for West. In addition to its prominent role in her most commercially successful play and her most important film, *She Done Him Wrong* (1933), "Frankie and Johnny" became a staple as West deliberately intertwined her popular Diamond Lil/ Lady Lou character with her own public persona throughout the remainder of her life. West not only featured the song prominently in stage revivals of *Diamond Lil* during the late 1940s, but also continued to perform the song late in life, as when she accepted an award from a USC film fraternity in 1968 and in a 1976 appearance on Dick Cavett's television special *Backlot USA*.[3]

Mae West established her public image during the 1920s and 1930s by defying convention in ways echoed by the inclusion of "Frankie and Johnny" in her funeral service: identifying with boldly assertive female figures of history and song; reveling in the secular while interrogating the sacred; and embracing vernacular and popular expressive forms rather than elite notions of culture. In so doing, she cast off Victorian notions of chastity and moral restraint in favor of a modernist sensibility centered on the pursuit of pleasure and experience, fashioning an audacious persona as the nation's preeminent icon of female sexuality. Despite West's symbolic whiteness, appropriations of African American performance proved key catalysts in her storied career.

West's engagement with "Frankie and Johnny" provides an extremely useful lens through which to understand her relationship to African American culture writ large. This is especially apparent in the first Hollywood film to feature West at center stage and as chief author, *She Done Him Wrong* (1933), wherein West delivers an energetic rendition of "Frankie and Johnny" in the lead role of Lady Lou and embodies the spirit of the ballad in a broader sense through the outlaw ethics enacted by her character. West certainly saw her work in these terms, writing retrospectively of her 1930s Hollywood career in her autobiography: "It was the Hollywood pattern to fear change, novelty and new material. I scared them, but they needed me to help a sagging box-office. However, I was an outlaw. I didn't conform or say 'Yes sir'."[4]

Arguably, Mae West remains best known today for her curvaceous figure and the seemingly endless recirculation of her quotable one-liners, such as "Come up sometime, and see me" and "Between two evils, I always pick the one I never tried before." As caricatures of bygone celebrity figures go, West could do worse. After all, she did carefully fashion much of her public persona around a larger-than-life sexual allure and continually repeated her most popular lines, many of which retain a sense of daring even today because of their flaunting of conventional mores regarding behavior deemed appropriate for women. Yet as the ongoing cottage industry of West publications attests, there remains much more to say.

Beyond hips and quips, one of the trademarks of West's work as a thespian was that she seldom accepted material as given to her. In an early role in the comedy revue *A La Broadway* (1911), for instance, the eighteen-year-old West cleverly refashioned a throwaway role as an Irish maid, Maggie O'Hara, into a show-stealing number featuring risqué lyrics and an assortment of dialect impressions.[5] In the mid-1920s, she began writing her own plays—including *Sex* (1926), *Diamond Lil* (1928), and *The Constant Sinner* (1931)—principally as a means of crafting her roles more precisely to her own liking.[6] Similarly, in her first Hollywood role, as Maudie Triplett in *Night After Night* (1932), West made memorable an otherwise pedestrian film by reworking the supporting character as originally scripted by Louis Bromfield and Kathryn Scola to reflect the charmingly free-spirited personality she had developed for the stage in 1920s New York, including the addition of her oft-quoted line "Goodness had nothing to do with it."

On the heels of West's successful supporting role in *Night After Night*, she proposed to the struggling Paramount Studios a film that would be based on her hit Broadway play *Diamond Lil* and deeply interwoven with elements inspired by the ballad "Frankie and Johnny." The play was a quintessential example of an established entertainment tradition that Marybeth Hamilton terms "urban sensationalism: popular theater that catered to prurience by lifting the veil on metropolitan vice."[7] Specifically, *Diamond Lil* featured "white slavery" (prostitution), drinking (when alcohol was outlawed by Prohibition), violence, and salacious song-and-dance numbers. Catching word of the film project, officials with the Motion Picture Producers and Distributors of America (MPPDA) repeatedly warned Paramount that West's new film could *not* be an adaptation of *Diamond Lil*.[8] Despite Paramount's repeated assurances to the MPPDA, however, this was precisely what West set out to do, capitulating only moderately to censors and the Motion Picture Production Code.

Like the play, the film is set in New York's Bowery district during the 1890s. West stars as Lady Lou, who leads a lavish lifestyle, partly as the result of the largesse of male suitors. As in the play, too, West balances her protagonist's potentially scandalous behavior with acts of virtue. On the one hand, Lou kills a criminal known as Russian Rita, albeit accidentally and in self-defense when Rita attacks her in a jealous rage; on the other hand, Lou secretly buys a building for a Salvation Army mission in the Bowery, despite not being a religious woman herself. In the main, the changes that West deployed in the film consisted of altering character names and substituting highly charged innuendo for the play's more direct displays of sexual attraction. For instance, West initially pitched her film to Paramount under the moniker *Ruby Red*, in a halfhearted effort to distance the film from *Diamond Lil*. Late in the process, though, West opted for the more assertive *She Done Him Wrong*. This revised title more explicitly connected the film's protagonist with "Frankie and Johnny," a popular song from the earlier play, but made the connection with a key difference: inverting the ballad's standard refrain "He was her man, but he done her wrong." This was a point that West insisted on with Paramount executives in order to stress female agency, both her own and, by extension, that of Frankie in the song.[9] Much to the consternation of censors, the film's congruity with West's popular play and its featured ballad were not lost on audiences; a California Theatre ad for *She Done Him Wrong* even played up the connections explicitly by promising, "You'll roar through your blushes at 'Diamond Lil's' own brawling, scarlet story of a 'Frankie & Johnnie' girl."[10]

One of West's most intrepid retentions from *Diamond Lil* was that *She Done Him Wrong*'s Lady Lou actively engages the romantic attentions of no less than five male characters over the course of the film:

- Gus Jordan (Noah Beery): West's paramour of record at the outset of the film, Jordan is a ward politician, owner of a saloon and concert hall, and—

unbeknownst to Lou—head of illegal counterfeiting and white slavery enterprises. Russian Rita helps oversee the last of his operations.

- Dan Flynn (David Landau): Flynn is working to gather evidence of Jordan's criminal activities for the police so that he can assume Jordan's position as Bowery boss. He confesses that the primary motive for these elaborate machinations is to displace Jordan as the recipient of Lou's affections.
- Chick Clark (Owen Moore): A career criminal and Lou's former lover, Chick is currently serving a prison term for an attempted robbery that he undertook to supply Lou with more diamonds to add to her already voluminous collection. Flynn played an unspecified role in Clark's apprehension by the police.
- Serge Stanieff (Gilbert Roland): Serge is Russian Rita's assistant and lover. A professional ladies' man, Serge aggressively pursues Lou's attentions from the moment they first meet.
- Captain Cummings (Cary Grant): At the outset of the film, Cummings appears as the officer in charge of a Salvation Army mission adjacent to Jordan's business. Only late in the film does the viewer discover that Cummings is actually a police detective known as the "Hawk," who is working undercover to gather evidence against Jordan's criminal enterprises.

In sum, this cohort includes a convicted jewel thief, a Bowery crime lord involved in counterfeiting and prostitution, a shady aspiring Bowery boss, an international gigolo, and a Salvation Army officer who turns out to be an undercover police detective.

For nearly ten minutes at the outset of the film, before West's first appearance on-screen, Jordan, Flynn, Stanieff, and a handful of other characters remark at length on Lou's singular magnetism. After alighting from her horse-drawn carriage, Lou bemusedly introduces herself to an impoverished mother and daughter as "the finest woman ever to walk the streets." Although Lou is well appointed with material finery by Gus Jordan, she is not cast as a conventional prostitute or kept woman. Rather, she openly flirts with other men in front of Jordan, trades verbal barbs with men, and helps earn her way by headlining the concert hall's musical entertainment.

It is on the stage of Jordan's establishment that Lou performs "Frankie and Johnny" as well as "A Guy What Takes His Time," a thinly veiled paean to female sexual pleasure, and "I Wonder Where My Easy Rider's Gone," another song drawn from African American sources. Although *She Done Him Wrong* is thoroughly laced with both explicit and implied references to "Frankie and Johnny," the film significantly departs from the historical ballad in that it is voiced by a white woman. To be sure, "Frankie and Johnny" had become a part of both "white" and "black" American musical cultures by the early 1930s, with considerable blurring and intermixing between the two. Nonetheless, it matters that this version is performed by a white woman—and not just any white woman, but Mae West, who, with this movie, became a potent national icon of white female sexuality. Just as Lou leans heavily on black musical material and style, to great acclaim, within the frame of the movie, the fact that West drew two of her three musical numbers from African American sources was far from incidental to the movie's success or to her own ascendance as a national celebrity.

From its onset, West's long show business career was inextricably tied to engagements with and appropriations of African American culture. Her childhood fascination with the African American blackface comedian Bert Williams is often remarked on in West biographies, and West's mother arranged for Mae to perform imitations of Williams at church socials as part of her early training. Likewise, her first chronicled performance, in an amateur talent show—a piece for which she won first place and which thus launched her show business career—was a rendition of a "coon song" titled "Movin' Day," and she continued to incorporate songs like Williams's "Nobody" and ragtime numbers in her acts well into her teenage years.[11] A few years later, the young adult West made her early Broadway reputation with a version of the scandalous "shimmy dance" that she had first witnessed during one of her regular trips to South Side black nightclubs while based in Chicago for eighteen months in 1916–1917.[12] She took formal dance lessons from African American instructors in Chicago and New York, and performed onstage alongside black musicians and dancers in the early 1920s, at a time when many white performers and entertainment critics still considered such "race mixing" déclassé.[13] In the first play she wrote, *Sex* (1926), West performed several musical numbers directly borrowed from African American vernacular culture, including "Shake That Thing," a risqué hit for Ethel Waters in 1925, a year before West's play.[14] Zora Neale Hurston recalled: "I noted that Mae West in *Sex* had much more flavor of the turpentine quarters than she did of the white bawd. I know that the piece she played on the piano is a very old jook composition. 'Honey let yo' drawers hang low' had been played and sung in every jook in the South for at least thirty-five years."[15] If US modernism of the 1920s was a self-consciously "mongrel" movement of cross-racial appropriations, as Ann Douglas argues, then Mae West was one of its most notable practitioners, drawing on African American culture as a particularly rich font of source material from an early age.[16] Still, essential as ragtime and the shimmy were to West's early professional successes, there is no richer terrain for sorting out her relationship to African American vernacular culture than the ballad "Frankie and Johnny."

Why was this song so appealing to West? Or to be more precise, why and how did "Frankie and Johnny" mesh so well with the iconoclastic public persona that Mae West carefully crafted for herself over the course of the 1920s and 1930s? When production began on *She Done Him Wrong*, West was already notorious for her flouting of gender and sexuality norms, both from her work on the stage during the 1920s and from her brief but memorable spot in the 1932 film *Night After Night*. In her play *Sex*, for example, West cast herself as Margy Lamont, a prostitute who defies the authority of her pimp, Rocky, and insists that her apartment is her domain, reminding him, "I'm paying the freight on this joint, and what I say goes"; who refuses to pay off a police officer in search of a bribe, asserting, "I don't see why I should pay for the privilege of working"; who seduces the son of a New England industrial magnate and even takes the initiative to climb atop him, in an overt act of seduction, before the stage lights dim; and finally, who leaves the promise of a respectable marriage and high society for life on the open seas with a retiring British naval lieutenant.[17] From this vantage, one can grasp why Frankie's act of agency in killing her man in response to his infidelity resonated with West's transgressive sensibilities. Equally significant, the song unmistakably establishes Lou's symbolic bond with African American culture, appropriating the form and aura of vernacular blackness, as so many of West's modernist contemporaries—both white creative artists and their middle-class New Negro Renaissance counterparts—were keen to do. In this particular borrowing, however, West's revisions to the Frankie and Johnny of ballad lore are even more telling than the stock verses that she belts out on stage. West's genius was to cast herself as a rebel in the Frankie mold, but with an important twist: namely, Lou would display power over men—and multiple men at that—rather than shedding tears or bullets over an unfaithful lover. In doing so, West portrayed modernist values, for women, as a compelling alternative to the stuffy dictates of Victorian moral sensibilities.

Lou consistently controls the terms of her relationships with men, encouraging or deferring each of her suitors' ardent passions to her advantage. Indeed, the ease and outright cynicism with which Lou pulls their strings is as arresting as her resolve to flirt openly, bawdily, and unapologetically with many men. For instance, while Dan Flynn aspires to usurp Gus Jordan's political clout, he does not yet possess the mantle of Bowery boss; consequently, Lou offers Flynn just enough encouragement to string him along in case his

FIGURE 5.1. Lady Lou handles Dan Flynn (*She Done Him Wrong*, 1933).

help is needed later. She allows him to pull her into his lap briefly, offering, "You know, I never did appreciate you before. But I do now," and places her arm enticingly around Flynn's neck—but without fully committing herself to Flynn, sexually or otherwise (figure 5.1).

Along similar lines, viewers soon learn that Lou had engaged in an affair with the jewel thief Chick Clark until he was sent to prison for a diamond heist—the spoils of which Lou still wears. Chick thus seems to be the most direct reference point of the film's title, *She Done Him Wrong*. In the play *Diamond Lil* and in early drafts of the film's screenplay, this point was reinforced by commentary from an anonymous barfly in Jordan's saloon, who began to talk about Lil/Lou's jilting of Chick after his arrest until Jordan's henchman, Spider Kane (Dewey Robinson), knocks him unconscious.[18] Even with this detail omitted from the final film, West issued a key reversal of the "Frankie and Johnny" ballad by placing her female protagonist in the role of the lover doing the jilting of male counterpart. When Kane suggests that it might be a good idea for Lou to visit Chick in prison, if only to placate her ex-lover's vengeful temper, her response suggests she has not thought about Chick since his arrest, over a year earlier. Moreover, Lou not only blatantly lies to Chick during the ensuing prison visit by claiming (falsely) that she has been and will remain faithful to him, but also openly announces her intent to do so ahead of time:

> SPIDER: Remember Lou, Chick's probably pretty sore.
> LOU: I'll make him think he's on a vacation.
> SPIDER: Yeah, he'll listen to you.
> LOU: Who won't? Once I get 'em, they're branded.

West's choice of imagery here is telling. To declare that men who fall under spell are "branded" and bound to act according to her whims suggests that she regards suitors as possessions; in effect, she reverses the dynamic more common to early twentieth-century male-female relationships, especially that of pimp and prostitute, as in Gus Jordan's white slavery enterprise. Implicitly, West also posits an analogous seductive power for herself over film audiences, thereby at least partially resisting the passive objectification imposed on many female film stars.

The scene depicting Lou's visit to Chick in Sing Sing prison opens with her strolling past a row of prison cells, enjoying a series of rapid-fire exchanges with male inmates, all of whom seem to know her by reputation, even if not by experience.

> PRISONER: Say, Lou, you gotta help me get out of this.
> LOU: Who, me?
> PRISONER: You gotta. I've been framed. You've got a lot of pull. You can get me out. It's a frame I tell ya! It's a frame!
> LOU: You're the right picture for it. (To Spider) One of the fastest guys in the business, but he's takin' his time now.

This sequence serves to enhance Lou's status as a legendary figure and augments the viewer's impression of her as someone with a razor-sharp wit who is fully at ease with rough male characters of a sort that presumably would instill fear in the average citizen.

When Lou arrives at Chick's cell, the ensuing action is a study in contrasts. While Lou is a model of calm detachment, Chick appears to be falling to pieces: his hands tremble, his voice quavers, and he seems unable to bear the idea of her leaving him. Despite Lou's attempt to appease Chick with the assurances of fidelity—"If I can wait a year, you can wait a year"—when the scene ends, he grips the bars of his cell in frustration and declares with an increasingly fevered pitch, "I can't wait! I can't wait! I can't wait!" As West recognized, this heightened emotionalism was more typical of a female film role; even the decision to name this character "Chick"—popularized via African American vernacular usage in the 1920s as a somewhat dismissive slang term for a woman—seems suggestive in this respect. Whereas ballad singers often depicted Frankie as driven to excessive emotion and violent retribution in the ballad, West casts Chick in that role, complete with his threat of violence against Lou if she does not remain loyal to him. In this manner, West challenges the prevailing supposition that hysteria is a quintessentially feminine condition.

After Chick Clark makes good on his promise to escape from prison (reportedly, killing a guard in the process), he sneaks into Lou's room and demands that she run off with him. When Lou bluntly dismisses him, "I tell you,

FIGURE 5.2. Chick Clark pleads with Lou (*She Done Him Wrong*).

Chick, you're through. Get out!" Chick is outraged: "You got a nerve to stand there and tell me to get out. Me jumpin' freights, crawlin' through the mud to get to you." Lou's terse, clipped language could be that of an iconic 1930s Hollywood gangster like Edward G. Robinson's Rico dismissing a displaced rival crime boss in *Little Caesar* (1931), while Chick's expectations that a heroic male quest for a love interest will be rewarded with admiration parallel the conventions of Victorian-era melodramatic romance. Chick again proves unable to control his passions and begins choking Lou with his bare hands. Yet he is soon overcome with emotion and drops to his knees, pleading for Lou's affections in tearful tones: "Don't you know what I feel for ya? Ain't you got a heart left in you for me?" (figure 5.2).[19] However much the film may ascribe certain conventionally "feminine" traits to Chick Clark, his instability and capacity for violence mean that he remains a threat. Lou therefore promises to rendezvous with Chick after her evening's turn on stage, but this obviously is not a promise she intends to keep.

As part of her power reversals, West scripts all of Lou's lovers—former, current, and aspiring—as being driven by passion far more than reason, at least with regard to their designs on Lou. For example, it is Flynn, not Lou, who exclaims, "When I said I was crazy about you, I didn't say how crazy," and he vows, "To get you, I'd even frame my own mother." Lou, on the other hand, remains calm, cool, and calculating throughout the film—always ready with a witty rejoinder and quick thinking enough to negotiate herself out of the tight predicaments that ensue from the inevitable collision of her numerous rival suitors. Serge, an assistant to Russian Rita, also is typical in this regard. From the moment he lays eyes on a nude portrait of Lou that hangs in Gus Jordan's saloon, Serge is desperate to find moments alone with Lou and consummate a sexual conquest. Toward this end, he gives her a diamond brooch that had been given to him by Rita, which Lou happily accepts.[20] But when Serge attempts to woo Lou with the sweeping declaration "I shall die to make you happy," she cavalierly replies, "Oh, but you wouldn't be much use to me dead." Again, the focus is brazenly on the instrumental benefit that a suitor might play for the female protagonist, rather than on platitudes or abstract ideals.

Not least among these benefits are Lou's troves of jewelry and other gifts connotative of luxury, such as a swan-shaped bed that Gus Jordan imported from France for her room above the concert hall. Lou's embrace of materialistic glamour also is part and parcel of the revisions that West works on the "Frankie and Johnny" ballad. As outlined in the introductory chapter, the ballads frequently cast Frankie in a subservient role, with stock verses in which she earns money (often implicitly or explicitly through prostitution) in order to outfit her man with a $100 suit of clothes. Lou's reversal of this equation could hardly be more pointed. It is Lou's stylish appearance that is much admired in the film, not that of any of her male suitors. Further, in the scenarios that West scripts, men such as Chick Clark, Serge, and Gus Jordan engage in criminal enterprises (theft, white slavery, and counterfeiting among them) in order to provide Lou with diamonds, expensive form-fitting gowns, and lavish furnishings. Equally significant, her appetite for these luxuries is unapologetically voracious rather than reserved and unassuming. Gus Jordan estimates the value of her diamonds at "pretty near half a million," and Lou counters Serge's "And now surely you have enough diamonds" with the pithy "Diamonds is my career." In short, Lou has effectively reversed the expected flow of wealth between the archetypal prostitute-and-pimp arrangement of Frankie and Johnny, and has enjoyed immense profitability and notoriety in the process. In her first stage appearance in the film, she carries a diamond-encrusted cane, an item that Frankie buys for Johnny in some versions of the ballad (figure 5.3).[21] A stage backdrop that features an advertisement for a diamond company, accompanied by the text "Our Lou wears them," suggests that she is collecting still more income off her dazzling persona by means of commercial endorsements (figure 5.4).

None of this is to deny that Lou displays considerable passion beyond a desire for material finery. Yet West fashions her protagonist's passion so that it seems more a matter of libidinal appetite than a conventional, idealistic contemplation of love, and at no point does it override her own best interests. To be sure, West had to make some concessions on this front for the film, relative to the more openly bawdy flavor of her stage play *Diamond Lil*. For instance, the play and early drafts of the film screenplay were much more explicit in their discussion of white slavery and sex; in the play, Lil directly asked Captain Cummings, "You ain't no virgin, are you?"[22] Reflecting how mindful West

FIGURE 5.3. Modernist music: Lady Lou performs "I Wonder Where My Easy Rider's Gone" (*She Done Him Wrong*).

FIGURE 5.4. Victorian music: An Irish tenor performs "More To Be Pitied than Censured," with Lou's diamond company endorsement in the background (*She Done Him Wrong*).

was of the tightrope she was walking with the medium of cinema, her initial draft of the screenplay, prepared with assistance from John Bright for Paramount Studios, followed an embrace between Lou and Serge with the note "WE FADE OUT an inch before the censor's scissors."[23] Nonetheless, what West did manage to work into her film is remarkable by the standards of the day. Most famously, Lou says to Captain Cummings, "You know, I always did like a man in a uniform. That one fits you grand. Why don't you come up sometime, and see me?" When Cummings politely declines, she looks him up and down salaciously before insisting, "Oh, you can be had." It bears emphasizing here that only later do viewers learn that Cummings is an undercover police detective and not a man of the cloth (figure 5.5). These antics would have come as no surprise to those familiar with West's theatrical work, for as soon as she began crafting scripts for herself, they centered on her roles as female protagonists whose charms proved irresistible to all men who came within their orbit. For instance, Margy Lamont of West's play *Sex* entertains the attentions of four male characters, maintaining control throughout over which ones she will see or turn away.

The sexual exploits of West's protagonist are less explicit on the screen than they had been on the stage with *Sex* or *Diamond Lil*, but it remains notable that Lou defies so many expectations of female "decency" *and* escapes punishment for doing so. In fact, like much of West's oeuvre, *She Done Him Wrong* staged a skillfully crafted contrast between Victorian and modernist cultural values. Whereas Victorian culture stressed the importance of reserved comportment, chasteness, and self-sacrifice for "proper" women, modernists like West championed quick-wittedness and the importance of adventurous plunges into visceral experiences of all sorts. Although her body seemed to hark back to an earlier, pre-flapper female standard, and though she frequently played roles set in the 1890s, West's connections with modernism were readily apparent. A scene with Captain Cummings in Lou's private rooms showcases the contrasts between Victorianism (Cummings) and modernism (Lou) quite pointedly. Offering Cummings a seat beside her, Lou encourages him, "Loosen up, unbend, you'll feel better." Here, West unmistakably is speaking as a modernist to old-fashioned moralizers generally. In one of the most famous exchanges scripted by West, Cummings plays the good monogamist by asking, "Haven't you ever met a man that could make you happy?" Lou replies, "Sure, lots of times." Even at the level of body language, Cummings maintains an upright, even stiff posture befitting of his sanctimonious tone, whereas Lou's movements in the scene are sensuously rolling, and she seems imminently aware of the seductive effects of her own body.

In all this, needless to say, the game was rigged. Like modernist writers such as H. L. Mencken and Sinclair Lewis, West was plainly setting up Victorian values as an outdated straw man, subject to her withering assault of wit, charm, and seduction throughout the film. Yet whereas Ann Douglas rightly notes that many modernists (including Mencken and Lewis) bitterly feminized the Victorian culture from which they wished to distance themselves, West successfully managed to cast modernism itself in feminine terms.[24] Not least, West stacks the deck against older mores by making modernist values appear more fun: by providing a pleasing visual spectacle for the film's audience

FIGURE 5.5. Lou entices Captain Cummings (*She Done Him Wrong*).

as well as its male characters; by gazing with admiration at her own material finery and beauty; and by engaging in smart-as-a-whip banter with male characters such as Captain Cummings and Serge. Most importantly, the relativism and flexibility of modernist values repeatedly allow Lou to emerge unscathed from tight spots that would trap a more rigidly moralistic character.

In dramatizing the contrasts between Victorian and modernist sensibilities, West's decision to create a period film plays a significant role. Her insistence on preserving the 1890s setting of *Diamond Lil* in *She Done Him Wrong* accomplished at least three ends for West. First, by design, locating Lou's scandalous actions in the historical past may have helped West somewhat temper the concerns of MPPDA officials. Specifically, tapping into a then-current entertainment vogue for tales of the Bowery in days gone by placed the film's treatment of drinking, prostitution, and other forms of vice at a safe historical remove.[25] Second, the full-figured womanhood prized in the earlier era was a much better match for West than the flapper style predominant in the metropolitan culture of the Roaring Twenties. As West explained to an interviewer in 1929: "That explains why I set *Diamond Lil* back in the old Bowery days to make it more distinctive. Get me? . . . Nowadays all the girls look alike—same build, slim and sexy, short skirts, same kind of stockings, same kind of paint, same kind of hairdress, and same kind of thoughts, if they'd only admit it."[26] On a related note, Emily Leider articulates a frequent line of argument regarding West's popularity during the Great Depression: "Even her voluptuous body worked to provide reassurance that abundance was around the corner and the sunken cheeks of hard times and breadlines would pass."[27] Third, returning to the 1890s heyday of Victorian cultural mores in the United States made the modernist sensibilities of Lou vividly stand out from her surroundings.

Beyond the unconventional nature of Lou's ethics with respect to sex and decency, West cleverly keys her juxtaposition between Victorian and modernist aesthetics to the soundtrack of *She Done Him Wrong*. West sets the tone musically in this regard early in the film when the pianist Ragtime Kelly plays "a brand new tune, just out," entitled "After the Ball," for Gus Jordan. The most popular sheet-music seller of the 1890s, this 1891 song by the composer Charles K. Harris was an apt choice for reinforcing the period setting and overall nostalgic aura of the film. Interestingly, Jordan responds, "Gee, Kelly, that'll be a great song for Lou." As West's subsequent musical numbers make clear, however, Jordan could hardly be further off base here.[28] With its measured pace, solemn delivery, and melodramatic narrative of a man who wrongly cast off his fiancée because of a case of mistaken identity, "After the Ball"—and the genre of sentimental parlor ballads as a whole—is precisely the type of music that West places in *contrast* with Lou's performances in *She Done Him Wrong*.

The musical number that best illustrates the contrast between Lou's modernity and Victorian sentimentality is a popular period tune entitled "She Is More to Be Pitied than Censured" (1894). This William Gray composition is performed on the stage of Jordan's establishment by a formally attired Irish tenor (Fred Santley), who sports a handlebar mustache as an exaggerated period touch (figure 5.4). The portion of the song audible in the film includes the following verses:

> *She is more to be pitied than censured,*
> *She is more to be helped than despised.*
> *She's only a lassie who ventured*
> *On life's stormy path, ill-advised.*
>
> *Do not scorn her with words fierce and bitter.*
> *Do not laugh (ha-ha) at her shame and downfall.*
> *For a moment just stop and consider,*
> *That a man was the cause of it all.*

West's savvy selection of this song aids her ambitions for the film, on two fronts. For one, the reminder that "fallen women" do not become stigmatized without a man's equal participation is certainly a notion with which West and her protagonist would sympathize. West's sympathy for this revisionist corrective notwithstanding, however, the song still constructs the fallen woman as an object of pity in need of aid from concerned listeners. While this might be well and good for other women, West would never accept such a state of despondency for one of her own characters. As West would later put it in her famous list titled "Things I'll Never Do": "I pity weak women, good or bad, but I can't like them. A woman should be strong either in her goodness or badness."[29] In this vein, through a combination of quick thinking and seductiveness, Lou negotiates her own way out of every predicament that confronts her in *She Done Him Wrong*, rather than passively awaiting rescue.

For emphasis, West implements a supporting character named Sally Glynn to serve as a counterpoint to her own Lady Lou. Early in the film, a distraught Sally enters Gus Jordan's establishment and attempts to poison herself, but she is thwarted at the last moment by a saloon employee, and promptly faints. Jordan's henchman, Spider Kane, then carries the unconscious young woman to Lou's room for rest and recovery.[30] Lou quickly deduces Sally's trouble and offers some pointed advice to the younger woman:

SALLY: How did you know there was a man?

LOU: There always is. You know, it takes two to get one in trouble.

SALLY: Oh, you know everything about me.

LOU: I wouldn't say that, but I am observant. . . . What was he—married?

SALLY: Yes, but I didn't know. I didn't know.

LOU: It makes no difference to me whether you did or not. Men's all alike, married or single. It's their game. I happen to be smart enough to play it their way. You'll come to it.

. . . .

LOU: Forget about this guy. See that you get a good one the next time.

SALLY: Who'd want me after what I've done?

LOU: Listen, when women go wrong, men go right after them.

One can easily imagine that West is speaking here through Lou not only to the character of Sally, but also to her female audience in general (figure 5.6). Clearly, West saw the last statement—"When women go wrong, men go right after them"—as a central part of her own strategy for building the appeal of her characters on stage and screen. Further, Lou's advice to Sally expresses a modernist disdain for prevailing notions that required women to maintain sexual purity and monogamy. The very nonchalance with which Lou dispenses this streetwise wisdom seems to make light of the overwrought, melodramatic treatment of crises of compromised female morality in Victorian plays and fiction.[31]

In the play *Diamond Lil*, Lil's response to Sally's "Oh, you know everything about me" also included the line, "The story is so old it should have been put to music long ago."[32] Arguably, it already had been: Sally's story is essentially identical to the narrative of "She Is More to Be Pitied than Censured," which is performed shortly after her initial appearance in the film. Like the unnamed woman in the song, Sally has been "done wrong" by a man and left

FIGURE 5.6. Lou comforts Sally Glynn (*She Done Him Wrong*).

in desperate circumstances and a fragile state of mental stability. Sally, too, is a "fallen woman" who seems debilitated by self-pity and by a fear of censure from her family and society. Despite Lou's attempt to help Sally, Gus Jordan and Russian Rita subsequently coerce the young woman into prostitution on the Barbary Coast, compounding Sally's victimization until she reappears near the end of the film as Captain Cummings's star witness against Jordan's white slavery enterprise.

Unlike the ballad protagonist Frankie, demure and Victorian-minded Sally does not manifest a desire for vengeance against the man who betrayed her; instead, in keeping with Victorian conventions, Sally turns her destructive impulses inward upon herself. Counteracting this impulse seems the crux of Lou's message to Sally: namely, don't decimate your sense of self-worth because of something as slight as a sexual indiscretion. It is no coincidence, I argue, that Lou's counsel on this point resonates with the spirit of a song such as Ma Rainey's "Trust No Man":

> *Trust no man, no further than your eyes can see*
> *He'll tell you that he loves you and swear it is true*
> *The very next minute he'll turn his back on you.*

As Sandra Lieb interprets this song: "Ma Rainey seems to tell women: don't blame yourself when your man leaves you; that's his nature. Thus, she encourages women to stop castigating themselves, accept the realities of relations between the sexes, and shift the blame and anger from themselves to the men who abandon them."[33] That said, it is revealing of Lou's character that she, unlike the female protagonist of "Frankie and Johnny," is unconcerned with exacting vengeance on the man who has done Sally wrong. While elsewhere in the film viewers see that Lou is more than capable of catalyzing violence between men and enacting violence herself when it proves necessary to her survival, in the case of Sally Glynn it seems that to express a thirst for vengeance would be to grant an inflated importance to the duplicitous man who left Sally in disgrace. To Lou, it seems, such a trifling man is not worth the bother. In Lou's advice to Sally, viewers therefore see another example of her conviction regarding the need for female self-reliance and agency as a corrective to the ideologies of chastity and self-blame that had structured the lives of Victorian-era American women.

Such contrasts also are readily apparent in West's choices of songs for her own character in the film, all of which mark striking departures from the likes of "After the Ball" and "She Is More to Be Pitied than Censured." Consider, for example, her first musical number in the film: "I Wonder Where

My Easy Rider's Gone" (1913), a hybrid ragtime-blues tune credited to the black songwriter Shelton Brooks and associated during the 1910s with the white vaudeville singer Sophie Tucker, who was billed as the "Last of the Red Hot Mamas."[34] That the date of this composition falls well after the supposed 1890s setting of the film is not anachronistic sloppiness on West's part as a writer; the numerous period signposts in the film's opening montage sequence belies such a conclusion. Rather, West deliberately chooses a more recent song as a means of indicating the freshness and modernity of her protagonist relative to everyone else in the film. Indeed, the pace and rhythm of Lou's song virtually jump off the screen with visual and aural energy when contrasted with the Irish tenor's staid delivery of "She Is More to Be Pitied than Censured."[35] Whereas he sings with a labored tempo and breaks his rigid posture only for stiff gestures with his arms, Lou bounces suggestively and energetically to the up-tempo pacing of "I Wonder Where My Easy Rider's Gone." She appears completely comfortable with her erotically charged body and openly flirtatious with her audience (figures 5.3–5.4).

The lyrics of these two musical numbers contrast in important ways as well. In *She Done Him Wrong*, West's version of the lyrics includes the following lines:

> *Ever since Miss Susie Johnson lost her Jockey Lee,*
> *There's been much excitement and more to be.*
>
> *You can hear her moanin' from early morn,*
> *I wonder where my easy rider's gone. [× 3] . . .*
>
> *I wonder where my easy rider's gone.*
> *He went and put my brand new watch in pawn.*
>
> *I see him comin' round that turn.*
> *What a trail that man can burn!*
> *He's goin' to win because my dough is on the nose.*
>
> *Just watch my Jockey easy ride in style,*
> *He'll hit that home stretch, winner by a mile.*
>
> *I want him to win this spree*
> *And keep a-goin' til he comes to me.*
> *Oh, I wonder where my easy rider's gone. [× 2]*

One quality of these lyrics that sets them apart from Victorian ballads of the 1890s is the embrace of a vernacular idiom, including slang phrases such as "my dough is on the nose" and West's proclivity for dropping the final *g* from words such as "moaning" and "going." In this respect, West loosely resembled fellow modernists such as H. L. Mencken, Ring Lardner, and Zora Neale Hurston, all of whom spent considerable energy in championing the virtues of American speech as a distinct variant of English.[36] Beyond simply capturing the distinctive flavor of working-class Bowery accents, West's deployment of vernacular was a way of signaling the modern and populist sensibilities of her creative work.

Even more jarring are the numerous and barely concealed erotic allusions that populate Lou's song. Notably, William Gray's "She Is More to Be Pitied than Censured" ventures only that the woman at its center is "a lassie who ventured / on life's stormy path, ill-advised," even if the cause of her shame and downfall are apparent enough by implication. Writing almost two decades later, Shelton Brooks also avoided direct references to sex, but incorporated double entendres that rather blatantly allude to female sexual longing; undoubtedly, this combination of coyness and candor was part of the song's appeal for West. The general public's lack of familiarity with the terminology of the song likely aided her as well. For instance, had members of the MPPDA been aware that "easy rider" here refers to a pimp and not just to a jockey, it seems unfathomable that the song would have been allowed to remain in the film. In any event, the reference to a pimp who has strayed from a woman connects this song to variants of "Frankie and Johnny" that imply a similar relationship between its title characters. Lou thus indicates her awareness of *some* women's dependence on such men, even to the extent of allowing an easy rider to pawn one's goods—a gesture that at least loosely parallels Frankie's use of her earnings to buy expensive clothing for Johnny in ballad lore. Significantly, though, Lou makes this acknowledgment at the remove of a third-person narrative, since the opening verse states that the relationship of dependence on a man here belongs to "Miss Susie Johnson," not to Lou herself.

West was well aware that her articulation of modernist aesthetics and her challenges to dominant gender codes hinged on her implementation of African American vernacular music as source material. Scholars have rightly pointed to the influence of the white nightclub impresario Texas Guinan on Mae West's showmanship and affinity for witty one-liners, but West's musical endeavors owed at least as much to her black contemporaries, songwriters and blueswomen in particular. As Jill Watts notes of West's early Hollywood years: "West now encouraged the public to associate her with black performance. She repeatedly acknowledged her debt to African-American culture, recounting her appropriation of the shimmy, ragtime, and blues from the black community. . . . As with the screen character, these details served to reentrench West's 'badness,' linking her with hypersexuality and the forbidden crossing of racial lines."[37] In *She Done Him Wrong*, West's use of songs of a recognizably African American musical style and origin matters because such adaptations, as much as anything else in the film, mark the modernity of Lou and, by only a slight extension, Mae West herself. In the context of the 1930s, of course, cross-racial cultural borrowings of the sort that West engaged in tended to flow with much greater profitability from black to white than the inverse. Replete with cross-racial appropriations, *She Done Him Wrong* catapulted Mae West to the status of international celebrity. By contrast, when the African American blues artist Ida Cox began billing herself as the "Sepia Mae West" in 1934 in an attempt to enhance her own marketability, she met with only modest success.[38]

West's decision to turn to a song by Shelton Brooks, who also supplied material to Bessie Smith, was far from anomalous; she knew African American composers such as Andy Razaf, James P. Johnson, and Perry Bradford. Razaf's biographer, Barry Singer, notes that West was "a frequenter of the black Gaiety Building publishing offices throughout the Twenties in search of fresh bawdy song material for her repertoire."[39] So too, West frequented the black nightclubs of Chicago and New York regularly throughout the late 1910s and 1920s, such as The Nest in Harlem's 133rd Street "Jungle Alley."[40] The initial theatrical run of *Diamond Lil* was backed by Owney Madden, West's onetime lover as well as a bootlegger and owner of the Cotton Club in Harlem—another of West's nightspots of choice.[41] Consequently, she was well acquainted with the music and dance performances of her black and white peers, and was very much in step with the newfound fascination of many white modernists with black music during the Harlem Renaissance. West displayed her familiarity with African American cabaret culture in her novel *The Constant Sinner* (1930), originally titled *Babe Gordon*, and its adaptation for the stage (1931); in both incarnations, the protagonist, Babe Gordon, frequents Harlem nightclubs and sporting events, and takes a black lover, Money Johnson, who has ties to vice.

In light of her immersion in the world of black entertainment, it should hardly be surprising that blueswomen were essential influences on the persona that West first put before the public in the stage play *Diamond Lil* (1928) and polished to tremendous effect in *She Done Him Wrong* and *I'm No Angel* (1933). During preproduction on *She Done Him Wrong*, West discovered that one of the major challenges was how to suggest, by metaphor, inference, and body language, that which she had been able to state or show more directly on the stage. Her screenplay drafts contain numerous references to nonverbal performance details, such as meaningful glances, a "slow, outrageous wink," and Lou's "swaggering" gait.[42] In refining the crasser elements and accustomed performance gambits traceable to her background in vaudeville and burlesque, what better place to look for guidance than the blueswomen of the day such as Ma Rainey and Bessie Smith? Recordings by these artists were conspicuously more frank in their treatment of sex than the music recorded by their white contemporaries, and often used only the thinnest veneer of coded language to veil sexually charged innuendo. Consider, to cite but one example, an excerpt from Smith's "Empty Bed Blues" (1928):

> *Bought me a coffee grinder, got the best one I could find [× 2]*
> *Oh he could grind my coffee 'cause he had a brand new grind*
>
> *He's a deep-sea diver with a stroke that can't go wrong [× 2]*
> *He can touch the bottom and his wind holds out so long*
>
> *He knows how to thrill me, and he thrills me night and day [× 2]*
> *He's got a new way of loving almost takes my breath away*

As scholars such as Angela Davis have demonstrated, blueswomen like Smith articulated a moral sensibility quite distinct from that promulgated by the commercial music targeted at white audiences—one that often (though not entirely consistently) encouraged women to claim sexual desire matter-of-factly, even enthusiastically, and rejected "mainstream values, especially those prescribing passivity in relations with men."[43]

While the level of explicitness that Smith and her contemporaries in the race-record industry offered listeners was not something that West could fully match within the censorship-imposed constraints of a Hollywood film, the provocative flavor of her lyrics suggest a connection. Penned by the white composers Ralph Rainger and Leo Robin, West's performance of "A Guy What Takes His Time," midway through *She Done Him Wrong*, bears an unmistakable imprint of blues influence:

> *A guy what takes his time, I'll go for anytime.*
> *I'm a fast movin' gal that likes 'em slow.*
> *Got no use for fancy drivin', wanna see a guy arrivin' in low.*
>
> *There isn't any fun in getting somethin' done*
> *If you rush when you have to make the grade.*
> *I can spot an amateur, appreciate a connoisseur at his trade*
> *Who would qualify, no alibis, to be the guy what takes his time.*[44]

Although tamer than Smith's "Empty Bed Blues," these lyrics are nonetheless rife with double entendre. Particularly when paired with West's provocative stage movements and facial expressions, the song conveys a forthright articulation of female eros comparable to that of peers like Smith and Rainey.

West likely drew inspiration from these same musical artists in crafting her stage persona as well. As West saw firsthand, the most successful blues singers of the 1920s worked diligently to create an impression of themselves as larger-than-life figures on stage. Bessie Smith, for instance, earned the moniker "Empress of the Blues" and drove home this stature with elaborate headdresses and other glittery, sequined attire, following the example earlier established by star performers like Ma Rainey.[45] In poet Robert Hayden's memorable image of Smith, "She came out on the stage in ostrich feathers, beaded satin, / and shone that smile on us and sang."[46] Hence, the famous jewel-encrusted form-fitting gowns that designer Edith Head crafted for Mae West in *She Done Him Wrong* may owe as much to the glamour displayed by contemporaneous blueswomen as to the dance hall singers of the 1890s, whom Lou ostensibly represents.[47] Likewise, the ability of Rainey and Smith to capture an audience's rapt attention—a quality that the poets Hayden and Sterling Brown and the singer Memphis Minnie so eloquently expressed—certainly was a quality that West desired for both herself and her screen characters.[48] Among the admiring remarks that one hears about Lou before she finally appears are revelations that she is the object of several men's unconcealed fantasies, that the real-life vaudeville impresario Tony Pastor "says she has it all over Della Fox" (a famous singer and comedienne of the 1890s), and that businesses are begging to use her image on promotional calendars, all of which attests that she is a kind of living legend. On stage, Lou is greeted with resounding applause from working-class Bowery denizens and "society folks" alike and captivates the entire audience throughout each of her three songs in the film.[49]

Like West's Lady Lou, blueswomen such as Ma Rainey and Bessie Smith fashioned self-images that extended beyond their performances. As Angela Davis puts it, "Blues women were expected to deviate from the norms defining orthodox female behavior, which is why they were revered by both men and women in black working-class communities."[50] Ida Cox recorded the iconic "Wild Women Don't Have the Blues," but it was Bessie Smith who most famously embodied this irreverent sensibility. Smith was notoriously uproarious, capable of drinking exploits, and not above the occasional brawl.[51] In addition, both Rainey and Smith were unapologetic and relatively open in their embrace of sex with multiple partners, and their sense of sexual liberty extended to bisexuality. Rainey's "Prove It on Me Blues" (1928) included the explicit refrain, "Went out last night with a crowd of my friends / They must have been women, 'cause I don't like no men."[52] West adamantly insisted that she remained exclusively heterosexual throughout her life, but she nonetheless wrote plays that featured homosexuality and cross-dressing in *The Drag* (1927) and *The Pleasure Man* (1928). West also frequented gay-friendly clubs both downtown in Greenwich Village and uptown in Harlem, where she was "among the few whites (Carl Van Vechten was another) allowed into the clubs along 140th Street that presented transvestite floor shows." As several of West's biographers have remarked, the drag performances of figures such as Bert Savoy and Julian Eltinge provided another vital thread of influence on her one-liners and "campy hyper-femme mannerisms." In addition, West's sexual liaisons frequently crossed class and racial lines, including affairs with African American boxers such as William Jones and Chalky Wright.[53] In general, West resembled Rainey and Smith in forthrightly claiming wide-ranging sexual desires, both onstage and off.

Significantly, too, the offstage exploits of Rainey and Smith hardly remained unknown to their fans; if anything, these qualities seem to have further endeared them to their admirers. Paramount Records marketed Rainey to black audiences not only as the "Mother of the Blues" but also as the "Paramount Wildcat."[54] With considerable success, West strove for a comparable blurring between her stage and screen exploits and the persona "Mae West," albeit not without some ambivalence. At least in part to allay censors' concerns, by late 1933 Paramount Studios had begun to issue a barrage of promotional material emphasizing that, in her private life, West never touched a drop of alcohol or smoked and that she led a quiet, reclusive life.[55] Yet with regard to sex, Paramount could not resist playfully suggesting of her considerable skills as a writer that West did "her best work in bed."[56] For her part, West generally remained discrete about her offscreen affairs of the 1920s and 1930s, even as she seemed to delight in hinting to reporters about her prowess on this front. For example, when asked by the Hollywood journalist Hedda Hopper how she knew so much about men, West famously replied, "Baby, I went to night school."[57]

West remained very much aware that no small part of her professional success in the world of 1930s movies was owed to her knack for "playing at sex," or "kid[ding] sex," rather than openly enacting scandalous behavior. As she explained to Hilary Lynn in 1936, "The reason people go for my pictures in a big way is that I don't make 'em afraid of sex. . . . I take sex with a laugh. I don't let it get me." Pointedly, too, West responded to Dana Rush's inquiry about how she managed to evade censorship of her characters' seemingly immoral actions: "I always use gags and wisecracks to get away from the sentimental. . . . I get a laugh and then where's all the tragedy?" For these reasons, she referred to her Diamond Lil/Lady Lou character as "a cheerful sinner."[58] West employed such playfulness with a purpose, however; she consistently used her deft comedic touch to mount substantial challenges to Victorian strictures regarding women and sexuality. She remarked to Lynn, "It's surprising how, in so many pictures you see nowadays, sex is something which causes suffering." West sought to unshackle sex for women from such rigid, puritanical constraints, and comic play proved an effective means to this end.[59]

Timing and context were fortuitous for the professional ambitions of both West and her blueswomen contemporaries. As the phonograph industry caught fire in the 1920s and companies pursued the race record market, female vocalists like Rainey and Smith were able to capture a sizable portion of that business; such economic clout contributed to their self-assurance, both on- and offstage. Rainey and Smith also exerted significant authority over the touring shows that they headlined on the Theater Owners Booking Association (TOBA) circuit during the 1920s, extending to details of costuming, choreography, and song selection.[60] Coincidentally, female performers enjoyed a comparable eminence in Hollywood at the time of West's celebrated arrival in Los Angeles. Actresses dominated the star system of early-1930s Hollywood. To review motion picture fan magazines from the first half of the 1930s is to encounter a world in which West and her female peers stood center stage, while male leads such as Clark Gable and James Cagney were, at best, secondary attractions. For example, a 1934 feature in *Silver Screen* entitled "The Four Big Shots of Hollywood" profiled Marie Dressler, Katharine Hepburn, Janet Gaynor, and Mae West; that nary a man appears among this group was no aberration.[61] Douglas Fairbanks Jr., a marquee star, famously—and temporarily—vowed to "quit Hollywood" in 1934 in a fit of pique due to the perceived dominance of female stars over their male counterparts. He explained, "My part in *Morning Glory* wasn't even a fair leading man's. Like all others in the cast, I was only a stooge for Katharine Hepburn."[62] Parallel to Rainey and Smith's trailblazing in the arena of music, West leveraged her stature to challenge expectations of female chasteness and decorum more decisively than did any of her female cinematic contemporaries. The repeated suggestion in mass media of the day that West defied these expectations both on-screen and off made the potential significance of such rebellions that much more powerful to audiences.

Despite West's affinity for contemporaneous African American female performers, the ways in which *She Done Him Wrong* counterposes Lou and her maid, Pearl, seem considerably less self-aware than the contrasts between Lou and the distraught "fallen woman" Sally Glynn. In most respects, West's scripting of Pearl leaves the actress Louise Beavers little opportunity to escape

FIGURE 5.7. Lou chastises Pearl
(*She Done Him Wrong*).

the orbit of the film industry's prevalent stereotypes of black women as un-educated, asexual, and possessing no apparent purpose other than to nurture white characters. In fact, Pearl's first moments on screen are accented by her singsong declaration "I just loves to work for you, Miss Lou." Even more, Pearl's exaggerated dialect is directly mocked by Lou. For instance, after Lou impatiently calls Pearl to her boudoir, the characters share this exchange:

> PEARL: I is coming. I is coming.
> LOU: Yeah, you is coming, your head is bending low. Now, get here before winter.
> PEARL: Well, here I is.
> LOU: Here you is. Listen, Eight Ball, what are you doing: working for me or sleeping for me?

Virtually the only depth granted to Pearl is shown in her final rejoinder in this exchange, "I ain't sleeping so much that I don't see what's going on around here."[63]

In an all-too-common trope, costuming contrasts between this pair high-light Lou's glamour against Pearl's ostensible lack thereof. As Watts observes, "While Pearl appears in the traditional black dress and apron, Lou's white-ness is often highlighted by her contrasting light gowns and sparkling dia-monds" (figure 5.7).[64] In part, these contrasts stem from the fact that West countenanced no on-screen rival to her own feminine allure. But West's biog-raphers paint a picture in which the star's offscreen relationships with her African American maids sometimes mirrored this cinematic scene. West's real-life maid, Lily Taylor, attended to her on-screen, too, in West's films *I'm No Angel* (1933) and *Belle of the Nineties* (1934), and West appears to have been none too pleased when Taylor left West's employ in order to pursue her own full-time film career.[65] For a performer who so readily acknowledged her debts to African American culture, these inconsistencies regarding her on- and off-screen relationships with black women remain profoundly disappointing.

MAE WEST'S PERFORMANCE OF "Frankie and Johnny" and the accompanying action late in the film bring many of the aforementioned themes and narrative threads to a dramatic crescendo. By the time Lou performs this song, she has played on the affections of Gus Jordan, Dan Flynn, Serge, Chick Clark, and Captain Cummings, from motives as diverse as financial enhancement, pragmatic self-protection, and erotic desire. When Spider tells Lou that Chick Clark has escaped from prison and is "out back in the alley," she seems startled, as if she had again forgotten all about Chick after the recent prison visit. She thinks for a minute and instructs Spider, "Take him up the back way to my room. I don't want the cops to get him. I'll figure somethin' out later," before heading to the stage for her third and final musical number of the film, "Frankie and Johnny." If Lou truly has no method in mind for dealing with Chick when she takes the stage, then she shows considerable resourcefulness in formulating a plan on the fly while in the spotlight.

As West delivers it, "Frankie and Johnny" seems about anything but pathos of the sort one finds in the renditions by a singer such as Huddie Ledbetter. Appearing in a body-hugging white gown and visually ablaze with sparkling diamonds and sequins, West bounces her hips and rolls her shoulders subtly but evocatively to the up-tempo rendition of the tune, casting a, by now, familiar spell over her audience.[66] Notably, too, West's Lady Lou sings of Frankie's murder of her unfaithful man without the least hint of remorse in her delivery. If anything, she delivers the song with a touch of mischief and enticement written in her smile, raised eyebrows, and subtle nods. Of course, the crowd goes for it like gangbusters.

At this point in the film, Lou has pressing concerns other than entertaining her audience. After Lou sees Chick Clark sneak into her room by way of the concert hall balcony, she uses a subtle nod of her head and flick of her eyes from the stage to indicate to Dan Flynn, who is in the audience, that he should head there. Flynn, no doubt, thinks this portends the sexual rendezvous with Lou for which he has been openly yearning throughout the film. Lil's seemingly flirtatious gaze certainly leads him to think as much. But when Flynn opens the door to Lou's room, he is felled by three rapid gunshots from Chick Clark, who likely had been anticipating Lou's entry, but had a score to settle with Flynn in any event. In one fell swoop, then, and with little more than quick thinking and a flutter of her eyelids, Lou manages to dispose of an undesired (and not particularly handsome) suitor, in Flynn, and to ensure that her vengeful ex-lover Chick will soon be returned to police custody.

The lyrics that Lou delivers before being interrupted by Chick's gunshots are conventional ones:

Frankie and Johnny were sweethearts,
Oh, how they could love!
Swore they'd be true to each other,
As true as the stars up above.
He was her man, and he was doing her wrong.

Frankie went 'round the corner
To get a bucket of beer.
Said to the man called the bartender,
"Have you seen my Johnny here?
He's my man, and he's doing me wrong."

"Ain't gonna tell you no stories,
Ain't gonna tell you no lies,
I saw your man Johnny leave 'bout an hour ago
With that gal named Nellie Bly.
He's your man, and he's doing you wrong."

Frankie went down to that hop spot
Brought along a great big forty-four
She went inside, and there she spied
Her Johnny on the floor
He was her man, and he was doin'— [song interrupted by gunshots][67]

Yet the film narrative that West forges around the song departs from this lyrical narrative substantially. As noted earlier, West cared very much that viewers perceive that Lou was doing men (especially Clark and Flynn) wrong; nowhere is that reversal of the ballad's chorus more readily apparent than in this climactic shootout scene, which unfolds simultaneously with Lou's performance of the ballad from which her movie derives its title. Further, whereas a common variant of the ballad attests, "Frankie went down to the pawnshop / She didn't go there for fun / She hocked all of her jewelry / Bought a pearl-handled 44 gun," Lou has no need to pawn her diamonds to get a gun, much less to use such a weapon herself. Still, if Lou doesn't literally pull the trigger as Frankie does in the ballad, she expertly pulls the strings that bring about Flynn's shooting and Clark's arrest by the police.

The way in which the scene is shot, cutting between medium close-ups of Lou on stage and wider angle shots of the action with Clark and Flynn on the balcony filmed over Lou's shoulder, helps suture the viewer into Lou's shoes quite directly as she plays catalyst to the action (figures 5.8–5.10). Lest this point regarding Lou's agency somehow still be lost on the viewer, West mimes Frankie's pistol-shooting action onstage immediately before the actual shooting on the upper balcony of the concert hall (figure 5.11). Interestingly, at least one poster for the movie promised an even more direct correspondence, showing a sultry Mae West leaning against a bar with a smoking pistol in her hand and a dead man, labeled "Mr. Low Gross," lying at her feet—a nod to both her box office clout and her outlaw persona (figure 5.12). There is doubtless more to say here about the phallic imagery inherent in the film's simulated gunplay, especially since West had at least a layperson's understanding of basic Freudian concepts. Even without a detailed psychoanalytic line of interpretation, it is clear that West was unabashedly signaling her protagonist's assertion of power over men through a symbolic usurpation of one of the most charged cinematic symbols of male authority, the gun. By leading Flynn to his death at precisely the moment when she is a glittering public spectacle of erotic impulses, West also suggests her character's potential as simultaneously a locus of sexual desire and a danger to would-be male suitors.

The level of conscious, painstaking design in the construction of this scene becomes fully apparent when one reviews the manuscripts of West's *Diamond Lil* and the series of revisions that the adapted screenplay underwent in the weeks leading up to the filming of *She Done Him Wrong*.[68] In *Diamond Lil* and early screenplay drafts, for example, Flynn is not ambushed by Clark's bullets without warning. Rather, Lil tells Flynn that Clark is in her room, and she unscrupulously plays on the conventions of chivalry by demanding: "Flynn, if you're gonna be my man, now's the time to prove it."[69] In this scenario, Lil is uncertain how the confrontation will unfold, but seems assured that at least one of her undesired suitors will be eradicated in short order. Interestingly, an alternative proposed by John Bright in a "revised final script" dated November 22, 1932, aimed to purify Lou's morality by taking the scheme to bring Dan Flynn and Chick Clark into confrontation out of her hands. In this version, the streetwise Spider Kane masterminds the plan to save Lou: he takes Chick to Lou's room, then tells Flynn that Lou wants to see him, and ensures a fatal shootout when he provides Chick Clark with a gun, telling him, "I got a hunch you might need this."[70] The film, by contrast, depicts Spider as an underling, subject to Lou's authority, and his final lines preceding Lou's going onstage to sing "Frankie and Johnny" are simply a threefold repetition of "All right, Lou" in response to her directives. Also notable is that virtually all of West's earlier versions of this scene portray Lou dancing a tango with the character Pablo Juarez (replaced by Serge in the film), to the tune "El Choclo," as the action between Flynn and Clark unfolds, essentially placing Lou in the role of passive bystander.[71] In contrast to these earlier possibilities,

FIGURES 5.8–5.10. Lou sets up Dan Flynn. 5.8: From the stage, Lou sees Chick Clark enter her room. 5.9: She nods for Flynn to head to her chambers. 5.10: Clark shoots Flynn as he opens the door to Lou's room (*She Done Him Wrong*).

the film representation presents Lou on center stage, unambiguously steering the action that leads to Flynn's demise and Clark's return to prison. What is more, she does so while performing "Frankie and Johnny," pointedly tying her own audacious actions to the ballad while making her crucial revision of its script crystal clear: namely, there is no doubt here that *she* done *him* wrong — and not just one man, but two.

Following this sequence of dramatic action, the film concludes in rapid-fire fashion with a police raid that rounds up Gus Jordan, Serge, and Chick Clark

FIGURE 5.11. Lou pantomimes Frankie's pistol shot (*She Done Him Wrong*).

for arrest. Lou, on the other hand, goes into the custody of Captain Cummings. Again, the film proves more compelling—and certainly more subversive of contemporaneous mores and gender role expectations—than its predecessor on the theatrical stage or in early screenplay drafts. The contrasts are illuminating enough to bear quoting one of the earlier screenplays at length:

> LIL: You makin' me think I was a lost soul or somethin'. Me layin' off my diamonds one by one—layin' off my paint and powder—layin' awake nights thinkin' I wasn't good enough for you. And you—just a common ordinary cop. Alright, Mr. Policeman, do your business. Give me the bracelets. They'll be a new kind of jewelry for me.
>
> LIL: Well, what are you standing there for? What are you waiting for? You want me, don't you?
>
> [Cummings takes Lil in his arms.]
>
> CUMMINGS: You know I want you.
>
> [Lil struggles slightly in his arms.]
>
> LIL: What are you trying to do to me? You know what I am, don't you?
>
> CUMMINGS: (warmly) I know you better than you think I do. I know that giving Jacobsen's Hall to the Mission isn't the only good thing you've done.
>
> LIL: I didn't do it for them. I did it for you.
>
> CUMMINGS: Then you'll believe me when I tell you that I'm mad about you—I want you.
>
> [Lil's arms go about his neck.]
>
> LIL: Oh, I always knew you could be had![72]

Contemporary fans of Mae West might not recognize the character portrayed here, since several aspects of this version of the closing scene cut against the

, , , Mae West, the famous exponent of sex in the theater, makes her Hollywood début. What's she like? Well, she's different, and startling, and amazing—see for yourself

FIGURE 5.12. Mae West kills "Mr. Low Gross": Poster for *She Done Him Wrong.*

grain of the legendary film persona for which she is known today. Perhaps most notably, this draft version of Lil expresses vulnerability ("You makin' me think I was a lost soul or somethin'"), self-doubt ("layin' awake nights thinkin' I wasn't good enough for you"), and guilt over her past behavior ("You know what I am, don't you?"). Just as noteworthy, she claims to have changed herself to adapt to the values of a male love interest and to have waited for that man to make the first move. Only Lil's final line—has she been gaming Cummings even with this final display of moroseness? — might lead one to perceive this incarnation of her as being noticeably different from other female film protagonists of her era.

West's final reworking of this material for the film shows a substantial change of spirit, and it helped cement the persona to which the actress would return in her future films. As with the earlier draft, this material picks up with the departure of the other criminals in the police wagon, but secludes Lil and Cummings in their own horse-drawn carriage.

> CUMMINGS: (taking her hand) Well, you surely don't mind my holding your hand.
>
> LOU: (withdrawing her hand into her lap) It ain't heavy. I can hold it myself. (Cummings grabs her hand again and holds it) You know, this is a dirty trick, and I could get real sore if I didn't have a lot of self-control.
>
> CUMMINGS: Well, so have I, but I'm beginning to lose it. You know, you remind me of a glittering palace of ice. (looking at the array of diamond rings on her hand, which he begins to remove)
>
> LOU: I ain't ice.
>
> CUMMINGS: I didn't say *you* were, but your diamonds are all going to the storehouse.
>
> LOU: You said I had a soul. I looked for it, but I didn't find it.
>
> CUMMINGS: You will.
>
> LOU: Where, in jail?
>
> CUMMINGS: No, that's not the place for you.
>
> LOU: Well, you got me, ain't you?
>
> CUMMINGS: Yeah, I got you. You're my prisoner and I'm going to be your jailer for a long, long time.
>
> (Cummings puts an engagement ring on Lou's finger.)
>
> LOU: Oh yeah?
>
> CUMMINGS: Yeah, and you can start doing that stretch right now.
>
> (Close-up on Lou's hand with the ring)
>
> LOU: Where'd you get that, dark and handsome?
>
> CUMMINGS: You bad girl!
>
> LOU: Umm, you'll find out.
>
> (Fade to black as the couple embraces in a kiss)

Several points of revision merit attention here. First, elements of self-doubt, vulnerability, and religiously inflected guilt are nowhere to be found. Nor does Lou express any feelings of repentance for her past actions, an unusual

FIGURE 5.13. Lou as reformed woman? (*She Done Him Wrong*).

feature remarked on in reviews at the time.[73] The focus here is on a character who has not altered from the one audiences have seen from the outset of the film (figure 5.13). Lou maintains a sense of autonomy by withdrawing her hand from Cummings's grasp, albeit temporarily; nothing in her dialogue or body language suggests weakness. And while both characters express themselves forcefully, the possibility that this "bad girl" will bring about changes in Captain Cummings seems decidedly more likely than the reverse; indeed, he has already begun to shed the patented self-control that until now seemed to be his central character trait.

In a broader context, during a brief period between 1929 and the onset of Joseph Breen's draconian reign as head of the film industry's Production Code Administration beginning in 1934, a number of Hollywood films featured female protagonists performing remarkable subversions of prevailing gender role expectations. Even in this context, West's transgressions stood out, and her first two starring roles, in *She Done Him Wrong* and *I'm No Angel*, proved especially important catalysts for triggering the end of this relative openness in US film depictions of female characters.[74] In hindsight, the swiftness and sternness of the reaction from Breen and other key players in Hollywood's censorship brigade does not appear especially surprising. After all, *She Done Him Wrong* was not a subtle tweaking of social mores; it was a trumpet blast of an assault on Victorian conventions regarding gender and sexuality. As noted earlier, Lou lavishes her romantic attentions on no less than five men during the course of the film, *and* she does so, in at least four of those cases, for reasons that seem motivated more by her own opportunistic advancement than by feelings of anything like "love" as characteristically portrayed in literary or cinematic romance narratives. Typically, even *one* such moral indiscretion would bring about the downfall, and probably the death, of the female protagonist in the literary antecedents of Hollywood's early-1930s tales of fallen women.[75] West's character, by contrast, escapes unpunished despite flagrantly flaunting convention in these ways.

In truth, West's character does considerably more than defy expected gender codes. Beyond the issues of sexual ethics, lest one forget, Lou was an accessory to the murder of Dan Flynn, in every sense that matters, albeit perhaps not in a strictly legal sense; and she killed Russian Rita by her own hand, in self-defense, when Rita attacked her in a wild fit of anger over Serge's affection for Lou. Yet whereas traditional ballads sometimes end with Frankie distraught and literally weeping over the grave of the lover she murdered, Lou expresses not even an ounce of remorse for Flynn's or Rita's death. And while Frankie in the ballads almost invariably insists on a moral justification for her fatal act of violence—"he was my man, but he done me wrong"—West's Lady Lou doesn't appear compelled to offer much in the way of moralistic rationales for *any* of her actions. In other words, West is at pains to show that her protagonist is consciously doing men wrong and getting away with it. Thus, while Lou's stockpile of diamonds may soon be turned over to the state, she nonetheless rides off into the proverbial sunset, with "dark and handsome" leading man Cary Grant in tow. It is difficult to imagine any other actress of the era pulling off such escapades in this manner, or essaying such a forthright rejection of the entrenched tropes of female grief, disavowal of past misdeeds, and moral redemption at the film's finale.

In many versions of the "Frankie and Johnny" ballad, Frankie escapes legal repercussions for a crime of which she is incontrovertibly guilty. Even here, though, West's subtle departure from the conventional "Frankie and Johnny" ballad is highly indicative of her larger ambitions. In those versions of the ballad that do not end with Frankie at the gallows or in jail, most often she is released by a sympathetic judge. For example, Mississippi John Hurt's 1928 recording of "Frankie" explains:

> *Frankie and the judge walked outta the stand,*
> *And walked out side by side*
> *The judge says, "Frankie, you're gonna be justified,*
> *Killin' a man, and he did you wrong."*[76]

As noted in the introductory chapter, this was essentially the outcome of Frankie Baker's real-life trial for the murder of Allen Britt in St. Louis in 1899. What is striking about West's work on this front is that Lou attains her freedom not by recourse to the mechanisms of the legal system, but instead by enchanting a police detective. Rather than being the passive recipient of a favorable verdict, Lou, through her powers of seduction, carves out her own means of escaping the consequences of her actions and underworld attachments. This strategy remains a conundrum for contemporary feminist scholars with regard to West's legacy: the unquestionably bold nature of her assertiveness is tempered by the fact that her sexual allure typically seems to constitute the primary weapon in her assault on male power. But should one expect otherwise from a performer who drew so deeply from the blues divas of the 1920s and early 1930s? Here, too, West articulated her message in terms already familiar to aficionados of African American vernacular expression, by joining a quick wit, self-confidence, and a glamorous image in a winning combination.

CHAPTER 6

THE LYNCHING OF JOHNNY:
STERLING BROWN'S SOCIAL REALIST CRITIQUE

ORIGINALLY PUBLISHED IN 1932, Sterling Brown's *Southern Road* has long been celebrated for its engagement with African American ballads, blues, spirituals, and work songs (figure 6.1). Alain Locke acclaimed Brown at the time as "New Negro Folk-Poet," citing his unparalleled knack for "portrayal of Negro folk-life true in both letter and spirit to the idiom of the folk's own way of feeling and thinking."[1] Likewise, in a more recent critical work on Brown, Joanne Gabbin notes his ability to capture "the language of the Black folk—the dialect, the idioms, the imagery, the style," and applauds the poet's penchant for "cross-pollinating" materials from African American folklore with elements derived from Western literary traditions.[2] Brown's relationship with folklore was indeed extensive. More so than any other intellectual of the 1920s and 1930s except Zora Neale Hurston, Brown sustained a deep engagement with African American folk communities, finding a welcome place in the homes, bars, and barbershops of rural southwestern Virginia; Jefferson City, Missouri; Nashville, Tennessee; and Washington, DC. Brown also wrote some of the earliest scholarly work appraising the merits of black vernacular music traditions as literature and as a form of collective social history.[3] Figures like W. E. B. Du Bois had paved the way in their studies of spirituals, and Brown followed suit with secular music forms such as ballads, work songs, and the blues—all of which he drew upon for his own creative work in *Southern Road*. In addition to Brown's use of established literary forms like the sonnet, the poetry of *Southern Road* directly refers to a range of secular and sacred works, including Bessie Smith's "Backwater Blues," W. C. Handy's "St. Louis Blues," the ballad of "John Henry," and spirituals such as "When the Saints Go Marching In."

It is unsurprising, then, that Brown found his way to a song as widely circulated as "Frankie and Johnny." Brown, however, was far more than a passive recipient of folk traditions, and his poem features several significant de-

FIGURE 6.1. Sterling Brown, 1944.

partures from conventional versions of the ballad. For one, Brown relocates the narrative away from its native St. Louis and into the rural South. Moreover, the poem transposes the all-black context of the ballad into a world that crackles with Jim Crow brutality. Specifically, Brown's Frankie is not a jilted black lover, but rather the white daughter of a sawmill worker. Readers also learn in the opening stanzas that she is a "halfwit" with "a crazy love of torment" who violently dismembers or otherwise wounds animals for the sheer enjoyment of it. For his part, Johnny is a black sharecropper who "had to slave it and never had much fun" in fields of sugar corn. Eventually seduced by Frankie into a series of covert sexual liaisons in the woods, at poem's end Johnny pays the price when Frankie's father spearheads his lynching.[4] In the terms offered by Adam Gussow's study of early twentieth-century blues music, Brown transforms "Frankie and Johnny" from a story of "intimate violence"—"the violence that black folk inflict on each other"—to an episode of "disciplinary violence . . . the white-on-black vigilantism . . . designed to terrorize, silence, and restrict the mobility of Southern black folk."[5] Precisely because the poem involves so many dramatic reinventions, it offers a valuable window onto Brown's ambitions as a poet concerned with social justice and a prime example of the extent to which creative artists altered the "Frankie and Johnny" ballad.

Relocating the "Frankie and Johnny" story from an urban red-light district in the Midwest to a southern sharecropping milieu exposes the deep ambivalence expressed toward the rural South throughout much of Brown's *Southern Road*. At the heart of these divided sentiments was the fact that the South was *both* the hub of rich African American folk traditions beloved by the poet *and* the site of tremendous daily hardships and occasional flagrant outbursts of violence under the Jim Crow social system. Thus, while Brown deeply treasured his experiences with the black folk communities of the South, he remained critical of the region's racial and class inequalities. S. Elmore Hurd, a Jamaican immigrant living in Boston, wrote a letter to commend the poet on this front: "Cut this book anywhere and it will bleed . . . drip the blood of men and women who sing in the storm."[6] Still, Brown recognized that this same aspect of his poetry would earn him the consternation of the "bourbon South" and likely diminish his readership.[7]

In the poems of *Southern Road*, Brown also is skeptical of the artifice of city life as well as the presentation of African American culture to mainstream audiences via white Harlem Renaissance cultural brokers like Carl Van Vechten and white-owned commercial venues such as The Cotton Club. Brown's poem "Cabaret" makes this abundantly clear by intercutting faux plantation scenarios set in a northern nightclub with snapshots of enforced black labor on the levees of a flood-stricken South.[8] In short, the gulf between the South as nostalgically imagined in Roaring Twenties musical revues and as the setting of African American lived experience could scarcely be more pronounced.

Yet Brown's treatment of the rural South emerges as severely vexed in its own right; as readers move from poem to poem, they encounter not only nightmarish spectacles of the sort that conclude "Frankie and Johnny," but also sketches that admiringly describe the resourcefulness and endurance of the region's black folk in the face of floods, meager crops, and racial violence. Taken collectively, the poems of *Southern Road* offer a biting revision of Southern literary traditions. Brown's subsequent publications, *Negro Poetry and Drama* (1937) and *The Negro in American Fiction* (1937), demonstrate how widely read he was in American literature and how critical he was of writers such as Thomas Nelson Page, who sought to glorify the plantation era of the antebellum South, and Thomas Dixon, who demonized postemancipation African Americans as conniving mulattoes and rapacious male beasts. Particularly given the influence of a work like Dixon's *The Clansman* (1905) and its adaptation by D. W. Griffith as the film *Birth of a Nation* (1915) in contributing to the real life resurgence of the Ku Klux Klan and white racial terrorism against African Americans, Brown recognized the high stakes of cultural representations of race and region. Thus, in much the way that Brown repeatedly advocated in his literary criticism, he sought in his poetry to displace the likes of Page and Dixon with work that blended artistry and an unflinching brand of social realism.[9]

As Gabbin chronicles in her seminal study of Brown's career, the poet arrived at his highly regarded debut volume after passing through an educational and experiential crucible that merged wide-ranging influences. Brown was shaped by an eclectic set of mentors who straddled the ostensible divide between high culture and folk culture. He was raised in a home that emphasized a love of books, and he was the product of a rigorous education at Dunbar High School (in Washington, DC), Williams College, and Harvard University. Brown came of age reading a wide variety of poetry: everything from Elizabethan sonnets to modern imagist verse, with Edwin Arlington Robinson and Robert Frost playing especially important roles in shaping Brown's craft. Brown admired how Robinson "took up the undistinguished, the failures, and showed the extraordinary in ordinary lives," and took inspiration from Frost's stoicism and democratic vision. Gabbin adds that the English poet A. E. Housman, while generally distinct from Brown in form, nonetheless influenced his tendency "to celebrate courage, strength, and manliness in his poems."[10]

In addition to these literary influences, from young adulthood Brown was fascinated by folk cultural forms of expression. He was immersed in the contemporary discourse of folklore scholarship, corresponding with prominent folklorists such as Benjamin Botkin, Lawrence Gellert, and the father-son team of John and Alan Lomax, and working in concert with all of them as an editor, informal collector, and dialogue partner during the 1930s and 1940s. Botkin, who was appointed national folklore editor of the Federal Writers' Project in 1938, shared a particularly vibrant correspondence with Brown throughout the 1930s. Brown offered advice on the politics of representation to Botkin for his journal *Folk-Say: A Regional Miscellany* (1929–1932) and solicited other African American poets to contribute work to the publication; Botkin responded in kind by offering remarkably detailed thoughts on the representation of folk dialect in Brown's poetry. Further, two critical essays by Brown and ten of the poems from *Southern Road* made their first appearance in *Folk-Say*.[11]

Although many of Brown's published views on the importance of folk expression postdate his debut volume of poetry, his early essays and the poems of *Southern Road* make clear that most of his core ideas on the subject had germinated by 1932. For example, in a 1930 essay entitled "The Blues as Folk Poetry," written for *Folk-Say*, Brown confidently asserted, "Blues of importance to students of folk life are still being produced, in considerable numbers and with a great degree of authenticity."[12] Thus, during an era when a majority of professional and amateur folklorists continued to adhere to a model of folklore productions as relics of the nation's past that continued to exist anachronistically in the present, Brown shared, with paradigm-shifting peers such as Botkin, Gellert, and the Lomaxes, a conviction that folklore and folk music were not ossified fossils representing only the past, but rather thriving, adaptive traditions and, thus, rich sources of social history from the vantage point of the folk or "common man." Moreover, the perception of a rapidly changing society in the 1920s and 1930s seemed to add gravity to folk expression as a kind of cultural anchor or touchstone for enthusiasts like Brown.

After the publication of *Southern Road*, Brown served as national editor for Negro Affairs for the Federal Writers' Project from 1936 to 1940, overseeing numerous publications that blended elements of folklore and social history. In personal correspondence drafted around the time that he left the project, Brown recalled his accomplishments in this position as including his own insightful essay for the FWP's guidebook *Washington: City and Capital* (1937); oversight of "Negro" material for several state guidebooks, as well as *The Negro in Virginia* (1940), which Brown aptly termed "a very readable new type of social historiography"; and "a study of the struggle for freedom including the Underground Railroad—the first history written by Negroes, a study of folklore, and a book of ex-slave narratives (far from the plantation tradition)."[13] Such work often was tough sledding, as when Brown had to wrangle over deletions to *The Negro in Virginia* requested by the FWP's director, John Newsom, involving descriptions of slaveholder cruelty, and to rebuff Newsom's puzzling suggestion that a chapter "on the harrowing subject of the punishment of slaves should close on a humorous note."[14] In the face of such obstacles, Brown's published essays and his correspondence as FWP editor repeatedly stress the importance of folk expression in forging "bottom-up" revisions of US history and displacing racist stereotypes with more accurate and diverse representations of African American life.

Like Botkin and Gellert, Brown looked to the folk not as exemplars of a simpler, idyllic past, but rather as informed commentators on matters of class and race-based social injustices, both historical and contemporary. In this vein, Brown served as an informal advisor for Gellert's *Negro Songs of Protest* (1936), which reported theretofore seldom documented social critiques embedded in African American secular music traditions.[15] As Brown explained in *Negro Poetry and Drama*, "Negro folksongs, from the earliest down to those uncovered by Lawrence Gellert, are invaluable to anyone seeking to know the American Negro. They constitute a very adept self-portraiture. . . . Equally convincing in light heartedness and tragedy, they put to shame much of the interpretation of the Negro from without."[16] Speaking at a gala concert hosted by the Library of Congress in 1940 to commemorate the seventy-fifth anniversary of the Thirteenth Amendment to the US Constitution, Brown contended that African American folk communities sang music of social comment "not loudly, but deeply." Riffing on Du Bois's term for the spirituals, Brown deemed secular folk music of protest "the sorrow songs of a bitter present."[17] Brown consistently urged students and scholars of folklore to examine more deeply this vital component of vernacular music, jokes, and tales.

Brown was insistent that creative artists as well as folklorists should attend to the protest dimension in representations of African American folk life. Consequently, Brown praised Zora Neale Hurston's "sensitive ear" for the rich nuances of the black folk idiom in her pathbreaking folklore study *Mules and Men*, but lamented:

> Her characters are naive, quaint, complaisant, bad enough to kill each other in jooks, but meek otherwise, socially unconscious. Their life is made to appear easy-going and carefree. This, to the reviewer, makes *Mules and Men* singularly *incomplete*. These people live in a land shadowed by squalor, poverty, disease, violence, enforced ignorance and exploitation. Even if browbeaten, they do know a smouldering resentment. Many folk-stories and songs from the South contain this resentment. . . . *Mules and Men* should be more bitter; it would be nearer the truth.[18]

By contrast, Brown lauded *Uncle Tom's Children*, the debut fiction volume by the social realist Richard Wright, as "a bitter transcript of reality, more powerful because of its poetic handling."[19] Even though his estimation of Hurston's work might seem narrowly prescriptive to twenty-first-century eyes, Brown clearly felt that any analysis that neglected to engage both the aesthetic and the political dimensions of folk expression was lacking.

Brown's relationship to folk expression was not purely a distanced, academic one. While teaching at Virginia Seminary and College (Lynchburg), Lincoln University (Jefferson City, Missouri), Fisk University (Nashville), and—from 1929 onward—Howard University (Washington, DC), he added a number of vernacular guides from his local communities to his list of teachers. At Lincoln, for example, Brown's students introduced him to local characters such as "Old Man McCorkle" and Slim Greer, as well as to the music of artists like Ma Rainey—all of whom featured prominently in the poet's subsequent work.[20] Lewis Jones, a colleague at Fisk University, recalled how "Sterling's preoccupation with folk culture led him to search out the local folk artists," invite local musicians to play at his house ("On occasion, Sterling would pick a few bars on his own box," says Jones), and regularly hang out at the barbershop of a storyteller named Will Gilchrist, or "Gillie."[21] Two other especially influential folk mentors were Mrs. Bibby, the sagacious mother of one of Brown's students at Virginia Seminary, and Calvin "Big Boy" Davis, a musician and raconteur who visited Brown's classrooms at Virginia Seminary and at Howard.[22] In addition to inspiring multiple poems in Brown's *Southern Road*, Bibby and Davis helped affirm the young poet's admiration for folk expression and crystallize his vision of folk culture's virtues: specifically, the qualities of wisdom born of experience, tenacity in the face of hardship, and pithy self-expression. Brown's relationship to folk culture thus bridged the academic and the participatory. In this regard, a letter that Brown sent to a Federal Writers' Project employee is suggestive of his own approach: "One word of advice. Don't rush the people. They may be suspicious. Just soak in the life. If you tell some of the folklore you know yourself that might help." He added in the same letter: "I heartily approve your going to the rural sections and not to the books. The latter might serve as guides to procedure. But a sympathetic approach to the people, which means no condescension and no marked curiosity, should help even more."[23] Put simply, Brown approached the folk as peers, even mentors, rather than as exotic research subjects, and he encouraged other writers to do likewise.

From this panoply of sources, Brown derived a nuanced sense of folklore as an artistically rich body of expression. Hence, he chose to include a substantial section titled "Folk Literature" alongside the work of more conventionally literary authors in his widely read 1941 anthology *The Negro Caravan*. Brown felt that spirituals, work songs, blues, and ballads ("Frankie and Johnny" among them), although often by anonymous authors, represented a kind of poetry in their own right; thus, their literary merits were not dependent on creative adaptations by poets such as himself. Further, in *Negro Caravan* and elsewhere, Brown adopted a much broader, more inclusive definition of folk expression than the one used by the majority of his antiquarian folklorist contemporaries. He articulated his vision at a national folklore symposium in 1942: "I have been much influenced recently by a trend toward the collecting and the using of a living folklore—the living speech of the people. I know some of the difficulties in defining this 'folk,' and I imagine that many of the people I have gone to are not folk. This hasn't bothered me particularly, since my interest was not scientific. I wanted to write of people with some accuracy as to their life and character. That gets one not into folklore, but into a living-people-lore."[24]

While Brown downplays the "scientific" aspects of his work, his grasp of folk expression was every bit as nuanced as most folklorists' of his day. What he describes as "living-people-lore" involved a jettisoning of unrealistic expectations that the "folk" would somehow remain in pristine isolation from the larger world's modernization and social conflicts. In this sense, he was ahead of his time, already in the 1930s and 1940s rejecting ideas of cultural purity that most professional folklorists would come to regard with skepticism by the 1970s. Brown was also well ahead of his time in insisting that most US folk traditions were "hybrid" rather than ethnically sealed off from one another. He noted, for instance, that "Negroes hand down fairly straight versions" of traditional Scotch-English ballads, and that "Leadbelly sings cowboy songs, yelling 'Ki-yi-yippy-yippy-yay' with his own zest." Of "Frankie and Johnny"— which he called "the most widely known tragedy in America"—Brown noted: "[It] is attributed to both white and Negro authorship. It could come from either; it probably comes from both; the tenderloin cuts across both sections."[25] In this regard, Brown saw ballads, blues, and work songs as profoundly American, democratic modes of expression.

Beyond the primary documents of folk expression, Brown was well acquainted with an international array of literary projects grounded in folklore—Irish, English, German, and French, as well as the work of New Negro peers such as Jean Toomer, Langston Hughes, and Hurston.[26] This was, then, an interest that Brown shared with many contemporary poets, perhaps most notably Hughes and Carl Sandburg. In advance of Hughes's first tour through the South, in 1931 (with Zora Neale Hurston), he wrote to Brown that he hoped his public readings would "encourage the reading of Negro authors, and be an incentive toward literary creation using the racial folklore and backgrounds as material."[27] Brown, too, was a tireless advocate for folk expression as a valuable mine of materials for literary artists, not least in the example of his own poetry. Both Hughes and Brown frequently incorporated references to specific African American folk songs, sacred and secular, in their verse, while also adopting and sometimes improvising on the formal structures associated with spirituals, blues, work songs, and ballads.

Numerous scholars have noted that Sandburg represented an important touchstone for Brown.[28] What has been less often remarked on is that Brown's disposition toward Sandburg was riddled with ambivalence. On the one hand, Brown could not but help feel the influence of Sandburg's pathbreaking emulation of vernacular voices; Sandburg affected an entire generation of poets in this regard. Yet as the Swedish American poet laureate of America's laboring classes traversed the country, weaving performances of "Frankie and Albert" and other African American folk songs into his stage repertoire, his interpretations raised questions of mimicry and appropriation for Brown and some of his contemporaries. The African American educator Horace Mann Bond wrote to Brown in 1931: "We heard Carl Sandburg recently at Chicago. He used his guitar to some effect. Most of his repertoire was made of Negro songs. . . . It makes me mad as hell to see the white bastards capitalizing on us, and poorly, too . . . only theirs is not genuine, or do you think? Maybe that's why the great white public takes to it." Brown's sly, even snarky, disdain regarding the commercialization of folk music by way of "the T.O.B.A. circuit, carnival minstrel troupes, and the returned prodigal with his songbag full" in a 1930 publication is a clear allusion to Sandburg's popular *American Songbag* anthology (1927) and leads one to suspect that Brown concurred with the thrust of Bond's sentiments.[29]

Brown's ideas regarding the hybrid nature of US folk music should make clear that his reservations regarding Sandburg were not strictly a matter of a white poet adapting African American folk expression. But Brown *did* care about authenticity, fidelity to vernacular culture, and—following the lead of his Williams College professor George Dutton—what he termed "critical realism." Whereas Brown found such qualities lacking in Sandburg's public performances, he sought to implement them in his own poetry. In part, Brown's sense of critical realism involved literary work that engaged real-life hardships and inequalities, and treated historical actors as three-dimensional human beings rather than as comic props or abject victims.[30] In the field of folk music, Brown found an exemplar of these ideals in Huddie Ledbetter: "A striking contrast to the favored house servant is such a folk character as Huddie Ledbetter, better known as Leadbelly, whose knowingness is stark rather than soft, and whose audience (certainly in his formative years) was his own kind of people, not the white quality. The bitter brew that Leadbelly concocted in the levee camps and jooks and prisons differs from the sugary potions that Remus and the other 'uncles' dispensed."[31] As suggested by his affinity for Ledbetter, Brown's conceptions of critical realism and authenticity in folk music were predicated upon a close connection to rural, noncommercial sources. Hence, he evaluated Ethel Waters's 1938 rendition of "Frankie and Johnny" rather harshly, despite a certain admiration for her talents: "In contrast to Bessie Smith, who became famous for 'folk' blues, Ethel Waters became famous for gamey, double-entendre, cabaret songs. Once the toast of the honky-tonks, she is now the toast of Broadway. Unfortunately, her version of 'Frankie and Johnny' was made after she became a stage star. She overdramatizes this folk classic too much for my taste."[32] Needless to say, attempting to bridge audience accessibility, fidelity to the folk idiom of performers like Smith and Ledbetter, and modernist literary aspirations was no easy feat, even for someone as prolific as Brown proved to be during the Depression decade.

When submitting the manuscript that became *Southern Road* to prospective publishers in 1929, Brown described his mission as interpreting "certain aspects of Negro character and folk life as I have observed them."[33] A brief consideration of selected poems shows that Brown approached this mission in multifaceted ways. The volume's opening poem, "Odyssey of Big Boy," channels the persona of the musician Calvin Davis into a first-person mock-epic autobiographical yarn that traces a sprawling geography of jobs held and women conquered, reaching from Kentucky southward to New Orleans and back north again to Washington, DC. With a repetition of each stanza's final line, echoing the form and cadence of "John Henry," the poem rings with musical quality:

> *I done had my women,*
> *I done had my fun;*
> *Cain't do much complainin'*
> *When my jag is done,*
> *Lawd, Lawd, when my jag is done.*[34]

However, the typical folk ballad would not be replete with references to numerous other African American ballad legends such as Casey Jones, Stagolee, and John Henry; nor would the ordinary folk ballad give a self-aware nod to the Western literary tradition of Homeric quests, as does Brown. In "When De Saints Go Ma'ching Home" and "Ma Rainey," Brown takes a different tack and masterfully evokes particular performative moments by Calvin Davis and Rainey in relation to their audiences, by intermixing descriptive verse with lyrical excerpts from the voices of the singers themselves.

In still another form of dialogue with folk music traditions, the poem "Southern Road" merges elements of blues and work songs into a hybrid structure that is folk derived and yet, ultimately, Brown's own. As Gabbin explains: "Using the basic stanzaic pattern of the blues, Brown slightly reorders it into shorter lines to accommodate the caesura and the 'grunt' that mark the work song. With the first four lines presenting the situation or the problem, and the last two lines resolving the problem or reacting to the situation, Brown emphasizes simultaneously the speaker's blues-ridden sense of hopelessness and despair, and a stoic brand of resilience that will keep him going."[35] For example, after sketching out the murder that landed the protagonist in prison and lamenting the forced separation from his wife, unborn child, and parents, he "lines out" from his spot on a chain gang:

> *White man tells me—hunh—*
> *Damn yo' soul;*
> *White man tells me—hunh—*

Damn yo' soul;
Got no need, bebby,
To be tole.[36]

At the same time, Brown's poem recounts the story of a particular convict and uses a loosely chronological narrative thread, qualities that depart from the archetypal abstraction and nonlinear structure characteristic of most folk blues and work songs. Consistently, then, Brown blends vernacular inspiration with poetic innovation to suit his own designs.

Brown deployed his vast knowledge of folk and Western poetic traditions in these and still other diverse ways, but his strongest affinity was for the form and characters of ballads. One reason for Brown's special attraction to the ballad, Gabbin recognizes, is that "the framework of the folk-ballad . . . has a built-in effect of elevating the deeds of the ordinary man to legendary status."[37] If anything, Brown goes to even greater lengths than folk ballads themselves to chronicle extraordinary qualities in "ordinary" lives. As a case in point, in "Ruminations of Luke Johnson," a black domestic worker named Mandy Jane carries out a daily ritual of discreetly making off with a basket of food from her white employers, an act that attains a sense of gravity that is every bit the equal of the action-packed heroics of Stagolee or John Henry.[38]

To be sure, heroic masculinity is a key virtue for Brown, as displayed in "The Odyssey of Big Boy" and "Strong Men"; the poet also bore a strong affection for tall tales, as reflected in his series of Slim Greer poems (in *Southern Road* and beyond), in which the title character embodies a trickster role. Far more often, though, Brown used his verse to spotlight anonymous everymen and women who bore enormous hardships—poverty, racial inequality, natural disasters—with stoicism. Hence, unlike the badman character of Lazarus in African American folklore, the protagonist of Brown's "Southern Road" does not escape the chain gang or go down with guns blazing against a sheriff's posse, but rather seems resigned to his fate:

Chain gang nevah—hunh—
Let me go;
Chain gang nevah—hunh—
Let me go;
Po' los' boy, bebby,
Evahmo' . . .[39]

Here, as Mark Sanders notes, Brown makes clear that the "articulation of alienation and existential angst" was hardly the exclusive purview of erudite modernists.[40] "Virginia Portrait," inspired by the aforementioned Mrs. Bibby from Brown's time at Virginia Seminary in the 1920s, also is representative in this regard:

> Even when winter settles on her heart,
> She keeps a wonted, quiet nonchalance,
> A courtly dignity of speech and carriage,
> Unlooked for in these distant rural ways.[41]

As different as these two examples are, in both cases Brown sought to replace long-standing stereotypes of African American ineptitude and subservience with elements of the heroic—a heroism no less striking for eschewing the flamboyant exploits typical of American folk balladry.

Compared with the foregoing poems, Brown's "Frankie and Johnny" has received little detailed attention. In some respects, this is understandable; it is by no means the most accomplished or formally innovative poem in *Southern Road*. Equally important in the poem's neglect, I suspect, is the fact that unlike many of the more celebrated works in the collection, "Frankie and Johnny" offers little in the way of a heroic impulse—a point to which I will return. In addition, "Frankie and Johnny" is the only poem in *Southern Road* in which Brown indexes a widely familiar folk music source and departs radically from the spirit of the folk original. As noted, Brown was aware of the ballad's typical elements and subsequently reprinted a standard version of "Frankie and Johnny" in *The Negro Caravan*. He also knew of the song's urban, midwestern roots, describing "St. James Infirmary" as "an old southwestern gambling song, part frontier, part folk Negro. St. Louis, Memphis, Little Rock, Oklahoma City, that type of town. Close cousin to 'Frankie and Johnny' and 'Stackolee.'"[42] Thus, Brown's relocation of the action from a bustling, urban frontier locale to the rural South, the transformation of Frankie's race from black to white, and the reworking of Johnny's identity from sporting man (pimp) and musician to sharecropper were conscious moves on the part of the poet.

Brown opens his poem with a couplet from the traditional lyrics serving as an epigraph: "Oh Frankie and Johnny were lovers / Oh Lordy how they did love!" (see text figure 6.1). The attribution of these lines to an "Old Ballad" is a way of insisting that "Frankie and Johnny" is a quintessentially American artifact, consistent with Brown's beliefs that this song's vitality owed to an admixture of African American and white contributions. The first stanza of the poem proper, however, promptly disrupts any nostalgia that the song might have called to mind for readers by the 1930s:

> *Frankie was a halfwit, Johnny was a nigger,*
> *Frankie liked to pain poor creatures as a little 'un,*
> *Kept a crazy love of torment when she got bigger,*
> *Johnny had to slave it and never had much fun.*

Brown immediately blurs the question whether readers should regard Frankie as an object of pity (an intellectually disabled "halfwit") or a sadistic monster (with her "crazy love of torment"). While traditional variants of the "Frankie and Johnny" ballad sometimes prove unclear on her status as heroine or antiheroine, its narrative tension arises from Frankie's dual status as a victim of Johnny's infidelity and the agent of Johnny's death, with lamentations from Johnny's mother adding weight to Frankie's guilt in versions like Huddie Ledbetter's. Brown's Frankie is simultaneously less a fully competent agent *and* capable of far greater cruelty than her folk music namesake. The impression of Frankie's unfeeling brutality grows in the second stanza, in which she enacts violence on a series of defenseless animals—butterflies, angleworms, dogs, and calves—all seemingly for the joy of "listening to their drawn out cries." The typical ballad motive of Frankie seeking vengeance against an injudicious or coldhearted adulterer is absent. Instead, Frankie's cruelty to animals in Brown's poem establishes her animalistic nature, which was a common mode of stigmatizing the "feeble-minded" as allegedly subhuman in the early decades of the twentieth century.[43] Meanwhile, the opening line's racial epithet and the choice of the slang term "slave" as a verb to describe Johnny's agricultural labors establish a setting in which very little has changed for African Americans in the rural South since the antebellum era.

The third stanza further complicates Brown's characterization of Frankie by adding additional backstory, and perhaps even something of an "explanation" for her cruelty:

> *Frankie took her pappy's lunch week-days to the sawmill,*
> *Her pappy, red-faced cracker, with a cracker's thirst,*
> *Beat her skinny body and reviled the hateful imbecile,*
> *She screamed at every blow he struck, but tittered when he curst.*

Here, the poem efficiently marks the class status of Frankie's father through his job at a sawmill and then promptly charts a course all too familiar in lit-

TEXT FIGURE 6.1. (*opposite*) Sterling Brown, "Frankie and Johnny," from *Southern Road*, ©1932 by Harcourt Brace and Company, Inc. Reprinted by permission of the Estate of Sterling A. Brown.

STERLING BROWN'S "FRANKIE AND JOHNNY" (1932)

Oh Frankie and Johnny were lovers
Oh Lordy how they did love!
OLD BALLAD

Frankie was a halfwit, Johnny was a nigger,
    Frankie liked to pain poor creatures as a little 'un,
Kept a crazy love of torment when she got bigger,
    Johnny had to slave it and never had much fun.

Frankie liked to pull the wings off of living butterflies,
    Frankie liked to cut long angleworms in half,
Frankie liked to whip curs and listen to their drawn out cries,
    Frankie liked to shy stones at the brindle calf.

Frankie took her pappy's lunch week-days to the sawmill,
    Her pappy, red-faced cracker, with a cracker's thirst,
Beat her skinny body and reviled the hateful imbecile,
    She screamed at every blow he struck, but tittered when he curst.

Frankie had to cut through Johnny's fields of sugar corn
    Used to wave at Johnny, who didn't *'pay no min'*—
Had had to work like fifty from the day that he was born,
    And wasn't no cracker hussy gonna put his work behind—.

But everyday Frankie swung along the cornfield lane,
    And one day Johnny helped her partly through the wood,
Once he had dropped his plow lines, he dropped them many times again—
    Though his mother didn't know it, else she'd have whipped him good.

Frankie and Johnny were lovers; oh Lordy how they did love!
    But one day Frankie's pappy by a big log laid him low,
To find out what his crazy Frankie had been speaking of;
    He found that what his gal had muttered was exactly so.

Frankie, she was spindly limbed with corn silk on her crazy head,
    Johnny was a nigger, who never had much fun—
They swung up Johnny on a tree, and filled his swinging hide with lead,
    And Frankie yowled hilariously when the thing was done.

erary and popular culture characterizations of southern poor whites: namely, depicting them as a morass of moral turpitude and psychosexual depravity. Frankie's "pappy" is driven to physical and psychological torture of his own offspring by "a cracker's thirst," suggesting that his actions spring from repugnant emotive impulses and appetites inherent to his race and class, rather than from reason. Although Brown's resorting to such a base brand of caricature might be disappointing from a critic who would go on to analyze the demeaning use of stereotypes against African Americans in US fiction, poetry, and drama with such aplomb, the well of stock images that Brown draws on here ran deep. The specter of unproductive citizenry was a subject of acute anxiety amid the economic stagnation of the Great Depression, and eugenicists of the day described southern poor whites generally, and the "feeble-minded" in particular, as degenerate threats to white racial purity, nothing less than uncivilized blights upon US civilization—or, to borrow from William Faulkner's description of *The Sound and the Fury* (1929), "a story of blood gone bad."[44] In addition, this representation of white southerners would have been familiar to the period's readers from examples such as the tenant-farming Lester family of Erskine Caldwell's novel *Tobacco Road*, also published in 1932. In the case of Brown's poem, is the reader intended to conclude that Frankie is merely a product of the violence inflicted so remorselessly upon her, a helpless "halfwit"? Perhaps in part, but the detail that she "tittered when he curst" and her "crazy love of torment" seem intended to mark Frankie as a sadomasochist, one who takes pleasure in provoking and receiving violence as well as in inflicting it.

The ensuing two stanzas mark the rising action of the poem as the characters' paths cross—first incidentally and then intimately—in ways verboten within Jim Crow society:

> *Frankie had to cut through Johnny's fields of sugar corn*
> *Used to wave at Johnny, who didn't* 'pay no min'—
> Had had to work like fifty from the day that he was born,
> And wasn't no cracker hussy gonna put his work behind—.

> *But everyday Frankie swung along the cornfield lane,*
> *And one day Johnny helped her partly through the wood,*
> *Once he had dropped his plow lines, he dropped them many times again—*
> *Though his mother didn't know it, else she'd have whipped him good.*

Here, Brown at first casts Johnny in a redeeming light by employing his vernacular voice to express disdain for Frankie's overtures, privileging the fidelity to labor necessitated by his social station over carnal pursuits. Even more, operating in a typically masculinist mode, Brown seems to credit Johnny's initial disdain of Frankie as a "cracker hussy." Whatever sympathy this verse enlists in readers is diminished, of course, when Johnny yields to Frankie's repeated temptations. As was his wont, Brown here invests parents with a greater sense of wisdom than their offspring, suggesting that Johnny's mother would have brought an end to his affair with Frankie had she but known of it. Lacking this "mother wit," Johnny pursues rendezvous with Frankie, leading to his ultimate demise. Just as the traditional ballad's tragic outcome typically is presaged by the refrain "He was her man, but he was doing her wrong," readers by now know that Frankie and Johnny's affair is destined to end ruinously.

The closing two stanzas bring the poem to a heavily foreshadowed but nonetheless tragic crescendo of violence:

Frankie and Johnny were lovers; oh Lordy how they did love!
But one day Frankie's pappy by a big log laid him low,
To find out what his crazy Frankie had been speaking of;
He found that what his gal had muttered was exactly so.

Frankie, she was spindly limbed with corn silk on her crazy head,
Johnny was a nigger, who never had much fun—
They swung up Johnny on a tree, and filled his swinging hide with lead,
And Frankie yowled hilariously when the thing was done.

Echoing the poem's epigraph, Brown here inserts his only direct quotation from the traditional ballad, but does so in a way that negates the line's usual sentimental associations. In the ballad, this line captures much of the tragedy inherent in the folk narrative, that is, Frankie really does love Johnny, notwithstanding the fact that she takes revenge on him for his infidelity with Nellie Bly. In Brown's poem, by contrast, this couplet assumes a decidedly sinister tone. As established at the outset of the poem, Frankie's actions appear to stem not from a broken heart, as in most "Frankie and Johnny" ballads, but rather from a sadistically twisted soul. Specifically, her soul has been warped by the corrupting influence of patriarchal, white supremacist violence. Frankie's father abuses her, seemingly, out of an admixture of his licentious "cracker's thirst" and his resentment of the ways that his daughter falls short of the southern belle ideal in her undernourished body and dysfunctional mind. Consequently, Frankie seems morally, and perhaps mentally, incapable of true affection.

For all these reasons, the prospect of cross-racial romance within the context of the Jim Crow South seems a fool's errand, at least in the poet's rendering. As Sanders puts it, "Frankie's particular form of dementia, manifested in masochism, ultimately serves as metaphor for the white obsession with violence and revenge."[45] In this treatment, Brown critically revises not only the "Frankie and Johnny" ballad, but also the fiction of authors such as Thomas Dixon. Dixon represents the ex-slave Gus as obsessed with the forcible sexual conquest of the white southern belle Marion Cameron, for which he meets a "justified" demise at the hands of the "heroic" Ku Klux Klan, led by Marion's brother, Great Dragon Ben Cameron. Brown overturns this formula by portraying the white female, Frankie, as the agent of African American Johnny's sexual seduction and death. In Brown's telling, Frankie, her father, and the lynch mob are the agents of savage, animalistic violence in a story that offers neither heroic action nor redemption.

Casting a white woman as a temptress and the malevolent agent of a black man's violent demise was a relatively common tack for politically engaged creative artists from the 1920s through the 1940s, and even beyond that in key texts of the Black Arts Movement such as Amiri Baraka's *Dutchman* (1964). For instance, the artist John Wilson's 1943 lithograph *Deliver Us from Evil* includes a tableau of a lynching party headed by a man in a suit and a police officer, apparently on behalf of a young white woman who stands between them with downcast eyes while smiling in a mirthful, self-satisfied manner (figure 6.2).[46] More famous is Gwendolyn Brooks's scathing depiction of a young black man named Sammy who pays "with [his] hide and heart" for his consuming desire for a "taste of pink and white honey," in "The Ballad of Pearl May Lee" from the poet's 1945 collection *A Street in Bronzeville*. The white "vixen," Pearl May Lee, mocks her conquest, "You got my body tonight, nigger boy. / I'll get your body tomorrow."[47]

An even closer parallel to Brown's poem is *Amber Satyr* (1932), by the white novelist Roy Flannagan, which was published the same year as *Southern Road*. Brown summarized Flannagan's plot succinctly as "a lynching that follows a white woman's relentless and frenzied pursuit of her hired man, a good-looking Negro."[48] Specifically, Sarah Sprouse is from a family widely regarded by the community as "white trash," and following her husband's demise from rheumatism, she recklessly pursues the mixed-race Luther Harris through a series of bold flirtations and impassioned letters. Unlike Brown's Johnny, Luther resists this powerful temptation, but nonetheless the lustful brothers of Sarah's late husband, Willis and Benjo Sprouse, are driven mad with envy and kill Luther when they discover Sarah's taboo, cross-racial overtures.[49] Notably, in each of these examples white men perpetrate the tangible acts of

FIGURE 6.2. John Wilson, *Deliver Us From Evil*, 1943. © Estate of John Wilson/ Licensed by VAGA, New York, NY.

violence, but it is a white female temptress who seems scapegoated, given the lion's share of blame.

Brown's subsequent autobiographical sketch "Georgia Nymphs" captures a nearly parallel experience in which an accidental encounter with a group of flirtatious young white women at a swimming hole outside an Alabama town causes Brown and his friend, Ed, to immediately, instinctively flee. But the young women seem to relish extending their torment of the poet by insisting on changing into their clothes in the house of Brown's host, while he and Ed wait nervously outside: "The largest, probably the oldest of the five, came to the back screen door. She was a strapping buxom blonde, in a scanty pair of trunks and a heavily packed brassiere. She looked us over coolly and then put on her act: a home talent variant of a Mae West grind, gentle bump and all. She tossed her head and rolled away with a curt laugh." Mirroring the blend of terror and titillation found in fictional sketches such as the swimming hole encounter in Richard Wright's "Big Boy Leaves Home" (1938), this episode leaves Brown and his friend menaced and in fear of violent retribution from the town's white men until they are able to escape on a bus bound for Atlanta that night.[50]

An essay entitled "Take Your Coat Off, Gene!" from the same posthumously published manuscript, *A Negro Looks at the South*, describes a stump speech by Georgia's segregationist governor Eugene Talmadge from Brown's position on the periphery of an unnamed town square amid a group of African American spectators. He recounts, "I was stared at also by the village belles, who gave me the once-over coolly. One strutted back and forth, looking over her shoulder. 'Lynch-bait,' muttered one of my new friends."[51] Brown's use of "coolly" in both sketches makes clear the degree of malevolent calculation he perceived in such cross-race flirtations. Thus, the figure of the white southern woman as femme fatale in "Frankie and Johnny" was not anomalous in the poet's broader corpus of writings.

Brown adds complexity to his portrait of Frankie when he informs the reader of Frankie's intellectual disability and her own victimization at the hands of her father. Even if one interprets Frankie's cruelty as a product of dissolute parenting, however, Brown leaves little room for readers' sympathy toward her. While her hands may not literally be stained with Johnny's blood, she remains far from blameless in the poet's eyes. By telling her father of her sexual liaisons with Johnny, Frankie presumably knows that she is sealing his death, as surely as if she lynched him with her own hands. As with the knife employed "to cut long angleworms in half" during her childhood, she uses her father and a mob of white men as a weapon to implement her own sadistic impulses.

There is little gainsaying the viciousness of the poem's final image: as Johnny is lynched, "Frankie yowled hilariously when the thing was done." Similar portrayals of the animalistic fury of white lynch mobs characterized Depression-era works such as "Flag Salute" (1934), by the African American schoolteacher Esther Popel, with its imagery of "the brutish, raucous howls / Of men, and boys, and women with their babes, / Brought out to see the bloody spectacle / Of murder in the style of '33!"[52] In a similar vein, the Jewish dancer Edith Segal choreographed an antilynching piece entitled *Southern Holiday* (1933) for the Red Dancers, in which she instructed performers to "dance with the torso low and energized, because it best emphasizes the animal-like nature of the lynchers."[53] As in these works, Brown's reversal shows lynchers to be dehumanized by their attempted dehumanization of African American victims. The fact that Frankie seems to gain pleasure from both receiving and inflicting pain—up to and including fatal levels of brutality on others—limits readers' pity for her circumstances.

In contrast to the traditional ballad, which often leaves room for listeners to feel some measure of sympathy for both Frankie and Johnny, Brown's radically retooled adaptation trains readers' sympathy solely on Johnny's status as victim. Further, whereas Gwendolyn Brooks as narrator caustically casts at least some element of blame on her black male protagonist, Sammy, for the foolhardiness and racial disloyalty of recklessly pursuing the sexual conquest of a white woman (for example, in the refrain "You had it coming surely"), Brown forgoes taking such an intensely disparaging tone toward his male protagonist. Even if Brown's Johnny appears imprudent for yielding to the temptation of sex with Frankie, his violent fate seems grotesquely out of proportion to such a misstep in judgment. Whether or not the reader deems the abused "halfwit" Frankie fully culpable for Johnny's death, in the same manner as her father and the lynch mob, in Brown's estimation she has been wrought into an instrument of the oppressively patriarchal and white supremacist ideology at the heart of Jim Crow society. Put another way, Brown seems to invoke Frankie's mental disability less as an affliction calling for sympathy than as a symbol of the intellectual backwardness of white Southern culture. Ironically, in this regard, Brown resembles the eugenicists of his day, who justified widespread programs of institutionalization and sterilization by characterizing the mentally disabled as atavistic throwbacks to an earlier stage of human civilization and as perversely hypersexual. Perhaps needless to say, the poet vigorously rejected these same eugenicists' nearly identical derogatory claims about African Americans.[54]

The master trope of Brown's debut volume is the road, which, says Sanders, "serves as a practical means of mobility, a means of escaping the particular confinements of Southern life," and, in a broader sense, "the movement from restrictive circumstance to greater possibility." Yet Johnny is afforded no access to the road's redemptive possibilities. Instead, "objectified, the black victim remains silent as he is literally consumed by a cultural pathology stronger than his individual ability to resist it."[55] This is not characteristic of Brown's most frequently discussed protagonists, such as Calvin "Big Boy" Davis and Mrs. Bibby, who endure and move on (psychologically, even if not geographically in Bibby's case) in the face of oppressive circumstances. Likewise, in "Strong Men," arguably Brown's most famous poem, the trajectory charted for African American (men)folk writ large is one of persistent progress stubbornly claimed in the face of life's numerous obstacles: "The strong men keep a-comin' on / The strong men git stronger."[56] Johnny's relative lack of agency might at first appear to be a curious contrast in this light. After all, Brown was enamored of the heroic impulse in American balladry. In his "Frankie and Johnny" adaptation, though, Brown forgoes the heroic strain of many folk ballads in favor of a harrowing indictment of white cruelty under Jim Crow.

In this regard, "Frankie and Johnny" spotlights a collision in Brown's literary project between the narrative impulse to show heroic underdogs triumphing over adverse forces, and the stark, uncompromising reality of the harsh consequences facing those African Americans who defied Jim Crow's racial and sexual orthodoxies.

Just as importantly, Brown would have had little evidence to convince him of the possibility of a successful counterinsurgency against Jim Crow at the time of *Southern Road*'s publication in 1932. If Brown's Johnny seems an inert victim in the face of the white mob's fatal onslaught, it bears keeping in mind that much of the active resistance mobilized among sharecroppers in rural southern communities by the Southern Tenant Farmers' Union did not take shape until 1934, two years after the publication of Brown's *Southern Road*.[57] Once such collective action emerged, Brown's poetry shifted accordingly. Brown's second poetry manuscript, *No Hiding Place*, reflects the surge of militancy among political organizers and creative artists in opposition to racial and class oppression during the years immediately following the appearance of *Southern Road*. Even in the numerous instances when the superior force of the "Cotton South" ultimately overmatches rebellion by black folk communities, *No Hiding Place* frequently grants its protagonists the heroic aura intrinsic to defiance of authority. As a case in point, the titular character of "Old Lem" recognizes the overwhelming odds posed by Jim Crow society:

They got the judges
They got the lawyers
They got the jury-rolls
They got the law
They don't come by ones
They got the sheriffs
They got the deputies
They don't come by twos
They got the shotguns
They got the rope
We git the justice
In the end
And they come by tens.

In contrast with Johnny from *Southern Road*, Lem narrates an incident in which "a buddy / Six foot of man / Muscled up perfect / Game to the heart" talks back to white authority figures at the local commissary and then refuses their warning to leave the county; instead, he stands boldly against the resulting mob, even though he knows that doing so will mean his death.[58] Within Brown's moral universe, the character granted heroism meets his end for speaking assertively "man to man," whereas the character who yields to the "weakness" of sexual dalliance with a white woman does not exit the scene on his own terms or in a way that readers might find admirable.

All that said, one ought not overdraw the contrasts between Brown's first two poetry volumes. Reexamined carefully, Sanders's assessment of Brown's second manuscript—that it is "much darker in mood, more severe in its condemnation" than the earlier collection—seems an apt description of the tone of poems like "Frankie and Johnny" in the debut volume.[59] In fact, within the pages of *Southern Road*, Brown's "Frankie and Johnny" falls between "Johnny Thomas" and "Sam Smiley," two poems that also conclude with the lynching of black men. "Johnny Thomas" describes the hard-luck story of a young man abused, in turn, by a teacher, his father, a "fancy woman," a sheriff, and a prison guard. Caught stealing in an ill-advised attempt to gain money and win back his avaricious love interest, Johnny meets his demise on the chain gang:

Guard lashed Johnny
An awful lick,
Johnny split his head
Wid a muddy pick.

Dey haltered Johnny Thomas
Like a cussed mule,
Dey hung Johnny Thomas
For a consarned fool.

Dropped him in de hole
Threw de slack lime on,
Oughta had mo' sense
Dan to evah git born.[60]

A repeated line in the poem seems to jab at Johnny by describing him as "a consarned fool," but the closing couplet suggests that his principal "foolishness" was simply the misfortune to be born a black man in the South. In this sense, the refrain seems akin to the treatment of racial oppression in folk music, as in the stock blues line: "Ain't but one thing, you know, this black man done wrong / Stayed in Mississippi a day too long."

Brown's "Sam Smiley" limns the portrait of a black veteran returning from the battlefields of World War I, dancing aboard ship in anticipation of reuniting with "the girl who beat all girls in France." Tragically, upon returning to the "shanties" of his home community, he discovers that his lover was raped and impregnated by a white man, which led her to take her own life and that of her unborn child. Emboldened and trained in violence from his time at war, Sam kills the culprit. Finally, the interracial cycle of violence concludes as a mob seeks out and lynches the protagonist.

> *The oaken leaves drowsed prettily,*
> *The moon shone down benignly there;*
> *And big Sam Smiley, King Buckdancer,*
> *Buckdanced on the midnight air.*[61]

Here, Brown ruptures the natural landscape's beauty with a grotesque lynching, but as in "Frankie and Johnny" his description refrains from graphically detailing the lynching itself, in the interest of achieving a more powerful literary effect. In contrast with the male protagonist of "Frankie and Johnny," though, Sam Smiley receives heroic attributes via his background as a war hero and in his striking back in vengeance at the man who violated his wife. Especially when paired sequentially with "Frankie and Johnny," Brown's poetry issues a devastating indictment of a social system that enacts such drastic disparities in punishment for interracial sex by white men and black men.[62]

The question remains why Brown might have desired to rework the "Frankie and Johnny" ballad as part of his critique of racial violence. Elsewhere in *Southern Road*, Brown goes to considerable lengths to illustrate the fact that African American culture possessed an internal richness and vitality above and beyond its engagement with racial oppression at the hands of whites, a key premise that he held in common with Zora Neale Hurston. At the same time, however, Brown situates his portraits of African American folk life—both the agonizing tragedies of flood survivors in "Children of the Mississippi" and the trickster-style tall tales of the Slim Greer poems—within contexts that are bounded and affected in multifold ways by the racist culture of Jim Crow society.

Certainly, black vernacular music traditions contained references to interracial violence, both coded and overt. As Adam Gussow documents in his study of the blues tradition, this included numerous oblique references to the "disciplinary violence" that whites inflict on African Americans, as in Little Brother Montgomery's "The First Time I Met You" (1936), and, less commonly, to instances of African American "retributive violence" against acts of white domination, as in Mamie Smith's "Crazy Blues" (1920).[63] Yet a reader would not be likely to mistake Brown's "Frankie and Johnny" for one of its vernacular counterparts. Beyond differences in meter and diction, Brown's style of social critique seldom surfaces in the same pointed, sustained, and systematic way within the musical traditions from which the poet drew so much inspiration. As a poet concerned with both aesthetic craft and social critique, perhaps Brown felt that the portrait of a fatal lover's quarrel within an African American community served the latter purpose less ably than the Jim Crow tragedy he creatively refashioned from the "Frankie and Johnny" source material.

Dramatically as Brown's "Frankie and Johnny" departs from standard versions of the ballad, the poet would likely have contested the notion that his reinvention was divorced from the spirit of folk expression. In "The Blues as Folk Poetry," Brown insisted: "It is a popular misconception that the Blues are merely songs that ease a woman's longing for her rambling man. . . . The cloudiest aspects of the sunny South get their due share of lines. There are 'Chain Gang Blues,' 'Prison House Blues,' 'Ball and Chain Blues.' The cell is sometimes lighted up as in 'He's in the Jailhouse Now' comic variations, but is just as often darkened." Elsewhere in the same essay, Brown noted the presence of songs about topics such as natural disasters, the boll weevil, and migration from the South as a form of escape. His description of the blues could just as easily describe his own poetry in works such as "Frankie and Johnny": "There is a terseness, an inevitability of the images dealing with suffering. Irony, stoicism, and bitterness are deeply but not lingeringly expressed."[64] Even in African American folk humor, Brown noted the presence of an "edge in numerous jokes about sharecropping and the law. Landlords who 'figure with a crooked pencil' are derided," and anecdotes "dealing with sadistic sheriffs and mobs are gruesome; yet they produce laughter, a sort of laughter out of hell."[65]

More to the point, Brown was well aware that increased public recognition of folk expression's dimensions of social criticism was crucial to the project of reshaping societal perceptions of the African American creators of that folklore. He argued in a 1950 essay, "The Negro creators of an important segment of American folklore should no longer be subjected to the condescension of the 'oh so quaint,' 'so folksy,' school. Looking on Negro lore as exotic *curiosa* becomes almost impossible if the body of available material is thoughtfully considered."[66] As noted earlier, Brown also insisted on the malleability of folk expression to meet changing social circumstances and community needs. And just as he remarked on "the folk habit of lifting what they want and using it how they will," Brown took the framework of the traditional ballad and recast its characters and milieu to forge a radically new "Frankie and Johnny."[67]

In weaving an antilynching critique into his adaptation of "Frankie and Johnny," Brown joined a sizable contingent of like-minded social realist contemporaries in poetry, fiction, drama, dance, and the visual arts. In poetry, Langston Hughes demonstrated one strategy common among poets and visual artists alike by analogizing lynching victims to Christ on the cross. In "Christ in Alabama," Hughes opines, "Christ is a nigger, / Beaten and black." Describing this figure as the product of a forced liaison between the "Mammy of the South" and a "White Master above," the poem concludes:

> Most holy bastard
> Of the bleeding mouth,
> Nigger Christ
> On the cross
> Of the South.[68]

This poem originally appeared in the December 1, 1931, issue of *Contempo*, which was devoted primarily to the Scottsboro Boys case, in which two white women accused nine young black men of raping them while stowing away on a train in Alabama. Thus situated, the poem invited readers to interpret the fate seemingly awaiting the Scottsboro Boys as a comparable kind of "legal lynching" and crucifixion, and raised the question of how ostensible Christians could perform such acts of blatant injustice.[69] Brown's "Frankie and Johnny" eschews the Christian symbolism of Hughes's poem, but is no less concerned with indicting racial violence. In much the way that Hughes urges his audience to reconsider the familiar biblical story of the crucifixion through the lens of baseless persecutions in the contemporary moment, Brown takes a popular-culture text that most readers will think they know—the "Frankie and Johnny" ballad—and rearticulates it to confront them with a damning social injustice.

From a strikingly different perspective, Richard Wright moves the narrator (and hence readers) from observer to victim of a lynching in his poem "Between the World and Me" (1935). In characteristic Wright fashion, his account pulls no punches:

> And then they had me, stripped me, battering my teeth into my throat till I
>   swallowed my own blood.
> My voice was drowned in the roar of their voices, and my black wet body slipped
>   and rolled in their hands as they bound me to the sapling.
> And my skin clung to the bubbling hot tar, falling from me in limp patches.
> And the down and quills of the white feathers sank into my flesh, and I moaned
>   in agony.
> Then my blood was cooled mercifully, cooled by a baptism of gasoline.
> And in a blaze of red I leaped to the sky as pain rose like water, boiling my
>   limbs.[70]

To the extent possible through the printed word, Wright wants his readers to experience the visceral trauma of lynching. Brown, on the other hand, chooses to bypass this level of excruciating detail in "Frankie and Johnny." Although Brown's restraint sets his work apart from Wright's, this distinction was one of strategy rather than of differing levels of commitment to social change. Looking back on his early career in a 1973 interview with Steven Jones and Steven Henderson, Brown recalled of his poetry: "I wanted it to be impassioned; that is, I wanted to have a feeling there that was communicated to the reader. I didn't want to yell; I wanted to make him yell, but I wanted to use a kind of language that would make him yell. . . . I wanted to communicate, and I found a language that was pithy, economical, metaphoric, imaginative, and . . . capable of expressing all ranges of human emotions."[71]

Aesthetic differences aside, Brown, like Wright, maintained close ties to leftist political organizations throughout the 1930s: he published poems in organs affiliated with the Communist Party USA, including *New Masses* and *New Challenge*, as well as in the labor-oriented anthology *Get Organized: Stories and Poems of Trade Union People* (1939); he spoke at multiple sessions of the American Writers' Congress, including acting as chair for a "folk session" in 1939; he presented a reading to the Labor Poets of America in New York City; and he boldly confronted anticommunist attacks on the Federal Writers' Project from the Dies committee and its allies.[72]

In the visual arts, Brown's leftist contemporaries also made frequent reference to lynching in their work. Perhaps most notably, two ambitious exhibitions focused on the antilynching cause were staged in New York City in 1935: *An Art Commentary on Lynching*, organized by Walter White of the NAACP and hosted by the Arthur Newton Galleries in midtown, and *The Struggle for Negro Rights*, cosponsored by the communist-affiliated John Reed Clubs, the International Labor Defense, and Louise Thompson's Vanguard collective, and staged at the American Contemporary Art Gallery in Greenwich Village.[73] Many of the artworks featured in these exhibitions illustrated the suffering of male lynching victims in grim, explicit detail. (Directly rendered victims of lynchings in these two shows were exclusively male, notwithstanding the occasional lynchings of black women, such as Mary Turner.)[74] Like Wright's poem "Between the World and Me," George Bellows's lithograph *The Law Is Too Slow* (1923), from the NAACP show, depicts a muscular victim being burnt alive, his arms chained behind his back around a stake, while a member of the surrounding mob of masked men leans forward to stoke the flames with a long pole (figure 6.3). Responding to real-life instances of such practices, Bellows's choice to render the ritual burning of the lynching victim seems intended to evoke the fires of hell and the barbarism of the lynching perpetrators. As

FIGURE 6.3. George Bellows, *The Law Is Too Slow*, 1923. Courtesy of the Metropolitan Museum of Art, New York, NY.

Dora Apel adds, "Though the image is somewhat ambiguous, blood seems to pour out between his legs, alluding to castration, as he throws back his head in pain."[75] A handful of works in these exhibitions went even further in their graphic representations of lynching violence.

Brown's poem, by contrast, devotes only a single line to the lynching act: "They swung Johnny on a tree, and filled his swinging hide with lead." While the lexical choice of "hide" suggests Johnny's bestialization in the eyes of the mob—in effect, reducing him to the status of Frankie's other animal victims— Brown does not linger on Johnny's mutilated corpse. Even here, though the

poet grants Johnny none of the defiance frequently displayed by his protagonists in the face of oppression, Brown seems at pains not to dwell overlong on
black victimization. Rather, this poem is ultimately more a character study of
the perpetrators of racial violence: Frankie, her father, and the accompanying
mob. In this regard, it is worth noting the art historian Margaret Rose Vendryes's critique of Bellows's print for rendering the African American man "as
not only a victim but a restrained virile beast . . . not unlike portrayals of the
devil in Western art."[76] Brown may well have feared enacting a comparable
dehumanization of the victim, in effect allowing white readers to dwell on
the violated black body in a manner loosely analogous to the practice of lynch
mob members claiming victims' body parts as gruesome souvenirs.[77]

A visual work more resonant with Brown's "Frankie and Johnny" is
George Biddle's lithograph *Alabama Code—"Our Girls Don't Sleep with Niggers"* (1933), from the *Struggle for Negro Rights* exhibition, which features a
white girl of indeterminate age seated on the lap of a balding white man who
sports a suit and tie (figure 6.4). The work does not render racial violence directly, but it was inspired by the Scottsboro Boys trials, and Biddle intended
the young girl to represent Victoria Price, one of the accusers in the case.

FIGURE 6.4. George Biddle,
*Alabama Code—"Our Girls
Don't Sleep with Niggers,"*
1933. Courtesy of the
Estate of George Biddle/
D. Wigmore Fine Art, Inc.,
New York, NY.

More broadly, the title's reference to the taboos against interracial sex in the Jim Crow South calls to mind the frequent use of accusations of sexual aggression by black men to rationalize acts of lynching; in its crudeness, the artist intended the title to evoke "that type of bigotted [sic], retrogressive, and sadistic . . . mentality in the South that makes such a racial attitude possible."[78] Like Brown's Frankie, the young woman in Biddle's lithograph appears to be both victim and victimizer. According to the art historian Frances Pohl, "Biddle, while impugning the moral character of the white Alabama girl, also suggests that she herself was being manipulated and used (both politically and sexually) by the white men who controlled the South." More subtly, noting that the girl pinches the man's knee while he fondles her breast, Dora Apel glosses this scene as "an apparent mutual seduction between the girl and the lecherous old man."[79] The suit and tie of Biddle's male figure suggests that sexual wantonness is not limited to the working-class "crackers" of Brown's verse, but the lithograph and poem still have much in common. In particular, both Biddle and Brown traffic in their own stereotypes of southern moral depravity and sexual license, albeit for reasons connected with social justice concerns. Namely, both creative artists recognize the necessity of dispelling the romantic mythology of kindly southern patriarchs and virtuous southern belles in order to expose the perversity of the Jim Crow social order and the complicity of white women in ritual violence against black men. In so doing, Biddle and Brown hoped to substantially change the national discourse on lynching.

Beyond battling for the hearts and minds of viewers on the issue of racial justice broadly, the two antilynching art exhibitions of 1935 sought concrete results. Political organizations and creative artists were united in seeking the passage of federal antilynching legislation. Specifically, the Costigan-Wagner bill of the mid-1930s would have instituted federal penalties for those committing lynching and for state government officials who failed to enforce the law. In the end, southern congressional obstructionism prevented the bill from passing, and Franklin Roosevelt never openly endorsed it, but the push for such legislation nonetheless served as a crucial rallying point for antiracist activism during the Depression decade as both political and artistic activists labored to keep the continuing crisis of racial violence in the public eye.[80] For his part, Brown was in dialogue with the NAACP's Walter White, one of the principal supporters of the Costigan-Wagner bill, during White's lobbying visits to the nation's capital.[81] To avoid descending into political agitprop, Brown's poetry does not include documentary evidence or statistical data of the sort found in White's *Rope and Faggot: A Biography of Judge Lynch* (1929), a book based on the light-skinned author's daring incognito (by passing for white) investigations of southern lynchings and race riots of the 1920s; none-theless, Brown's poem offers a clear moral injunction that is in keeping with the spirit of White's work. Addressing a gathering of the radical National Negro Congress in Philadelphia in 1937, Brown declared: "Those artists who are struggling to portray a changing world and, in their own way, to speed that change—are having no easy time. The misery, and tragedy that they must in-clude in their portrait of the real America, are unwelcome to the many readers who want as slick a reality as the paper of the magazine they read. . . . But the Negro artist who will be worth his salt must join with those who are recording a world of injustice and exploitation, a world that must be changed."[82] Like his social realist peers, Brown deployed artistic representations of racial vio-lence in poems such as "Frankie and Johnny" both to advocate for the con-crete measure of a federal antilynching bill and to dramatize the disparity be-tween the nation's lofty democratic ideals and its decidedly antidemocratic practices toward African Americans.

To the extent that Brown draws on and reshapes folk expression in service of a radical political critique, his poetry anticipates, and is roughly comparable to, the revisionary practice of his contemporary Woody Guthrie. In addi-tion to interpreting scores of folk music standards and crafting original songs, Guthrie occasionally penned new lyrics for familiar folk songs and hymns, as when he set the words of "This Land Is Your Land" to the melody of the Carter Family's "When the World's on Fire," itself an adaptation of an older Baptist hymn titled "Oh My Lovin' Brother."[83] Likewise, Huddie Ledbetter, much admired by Brown, adapted an up-tempo sukey jump song for the World War II context by replacing lines such as "I'm gonna tear your playhouse down" with "We're Gonna Tear Hitler Down."[84] In the 1910s, the activist Joe Hill had employed a similar practice for the Industrial Workers of the World's labor-organizing campaigns—for example, his song "The Preacher and the Slave" retools the Salvation Army hymn "In the Sweet Bye and Bye" into a cri-tique of organized religion's otherworldly focus. Several of Hill's songs were then published for wider audiences in the IWW's *Little Red Song Book*. As the scholar Cary Nelson explains, this practice had at its heart a "subversive aim: to empty out the conservative, sentimental, or patriotic values of the existing songs while replacing them with radical impulses."[85]

The "Frankie and Johnny" ballad tradition is neither patriotic nor conserva-tive, but many incarnations of the ballad are given over to romantic sentiment of a sort that likely did not mesh well with Brown's proclivity for stoicism. Moreover, the red-light setting and black-on-black violence of the traditional ballad might, for Brown, have smacked too much of the knife fights and other violence portrayed for comic effect in numerous musical numbers and illustrations stemming from the early twentieth-century "coon song" phenomenon and blackface minstrelsy.

In addition, an assertive female protagonist of the sort featured in most variants of the "Frankie and Johnny" ballad might not have found a home in Brown's masculinist ethos. Brown was well aware of the presence of black female ballad characters who demonstrated meaningful agency: besides anthologizing a standard version of "Frankie and Johnny" in *The Negro Caravan*, Brown elsewhere singled out as an admirable folk heroine Polly Ann from the John Henry tradition, who in some variants, when her man falls ill, steps in and hammers steel "like a natural man."[86] But in his own poetry, Brown typically casts female heroism as the stoic endurance of hardship rather than as aggression of the sort found in Frankie's shooting of Johnny in ballad lore: to wit, Mandy Jane's stealthy theft of food from the kitchen of her white employers in "Ruminations of Luke Johnson" rather than the brash male defiance of expected black deference toward white authority at the heart of "Old Lem."

Like Guthrie and Hill, Brown employed his verse in "Frankie and Johnny" as a means of pouring new, politicized wine into the bottles of familiar folk standards. In so doing, Brown hoped to spark recognition among the folk themselves and to transform the general reader's understanding of folk lives, especially those of African Americans in the rural South. Specifically, notes Sanders, "it is Brown's familiarity with rural folk form and his reproduction of rural folk voices that allow him to claim an agency and modernity on the part of poor agrarian blacks heretofore stigmatized as 'premodern.'"[87] As throughout so much of Brown's career as a poet, teacher, and literary critic, his aim in "Frankie and Johnny" was to render racial caricatures obsolete by forging new portraits suffused with critical realism and addressed to contemporary social justice concerns.

AFRICAN AMERICAN WOMEN'S VOICES
AND THE TIGHTROPE OF RESPECTABILITY

GIVEN THE ROOTS of the ballad "Frankie and Johnny" in the exploits of an African American female protagonist, one of the undeniably curious features of this study is its lack of focus on the work of black female creative artists of the 1930s. To be sure, blueswomen sang of brash exploits aplenty, including accounts of violent revenge on unfaithful male lovers, such as Ida Cox's "How Can I Miss You When I've Got Dead Aim?" (1925) and Bessie Smith's "Send Me to the 'Lectric Chair" (1927).[1] In a similar vein, Margaret Walker crafted folklore-flavored poetry such as her tribute to Kissie Lee, who, like Thomas Hart Benton's Frankie, deals with a man who "done her dirt long time ago" by gunning him down in a saloon: "And he was making for the outside door / When Kissie shot him to the floor."[2] However, none of the period's most likely candidates seem to have pursued a "Frankie and Johnny"–themed project outside of the realm of music, despite the song's widespread appearances in film, drama, dance, poetry, and the visual arts of the Depression decade.

At first blush, the outlaw antics and protofeminist sensibilities of the ballad's protagonist might seem resonant with the work of an author such as Zora Neale Hurston. For instance, Hurston recounted in *Mules and Men* (1935) an episode in which she invented a cover story for herself as a bootlegger on the run from the law in an effort to win over the residents of a Florida sawmill camp, since members of that community initially regarded her with suspicion as an outsider.[3] Moreover, in works of both folklore and fiction, Hurston chronicled the vibrantly expressive culture of southern juke joints and work gangs even when such material shaded toward the bawdy and raucous, relative to bourgeois standards of the day. Yet Hurston did not avail herself of "Frankie and Johnny" in any of her extant novels, plays, or scholarly books and essays. One might reasonably ask why not. Given Hurston's self-framing as a purveyor of authentic African American folk culture, it seems likely that the very popularity of the ballad and its transcendence of strict racial bounds may have limited its appeal for her. After all, Hurston repeatedly contrasted her own presentations of folk material with what she saw as the commercialized and exoticized offerings of Harlem cabarets and vaudeville theater—and "Frankie and Johnny" was certainly among the most popular songs in such settings.[4]

In the case of Katherine Dunham, a contemporary who blended ethnographic research and creative artistry much like Hurston, the reasons for the absence of a "Frankie and Johnny" work seem clear. Formally trained in ballet and modern dance, and with a degree in social anthropology from the University of Chicago (with a thesis on Haitian dance), Dunham became a colleague of Ruth Page at the Chicago branch of the Federal Dance Project in 1937. In keeping with the practice of many of the New Deal cultural organizations, though, Dunham was assigned to head a separate Negro Unit of the FDP. In this context, Dunham drew on her recent ethnographic research in Martinique as the basis for her FDP debut, *L'Ag'Ya* (1938), which blended elements of the island's folk dance traditions with ballet.[5] Dunham sustained these dual interests in choreography and ethnography throughout the remainder of her illustrious career, so it is not surprising that by 1944 Dunham was actively contemplating "Frankie and Johnny" as the basis for a new work. By chance, though, Ruth Page and Bentley Stone were, at that same time, planning a revival of their own 1938 *Frankie and Johnny* ballet (this time with Ruthanna Boris and Frederick Franklin in the title roles), and both Page and her husband-agent, Thomas Fisher, feared the diluted attention that might result from a simultaneous dance production on the same theme. Whether because of Fisher's conversation with Dunham about these concerns or because of the demands of other projects on her attention, her "Frankie and Johnny" project never materialized.[6]

In the mid-1940s, a talented young painter named Rose Piper executed a series of paintings based on vernacular African American music of the South, drawing on Sterling Brown for advice and encouragement. Incorporating elements of cubist abstraction in a novel fashion, Piper depicted pathos-filled figures amid imagery of trains and impoverished rural landscapes, all of which were hallmarks of the blues and, not incidentally, Brown's poetry. Titles such as *Back Water* (1946) and *Grievin' Hearted* (1947) made direct reference to 1920s blues songs of the same titles, and another painting, *The Death of Bessie Smith* (1947), transformed the famed singer's much-mythologized demise into an iconography of martyrdom.[7] Although Piper was immersed in the expressive culture of rural "low-down folk," her nearly exclusive focus on the blues as a genre meant that a ballad such as "Frankie and Johnny" seems never to have come under consideration for her canvases.

Although historians typically decline to engage in counterfactual speculation of the sort found in the preceding paragraphs, I have paused briefly to ponder the cases of Hurston, Dunham, and Piper to emphasize the range of factors that can lead creative artists toward or away from particular topics. Definitions of authenticity—whether structured by perceived degrees of commodification, racial specificity (or lack thereof), or a fixation on particular genres—often play a role in this regard, as can matters of timing, expedience, and professional conflict. Beyond such factors, the "politics of respectability" loomed large over early twentieth-century African American cultural production. As the scholar Evelyn Brooks Higginbotham succinctly explains, late nineteenth- and early twentieth-century African American intellectuals generally fashioned the politics of racial uplift in terms that called for African American public figures to be exemplars of dignity and rigorous Victorian morality: "Black leaders argued that 'proper' and 'respectable' behavior proved blacks worthy of equal civil and political rights. Conversely, nonconformity was equated with deviance and pathology and was often cited as a cause of racial inequality and injustice." Higginbotham observes that this logic posed particular consequences for folk culture: "The politics of 'respectability' disavowed, in often repressive ways, much of the expressive culture of the 'folk,' for example, sexual behavior, dress style, leisure activity, music, speech patterns, and religious worship patterns."[8]

This framework continued to exert a strong influence on African American culture during the New Negro Renaissance, especially since racial uplift organizations like the NAACP and the Urban League were such important patrons of the creative arts. Essays, editorials, and reviews from African American newspapers and journals such as the *Crisis* and *Opportunity* regularly called on creative artists to be a "credit to the race" and to displace racial stereotypes with redemptive representations. Creative artists who eschewed such an approach risked weighty rebuke from uplift-minded African Americans.[9] Even an author of the stature of the young Langston Hughes found that his second poetry volume, *Fine Clothes to the Jew* (1926), was harangued by African American critics because of his overly warm embrace of the "low-down folks," blues forms, sexuality, and cabaret settings. A reviewer for the *Philadelphia Tribune* lamented that the poet's "obsession for the more degenerate elements" of African American life resulted in a volume that was "a study in the perversions of the Negro."[10] These imperatives were imposed even more rigorously on female African American artists: for one high-profile example, witness the considerable clamor raised in response to Josephine Baker's exotically themed dance performances at the Plantation Club in New York City and even overseas at Paris's Folies Bergère.[11]

From this vantage, the fact that, whether spun as comedy or tragedy, "Frankie and Johnny" portrays a relationship between a black man and a black woman that culminates in trauma and violence matters greatly. Even more, the song and its adaptations typically included overt references to vice and infidelity. "Frankie and Johnny" was, as one folklorist put it, "a capital example of the ballad of low life."[12] Hence, as discussed in chapter 6, it is telling that the poet Sterling Brown was at pains to radically revise the racial dynamics and geography of the ballad tradition in his literary adaptation. The range of responses among African American women to such constraints can be suggested by a brief consideration of two women's relationships to "Frankie and Johnny" during the 1930s: the singer and theatrical performer Ethel Waters's recording of the song for Bluebird in 1938, which challenged the politics of respectability without overstepping such bounds far enough to risk censure; and Frankie Baker's unsuccessful attempts to wrest control of her identity and reputation from what she saw as the song's ignoble imagery, through two lawsuits against film adaptations of the ballad that bore her name. By these means, Baker strove to claim for herself some measure of the respectability that Waters daringly flaunted through her performances of the song.

For those familiar with Ethel Waters primarily through her matronly roles in films such as *Cabin in the Sky* (1943), *Pinky* (1949), and *The Member of the Wedding* (1952), it may come as a surprise that her early career traded substantially in the erotic. As recounted in her autobiography, *His Eye is on the Sparrow* (1951), Waters's upbringing in Chester, Pennsylvania, was a rough one. She grew up in a working-class environment that, like the fictionalized world of "Frankie and Johnny," was rife with prostitution and other forms of vice. Following an abusive, short-lived marriage at the age of thirteen, Waters established economic independence while still a teen through a career on the vaudeville stage. In this context, she became known as "Sweet Mama Stringbean" because of her lithe physique, and she forged her early reputation as a shimmy dancer—as did a young Mae West in this same era.[13] In another parallel with West, an important part of Waters's early career was predicated on her seductive magnetism. As the African American novelist William Gardner Smith recollected in a profile of Waters for the journal *Phylon*: "She did the hottest shake dance of her, or any other, day. She used to hold her arms far out from her body, to give the freest movement to all parts of her anatomy; she wore tassels on her hips sometimes, and a large buckle on her belt, to accentuate the movements of her body. She could squirm, twist, shake and vibrate in a way which was absolutely uncanny."[14]

When Waters became established as a star of the Theater Owners Booking Association (TOBA) circuit and race records in the 1920s, her flirtation with sexual boundaries continued. Most notable in this regard was her hit song "Shake That Thing" (1925), which became a signature Waters number for the next decade. In this respect, of course, Waters was operating in parallel not only to West, but also to her African American blueswomen peers such as Bessie Smith, with whom Waters performed early in her career.[15] As discussed in chapter 5, early blues songs of the 1920s by artists like Smith trafficked heavily in double entendre. With lyrics like "Why, there's old Uncle Jack, the jellyroll king, / He's got a hump in his back from shakin' that thing," Waters sometimes barely bothered to clothe her sexually charged imagery in metaphors.

But whereas West repeatedly, provocatively, and deliberately overstepped the bounds of "good taste" vis-à-vis sexual innuendo, Waters possessed qualities of mirth and charm that enabled her "to make the most torrid lines and otherwise lascivious movements seem respectable."[16] In the aforementioned profile of Waters, for example, William Gardner Smith followed up his remarks about the performer's tantalizing allure by remarking, "And yet—who ever felt the slightest sense of vulgarity? One had the impression that she could bathe in mud and still remain clean."[17] Commentators at the time and subsequent scholarly evaluations largely agree that this capacity to simultaneously convey transgression and respectability was crucial to Waters's success as a recording artist and onstage in numerous musical revues during the 1920s and 1930s.[18]

Waters's performances of "Frankie and Johnny" expertly negotiated this balancing act (figure 7.1). As chronicled by the biographer Donald Bogle, Waters first performed "Frankie and Johnny," to considerable acclaim, in an otherwise forgettable Billy Rose revue entitled *The Crazy Show* at Casa Mañana in Fort Worth, Texas, in 1938.[19] Later in the same year, she recorded the song for Bluebird. In the Bluebird rendition, Waters focuses primarily on Frankie's enactment of revenge on Johnny. After a standard opening ("Frankie and Johnny were sweethearts / Boy, how they could love"), Waters bypasses the usual search-for-Johnny and conversation-with-a-bartender motifs, instead moving directly to Frankie's happenstance discovery—on her own—through a hotel window of Johnny "lovin' up old Nellie Bly." Three full stanzas then detail Frankie's leap to action: first, buying a "forty-four gun" from "her favorite pawn shop," and then setting out for Nellie's room garbed in a "long red

FIGURE 7.1. Ethel Waters, 1938. Photograph by Carl Van Vechten. Courtesy of the Van Vechten Trust/Yale Collection of American Literature, Beinecke Rare Book Room and Manuscript Library, New Haven, CT.

kimono." The stanza describing her arrival at Nellie's brothel offers an especially fiery depiction of Frankie:

Then back Frankie dashed to that hotel
Started yanking that bell
She said, "Stand back, you madam and floozies,
Or I'll blow each and every one of you straight to hell.
I want my man who's done me wrong!"

Sure enough, paying little heed to Johnny's "panic" and "screaming 'Oh Frankie, don't shoot!'" she follows through with resolve:

Three times she pulled a trigger on a forty-four gun
The gun went root-toot-toot
She'd nailed her man who'd done her wrong

Waters concludes by skipping the more typical treatment of Johnny's funeral and Frankie's grief in favor of the relatively unusual device of showing Frankie facing punishment for her crime. Specifically, Waters describes the protagonist imprisoned in "a dungeon / Way up in a dark, dingy cell / In the southeast corner of a jail / Where the wind seemed like it blew straight from hell," followed by a trip to the gallows. Thus, even though Waters never became identified with "Frankie and Johnny" as thoroughly as did Mae West, she mirrored West in selecting a variant of the song that emphasized Frankie's agency and defiance of prevailing societal expectations of female passivity and restraint.

At least two factors characteristic of Waters's early career, however, temper the rebellious elements of her performance of the song. For one, Waters ends on a note of reverence while Frankie is atop the scaffold:

But the day Frankie mounted the scaffold
She was just as calm as any gal could be
And raising her eyes to heaven she cried
"Lord, I'm coming to thee!
I'm sorry I killed my man who done me wrong."

Conspicuously, in spite of her expression of remorse, Waters's Frankie seems convinced that she is bound for heaven and that she owes her apology to a higher power, not Johnny. With this closing stanza, Waters's "Frankie and Johnny" interweaves notes of Victorian sentimentality and sanctity with the song's earlier moments of impassioned violence and outlaw behavior. Just as this version of Frankie seems cool and composed at the moment of her impending execution, Waters delivers lines such as "I'll blow each and every one of you straight to hell" with a smooth, intimate style that, arguably, has as much in common with the work of a white pop crooner like Ruth Etting or a male blues crooner like Leroy Carr as with the powerful, belting style of blues vocals and moans of Ma Rainey or Bessie Smith.[20] Backing music from a string section enhances the record's sense of polish and refinement. By the early 1940s, Waters's career was shifting focus to stately roles for the silver screen, but as late as 1938 "Frankie and Johnny" provided a vehicle for the star to extend her trademark balance of daring and decorum, putting across a tale of love gone awry on the wrong side of the tracks, in a manner that seemed unthreatening—or, at least, acceptably salacious—to both white and black middle-class audiences.

From a twenty-first-century vantage point, it may seem that Ethel Waters muted her Frankie from staging a full-scale rebellion against social expectations for women, but it bears emphasizing that her interpretation of the song nonetheless defied the considerable pressure on African American women of the day to adopt a demure disposition. The imperative to fashion a "respectable" public persona emerged with special poignancy in the experiences of Frankie Baker during the 1930s and early 1940s. As detailed in the opening chapter, Baker's shooting of Allen Britt in 1899 seems the most likely inspiration for the ballad "Frankie and Johnny" (née "Frankie and Albert"), at least in the song's twentieth-century incarnations. After her acquittal at trial, Baker remained in St. Louis for roughly two years before moving to Omaha, Nebraska, circa 1901; she relocated again in 1915, this time to Portland, Oregon. As Baker explained to the Portland journalist Dudley McClure in the mid-1930s, part of the appeal of the Pacific Northwest had been the prospect of escaping her past, since the ballad had made her notorious in St. Louis and, eventually, in Omaha as well. In Portland, Baker hoped that she might be able to "grow old gracefully . . . without being constantly reminded of the old gun-shooting episode."

Around 1925, after a decade's residence in Portland's North End red-light district (where she was subject to a series of arrests on morals charges), Baker, at nearly fifty years old, sought respectability by leaving prostitution, opening a shoeshine parlor, and moving to a new Portland neighborhood.[21] But she was not destined for a peaceful life. For one, she explained, "Frankie and Johnny" seemed to follow her to each new stage of her life, providing a haunting reminder of the earlier tragedy and stigmatizing her in the eyes of local communities once the connections between her and the song were discovered. She testified that during her time in Omaha, "I'd come out of my house and every chick and child would start singing that song at me. I'd walk down the street, and they'd follow me singing that song." Likewise, in Portland, by the 1930s: "I just couldn't get away from it. . . . It was humiliating and harrying. I just got sick and tired of it. I heard it on the street and I heard it on the phonograph and I heard it on the radio. And then the movie came along with that song in it. That movie [a 1936 film entitled *Frankie and Johnnie* by Republic Pictures] . . . was more than any mortal woman could bear."[22] Further, Baker's ill health had limited her work options by the mid-1930s, even as the ballad bearing her name flourished across diverse media.

Clearly, Baker was well aware of the proliferation of "Frankie and Johnny" in 1930s America. In fact, as the scholar John David notes, "Despite the fact that Frankie ran away from St. Louis to 'escape' her past, her principal hobby was collecting books and articles about 'Frankie and Johnny.' The records were kept hidden in a bureau drawer." In March 1935, with her funds dwindling, Baker filed a lawsuit against Paramount and Mae West, accusing *She Done Him Wrong* of inflicting "public scandal, infamy, shame and disgrace" on the plaintiff.[23] As Baker explained to McClure: "They've been writing about me and making money for years. One fellow made $25,000 on a book about Frankie and Johnny—and here I am sick and almost broke. Now this Mae West makes a picture and sings "Frankie and Johnny" and takes things right out of my life. I'm good and sore. The picture made millions and they got to pay me from now on."[24] The allusion here appears to be to either John Huston's or John Held Jr.'s book, although she vastly overestimates the publication's profitability for the author in either case. So too did Baker's attempt to garner $100,000 in redress from Paramount and West prove overambitious, since the suit never made it to trial.

Nonetheless, Baker persisted, hiring attorneys to file a second legal claim in April 1938, this one against Republic Pictures for its film *Frankie and Johnnie* (1936), which features the white actors Helen Morgan and Chester Morris in the title roles and is set in a St. Louis "sporting house" in 1870 (figure 7.2). The film was shot in 1934, but encountered opposition from the newly strengthened Production Code Administration of Joseph Breen, and, consequently, was shelved for two years before a heavily edited version finally hit theaters in 1936. The theatrical release omitted all explicit references to prostitution, introduced a supporting character to shoot Johnnie instead of Frankie, and even neglected to include "Frankie and Johnny" among the songs performed by Morgan.[25] In her suit against Republic, Baker sought $200,000 in dam-

FIGURE 7.2. Frankie Baker at the time of her lawsuit against Republic Pictures, with (*from left*) Joseph McLemore and Robert Witherspoon (her attorneys), and Charles Marshall, Mariah Jones, and Richard Clay (witnesses). *St. Louis Post-Dispatch*, February 17, 1942.

ages for the film's portrayal of the titular heroine as "a woman of unchaste character, a harlot, . . . an adulteress, . . . a person of lewd character, and a murderess."[26]

This case, which eventually went to trial in 1942, featured the spectacle of the folk song researcher Sigmund Spaeth as a star witness for the defense. Since Spaeth had served as advisor for the film and even played a bit role in it, he was hardly an unbiased commentator. Nonetheless, Spaeth marshaled his academic training and his air of authority as the former host of the popular NBC radio program *The Tune Detective* (1931–1933) to insist that the ballad's origins predated Baker's 1899 affair. Adopting a passive-aggressive demeanor toward Baker on the witness stand, he claimed, "I'm glad to see Frankie is such a nice woman. I always thought she should have been punished severely."[27] Sounding an even harsher note, Republic's attorney, Hugo Monnig, argued:

> Frankie Baker wants to appropriate for her own use one of the finest ballads in American folklore. If you give her a verdict, she will have a claim against

everybody who ever sang the song. Send her back to Portland, Oregon, and her shoe shine business; for an honest shine, let her have an honest dime. Don't make her a rich woman because forty years ago she shot a little colored boy here in St. Louis.

The jury seems to have concurred, deliberating for just over an hour before delivering a unanimous verdict for Republic Pictures.[28] The outcome was surely a disappointment to Baker, and she returned to Portland to live out the remainder of her life in relative poverty. But the testimony of Baker and her acquaintances from turn-of-the-century St. Louis reveals that more was at stake in her legal cases than a quest for financial remuneration alone. She also insistently tried to reclaim control of the narrative of her own life and reputation from the song and its popular adaptations.

While the nation was captivated by the story of "Frankie and Johnny" across the early decades of the twentieth century—and never more so than during the 1930s—Frankie Baker found considerably less charm in the tale as a representation of her own past. In her conversations with McClure in 1935, Baker acknowledged having been a "queen sport" and "the saddle-colored belle of Darktown" during her St. Louis years, and having devoted much of her income to outfitting Allen Britt in fancy shoes, pants, waistcoats, and "the other accoutrements of a 'dandy' in the good old days." She also described for McClure an earlier incident in which a "sportin' girl" had attacked her with a knife over Baker's affections for a man who was the rival's beau and pimp, leaving a noticeable scar on the left side of Baker's face.[29]

By contrast, in her statements as part of the lawsuit against Republic Pictures, Baker was at considerable pains to distinguish between the ballad's tropes and her own accounting of the events around Britt's death in St. Louis in 1899. She emphasized three points of discrepancy in particular. First, although Baker affirmed that Britt was seeing a young woman named Alice Pryor on the side, she claimed that she had not been bothered by that fact and explained that on the night of the shooting: "I went straight to our home at 212 Targee Street and went to bed. . . . I wasn't going to let his philandering worry me. I had had experience. Albert wasn't even at Alice's house. They were together, all right, but were at a party in a friend's home. [He] was drinking and, as always, was entertaining at the piano."[30] Second, on a related note, Baker repeatedly insisted that her boyfriend's dalliance with Pryor was not her motive for the shooting; rather, she testified that she shot Britt with a pistol only after he attempted to attack her with a knife. Despite the fact that the *St. Louis Post-Dispatch* misreported the incident at the time, stating that Baker killed Britt with a knife in a fit of jealousy, Baker's motive of self-defense was, in fact, accepted by the coroner's jury and by Judge Willis Clark during her criminal trial in 1899; Baker later recalled that she even received her gun back from the court following her trial.[31] Baker explained, "I was afraid of Albert. He beat me unmercifully a few nights before the big blow-off. My eye was festered and sore from that lacin' when I went before Judge Clark. He noticed it, too." Baker called on her acquaintance Richard Clay, the primary informant for John Huston's research into the ballad's origins, along with the father of the deceased, George Britt, to affirm her account on these matters.[32]

In a third point of departure from the "Frankie and Johnny" ballad tradition, Baker averred that she felt no significant remorse over Britt's death: "He knew he was wrong. I felt sorry for him. Sometimes they sing that I sobbed and cried, but that's wrong, too. I felt terrible, of course, but I simply had protected myself. I had nothing to cry about. I didn't feel smart about it, either. I didn't go to his funeral because I couldn't. I was in jail."[33] Witnesses for Baker in the Republic Pictures trial even went so far as to claim that Frankie had been "a good Christian woman," that she had dressed in modest "calico and gingham dresses," that Britt likewise had dressed humbly, and that Targee Street had been the "quiet, respectable home of substantial Negro folks." Interestingly, Clay offered his corrections in counterpoint to a photostat of Thomas Hart Benton's *Frankie and Johnny* mural (1935–1936), which was provided as a prompt for his responses by one of Republic Pictures' attorneys.[34] Dubious though portions of this supporting testimony may have been, Frankie Baker understandably cared about how her past experiences were represented in her present moment of the 1930s and early 1940s.

That the apparent facts of the case as adjudicated at the time of Britt's death so quickly gave way to a lyrical story line centered on the jealousy of a woman scorned was certainly owed, in part, to artists' penchant for the kind of love-gone-wrong dramatic action that characterized the American ballad genre. But the one-sidedness of this battle of competing narratives—in which the melodramatic love triangle of the ballad almost entirely displaced the self-defense against domestic assault of Frankie Baker's experience—also speaks to a larger cultural silencing of women's experiences with violence. This silencing proved especially pernicious for African American women, who often found their accounts of domestic violence and sexual assault downplayed or ignored by both the justice system and even some members of social movements ostensibly aimed at African American liberation.

In the face of such indifference, blueswomen's songs offered some of the few instances of widely circulated public testimonies on the topic. For example, in "Black Eye Blues" (1928) Ma Rainey warns her man:

Take all my money, blacken both of my eyes
Give it to another woman, come home and tell me lies
You low down alligator, just watch me
Sooner or later gonna catch you with your britches down.[35]

Likewise, in "Cell Bound Blues" (1924), Rainey describes taking revenge on a domestic abuser, in a manner roughly parallel to Baker's shooting of Britt:

I walked in my room the other night
My man walked in and begin to fight

I took my gun in my right hand,
"Hold him, folks, I don't want to kill my man."

When I did that, he hit me 'cross my head
First shot I fired, my man fell dead.[36]

As Paige McGinley astutely remarks, such songs are best understood as theatrical narratives rather than strictly autobiographical statements, but the use of a first-person voice by a singer such as Rainey allowed her songs to speak with special poignancy to a number of African American women's lived experiences.[37]

In conjunction with the mid-twentieth-century civil rights movement, activists such as the young Rosa Parks and the attorney Karen (Galloway) Bethea-Shields performed important work for racial and gender equality by chronicling black women's testimonies regarding cases of white male sexual assault.[38] Operating outside the context of an organized social movement, Frankie Baker's ambitions via her lawsuits do not seem to have been as expansive as those of Parks and Bethea-Shields, but she did seek to use her testimony (and that of her St. Louis acquaintances) for parallel ends on a personal level. Specifically, Baker sought to put her motives and actions on higher moral ground than had most iterations of the "Frankie and Johnny" ballad or its adaptations. While not exactly claiming a bourgeois identity, Baker attempted to stake out a morally justified narrative of the incident by repositioning self-defense against domestic assault at its center and, in the process, to reclaim an important modicum of public respectability for herself.

Predictably, the judge and jury were not convinced by Baker's claims. She failed to win the day not only in her two lawsuits but also in the larger struggle to control the narrative of her own past. Instead, the type of stories told in "Frankie and Johnny" songs prevailed, and they continue to enjoy a vital existence in the twenty-first century. If anything, media coverage of Baker's legal actions enhanced the visibility of the "Frankie and Johnny" ballad and its cinematic adaptations by both Paramount and Republic Pictures. For their part, most journalists appear to have been even more dismissive of Baker's claims than were the jurors in the Republic Pictures trial. For instance, following the trial's conclusion, a *St. Louis Post-Dispatch* editorial lightheartedly mocked:

> What does it matter when that mournful old ballad first got going—whether it was after Frankie shot Johnny in 1899 in self-defense, or before the Civil War, as Sigmund Spaeth testified? The important thing is that it is sung wherever baritones gather on good terms, that it is imperishably part of the nation's folklore.
>
> Goodby, Frankie; no hard feelings, and we hope you had a good visit among home folks.[39]

Little wonder, then, that Baker felt as if the agency to script her own identity had long since been usurped by the omnipresent ballad and its adaptations.

Baker's relative powerlessness in these matters is instructive on at least two counts. First, it seems telling that even as a female African American character took center stage in the arena of American culture during the 1930s, authorship of "Frankie and Johnny" scripts so often remained in other hands. In this sense, Frankie Baker's lack of authority to (re)shape her own narrative in the courtroom, in the pages of newspapers, or in popular consciousness might have resonated with a contemporaneous generation of aspiring female African American artists, struggling for prominence. In spite of several important early successes by the likes of Hurston, Dunham, Piper, and Ethel Waters, the goal of widespread visibility for African American women's self-representations in the creative arts awaited greater fulfillment in later generations.

Second, in a broader sense, the drowning out of Baker's voice by the presumed expertise of the scholar Sigmund Spaeth at trial reflects the way in which many of those who most influenced the shape and flow of folk narratives in early twentieth-century American culture—Page and Stone, the Lomaxes, Benton, Huston, Covarrubias, Held, West, and Brown in the case of "Frankie and Johnny"—were members of the formally educated middle and creative classes. Put another way, the story of folklore's increasing pervasiveness in 1930s America hinged on an engagement with vernacular culture by creative artists and other intellectuals, more than on an unmediated eruption of the voices of the folk themselves. One might even venture that what gained wide purchase as "folk" in the period was a kind of cross-class (and quite often cross-racial) translation as often as it was what scholarly specialists would term the unvarnished primary materials of folklore itself. Even Huddie Ledbetter, who undeniably was rooted in vernacular traditions, found his public persona shaped to a significant degree by interlocutors such as John and Alan Lomax, record company personnel, and leaders of the Popular Front social movement.

All that said, I have tried to emphasize that one should not imagine the "folk" as cultural isolates; the folk of twentieth-century America were neither apart from nor unaware of the wider spectrum of US cultural expression—as seen in Ledbetter's affinity for the music of Gene Autry and Jimmie Rodgers and his concern with cutting a sharp, urbane image as a professional musician. The vogue for the vernacular in the 1920s and 1930s was not simply a matter of creative artists and enthusiast scholars trekking lost highways to seek out folk authenticity; rather, those born in vernacular-rich communities, like Ledbetter and Ethel Waters, assertively reached out to embrace the larger cultural milieu in their own right. The phenomenon of "Frankie and Johnny" in the 1930s thus might be framed as a particularly vital intensification of exchanges across divides of race and levels of culture of a sort that had been in motion long before the crystallization of this particular ballad at the dawn of the twentieth century.[40] Granted, members of the local color and plantation school generation of US arts and letters during the late nineteenth and early twentieth centuries all too often drew on approximations of folk materials to shore up the supposed naturalness of racial segregation and class inequalities by portraying the folk as exotic "others" or antiquarian curiosities. By contrast, as the United States sought to navigate its way through the tough times of the Great Depression, creative artists of the 1930s more often turned to vernacular culture to forge broadly representative *American* stories, in which the folk embodied that which best defined the distinctive spirit of the nation. As a result, "Frankie and Johnny" managed to cross significant barriers of class, racial, and cultural hierarchies, bringing African American folk expression to the center of US fine arts and popular culture in the process.

CHAPTER 1. FRANKIE AND JOHNNY TAKE CENTER STAGE: AFRICAN AMERICAN FOLK CULTURE IN 1930S AMERICA

1. Details for the ensuing description of Page and Stone's *Frankie and Johnny* derive primarily from a film of the ballet available online from the Chicago Film Archives, www .chicagofilmarchives.org/collections/index.php/Detail/Object/Show/object_id/8709. Other valuable sources include George Dorris, "*Frankie and Johnny* in Chicago and Some Problems of Attribution," *Dance Chronicle* 18, no. 2 (1995), 179–188; Cyril W. Beaumont, *Supplement to Complete Book of Ballets* (London: Beaumont, 1942), 88–91; John Martin, *Ruth Page: An Intimate Biography* (New York: Dekker, 1977), 93–95; Marcia B. Siegel, *The Shapes of Change: Images of American Dance* (Boston: Houghton Mifflin, 1979), 110–113; and Lindsey Virginia Boone, "Ruth Page and Jerome Moross's *Frankie and Johnny*: Its History in 1938 and 1945" (2007), *Electronic Theses, Treatises and Dissertations*, paper 3534.

2. Beaumont, *Supplement to Book of Ballets*, 89.

3. A program note by Moross described the relationship between the protagonists without equivocation: "Faithful Frankie loves Johnny madly. Johnny loves Frankie too, gladly accepting the money she makes from the other men"; quoted in Laura Rosenberg and Richard Rosenberg, "The Ballad and Scandalous Life of Frankie and Johnny," *American Classics: Jerome Moross: Frankie and Johnny, Those Everlasting Blues, Willie the Weeper*, Naxos CD 8.559086, 2002.

4. Siegel, *Shapes of Change*, 110.

5. Hallie Flanagan, *Arena: The History of the Federal Theatre* (New York: Bloom, 1940), 142.

6. Siegel aptly likens this moment to a "sight gag" from the era of silent movies. More broadly, she argues that Page and Stone conveyed the story of Frankie and Johnny "in the manner of a traditional tall tale, with the slapstick disrespect of a minstrel show" (*Shapes of Change*, 111–112).

7. Janet Gunn, "Federal Ballet Burlesque—Critic," *Chicago Herald and Examiner*, June 21, 1938.

8. Martin, *Ruth Page*, 112; Ruth Page, *Page by Page*, ed. Andrew Mark Wentink (New York: Dance Horizons, 1978), 68–69. Martin explains that in the following year, the ballet was allowed to appear in Boston following compromises with censors to remove some of the work's more irreverent material.

9. Cecil Smith, "Frankie-Johnny Ballet a Wow with Audience," *Chicago Daily Tribune*, June 20, 1938.

10. Claudia Cassidy, "On the Aisle: *Frankie and Johnny* Back, No Better or Even Better, Depending on Point of View," *Chicago Daily Tribune*, October 1, 1945; see also Cassidy, "*Frankie and Johnny* Bawdy and Disappointing Ballet," *Chicago Journal of Commerce*, July 3, 1938.

11. Beaumont, *Supplement to Book of Ballets*, 90; Boone, "Page and Moross's *Frankie and Johnny*," 32.

12. Jane Becker, *Selling Tradition: Appalachia and the Construction of an American Folk, 1930–1940* (Chapel Hill: Univ. of North Carolina Press, 1998), 5.

13. Rachel Clare Donaldson examines the "boom" of interest in folk music during the early 1960s and its indebtedness to the earlier 1930s generation: *"I Hear America Singing": Folk Music and National Identity* (Philadelphia: Temple Univ. Press, 2014), 129–157.

14. For more on the earliest known versions of "Froggie Went A-Courting," see Evelyn Kendrick Wells, *The Ballad Tree: A Study of British and American Ballads, Their Folklore, Verse, and Song* (New York: Ronald, 1950), 159–160. For more on the song's proliferation in the early twentieth-century United States, see Dorothy Scarborough, *A Song Catcher in the Southern Mountains: American Folk Songs of British Ancestry* (New York: Columbia Univ. Press, 1937), 244–248.

15. William A. Wilson, "Herder, Folklore, and Romantic Nationalism," *Journal of Popular Culture* 6, no. 4 (Spring 1973): 819–835.

16. "The Method of Folklore," in Andrew Lang, *Custom and Myth* (London: Longmans, Green, 1884), 11.

17. Alan Dundes, "Who Are the Folk?," in Dundes, *Interpreting Folklore* (Bloomington: Indiana Univ. Press, 1980), 2–4.

18. William Wells Newell, "On the Field and Work of a Journal of American Folklore," *Journal of American Folklore* 1, no. 1 (April–June 1888): 1–7.

19. Benjamin Filene, *Romancing the Folk: Public Memory and American Roots Music* (Chapel Hill: Univ. of North Carolina Press, 2000), 12–15.

20. Alan Lomax, *Cowboy Songs and Other Frontier Ballads*, rev. ed. (New York: Macmillan, 1938), xxv.

21. Filene, *Romancing the Folk*, 16–27; Donaldson, *"I Hear America Singing,"* 9–12.

22. Sandburg, *The American Songbag* (San Diego: Harcourt Brace Jovanovich, 1990 [1927]), 75.

23. Filene, *Romancing the Folk*, 39–46; Donaldson, *"I Hear America Singing,"* 17; Scott Reynolds Nelson, *Steel Drivin' Man: John Henry: The Untold Story of an American Legend* (New York: Oxford Univ. Press, 2006), 135–138.

24. Elijah Wald, *Escaping the Delta: Robert Johnson and the Invention of the Blues* (New York: HarperCollins, 2004); Karl Hagstrom Miller, *Segregating Sound: Inventing Folk and Pop Music in the Age of Jim Crow* (Durham, NC: Duke Univ. Press, 2010); Edward P. Comentale, *Sweet Air: Modernism, Regionalism, and American Popular Song* (Urbana: Univ. of Illinois Press, 2013).

25. Barry Mazor, *Ralph Peer and the Making of Popular Roots Music* (Chicago: Chicago Review Press, 2015), 37–45, 52–57, 93–117, 133–134.

26. Barry Mazor, *Meeting Jimmie Rodgers: How America's Original Roots Music Hero Changed the Pop Sounds of a Century* (Oxford: Oxford Univ. Press, 2009), 173.

27. Hurston, WPA Manuscripts, Florida File, Archive of American Folk Song, quoted in Comentale, *Sweet Air*, 69.

28. John Szwed, *Alan Lomax: The Man Who Recorded the World* (New York: Viking, 2010), 143, 184–185; Mazor, *Ralph Peer*, 189. For a full copy of the letter in which this declaration appears, see Ronald D. Cohen, ed., *Alan Lomax, Assistant in Charge: The Library of Congress Letters, 1935–1945* (Jackson: Univ. of Mississippi Press, 2011), 129–131.

29. Erich Nunn, *Sounding the Color Line: Music and Race in the Southern Imagination* (Athens: Univ. of Georgia Press, 2015), 35–44; Alan Lomax, *Mister Jelly Roll: The Fortunes of Jelly Roll Morton, New Orleans Creole and "Inventor of Jazz"* (New York: Duell, Sloan and Pearce, 1950).

30. Mazor, *Meeting Jimmie Rodgers*, 13–16; Mazor, *Ralph Peer*, 53, 100–107, 111–114;

Miller, *Segregating Sound*, 71–84, 121–123, 275–282; Paige A. McGinley, *Staging the Blues: From Tent Shows to Tourism* (Durham, NC: Duke Univ. Press, 2014), 85–86; Wald, *Escaping the Delta*, 33–35, 79–80, 96–98.

31. W. C. Handy, *Father of the Blues: An Autobiography* (New York: Da Capo, 1991 [1941]), 76–77.

32. Cecil Brown, "We Did Them Wrong: The Ballad of Frankie and Albert," in *The Rose and the Briar: Death, Love, and Liberty in the American Ballad*, edited by Sean Wilentz and Greil Marcus (New York: Norton, 2005), 143–145.

33. Wald, *Escaping the Delta*, chaps. 2 and 3; Miller, *Segregating Sound*, esp. chaps. 6 and 7; Jeffrey Todd Titon, *Early Downhome Blues: A Musical and Cultural Analysis*, 2nd ed. (Chapel Hill: Univ. of North Carolina Press, 1994), 237–241.

34. S. Nelson, *Steel Drivin' Man*, 138–142; see also Yuval Taylor, *Faking It: The Quest for Authenticity in Popular Music* (New York: Norton, 2007), 64–65.

35. David Gilbert, *The Product of Our Souls: Ragtime, Race, and the Birth of the Manhattan Musical Marketplace* (Chapel Hill: Univ. of North Carolina Press, 2015), 33–37.

36. "The Real Value of Negro Melodies," *New York Herald*, May 21, 1893, reprinted in John C. Tibbetts, ed., *Dvořák in America, 1892–1895* (Portland, Ore.: Amadeus, 1993), 355–359.

37. For a detailed analysis of Du Bois's use of musical epigraphs in *The Souls of Black Folk*, see Eric J. Sundquist, *To Wake the Nations: Race in the Making of American Literature* (Cambridge, Mass.: Belknap, 1993), 490–525.

38. Paul Allen Anderson, *Deep River: Music and Memory in Harlem Renaissance Thought* (Durham, NC: Duke Univ. Press, 2001), 13–29, 49–56; Ronald M. Radano, "Soul Texts and the Blackness of Folk," *Modernism/Modernity* 2, no. 1 (January 1995): 71–95.

39. Gilbert, *Product of Our Souls*, 2–3, 178–182.

40. Ibid., 132–136, 152–160, 178–188.

41. Alain Locke, foreword to *The New Negro* (New York: Macmillan, 1992 [1925]), xxv–xxvii (emphasis added).

42. James Weldon Johnson, *God's Trombones: Seven Negro Sermons in Verse* (New York: Penguin, 1990 [1927]), 5.

43. James Weldon Johnson, "Preface to the First Edition," *The Book of American Negro Poetry* (New York: Harcourt, Brace, 1931 [1922]), 9.

44. Du Bois, *The Souls of Black Folk* (Boston: Bedford, 1997 [1903]), 39.

45. Ibid., 43.

46. Shane White and Graham White, *Stylin': African American Expressive Culture from Its Beginnings to the Zoot Suit* (Ithaca, NY: Cornell Univ. Press, 1998), 225–237.

47. Langston Hughes, "The Negro Artist and the Racial Mountain," *Nation*, June 23, 1926, 692–693.

48. Steven C. Tracy, *Langston Hughes and the Blues* (Urbana: Univ. of Illinois Press, 1988), 117–123; see also Anderson, *Deep River*, 170–186.

49. Comentale argues that the themes of modernism, the concern with aesthetic innovation, and the shaping influence of new technology on changing forms of cultural expression all extended well beyond the realm of well-educated modernist writers and artists; moreover, early recorded blues and country music provided vernacular modernists with "a flexibility and range well beyond that of any modernist painting or poem" (*Sweet Air*, 7–11).

50. The two most insightful overviews of Hurston's career are Robert E. Hemenway, *Zora Neale Hurston: A Literary Biography* (Urbana: Univ. of Illinois Press, 1977), and Valerie Boyd, *Wrapped in Rainbows: The Life of Zora Neale Hurston* (New York: Scribner, 2003).

51. Du Bois, *The Souls of Black Folk*, 38; Zora Neale Hurston, *Mules and Men* (Bloomington: Indiana Univ. Press, 1978 [1935]), 4–5.

52. E. E. Cummings, *HIM* (1927), reprinted in George Firmage, ed., *The Theatre of E. E. Cummings* (New York: Liveright, 2013), 42–49 (act 2, scene 5); Richard S. Kennedy, *Dreams in the Mirror: A Biography of E. E. Cummings* (New York: Liveright, 1980), 290–293.

53. Robert Crawford, *Young Eliot: From St. Louis to "The Waste Land"* (New York: Farrar, Straus and Giroux, 2015), 21–22.

54. Eric Sigg, "Eliot as a Product of Americana," in *The Cambridge Companion to T. S. Eliot*, ed. A. David Moody (Cambridge: Cambridge Univ. Press, 1994), 20–21.

55. David Chinitz, *T. S. Eliot and the Cultural Divide* (Chicago: Univ. of Chicago Press, 2003), 28–44; Sigg, "Eliot as a Product of Americana," 20–23; John Russell David, "Tragedy in Ragtime: Black Folktales from St. Louis" (PhD diss., St. Louis Univ., 1976), 87–92; David Ewen, *The Life and Death of Tin Pan Alley: The Golden Age of American Popular Music* (New York: Funk and Wagnalls, 1964), 81–82. Mama Lou's real name was Letitia Lula Agatha Fontaine; see William Howard Kenney, *Jazz on the River* (Chicago: Univ. of Chicago Press, 2005), 97.

56. Geoffrey Grigson, *Recollections: Mainly of Writers and Artists* (London: Hogarth, 1984), 56–57.

57. Howard Pollack, *Aaron Copland: The Life and Work of an Uncommon Man* (New York: Holt, 1999), 291–295, 314–325, 334–335, 363–374, 388–406.

58. Jerome Moross, interview, *New York Evening Journal*, 1933, cited in Rosenberg and Rosenberg, "Ballad of Frankie and Johnny."

59. Charles Turner, "Jerome Moross: An Introduction and Annotated Worklist," *Notes* 61, no. 3 (March 2005): 662, 689, 699.

60. In Heyward's novel, Bess leaves town with a group of unnamed men on a riverboat bound for Savannah, Georgia; see DuBose Heyward, *Porgy* (New York: Grosset and Dunlap, 1925), 195–196.

61. Ellen Noonan, *The Strange Career of Porgy and Bess: Race, Culture, and America's Most Famous Opera* (Chapel Hill: Univ. of North Carolina Press, 2012), 1–9, 75–76, 104–107, 145–149, 176–177; see also Hollis Alpert, *The Life and Times of Porgy and Bess: The Story of an American Classic* (New York: Knopf, 1990), and James M. Hutchinson, *DuBose Heyward: A Charleston Gentleman and the World of Porgy and Bess* (Jackson: Univ. of Mississippi Press, 2000).

62. The list of useful publications on New Deal cultural projects is far too extensive to catalogue here, but among the more insightful are Karl Ann Marling, *Wall to Wall America: A Cultural History of Post Office Murals in the Great Depression* (Minneapolis: Univ. of Minnesota Press, 1982); Barbara Melosh, *Engendering Culture: Manhood and Womanhood in New Deal Public Art and Theater* (Washington, DC: Smithsonian Institution Press, 1991); Rena Fraden, *Blueprints for a Black Federal Theatre, 1935–1939* (Cambridge: Cambridge Univ. Press, 1994); Kenneth J. Bindas, *All of This Music Belongs to the Nation: The WPA's Federal Music Project and American Society* (Knoxville: Univ. of Tennessee Press, 1995); and Victoria Grieve, *The Federal Art Project and the Creation of Middlebrow Culture* (Urbana: Univ. of Illinois Press, 2009). Highly informative accounts by former participants include Hallie Flanagan, *Arena* (cited above), and Jerre Mangione, *The Dream and the Deal: The Federal Writers' Project, 1935–1943* (Philadelphia: Univ. of Pennsylvania Press, 1983).

63. *How Long, Brethren?* featured white dance performers backed by a full orchestra and a chorus of African American vocalists. Payton and Browne's productions were written and performed by members of the Federal Theatre Project's Negro Units; see Flanagan, *Arena*,

199; Fraden, *Blueprints*, 112, 177–179; Ellen Graff, *Stepping Left: Dance and Politics in New York City, 1928–1942* (Durham, NC: Duke Univ. Press, 1997), 93–95; and Susan Manning, "Black Voices, White Bodies: The Performance of Race and Gender in *How Long Brethren*," *American Quarterly* 50, no. 1 (March 1998), 24–46.

64. Page, *Page by Page*, 64.

65. Sonnet Retman, *Real Folks: Race and Genre in the Great Depression* (Durham, NC: Duke Univ. Press, 2011), 3.

66. Alan Lomax, *The Folk Songs of North America in the English Language* (Garden City, NY: Doubleday, 1960), 557.

67. These and other theories regarding the origins of "Frankie and Johnny" are gathered in Belden Kittredge [Vance Randolph], *The Truth about Frankie and Johnny, and Other Legendary Lovers Who Stalked across the American Scene* (Girard, Kans.: Halderman-Julius, 1945), 3–14; and Bruce Redfern Buckley, "Frankie and Her Men: A Study of the Interrelationships of Popular and Folk Traditions" (PhD diss., Indiana Univ., 1961), 14–36.

68. G. Legman and Vance Randolph, *Roll Me in Your Arms: "Unprintable" Ozark Folksongs and Folklore*, vol. 1 (Fayetteville: Univ. of Arkansas Press, 1992), 479–480.

69. John Huston, *Frankie and Johnny* (New York: Boni, 1930), 104–112; "The 'Frankie and Johnny' Episode of 1899," *Missouri Historical Review* 36, no. 1 (October 1941): 75–77; John R. David, "Frankie and Johnnie: The Trial of Frankie Baker," *Missouri Folklore Society Journal* 6 (1984): 1–30; C. Brown, "We Did Them Wrong," 123–145.

70. For a description of St. Louis's Chestnut Valley community, see Cecil Brown, *Stagolee Shot Billy* (Cambridge, Mass.: Harvard Univ. Press, 2003), 84–92. For more on the reputation of St. Louis's "pocket neighborhoods" of working-class African Americans for saloons, vice, and violence, see David, "Tragedy in Ragtime," 59–93.

71. Baker's friend, Pansy Marvin, and Marvin's boyfriend also shared the Targee Street apartment. Marvin was a key witness in the coroner's inquest following Britt's death; see Kittredge, *Truth about Frankie and Johnny*, 13–16; David, "Frankie and Johnnie," 6–7.

72. *Missouri Historical Review*, "'Frankie and Johnny' Episode," 76–77; see also David, "Frankie and Johnnie," 14, 20–21; C. Brown, "We Did Them Wrong," 143–144; Bruce Olsen, "Frankie and Johnny: He Done Her Wrong Right Here in St. Louis," *Bluesletter: The Monthly Magazine of the St. Louis Blues Society* 61 (July 2013): 5.

73. Kittredge, *Truth about Frankie and Johnny*, 13–14; David, "Frankie and Johnnie," 6–7.

74. David, "Frankie and Johnnie," 3–5; Legman and Randolph, *Roll Me in Your Arms*, 477–479; James J. Fuld, *The Book of World-Famous Music: Classical, Popular and Folk* (New York: Crown Publishers, 1966), 195–196.

75. C. Brown, "We Did Them Wrong," 127.

76. Spaeth, *Read 'Em and Weep: The Songs You Forgot to Remember* (New York: Doubleday, Page, 1927), 34.

77. That Frankie would solicit information from a bartender or saloonkeeper makes a certain amount of sense, since saloons in cities like St. Louis in the 1890s operated as hubs for community organizations, and their proprietors were sought out by police for information pertaining to criminal cases; see David, "Tragedy in Ragtime," 80–81.

78. C. Brown, "We Did Them Wrong," 128.

79. Buckley provides a meticulous analysis of the ballad's archetypal verses and the numerous variations of each one ("Frankie and Her Men," 37–107).

80. Adam Gussow, *Seems like Murder Here: Southern Violence and the Blues Tradition* (Chicago: Univ. of Chicago Press, 2002), 195–200, 206–211, 219.

81. Buckley identified fifty versions of the ballad featuring references to Frankie's trial, nineteen of them specifically noting her acquittal, twenty-seven indicating a guilty verdict, and others vague about the trial's outcome ("Frankie and Her Men," 96–99).

82. This closing stanza appears at least as early as Frank Crumit's popular 1927 recording of the song with the variant spelling "Frankie and Johnnie" (Victor 20715-A). The stanza did not appear in Crumit's earlier 1921 recording of the song with the Paul Biese Trio (Columbia A3459), which was based on the Leighton Brothers and Ren Shields's 1912 version.

83. A. Lomax, *Folk Songs of North America*, 558.

84. Emily Wortis Leider, *Becoming Mae West* (New York: Da Capo, 1997), 130–132; Jack Shadoian, *Dreams and Dead Ends: The American Gangster Film*, 2nd ed. (New York: Oxford Univ. Press, 2003), 29–30.

85. A. Lomax, *Folk Songs of North America*, 558.

86. David, "Frankie and Johnnie," 5, 9–17.

CHAPTER 2. LEAD BELLY'S NINTH SYMPHONY: HUDDIE LEDBETTER AND THE CHANGING CONTOURS OF AMERICAN FOLK MUSIC

1. John A. Lomax and Alan Lomax, *Negro Folk Songs as Sung by Lead Belly* (New York: Macmillan, 1936), xiii. Alan was the primary author for the section "Lead Belly Tells His Story" (3–28), and John Lomax wrote the sections "Finding Lead Belly," "Traveling with Lead Belly," and "New York City and Wilton" (29–64).

2. For more on the race and gender ideologies reflected in Bing Crosby's ascent to the pinnacle of US popular music during the 1930s, see Allison McCracken, *Real Men Don't Sing: Crooning in American Culture* (Durham, NC: Duke Univ. Press, 2015), 28–31, chap. 6.

3. Paige A. McGinley, *Staging the Blues: From Tent Shows to Tourism* (Durham: Duke Univ. Press, 2014), 81.

4. For more on the trials of the Scottsboro Boys and their place in Popular Front culture, see Dan T. Carter, *Scottsboro: A Tragedy of the American South* (Baton Rouge: Louisiana State Univ. Press, 1969); Robin D. G. Kelly, *Hammer and Hoe: Alabama Communists during the Great Depression* (Chapel Hill: Univ. of North Carolina Press, 1990); and Mark Naison, *Communists in Harlem during the Depression* (New York: Grove, 1983), 57–89.

5. Photo: Item 38, Subseries 03.07: Collected Photos of Various Performers, Series 3: Graphic Images, box 28 of 30, Alan Lomax Collection, American Folklife Center 2004/004, Library of Congress.

6. "Songs Win Cash and Stage Bids for Lead Belly," *New York Herald Tribune*, January 5, 1935, Huddie Ledbetter Files, folder 3 (1930s–1950s), American Folklife Center, Library of Congress (hereafter cited as Ledbetter Files).

7. Lomax and Lomax, *Negro Folk Songs*, 9–10. In an alternate explanation, Ledbetter once said that he turned to a twelve-string guitar after difficulty with too many strings breaking on his six-string model—on one occasion, he was left onstage with a single remaining string to play; see Charles Wolfe and Kip Lornell, *The Life and Legend of Leadbelly* (New York: HarperCollins, 1992), 49–52.

8. Wolfe and Lornell, *Life and Legend of Leadbelly*, 11.

9. Seeger, "Leadbelly," in *The Leadbelly Songbook: The Ballads, Blues, and Folksongs of Huddie Ledbetter*, ed. Moses Asch and Alan Lomax (New York: Oak, 1962), 7. Ledbetter's fellow musician Brownie McGhee provides additional salient commentary about Huddie's professional code: "Your necktie on, your shoes shined. . . . That was his standards. . . . When

he left the house going somewhere, he was always a gentleman. With his necktie, his shoes polished, his guitar in his case" (quoted in Wolfe and Lornell, *Life and Legend of Leadbelly*, 227–228).

10. Mike Alegria, "Leadbelly as I Knew Him in New York," in *Jazz Music: A Tribute to Huddie Ledbetter* (London: Jazz Music Books, 1946), 15. Ledbetter generally rendered the nickname "Lead Belly" as two words, so I have opted for that form except in direct quotations that render the moniker as "Leadbelly."

11. Library of Congress recordings 119-B-1 through 120-B-5, American Folklife Center; see also Wolfe and Lornell, *Life and Legend of Leadbelly*, 114. Ledbetter's familiarity with cowboy songs paralleled the presence of African Americans among the informants for John Lomax's *Cowboy Songs and Other Frontier Ballads* (1910); see Erich Nunn, *Sounding the Color Line: Music and Race in the Southern Imagination* (Athens: Univ. of Georgia Press, 2015), 16–22. Badman ballads typically feature characters who forcefully defy authority, becoming both feared and admired in their communities; see John W. Roberts, *From Trickster to Badman: The Black Folk Hero in Slavery and Freedom* (Philadelphia: Univ. of Pennsylvania Press, 1989), 173–184.

12. John Szwed, *Alan Lomax: The Man Who Recorded the World* (New York: Viking, 2010), 59.

13. Wolfe and Lornell, *Life and Legend of Leadbelly*, 16–19; Benjamin Filene, *Romancing the Folk: Public Memory and American Roots Music* (Chapel Hill: Univ. of North Carolina Press, 2000), 72; Elijah Wald, *Escaping the Delta: Robert Johnson and the Invention of the Blues* (New York: HarperCollins, 2004), 43–45, 53–61; Karl Hagstrom Miller, *Segregating Sound: Inventing Folk and Pop Music in the Age of Jim Crow* (Durham, NC: Duke Univ. Press, 2010), 1–7, 71–72, 222.

14. Quoted in Wolfe and Lornell, *Life and Legend of Leadbelly*, 43. Also obscured was the fact that "race records" by the likes of Blind Lemon Jefferson seem to have sold well in stores in rural white communities (Miller, *Segregating Sound*, 78).

15. Jeffrey Todd Titon, *Early Downhome Blues: A Musical and Cultural Analysis*, 2nd ed. (Chapel Hill: Univ. of North Carolina Press, 1994), 27–28, 59–60, 207–210, 241–253; Miller, *Segregating Sound*, 225–227.

16. Barry Mazor, *Ralph Peer and the Making of Popular Roots Music* (Chicago: Chicago Review Press, 2015), 57.

17. Miller, *Segregating Sound*, 2–6; see also Mazor, *Ralph Peer*, 76, 92.

18. Mazor, *Ralph Peer*, 111–118, 142–149; Mazor, *Meeting Jimmie Rodgers: How America's Original Roots Music Hero Changed the Pop Sounds of a Century* (Oxford: Oxford Univ. Press, 2009), 45, 56–57, 87–89.

19. Miller, *Segregating Sound*, 209, 237–240; Nolan Porterfield, *Jimmie Rodgers: The Life and Times of America's Blue Yodeler* (Urbana: Univ. of Illinois Press, 1979), 158–159; Mazor, *Meeting Jimmie Rodgers*, 13–16, 26–27, 51–52, 175, 209.

20. Wolfe and Lornell, *Life and Legend of Leadbelly*, 16–17, 42–48.

21. Sean Killeen, "Chronology: 1900–1910," *Lead Belly Letter* 4, no. 1 (Winter 1994): 7; Wolfe and Lornell, *Life and Legend of Leadbelly*, 82–84.

22. McGinley, *Staging the Blues*, 85–91.

23. John Cowley, "Leadbelly's Library of Congress Recordings, 1933–1940s: Part One, Take a Whiff on Me," *Blues and Rhythm* 59 (March–April 1991): 17; see also Wolfe and Lornell, *Life and Legend of Leadbelly*, 91.

24. Ross Russell, "Illuminating the Leadbelly Legend," *Down Beat*, August 6, 1970, 33.

"Aggravatin' Papa" was a song first popularized, in separate recordings, by Bessie Smith and the Virginians (a white jazz band) in 1923.

25. John Lomax, draft of material for *Negro Folk Songs as Sung By Lead Belly*, folder 428, John A. and Alan Lomax Papers, American Folklife Center 1933/001 (hereafter cited as Lomax Papers); see also Miller, *Segregating Sound*, 238, 245–246; Filene, *Romancing the Folk*, 71–72; Wolfe and Lornell, *Life and Legend of Leadbelly*, 89–91; Mazor, *Meeting Jimmie Rodgers*, 52–53.

26. Wolfe and Lornell, *Life and Legend of Leadbelly*, 85–87.

27. Ibid., 104–108.

28. Jerrold Hirsch, "Modernity, Nostalgia, and Southern Folklore Studies," *Journal of American Folklore* 105, no. 416 (Spring 1992): 190–191; Szwed, *Alan Lomax*, 31–32; Filene, *Romancing the Folk*, 52–56.

29. John A. and Alan Lomax, *American Ballads and Folk Songs* (New York: Dover, 1994 [1934]), 105–110, 117–118; Engels, "Views and Reviews," *Musical Quarterly* 21, no. 1 (January 1935): 108. Later generations of scholars critiqued this volume for the way in which the Lomaxes pieced together material from different versions of a given song into new, composite constructs—something that Lomax had done with his earlier *Cowboy Songs* as well; see Nolan Porterfield, *Last Cavalier: The Life and Times of John A. Lomax, 1867–1948* (Urbana: Univ. of Illinois Press, 1996), 153–155, 335. As Alan Lomax explained in relation to *American Ballads and Folk Songs*, "There wasn't room for 25 versions of 'John Henry.' Instead, I spent a delightful week making a composite of everything that everybody had collected about John Henry"; see Matthew Barton, "The Lomaxes," in *The Ballad Collectors of North America: How Gathering Folksongs Transformed Academic Thought and American Identity*, ed. Scott B. Spencer (Lanham, Md.: Scarecrow, 2012), 153.

30. On Alan Lomax's similar position, early in his career, regarding the importance of isolation to folk music authenticity, see Szwed, *Alan Lomax*, 37–39. But as noted in chapter 1, Alan Lomax reversed his thinking on the relevance of commercial music by the late 1930s.

31. John A. Lomax, "'Sinful Songs' of the Southern Negro," *Musical Quarterly* 20, no. 2 (April 1934): 181.

32. Miller, *Segregating Sound*, 262; Nunn, *Sounding the Color Line*, 78–84; Benjamin Filene, "'Our Singing Country': John and Alan Lomax, Leadbelly, and the Construction of an American Past," *American Quarterly* 43, no. 4 (December 1991): 618–619. Although John Lomax privately detested the harsh prison conditions that he witnessed, and even wrote letters to state governors to this effect, in his published writings he left the deplorable contexts under which he collected much of his material essentially unaddressed (Szwed, *Alan Lomax*, 64).

33. Barton, "The Lomaxes," 152, 166; Filene, *Romancing the Folk*, 56; Inga Arvad, "Did You Happen to See—Alan Lomax?," *New York Times Herald*, October 2, 1941.

34. Alan Lomax, "Sinful Songs of the Southern Negro," *Southwest Review* 19, no. 2 (Winter 1934): 105–131, reprinted in Alan Lomax, *Selected Writings, 1934–1997*, ed. Ronald D. Cohen (New York: Routledge, 2003), 9–31 (see esp. 10, 15, 19–21); Lomax and Lomax, *Negro Folk Songs*, 34–38, 44–45.

35. Miller, *Segregating Sound*, 242.

36. Wolfe and Lornell, *Life and Legend of Leadbelly*, 125–126.

37. Szwed, *Alan Lomax*, 89.

38. "Proceedings of the Modern Language Association of America," *PMLA* 49 (1934): 1325; Lomax and Lomax, *Negro Folk Songs*, 45; Porterfield, *Last Cavalier*, 342–343. McGinley

notes that John Lomax himself had performed folk songs at previous annual meetings of the MLA before ceding the stage to Ledbetter in 1934 (*Staging the Blues*, 101).

39. Wolfe and Lornell, *Life and Legend of Leadbelly*, 134–136; see also Miller, *Segregating Sound*, 272.

40. J. Lomax, "'Sinful Songs,'" 177–179.

41. In the course of the next five years, Alan Lomax went on to attempt similar joint documentation of musicians' life stories and repertoires with "Jelly Roll" Morton, Woody Guthrie, and Aunt Molly Jackson. Only in Morton's case did a biography eventually come to fruition, however: Lomax, *Mister Jelly Roll: The Fortunes of Jelly Roll Morton, New Orleans Creole and "Inventor of Jazz"* (New York: Grove, 1950).

42. Lomax and Lomax, *Negro Folk Songs*, 6.

43. Ibid., xiii.

44. Szwed, *Alan Lomax*, 67.

45. Alan Lomax, "Frankie and Albert," in Lomax and Lomax, *Negro Folk Songs*, 192.

46. Ibid.

47. Wolfe and Lornell, *Life and Legend of Leadbelly*, 30–34.

48. Tera Hunter, *To 'Joy My Freedom: Southern Black Women's Lives and Labors After the Civil War* (Cambridge, Mass.: Harvard Univ. Press, 1997), 162.

49. Wolfe and Lornell, *Life and Legend of Leadbelly*, 36.

50. Joe Brown, "Reflections on Leadbelly," *Folk Music*, June 1964, 12.

51. Russell, "Illuminating the Leadbelly Legend," 12. (Russell seems to reverse the typical use of "easy rider" for pimp in his formulation.) In this vein, some versions of Ledbetter's song "Fannin Street" (also known as "Mister Tom Hughes' Town") — including the first one he recorded for the Lomaxes at Angola in 1934 — included the lines, "Got a woman living on the backside of the jail, / Making an honest living by the working of her tail"; see Filene, *Romancing the Folk*, 67, 249.

52. Wolfe and Lornell, *Life and Legend of Leadbelly*, 27–28, 31, 58–59, 70–74, 95–96.

53. Ibid., 148.

54. Lomax and Lomax, *Negro Folk Songs*, 50–51; "Lead Belly Gets a Bad Scare as Fiancée Rolls In," *New York Herald Tribune*, January 14, 1935, 30, Ledbetter Files, folder 3 (1930s–1950s).

55. For more on the Lomaxes and racial ideology, see Patrick B. Mullen, *The Man Who Adores the Negro: Race and American Folklore* (Urbana: Univ. of Illinois Press, 2008), chaps. 3 and 4; and Hirsch, "Modernity, Nostalgia, and Folklore," 185–188, 191–198.

56. John Lomax, draft of the introduction to *Negro Folk Songs as Sung by Lead Belly*, in Lomax Papers, folder 428.

57. Wolfe and Lornell, *Life and Legend of Leadbelly*, 161; Szwed, *Alan Lomax*, 67–69.

58. Ledbetter recorded the song three times in Wilton, once on January 20 (LC 127-A and 127-B) and twice more in March (LC 148-A and 148-B, and LC 157-A); LC 157-A lacks the extensive spoken interludes of the two earlier Connecticut recordings. All three recordings were released on the Document Records series *Leadbelly: The Remaining Library of Congress Recordings*; volume 2 (1935) contains LC 127-A and 127-B; volume 3 (1935) contains LC 148-A and 148-B; and volume 4 (1935–1938) contains LC 157-A. Alan Lomax combined and performed his own edits on the material from the first two lengthier renditions for the version that appears in *Negro Folk Songs as Sung by Lead Belly*. Text figure 2.1 transcribes the first of the Wilton recordings.

59. John Lomax, draft of material for *Negro Folk Songs*, in Lomax Papers, folder 428; Alan

Lomax, "Frankie and Albert," in Lomax and Lomax, *Negro Folk Songs*, 192. In his review of *Negro Folk Songs as Sung by Lead Belly*, the Harlem Renaissance luminary James Weldon Johnson also took special note of Ledbetter's "spoken or chanted continuity monolog which he uses to amplify the story or illustrate the action of some of his songs" ("'Lead Belly,' Who Sang His Way Out of Jail: The Amazing Story of a Strutting Genius of American Folk-Song," *New York Herald Tribune*, February 21, 1937).

60. LC 127-A and 127-B; LC 148-A and 148-B.

61. In a March 1935 recording (LC 148-A and 148-B), Ledbetter emphasizes the latter point with an additional verse in which Frankie speaks to the departed Albert at his graveside:

Frankie says, "I told you
[unintelligible] years ago
Catch you with that woman
You won't live no more
Killed you man, 'cause you done me wrong."

62. Alan Lomax, "Frankie and Albert," in Lomax and Lomax, *Negro Folk Songs*, 192.

63. Bruce Redfern Buckley, "Frankie and Her Men: A Study of the Interrelationships of Popular and Folk Traditions" (PhD diss., Indiana Univ., 1961), 91–93. When Ledbetter repeats this two-verse exchange later in the same recording, he alters Mrs. Johnson's lines to refer to Albert as the "Only *support* I've got."

64. Denis Preston, "Negro Sinful Songs: A Review," in *Jazz Music: A Tribute to Huddie Ledbetter* (London: Jazz Music Books, 1946), 24.

65. The detail of blood flowing from Albert is rare, appearing in only one of over one hundred variants from Buckley's study that described the shooting ("Frankie and Her Men," 72–78).

66. LC 119-B-6.

67. LC 125-A.

68. LC AFS 725-B-2.

69. For more on Hurt's Okeh recording sessions, see Philip R. Ratcliffe, *Mississippi John Hurt: His Life, His Times, His Blues* (Jackson: Univ. Press of Mississippi, 2011), 56–66; Yuval Taylor, *Faking It: The Quest for Authenticity in Popular Music* (New York: Norton, 2007), 30–36, 48.

70. For more on Hurt's guitar techniques, see Ratcliffe, *Mississippi John Hurt*, 21, 26–28.

71. I am indebted to Harrison Wallace for discussions of the aesthetic contrasts between Ledbetter's and Hurt's vocals and guitar work. Taylor suggests that the lack of projection in Hurt's vocals and guitar work may owe both to his experience of playing for relatively small gatherings in Avalon and to his awareness of how such an intimate style might resonate with audiences (*Faking It*, 73–74).

72. For more on Smith's *Anthology*, see Robert Cantwell, *When We Were Good: The Folk Revival* (Cambridge, Mass.: Harvard Univ. Press, 1996), chap. 6.

73. For a more detailed analysis of Hurt's popularity with folk music enthusiasts of the 1960s, see Taylor, *Faking It*, 81–96.

74. Lomax and Lomax, *Negro Folk Songs*, 187.

75. John Garst and John Cowley, "Behind the Song," *Sing Out!* 45, no. 1 (Spring 2001): 69–70.

76. The Library of Congress call number for the Angola versions of "Ella Speed" are LC

120-B-5 (1933) and LC 125-B (1934). The lengthier, Wilton recording of this ballad spans LC 54-A and 54-B. Again, Alan Lomax appears to have reordered and edited the material that Ledbetter recorded for presentation in the pages of *Negro Folk Songs as Sung by Lead Belly*.

77. New words and new musical arrangement by Huddie Ledbetter. Collected and adapted by John A. Lomax and Alan Lomax TRO-© copyright 1936 (renewed), 1959 (renewed), Folkways Music Publishers, Inc., New York, NY, and Global Jukebox Publishing, Marshall, Texas. Used by permission. In an annotation, Alan Lomax clarifies, "So lazy and trifling 'he wouldn't hit a lick at a snake if it started to bite him'" (*Negro Folk Songs*, 188).

78. Alan Lomax annotates this line as follows: "'They put you under the pen' means 'gonna hang you or 'lectrocute you an' bury you. When you kill a woman, mean you gone'" (*Negro Folk Songs*, 189).

79. Lomax and Lomax, *Negro Folk Songs*, 37–38.

80. Ibid., 62.

81. Sean Killeen, "Lead Belly and the New York Folklore Society," *Lead Belly Letter* 4, nos. 2–3 (Spring/Summer 1994): 5.

82. Ibid., 13. In a similar vein, Martha Stumpf later recalled of Ledbetter's 1944 performance at Mills College, in Oakland, California: "He was a shock because he was so distinctively different from the other smoother folk singers"; quoted in Sean Killeen, "Lead Belly at Mills College," *Lead Belly Letter* 5, nos. 1–2 (Winter–Spring 1995): 3.

83. Quoted in Sean Killeen, "Lead Belly and the New York Folklore Society," 1, 4–5, 12–13; Killeen, "Far above Cayuga's Waters—Lead Belly at Cornell," *Lead Belly Letter* 4, no. 1 (Winter 1994): 3, 8; Lomax and Lomax, *Negro Folk Songs*, 52; Wolfe and Lornell, *Life and Legend of Leadbelly*, 170–176. With commercial opportunities lacking, and the Popular Front greatly diminished, in the last five years of his life (c. 1944–1949) Ledbetter returned to the circuit of academic audiences, where he had first attained national fame.

84. David A. Jasen and Gene Jones, *Spreadin' Rhythm Around: Black Popular Songwriters, 1890–1930* (New York: Schirmer, 1998), 23–25.

85. Alan Lomax to Charles Wolfe and Kip Lornell, June 20, 1992, quoted in Wolfe and Lornell, *Life and Legend of Leadbelly*, 197.

86. Lomax and Lomax, *Negro Folk Songs*, 52–53.

87. Miller, *Segregating Sound*, 245–246.

88. Titon, *Early Downhome Blues*, 235–260; Filene, *Romancing the Folk*, 49, 58–59; Miller, *Segregating Sound*, 2–6.

89. *New York Herald Tribune*, January 3, 1935. The text of the article is reprinted in Wolfe and Lornell, *Life and Legend of Leadbelly*, 139–142.

90. For a full transcript of the *March of Time* newsreel, see Herman Gebhard, "'March of Time' 1935: Leadbelly," *Living Blues* 30 (November–December 1976): 26–27. The video is available via websites such as YouTube. For additional analysis of the newsreel, see McGinley, *Staging the Blues*, 110–112.

91. "Songs Win Cash," *New York Herald Tribune*, January 5, 1935, Ledbetter Files.

92. "Lead Belly: Bad Nigger Makes Good Minstrel," *Life*, April 19, 1937, 38–40.

93. Filene provides an excellent analysis of this photograph and John Lomax's complicity in creating a "thoroughly exoticized" representation of Ledbetter (*Romancing the Folk*, 58–64).

94. Killeen, "Far above Cayuga's Waters," 8.

95. On the Lomaxes' disapproval of media portrayals of Ledbetter, see Szwed, *Alan Lomax*, 65–66, 72–73, and Wolfe and Lornell, *Life and Legend of Leadbelly*, 142.

96. Sean Killeen, "Harvard: Lead Belly's Education and Graduation," *Lead Belly Letter* 1, no. 2 (Winter 1991): 3; Filene, *Romancing the Folk*, 62–63; Porterfield, *Last Cavalier*, 343–344, 356–359; Nunn, 84–88; Lomax and Lomax, *Negro Folk Songs*, 24–26.

97. Taylor, *Faking It*, 58.

98. Wolfe and Lornell, *Life and Legend of Leadbelly*, 155; Hurston, "The 'Pet Negro' System," *American Mercury*, May 1943, 594.

99. Lomax and Lomax, *Negro Folk Songs*, 59, 63; Wolfe and Lornell, *Life and Legend of Leadbelly*, 168–169. Elsewhere in the same narrative, John Lomax confides, "Since then I have often wondered what were his thoughts as he held the car steadily on the highway. I did not know then. I do not know now" (35).

100. Unlabeled newspaper clippings in Ledbetter Files, folder 3 (1930s–1950s); Jack Schiffman, *Harlem Heyday: A Pictorial History of Modern Black Show Business and the Apollo Theatre* (Buffalo: Prometheus, 1984), 53–54; Wolfe and Lornell, *Life and Legend of Leadbelly*, 188.

101. Lomax and Lomax, *Negro Folk Songs*, 36.

102. Wolfe and Lornell, *Life and Legend of Leadbelly*, 188.

103. McGinley, *Staging the Blues*, 114–117.

104. For one of the most detailed firsthand descriptions of a Ledbetter performance, see Frederic Ramsey Jr., "At the Vanguard, and After," in *Jazz Music: A Tribute to Huddie Ledbetter* (London: Jazz Music Books, 1946), 6, 7–8.

105. Mazor, *Ralph Peer*, 69; Wolfe and Lornell, *Life and Legend of Leadbelly*, 156–160; Szwed, *Alan Lomax*, 69–70; see also Miller, *Segregating Sound*, 189–197, 217–227; Wald, *Escaping the Delta*, 52–55.

106. For the sake of space, I have foregone discussion of later recordings such as *Negro Sinful Tunes* (1939) on Samuel Pruner's Musicraft label and Ledbetter's sessions for Moe Asch's owner-operated Folkways label during the 1940s. Although they captured a much fuller range of Ledbetter's repertoire, these records also resulted in only modest sales. For more on Ledbetter and Musicraft, see Wolfe and Lornell, *Life and Legend of Leadbelly*, 212–213. For more on Ledbetter and Folkways, see Peter D. Goldsmith, *Making People's Music: Moe Asch and Folkways Records* (Washington, DC: Smithsonian Institution Press, 1998), 98–110, 194–196.

107. Following the concert, Caspar sought out a copy of *Negro Folk Songs as Sung by Lead Belly* "to learn more about Lead Belly and to try to play his songs" (Killeen, "Far above Cayuga's Waters," 8).

108. "Lead Belly: 'Take This Hammer' Memorial Concert" program flyer, January 28, 1950, Ledbetter Files, folder 3 (1930s–1950s).

109. Peer to John Greenway, March 28, 1955, quoted in Mazor, *Ralph Peer*, 1.

110. Lieberman, *"My Song is My Weapon": People's Songs, American Communism, and the Politics of Culture, 1930–50* (Urbana: Univ. of Illinois Press, 1989), 158; Richard A. Reuss, *American Folk Music and Left-Wing Politics, 1927–1957*, with JoAnne C. Reuss (Lanham, Md.: Scarecrow, 2000), 233–235; Cantwell, *When We Were Good*, 178–179.

111. Rachel Donaldson, *"I Hear America Singing": Folk Music and National Identity* (Philadelphia: Temple Univ. Press, 2014), 21. Michael Denning provides an important counterpoint: "The latter-day success of the folk music revival—of the music of Woody Guthrie, Huddie Ledbetter, and Pete Seeger—has often led historians and cultural critics to assume that folk music was the soundtrack of the Popular Front. This is not true: the music of the young factory and office workers who made up the social movement was overwhelm-

ingly jazz" (Denning, *The Cultural Front: The Laboring of American Culture in the Twentieth Century* [London: Verso, 1997], 329). While comparative sales numbers support the basic thrust of Denning's point, key members of the Popular Front labored extensively to *try* to make folk music serve such ambitious purposes, with several notable successes. For more on the topic of folk music in relation to Popular Front culture, see Reuss, *American Folk Music*, 115–140; Cantwell, *When We Were Good*, chap. 4; and Lieberman, *"My Song is My Weapon,"* chap. 2.

112. Guthrie to Moses Asch, January 2, 1946, quoted in Donaldson, *"I Hear America Singing,"* 46.

113. See Comentale, *Sweet Air: Modernism, Regionalism, and American Popular Song* (Urbana: Univ. of Illinois Press, 2013), 122, 133; Taylor, *Faking It*, 125.

114. "Lead Belly to Show N.Y.U. Students How He Sings His Way Out of Jails," February 1935 article reprinted without bibliographic details in Tiny Robinson and John Reynolds, eds., *Lead Belly: A Life in Pictures* (Göttingen, Germany: Steidl, 2008), 49; Porterfield, *Last Cavalier*, 348; Szwed, *Alan Lomax*, 65–67, 76; Wolfe and Lornell, *Life and Legend of Leadbelly*, 137–138.

115. Wolfe and Lornell, *Life and Legend of Leadbelly*, 191–193, 203–210, 214–216; McGinley, *Staging the Blues*, 119–127; Szwed, *Alan Lomax*, 160; Henrietta Yurchenco, *A Mighty Hard Road: The Woody Guthrie Story* (New York: McGraw-Hill, 1970), 98–102; Guthrie, "Leadbelly Is a Hard Name," in Moses Asch, ed., *American Folksong* (New York: Oak, 1961), 9–10.

116. For more on White's *Contribution* mural, see Breanne Robertson, "Pan-Americanism, Patriotism, and Race Pride in Charles White's Hampton Mural," *American Art* 30, no. 1 (Spring 2016): 52–71. White also crafted at least two later images of Ledbetter: the painting *Goodnight Irene* (1952), currently held by the Nelson-Atkins Museum of Art in Kansas City, Missouri, and a graphite illustration of Ledbetter produced to aid in the promotion of Gordon Parks's feature film *Leadbelly* (1976).

117. On Alan Lomax's early political radicalism, see Szwed, *Alan Lomax*, 27–29. He remained active in Popular Front culture throughout the late 1930s and early 1940s, and faced scrutiny from the FBI because of his leftist political activities during these years. See, for example, Szwed, *Alan Lomax*, 141, 150, 189.

118. For full transcripts of many of the *Back Where I Come From* radio broadcasts, see box 11.03.02, Alan Lomax Collection, American Folklife Collection 2004/004 (hereafter cited as A. Lomax Collection). The episode on western songs aired on November 20, 1941, the episode on railroad songs aired April 15, 1941, and the episode about Ledbetter aired on February 14, 1941. For full transcripts of many of the *Wellsprings of Music* radio broadcasts, see box 04.01, A. Lomax Collection; see also Donaldson, *"I Hear America Singing,"* 67–73.

119. Several sources from the time suggest that Nick Ray, the director of *Back Where I Come From*, began using Josh White to voice the narrative pieces written for Ledbetter because of White's smoother elocution. Woody Guthrie was so disgusted by this maneuver that he quit the program (Szwed, *Alan Lomax*, 165–167).

120. Killeen, "Chronology: 1941," *Lead Belly Letter* 2, nos. 2–3 (Spring–Summer 1992): 7; Killeen, "Chronology: After the War," *Lead Belly Letter* 1, no. 4 (Fall 1991): 7; Barney Josephson and Terry Trilling-Josephson, *Café Society: The Wrong Place for the Right People* (Urbana: Univ. of Illinois Press, 2009), 289–290.

121. Reuss, *American Folk Music*, 134.

122. Guthrie, "Leadbelly Is a Hard Name," 9–14; Yurchenco, *Mighty Hard Road*, 103–105; Szwed, *Alan Lomax*, 159–160.

123. Cary Nelson, *Repression and Recovery: Modern American Poetry and the Politics of Cultural Memory, 1910–1945* (Madison: Univ. of Wisconsin Press, 1989), 58–62; Gibbs M. Smith, *Joe Hill* (Salt Lake City: Univ. of Utah Press, 1969), 15–42.

124. Szwed, *Alan Lomax*, 105.

125. Words and music by Huddie Ledbetter. Edited and with new additional material by Alan Lomax TRO-© Copyright 1959 (renewed) Folkways Music Publishers, Inc., New York, NY. Used by permission.

126. Richard Wright, "Huddie Ledbetter, Famous Negro Folk Artist, Sings the Songs of Scottsboro and His People," *Daily Worker*, August 12, 1937, 7. In one example of peer criticism, Alan Lomax described a backstage encounter with the jazz musician-composer Mary Lou Williams: "Mary Lou Williams had no use at all for Lead Belly. . . . 'I went up to see Mary Lou. She's got no use for me—tole me my stuff was Uncle Tom.' He told her her mouth was sweet as cinnamon. She fobbed him off" (notes for a letter to Frederic Ramsey Jr., n.d., 6, A. Lomax Collection, folder 03.01.05).

127. Reuss, *American Folk Music*, 138. This incident also is recounted in Naison, *Communists in Harlem*, 212–213, and Filene, *Romancing the Folk*, 72.

128. Killeen, "Testimony: Burl Ives," *Lead Belly Letter* 5, nos. 1–2 (Winter–Spring 1995): 9.

129. Wright, "Huddie Ledbetter," 7.

130. Ramsey, "At the Vanguard," 8.

131. Wright, "Huddie Ledbetter," 7.

132. Ibid. Wright was not alone among radical writers in castigating John Lomax. Lawrence Gellert, who collected two volumes of songs full of biting social criticism from African Americans in the South during the 1930s, blasted Lomax's racist attitudes toward Ledbetter, along with his methods of collecting songs from southern prisons: "I'll wager that many a work-tired Negro in dirty bedraggled stripes was yanked off a rock-pile by bribed plug ugly guards and ordered to 'sing for the gentlemen'" (Gellert, "Entertain Your Crowd," *New Masses*, November 20, 1934, 19); see also Lew Ney, "A Southerner's Prejudices," and Gellert, "Lawrence Gellert's Reply," both in *New Masses*, December 11, 1934, 21–22. Gellert's complaints that Lomax ignored the radical strand of African American folk songs is complicated by the fact that Gellert appears to have fabricated some of the material in his own collections, *Negro Songs of Protest* (1936) and *Me and My Captain: Chain Gang Negro Songs of Protest* (1939). For more on Gellert, see Bruce M. Conforth, *African American Folksong and American Cultural Politics: The Lawrence Gellert Story* (Lanham, MD: Scarecrow, 2013).

CHAPTER 3. PISTOL PACKIN' MAMA: IMPERILED MASCULINITY IN THOMAS HART BENTON'S *A SOCIAL HISTORY OF THE STATE OF MISSOURI*

1. Archie Green, "Tom Benton's Folk Depictions," in *Thomas Hart Benton: Chronicler of America's Folk Heritage*, ed. Linda Weintraub (Annandale-on-Hudson, N.Y.: Edith C. Blum Art Institute, 1984), 33.

2. Justin Wolff, *Thomas Hart Benton: A Life* (New York: Farrar, Straus and Giroux, 2012), 10–12, 186–190; Henry Adams, *Thomas Hart Benton: An American Original* (New York: Knopf, 1989), 134–146; Linda Weintraub, introduction to Weintraub, *Thomas Hart Benton*, 9; Karal Ann Marling, "Thomas Hart Benton's Epic of the Usable Past," in *Thomas Hart Benton: Artist, Writer, and Intellectual*, ed. R. Douglas Hurt and Mary K. Dains (Columbia: State Historical Society of Missouri, 1989), 122. For the artist's own detailed account of these

travels see chaps. 4–7—"The Mountains," "The Rivers," "The South," and "The West"—of Thomas Hart Benton, *An Artist in America*, 4th ed. (Columbia: Univ. of Missouri Press, 1983 [1937]).

3. Wolff, *Thomas Hart Benton*, 164–167, 170–173, 184–185.

4. Alan Buechner, "Thomas Hart Benton and American Folk Music," in Weintraub, *Thomas Hart Benton*, 71; Benton, *Artist in America*, 113; Green, "Benton's Folk Depictions," 59; Leo G. Mazow, *Thomas Hart Benton and the American Sound* (University Park: Pennsylvania State Univ. Press, 2012), 91, 100–104.

5. Mazow, *Benton and the American Sound*, 88–93. Mazow borrows the term "anthological modernism" from Joann Mancini and elaborates it with specific reference to Benton; see J. M. Mancini, "'Messin' with the Furniture Man': Early Country Music, Regional Culture, and the Search for an Anthological Modernism," *American Literary History* 16 (Summer 2004): 208–237.

6. Wolff, *Thomas Hart Benton*, 79–80, 114–115, 171–172, 201–202, 222–224.

7. Desmond Rochfort, *Mexican Muralists: Orozco, Rivera, Siqueiros* (San Francisco: Chronicle, 1993), 20–21, 33–40.

8. Walter Kalaidjian, *American Culture between the Wars: Revisionary Modernism and Postmodern Critique* (New York: Columbia Univ. Press, 1993), 111.

9. Patrick Marnham, *Dreaming with His Eyes Open: A Life of Diego Rivera* (New York: Knopf, 1998); Bertram D. Wolfe, *Diego Rivera: His Life and Times* (New York: Knopf, 1943); and Rochfort, *Mexican Muralists*, 50–81.

10. Helen Delpar, *The Enormous Vogue of Things Mexican: Cultural Relations between the United States and Mexico, 1920–1935* (Tuscaloosa: Univ. of Alabama Press, 1992), 139–156. The most famous of the controversies surrounding the work of Mexican muralists in the United States involved Rivera's *Man at the Crossroads* mural for the newly constructed Rockefeller Center in New York City, but other murals by Rivera, Orozco, and Siqueiros also engendered heated criticism. On the Rockefeller Center controversy, see Laurance P. Hurlburt, *The Mexican Muralists in the United States* (Albuquerque: Univ. of New Mexico Press, 1989), 159–174; Kalaidjian, *American Culture between the Wars*, 118–122; Catha Paquette, *At the Crossroads: Diego Rivera and His Patrons at MoMA, Rockefeller Center, and the Palace of Fine Arts* (Austin: Univ. of Texas Press, 2017).

11. Delpar, *Enormous Vogue*, 24–25, 157–161; James Oles, *South of the Border: Mexico in the American Imagination, 1914–1947* (Washington, DC: Smithsonian Institution Press, 1993), 57–73, 173–203; Lizzetta LeFalle-Collins and Shifra M. Goldman, *In the Spirit of Resistance: African American Modernists and the Mexican Muralist School* (New York: American Federation of the Arts, 1996).

12. Richard D. McKenzie, *The New Deal for Artists* (Princeton, NJ: Princeton Univ. Press, 1973), 5–10; Karal Ann Marling, *Wall-to-Wall America: A Cultural History of Post-Office Murals in the Great Depression* (Minneapolis: Univ. of Minnesota Press, 1982), 30–32.

13. Thomas Hart Benton, *An American in Art: A Professional and Technical Autobiography* (Lawrence: Univ. Press of Kansas, 1969), 61–62.

14. Rachel Clare Donaldson, *"I Hear America Singing": Folk Music and National Identity* (Philadelphia: Temple Univ. Press, 2014), 32.

15. Adams, *Benton: An American Original*, 225–227; Wolff, *Thomas Hart Benton*, 194, 237–238, 253–254.

16. Benton, *Artist in America*, 113–114.

17. Mazow, *Benton and the American Sound*, 10.

18. Benton, *Artist in America*, 256–257, 287–290, 337; Wolff, *Thomas Hart Benton*, 212–

213; Buechner, "Benton and American Folk Music," 71–73; Green, "Benton's Folk Depictions," 33, 49; Vivian Green Fryd, "'The Sad Twang of Mountain Voices': Thomas Hart Benton's *Sources of Country Music*," in *Reading Country Music: Steel Guitars, Opry Stars, and Honky-Tonk Bars*, ed. Cecelia Tichi (Durham, NC: Duke Univ. Press, 1998), 259–260; Adams, *Benton: An American Original*, 176–178, 314; Thomas Hart Benton, interview by Paul Cummings, July 23, 1973, 30 (hereafter cited as Benton, interview by Cummings), Thomas Hart Benton Papers, Archives of American Art (hereafter cited as Benton Papers). Mazow provides a rich discussion of the Decca album (101–102) and the *Art for Your Sake* radio broadcast, noting that the script was entitled "The America of Mister Thomas Hart Benton, Including the Folksongs" (*Benton and the American Sound*, 129–135).

19. Quoted in Bob Priddy, *Only the Rivers Are Peaceful: Thomas Hart Benton's Missouri Mural* (Independence, MO): Independence Press, 1989), 45.

20. Wolff, *Thomas Hart Benton*, 212–213.

21. Hand-sketched musical notation sheets in the Benton Papers, microfilm roll 2328; see also Benton, *Artist in America*, 257; Green, "Benton's Folk Depictions," 59; Adams, *Benton: An American Original*, 178. Benton's papers include copies of songbooks focused on folk hymns and shape-note singing, as well as extensive notes for his *Sources of Country Music* mural.

22. Adams, *Benton: An American Original*, 236–238; Wanda M. Corn, *Grant Wood: The Regionalist Vision* (New Haven, Conn.: Yale Univ. Press, 1983), 43–46. A photograph of Benton and Wood in Victorian costume appears in Adams, *Benton: An American Original*, 238.

23. Craven, "Thomas Hart Benton," *Scribner's Magazine*, October 1937, 38.

24. Benton, *Artist in America*, 37; Wolff, *Thomas Hart Benton*, 112–113, 133.

25. Quoted in Adams, *Benton: An American Original*, 301.

26. Erika Doss, *Benton, Pollock, and the Politics of Modernism: From Regionalism to Abstract Expressionism* (Chicago: University of Chicago Press, 1991), 91–92.

27. Mazow, *Benton and the American Sound*, 86–87. Unfortunately, these murals are now lost, and images of them survive only in black-and-white reproductions in a Whitney Museum of American Art brochure.

28. Fryd, "'Sad Twang of Mountain Voices,'" 259. A few years after his Missouri State Capitol project, Benton completed *Wreck of the Ole '97*, a painting based on Vernon Dalhart's landmark million-selling country music record (Adams, *Benton: An American Original*, 179). Alan Buechner catalogues nine paintings, ten murals, nine lithographs, and eleven pencil drawings "devoted *entirely* or *in part* to musical subjects" from Benton's full career ("Benton and American Folk Music," 74–75). For the fullest treatment of the role of music in relation to Benton's art, see Mazow, *Benton and the American Sound*; his work demonstrates that music and sound more broadly affected not only Benton's choice of subject matter, but also his formal aesthetics.

29. Ray M. Lawless, "Thomas Hart Benton's Jealous Lover and Its Musical Background," *Register of the Museum of Art* (June 1961): 38.

30. Adams, *Benton: An American Original*, 124–129, 160–166, 184–187. For more on Benton and African American representation, see Richard J. Powell, "'Dem Shoes': Thomas Hart Benton's *Romance*," in *American Epics: Thomas Hart Benton and Hollywood*, ed. Austen Barron Bailly (Salem, Mass.: Peabody Essex Museum, 2015), 83–87.

31. For a discussion of the elements of social criticism contained in Benton's earlier murals, see Matthew Baigell, "Thomas Hart Benton and the Left," in Hurt and Dains, *Benton: Artist, Writer, and Intellectual*, 3–9.

32. Nancy Edelman, *The Thomas Hart Benton Murals in the Missouri State Capitol* (Kansas City: Missouri State Council on the Arts, 1975), 7–8.

33. Kathleen A. Foster, Nanette Esseck Brewer, and Margaret Contompasis, *Thomas Hart Benton and the Indiana Murals* (Bloomington: Indiana Univ. Art Museum, 2000); Adams, *Benton: An American Original*, 192–207.

34. Benton, *Artist in America*, 258, 270.

35. Green, "Benton's Folk Depictions," 57.

36. Benton, *American in Art*, 71–72.

37. Benton to Matthew Baigell, November 16, 1967, Benton Papers, microfilm roll 2325. Benton used similar stylized dividers in his New School murals of 1930; see Benton, *American in Art*, 64; Adams, *Benton: An American Original*, 171–172; Edelman, *Thomas Hart Benton Murals*, 11–14, 32.

38. Wolff, *Thomas Hart Benton*, 205.

39. See Matthew Baigell and Allen Kaufman, "The Missouri Murals: Another Look at Benton," *Art Journal* 36, no. 4 (Summer 1977): 314–317; Edelman, *Thomas Hart Benton Murals*, 20–32; Wolff, *Thomas Hart Benton*, 257–258; Doss, *Benton, Pollock, and Modernism*, 131; Adams, *Benton: An American Original*, 264–265. Some of these same points of critique were present in earlier Benton mural projects as well, such as his *American Historical Epic* series (1921–1926) and his *Social History of the State of Indiana* (1932–1933). Benton's inclusion of the Ku Klux Klan in the Indiana murals aroused particular controversy; see Kathleen A. Foster, "Thomas Hart Benton and the Indiana Murals," in Foster, Brewer, and Contompasis, *Benton and the Indiana Murals*, 16–17.

40. Matthew Baigell, *Thomas Hart Benton* (New York: Abrams, 1974), 142.

41. Adams, *Benton: An American Original*, 264.

42. "Thomas Benton Paints a History of His Own Missouri," *Life*, March 1, 1937, 35.

43. Quoted in Priddy, *Only the Rivers*, 84. Priddy provides the most thorough sampling of the critical and laudatory reactions to Benton's Missouri murals (83–124).

44. *Life*, "Thomas Benton Paints," 33; Benton, *Artist in America*, 281–283.

45. Wolff, *Thomas Hart Benton*, 259.

46. Quoted in Priddy, *Only the Rivers*, 110. As Justin Wolff observes, "For an artist who paid so much lip service to the public and popular taste, he proved remarkably inhospitable to comments and advice about his subjects and execution" (*Thomas Hart Benton*, 255).

47. Benton, "The Missouri Mural and its Critics" (1937), reprinted in Priddy, *Only the Rivers*, 265.

48. Benton, *American in Art*, 71.

49. Thomas Hart Benton, interview by Milton Perry regarding his *Independence and the Opening of the West* mural, April 21, 1964, 26, Benton Papers, microfilm roll 2325; Benton, interview by Cummings, 45.

50. Benton, "First notes—Missouri Mural," 3–13, Benton Papers, microfilm roll 2327; Edelman, *Thomas Hart Benton Murals*, 11–17; Benton, *American in Art*, 72.

51. Benton, interview by Cummings, 45; see also Benton, *Artist in America*, 255; Edelman, *Thomas Hart Benton Murals*, 11, 17–19; Adams, *Benton: An American Original*, 274–275. For a detailed overview of the real-life models for many of the mural's figures, see Priddy, *Only the Rivers*, 47–57.

52. Benton, *Artist in America*, 273. Benton employed similar research methods for his earlier *Social History of the State of Indiana* mural project (1933): Benton, "The Thirties," reprinted in Priddy, *Only the Rivers*, 227–228; Benton, *American in Art*, 69–70; Doss, *Benton, Pollock, and Modernism*, 100–101; Nanette Esseck Brewer, "The Anatomy of a Mural: Thomas

Hart Benton's Preparatory Drawings," in Foster, Brewer, and Contompasis, *Benton and the Indiana Murals*, 81–104.

53. Benton, *Artist in America*, 144; Priddy, *Only the Rivers*, 38–39; Baigell, *Thomas Hart Benton*, 138; Adams, *Benton: An American Original*, 239, 254, 312. Benton's illustrations appeared in an edition of *Adventures of Huckleberry Finn* that was published in 1942; he also provided illustrations for editions of Twain's *The Adventures of Tom Sawyer* in 1939 and *Life on the Mississippi* in 1944.

54. Henry Adams asserts that during Benton's youth, when he first read *Huckleberry Finn*, it was still "a book most people in Neosho [Benton's home town] regarded as indecent because of its frank presentation of the friendship between Huck and . . . Jim" (*Benton: An American Original*, 17).

55. For a sampling of the continued debate surrounding Twain's *The Adventures of Huckleberry Finn*, see Shelley Fisher Fishkin, *Lighting Out for the Territory: Reflections on Mark Twain and American Culture* (New York: Oxford Univ. Press, 1997); Jocelyn Chadwick-Joshua, *The Jim Dilemma: Reading Race in "Huckleberry Finn"* (Jackson: Univ. Press of Mississippi, 1998); and Sharon E. Rush, *Huck Finn's "Hidden" Lessons: Teaching and Learning across the Color Line* (Lanham, Md.: Rowman and Littlefield, 2006). It seems suggestive that Benton's Jim remained "the most prominently portrayed black man in the capitol for almost a half-century, until a bust of George Washington Carver was unveiled in 1982," according to Bob Priddy (*Only the Rivers*, 50).

56. Quoted in Priddy, *Only the Rivers*, 174.

57. Quoted in ibid., 117.

58. Cecil Brown, "We Did Them Wrong: The Ballad of Frankie and Albert," in *The Rose and the Briar: Death, Love, and Liberty in the American Ballad*, ed. Sean Wilentz and Greil Marcus (New York: Norton, 2005), 139. The lyrics for an even more profane version—dated to 1931, but said to have been heard "on a ranch near Boise, Idaho, between 1910–1912"—is reprinted in Gershon Legman and Vance Randolph, *Roll Me in Your Arms: "Unprintable" Ozark Folksongs and Folklore*, vol. 1 (Fayetteville: Univ. of Arkansas Press, 1992), 482–484. The latter includes the stanza: "She shot him once, she shot him twice, / Hit in the middle of his big black ass; / The whores and pimps huddled there, Waitin' for his soul to pass. / For he was her man, and he was doin' her wrong."

59. Bruce Redfern Buckley, "Frankie and Her Men: A Study of the Interrelationships of Popular and Folk Traditions" (PhD diss., Indiana Univ., 1961), 96–99.

60. Shortly after completing *A Social History of the State of Missouri*, Benton crafted lithographs of the three mythology panels from the murals and a sorghum mill tableau and sold them for $20 each through the national distribution network of Associated American Artists. In his *Frankie and Johnnie* lithograph, the figures have slightly wider eyes and more exaggerated lips than their counterparts in his mural, and the image makes clear that the line of fire from Frankie's revolver toward Johnny's buttocks was not an accident. For more on the lithographs of this scene, see Priddy, *Only the Rivers*, 129–130, and Green, "Benton's Folk Depictions," 57. This work is reproduced in Creekmore Fath, *The Lithographs of Thomas Hart Benton* (Austin: Univ. of Texas Press, 1979 [1969]), 42–43.

61. Benton, *Artist in America*, 132.

62. For audio and sheet music artwork of May Irwin's "Bully Song" (1896), see Johns Hopkins University's Lester S. Levy Sheet Music Collection, http://levysheetmusic.mse .jhu.edu/catalog/levy:142.048; see also David A. Jasen and Gene Jones, *Spreadin' Rhythm Around: Black Popular Songwriters, 1890–1930* (New York: Schirmer, 1998), 24–25, and Marlon Riggs, *Ethnic Notions* (San Francisco: California Newsreel, 1986).

63. Benton, *Artist in America*, 18–21.

64. For example, see Benton to his father, September 4, 1906; Benton to Nat Benton (brother), October 26, 1906; Benton to his father, March 24, 1907, Benton Papers, microfilm roll 2325.

65. Edelman, *Thomas Hart Benton Murals*, 2; see also Doss, *Benton, Pollock, and Modernism*, 129–131.

66. Margaret Rose Vendryes, "Hanging on Their Walls: *An Art Commentary on Lynching*, the Forgotten 1935 Art Exhibition," in *Race Consciousness: African-American Studies for the New Century*, ed. Judith Jackson Fossett and Jeffrey A. Tucker (New York: New York Univ. Press, 1997), 159, and Marlene Park, "Lynching and Antilynching: Art and Politics in the 1930s," *Prospects* 18 (1993): 333.

67. Benton to his father, September 4, 1906; Benton to his father, March 24, 1907; Benton to Thomas Craven, July 28, 1918, Benton Papers, microfilm roll 2325; Benton, Cummings interview, 30; Benton, *Artist in America*, 50, 130, 138, 162, 184–187, 197.

68. John Lomax, *Cowboy Songs and Other Frontier Ballads*, rev. ed. (New York: Macmillan, 1938), 152–155; John Lomax and Alan Lomax, *Best Loved American Ballads* (New York: Grosset and Dunlap, 1947), 283 (this collection was later republished with the title *Folk Song U.S.A.*). The Lomaxes regularly combined verses from different sources for their folk song publications, but John credited the *Cowboy Songs* version of "Jesse James" at least in part to "a Missouri Negro" named Billy Gashade.

69. Mazow, *Benton and the American Sound*, 39.

70. Quoted in Priddy, *Only the Rivers*, 121.

71. For a fuller history of these stereotypes, see Joseph Boskin, *Sambo: The Rise and Demise of an American Jester* (New York: Oxford Univ. Press, 1986), and Michael D. Harris, *Colored Pictures: Race and Visual Representation* (Chapel Hill: Univ. of North Carolina Press, 2003), chap. 3. For more on the perpetuation of such stereotypes in Depression-era film, see Donald Bogle, *Toms, Coons, Mulattoes, Mammies, and Bucks: An Interpretive History of Blacks in American Films*, 4th ed. (New York: Continuum, 2002), esp. chap. 3.

72. Doss, *Benton, Pollock, and Modernism*, 37 (emphasis in the original), 70, 80–85.

73. Baigell and Kaufman, "Missouri Murals," 317; Doss, *Benton, Pollock, and Modernism*, 130–131; Marling, "Thomas Hart Benton's Epic," 121; Priddy, *Only the Rivers*, 118.

74. Adams, *Benton: An American Original*, 266; Wolff, *Thomas Hart Benton*, 34, 45.

75. Quintin Slovek, "Thomas Hart Benton's Urban Missouri," unpublished essay, October 2013; copy in author's possession; used by permission.

76. Doss points out that industries like construction remained highly segregated during the Depression (*Benton, Pollock, and Modernism*, 86); see also Matthew Baigell, "Recovering America for American Art," in Weintraub, *Thomas Hart Benton*, 29; Adams, *Benton: An American Original*, 165–166.

77. Mazow, *Benton and the American Sound*, 10–11, 27–30.

78. Lawless, "Benton's Jealous Lover," 32–35.

79. Baigell, *Thomas Hart Benton*, 20; see also Fryd, "'Sad Twang of Mountain Voices,'" 271; Wolff, *Thomas Hart Benton*, 53–54, 66; Green, "Benton's Folk Depictions," 60.

80. See, for example, "Autograph Stamp No Lure to Artist," *Kansas City Star*, May 5, 1971, which includes photos of a sculpture diorama and a painting of a football game entitled *Forward Pass*, which Benton modeled after an ancient Etruscan sculpture of a battle scene (Benton Papers, microfilm roll 2328); see also Adams, *Benton: An American Original*, 16, 20, 26, 84; Doss, *Benton, Pollock, and Modernism*, 35–37.

81. Floyd Taylor, "Thomas Hart Benton Says Art Belongs in Clubs and Saloons, Not

Museums," *New York World-Telegram*, April 5, 1941, quoted in Adams, *Benton: An American Original*, 303. In another egregious attack, titled "Farewell to New York," Benton charged, "It is not all right when, by ingratiation or subtle connivance, precious fairies get into positions of power and judge, buy, and exhibit American pictures on a base of nervous whim and under the sway of those overdelicate refinements of taste characteristic of their kind" (reprinted in Benton, *Artist in America*, 265). Justin Wolff offers the most insightful analysis of Benton's troubled disposition toward homosexuality, attributing it in part to attitudes inherited from the artist's father, in part to a sublimated response to an attempted solicitation by his music tutor, Mr. Calhoun, during his teen years in Neosho, Missouri, and in part to a traumatic sexual molestation during Benton's art school days in Chicago by a mentor and friend that Benton referred to as "Hudspeth" (*Thomas Hart Benton*, 35–36, 73–75, 271–274); see also Adams, *Benton: An American Original*, 28–30.

82. Benton to his sister Mildred (c. 1918), quoted in Adams, *Benton: An American Original*, 84.

83. "Mr. Benton Will Leave Us Flat," *New York Sun*, April 12, 1935, reprinted in Adams, *Benton: An American Original*, 242.

84. Benton, "The Intimate Story: Boyhood," manuscript, 19–24, Benton Papers, microfilm roll 2325.

85. Priddy, *Only the Rivers*, 76.

86. Benton, *Artist in America*, 79–80.

87. Ibid., 22.

88. Adams, *Benton: An American Original*, 38.

89. Benton, *Artist in America*, 37. For further analysis of Benton's vexed disposition toward women, see Doss, *Benton, Pollock, and Modernism*, 35–36.

90. In his 1936 lithograph version of *Frankie and Johnnie* for Associated American Artists, Benton enlarged the relative size of this portrait within the composition and stripped the performer down to her stockings and a hat; see Fath, *Lithographs of Benton*, 42–43.

91. Baigell and Kaufman, "Missouri Murals," 317.

92. Barbara Melosh, *Engendering Culture: Manhood and Womanhood in New Deal Public Art and Theater* (Washington, DC: Smithsonian Institution Press, 1991), 1–12.

93. Baigell and Kaufman, "Missouri Murals," 317.

94. As Benton explained in an unpublished essay, the well-dressed figure in the *Politics, Farming, and Law in Missouri* panel was modeled after a St. Louis political operative named Mr. Sharkey, who was raising objections with the governor about the artist's depiction of African Americans in the *Social History of the State of Missouri* murals. As a salve to this criticism, Benton created a spot for a well-dressed black spectator and modeled it after the aggrieved Mr. Sharkey (Benton, "The Thirties," reprinted in Priddy, *Only the Rivers*, 254–256).

95. Quoted in Priddy, *Only the Rivers*, 120.

96. Doss, *Benton, Pollock, and Modernism*, 131.

97. Baigell and Kaufman, "Missouri Murals," 319.

CHAPTER 4. WHITEFACE MARIONETTES: JOHN HUSTON'S COMIC MELODRAMA

1. John Huston, *An Open Book* (New York: Knopf, 1980), 53; "Frankie, Fat and 58, Silent About Johnny," *New York Telegram*, October 30, 1930. It appears that Huston misidentifies the name of Ruth Squires's mentor. More likely, Squires worked with Remo Bufano. Although he was abroad for half of 1929 on a Guggenheim fellowship to Europe, Bufano

orchestrated numerous puppet theater productions in Greenwich Village (particularly at the Provincetown Playhouse) during the late 1920s and early 1930s before serving as director of the New York Marionette Division of the WPA's Theater Project from 1934 to 1939. For more on Bufano's work, see Bufano, *Magic Strings: Marionette Plays with Production Notes* (New York: Macmillan, 1939); Arthur Richmond, ed., *Remo Bufano's Book of Puppetry* (New York: Macmillan, 1955); and John Bell, "New York Puppet Modernism: Remo Bufano and Jane Heap," in *American Puppet Modernism: Essays on the Material World in Performance* (New York: Palgrave Macmillan, 2008), 71–96.

2. Stuart Kaminsky, *John Huston: Maker of Magic* (Boston: Houghton Mifflin, 1978), 4. A *New York Telegram* feature suggests in passing that Huston's mother assisted with his research on *Frankie and Johnny*, but provides no details ("Frankie, Fat and 58").

3. Axel Madsen, *John Huston* (Garden City, NY: Doubleday, 1978), 6.

4. In his autobiography, *An Open Book*, Huston mentions only running this initial $500 up to a sum of $11,000 through an exceptional lucky streak with the dice (54). In his conversations with the biographer Axel Madsen, he amended this story by admitting to losing the money (25).

5. Lest I exaggerate Huston's research endeavors, twelve of his thirteen ballad variants were collected by other researchers, and at least nine of these items had been previously published. Such compilation practices were fairly standard for folklorists of the time.

6. John Huston, *Frankie and Johnny* (New York: Boni, 1930), 104–111. Huston traced the etymology of his preferred term for pimp, "mack," to the French term *maquereau* by way of New Orleans.

7. Sonnet Retman, *Real Folks: Race and Genre in the Great Depression* (Durham, NC: Duke Univ. Press, 2011), 14.

8. Lawrence Grobel, *The Hustons* (New York: Scribner's Sons, 1989), 130.

9. Richard Krakeur to Robert Milton, March 3, 1945; from Mark Cohen (attorney) to John Huston, May 31, 1945, John Huston Papers, folder 73.f-664, Margaret Herrick Library, Academy of Motion Picture Arts and Sciences (hereafter cited as Huston Papers).

10. Huston, *Frankie and Johnny*, 79.

11. Ibid., 32.

12. Eugene O'Neill, *All God's Chillun Got Wings* (1924), act 1, scene 3.

13. Grobel, *Hustons*, 108–112, 121.

14. Huston, *Frankie and Johnny*, 17.

15. Bruce Buckley's study of the ballad finds Frankie brought to trial in roughly fifty of the more than two hundred versions that he compiled; of these, in fourteen variants she is hanged, and in six she is sentenced to the electric chair ("Frankie and Her Men: A Study of the Interrelationships of Popular and Folk Traditions," PhD diss., Indiana Univ., 1961), 96–103.

16. Huston, *Frankie and Johnny*, 20.

17. Ibid., 22 (emphasis added). For emphasis, Frankie repeats this point—"Let them hear my tale how I loved an' done wrong"—in the closing lines of the prologue (23).

18. Cecil Brown, "We Did Them Wrong: The Ballad of Frankie and Albert," in *The Rose and the Briar: Death, Love, and Liberty in the American Ballad*, ed. Sean Wilentz and Greil Marcus (New York: Norton, 2005), 128–130.

19. John Held Jr., *The Saga of Frankie and Johnny* (New York: Potter, 1972 [1930]), 48–49.

20. Huston, *Frankie and Johnny*, 79, 81.

21. Ibid., 35–36.

22. Ibid., 37, 39.

23. Ibid., 59.

24. "Those Famous Lovers, Frankie and Johnny," *New York Times Book Review*, November 30, 1930, 12.

25. Huston, *Frankie and Johnny*, 71.

26. Ibid., 73–75. Buckley found approximately thirty-eight versions of the ballad that included verses in which Frankie issued a dire warning to others not to impede the search for her unfaithful lover ("Frankie and Her Men," 62–65).

27. Huston, *Frankie and Johnny*, 77–79.

28. Ibid., 89–90.

29. Ibid., 105. Huston does not identify the source of this quotation in his essay, but it appears to be Richard Clay, who later appeared as a witness for Frankie Baker in her lawsuit against Republic Pictures—a story elaborated in the epilogue to this book.

30. Ibid., 80.

31. Ibid., 47.

32. Ibid., 57–58.

33. Ibid., 34.

34. Ibid., 67–70.

35. William Fadiman, "Re: St. Louis Legend—John Huston and Anthony Veiller," February 7, 1964, Huston Papers, folder 72.f-664.

36. Huston, *Frankie and Johnny*, 106–107.

37. "Frankie, Fat and 58."

38. Gail Bederman, *Manliness and Civilization: A Cultural History of Gender and Race in the United States, 1880–1917* (Chicago: Univ. of Chicago Press, 1995), 18–19.

39. Huston, *Frankie and Johnny*, 29–31.

40. Ibid., 76–77.

41. Unless otherwise noted, references to Huston's 1960s screenplay adaptation of Frankie and Johnny refer to an undated manuscript in the Huston Papers, folder 72.f-657. From details in associated correspondence and another closely related draft dated August 5, 1963 (folder 73.f-663), it seems reasonable to date the first screenplay to c. 1963.

42. Ernest Anderson to Huston, May 18, 1965, Huston Papers, folder 93.f-876.

43. John Huston, draft of *Frankie and Johnny* screenplay, n.d. (c. 1963), 3, Huston Papers, folder 72.f-657.

44. Ibid., 28–30. One wonders about the possible influence of film stars like Mae West on the newly competent incarnation of Frankie in Huston's 1960s screenplays.

45. Cecil Brown, *Stagolee Shot Billy* (Cambridge, Mass.: Harvard Univ. Press, 2003), 11–12, 21–36; Buckley, "Frankie and Her Men," 68–69, 77–78, 84–91, 96. The connections are extensive enough that Cecil Brown tentatively proposes that the two ballads may have been penned by the same composer, St. Louis's Bill Dooley; see C. Brown, "We Did Them Wrong," 142–145.

46. C. Brown, *Stagolee Shot Billy*, 48–59; John W. Roberts, *From Trickster to Badman: The Black Folk Hero in Slavery and Freedom* (Philadelphia: Univ. of Pennsylvania Press, 1989), 207–211. Brown's research suggests that Stagolee's real-life inspiration, Lee Shelton, likely had some involvement with prostitution as well, whether as a "go-between" or a pimp (38–39, 46–48).

47. Huston, draft of *Frankie and Johnny* screenplay, n.d. (c. 1963), 28–30, Huston Papers, folder 72.f-657.

48. Ibid., 51.

49. Ibid., 52–55.

50. Huston, *Open Book*, 53.

51. Grobel, *Hustons*, 114.

52. Huston, *Open Book*, 53.

53. Grobel, *Hustons*, 129–30.

54. George Gershwin, "Rhapsody in Catfish Row: Mr. Gershwin Tells the Origin and Scheme for His Music in That New Folk Opera Called 'Porgy and Bess,'" *New York Times*, October 20, 1935; Walter Rimler, *George Gershwin: An Intimate Portrait* (Urbana: Univ. of Illinois Press, 2009), 83–86; Deena Rosenberg, *Fascinating Rhythm: The Collaboration of George and Ira Gershwin* (New York: Dutton, 1991), 263–319.

55. Huston, *Open Book*, 130–131; see also "Gossip of the Rialto: News and Gossip of the Broadway Sector," *New York Times*, June 1, 1930.

56. William de Lys to John Huston, July 14, 1952, Huston Papers, folder 73.f-664; Alexis Greene, *Lucille Lortel: The Queen of Broadway* (New York: Proscenium, 2004), 116–119; Whitney Bolden, *Morning Telegraph*, October 30, 1952, quoted in Greene, *Lucille Lortel*, 118–119; David Harold Cox, *Irwin Bazelon: A Bio-Bibliography* (Westport, Conn.: Greenwood, 2000), 65.

57. Ronald Bennett to John Huston, February 20, 1953; Bennett to Huston, August 24, 1953; clippings sent from Bennett to Huston: "Old Ballad Dramatized," *Los Angeles Times*, April 22, 1953; "Hollywood Battlements," *Los Angeles Examiner*, April 15, 1953; and "Blues Ballad Dramatized," *Dance News*, June 1953, Huston Papers, folder 73.f-664. In addition, the play was performed by community theatrical groups in Woodstock, New York, and Chagrin Falls, Ohio; see Randy Echols to John Huston, n.d. (c. 1950), and William R. Dempsey to John Huston, April 29, 1955, Huston Papers, folder 73.f-664.

58. Paul McPharlin, *The Puppet Theatre in America: A History, 1524–1948* (Boston: Plays, Inc., 1969 [1949]), 351.

59. Ibid., 469. Squires's mentor, Remo Bufano, staged children's plays such as *Cinderella* and *The Fox and the Grapes* at the New York City's Provincetown Playhouse during the 1928 and 1929 seasons (405–06).

60. McPharlin, *Puppet Theatre in America*, 331–357; Ryan Howard, *Paul McPharlin and the Puppet Theater* (Jefferson, NC: McFarland, 2006), 32–42, 59–63; Bell, "New York Puppet Modernism," 74–91.

61. Howard, *Paul McPharlin*, 58. Ruth Squires, who originally performed Huston's *Frankie and Johnny*, later worked with McPharlin in the Marionette Fellowship of Detroit in 1932–33 (212).

62. A small sampling of books on this topic includes Houston Baker, *Modernism and the Harlem Renaissance* (Chicago: Univ. of Chicago Press, 1989); Ann Douglas, *Terrible Honesty: Mongrel Manhattan in the 1920s* (New York: Noonday, 1995); Richard Powell and David A. Bailey, *Rhapsodies in Black: Art of the Harlem Renaissance* (Berkeley: Univ. of California Press, 1997); Miriam Thaggert, *Images of Black Modernism: Verbal and Visual Strategies of the Harlem Renaissance* (Amherst: Univ. of Massachusetts Press, 2010); James Smethurst, *The African American Roots of Modernism: From Reconstruction to the Harlem Renaissance* (Chapel Hill: Univ. of North Carolina Press, 2011); James Donald, *Some of These Days: Black Stars, Jazz Aesthetics, and Modernist Culture* (New York: Oxford Univ. Press, 2015).

63. Huston, *Open Book*, 143–144.

64. As a sign of this close relationship, Van Vechten wrote the preface for Covarrubias's *The Prince Wales* and the volume featured the artist's rendering of Van Vechten among its gallery of caricatures; see Beverly J. Cox and Denna Jones Anderson, *Miguel Covarrubias Caricatures* (Washington, DC: Smithsonian Institution Press, 1985), 42. For more on Van

Vechten's role in the New Negro Renaissance, see Emily Bernard, *Carl Van Vechten and the Harlem Renaissance: A Portrait in Black and White* (New Haven, Conn.: Yale Univ. Press, 2012), esp. chap. 3.

65. Miguel Covarrubias, "Enter, the New Negro, a Distinctive Type Recently Created by the Coloured Cabaret Belt in New York," *Vanity Fair*, December 1924, 60–61.

66. Adriana Williams, *Covarrubias* (Austin: Univ. of Texas Press, 1994), 55.

67. Covarrubias, "Enter, the New Negro," 60.

68. This same illustration was retitled *At Leroy's* and stripped of its earlier caption in Covarrubias's *Negro Drawings* (New York: Knopf, 1927), 42. In the latter publication, the image is rendered in color.

69. W. E. B. Du Bois, "The Browsing Reader," *Crisis* 37, no. 4 (April 1930): 129.

70. Huston, *Frankie and Johnny*, 88–91.

71. Ibid., 87.

72. Ibid., 86.

73. Held, *Saga of Frankie and Johnny*, 6–7.

74. Ibid., 24.

75. "Chicago Police Close 'Frankie and Johnnie,'" *New York Times*, June 13, 1929; "Chicago Police Open Drive to Purify Legitimate Stage," *Washington Post*, June 15, 1929; "Play 'Frankie and Johnnie' Raided by Police as Indecent; Fifteen Arrests are Made," *New York Times*, September 11, 1930; "'Frankie, Johnny' Cast Faces Trial," *Washington Post*, September 14, 1930. Kirkland's play—set in 1849 St. Louis—seems to have suffered from some of the same problems of divided focus that plagued Huston's work. The reviewer J. Brooks Atkinson opined, "The trouble is that 'Frankie and Johnnie' never quite makes up its mind just what kind of play it intends to be. In the first act it is, by periods, local color, melodrama, farce and burlesque. Later it turns its attention more straightforwardly to the sentimental love story" (Atkinson, "'Frankie and Johnnie' Full of 1849 Color," *New York Times*, September 26, 1930).

CHAPTER 5. THE FINEST WOMAN EVER TO WALK THE STREETS: MAE WEST'S OUTLAW EXPLOITS IN *SHE DONE HIM WRONG*

1. Jill Watts, *Mae West: An Icon in Black and White* (New York: Oxford Univ. Press, 2001), 314.

2. Ibid., 59; Simon Louvish, *Mae West: It Ain't No Sin* (New York: Dunne, 2005), 99–100.

3. Watts, *Mae West: Icon*, 261, 292–293, 308.

4. Mae West, *Goodness Had Nothing to Do With It* (New York: Avon, 1959), 135.

5. Watts, *Mae West: Icon*, 32–33.

6. The authorship of several of West's projects was contested. For example, Mark Linder claimed that West's play *Diamond Lil* (1928) was based on his own play *Chatham Square*, which he had pitched to West. West does seem to have borrowed Linder's setting and the character of Chick Clark from Linder's script, but little else in the way of plot or her protagonist, Lady Lou; see Watts, *Mae West: Icon*, 98–104; Louvish, *Mae West: Ain't No Sin*, 150–151; Emily Wortis Leider, *Becoming Mae West* (New York: Da Capo, 1997), 186. West also tended to diminish the contributions of male collaborators, as she did with John Bright and Harry Thew regarding the screenplays for *She Done Him Wrong* (Leider, *Becoming Mae West*, 252; Louvish, *Mae West: Ain't No Sin*, 211). Nonetheless, I concur with West biographers such as Watts, Leider, and Louvish that the dialogue and protagonists in her plays and the film *She Done Him Wrong* unambiguously bear her imprint.

7. Marybeth Hamilton, *"When I'm Bad, I'm Better": Mae West, Sex, and American Entertainment* (Berkeley: Univ. of California Press, 1995), 6.

8. The MPPDA's Motion Picture Production Code lacked rigorous implementation measures while under the leadership of Will Hays, from 1930 to mid-1934. West's *She Done Him Wrong* and *I'm No Angel* (1933) were among the movies most responsible for the hiring of Joseph Breen in 1934 and the establishment of the Production Code Administration to enforce the Code's restrictions on the display of sexually suggestive content and criminal activities; see Lea Jacobs, *The Wages of Sin: Censorship and the Fallen Woman Film, 1928–1942* (Berkeley: Univ. of California Press, 1995), 27–42, 106–116; Ramona Curry, *Too Much of a Good Thing: Mae West as Cultural Icon* (Minneapolis: Univ. of Minnesota Press, 1996).

9. Leider, *Becoming Mae West*, 248; Curry, *Too Much*, 34.

10. *She Done Him Wrong* clippings file, Mae West Collection compiled by Dolly Dempsey, box 2, Margaret Herrick Library, Academy of Motion Picture Arts and Sciences (hereafter cited as West Collection).

11. Ruth Biery, "The Private Life of Mae West," *Movie Classic* 5, no. 5 (January 1934): 57; Watts, *Mae West: Icon*, 12–22; Leider, *Becoming Mae West*, 33–34, 41.

12. Malcolm H. Oettinger, "Literary Lil," *Street and Smith's Picture Play* 39, no. 1 (September 1933), 26; see also Watts, *Mae West: Icon*, 47–53; Hamilton, *"When I'm Bad,"* 26–27; West, *Goodness*, 60.

13. Watts, *Mae West: Icon*, 60–69.

14. "Shake That Thing" also was recorded by the blues singer Papa Charlie Jackson in 1925, but Waters's version made the more significant impression on West and the general public; see Randall Cherry, "Ethel Waters: 'Long, Lean, Lanky Mama,'" in *Nobody Knows Where the Blues Come From: Lyrics and History*, ed. Robert Springer (Jackson: Univ. of Mississippi Press, 2006), 275.

15. Zora Neale Hurston, "Characteristics of Negro Expression," in *The Sanctified Church: The Folklore Writings of Zora Neale Hurston* (Berkeley, Calif.: Turtle Island, 1981), 65–66.

16. Ann Douglas, *Terrible Honesty: Mongrel Manhattan in the 1920s* (New York: Noonday, 1995), esp. chap. 9.

17. West, *Sex*, reprinted in *Three Plays by Mae West*, ed. Lillian Schlissel (New York: Routledge, 1997 [1926]), 36, 51, 59–79, 91–92.

18. Mae West and John Bright, *Ruby Red*, first script, November 8, 1932, A-10, West Collection, box 2.

19. Song lyrics for "Diamond Lil" among West's papers suggest that Lil escapes from Chick's chokehold by having sex with him, including a verse that says, "Then he grabbed me by the throat / And he meant to kill me dead / I gave him one of my movements / And he lays me on the bed instead" (West, "Diamond Lil" song lyrics, West Collection, box 2).

20. Racist essentialism also makes an appearance here as Serge fawns, "The men of my country go wild about women with yellow hair"—a line even more charged when the character was Pablo Juárez from Rio de Janeiro in *Diamond Lil* and in early drafts of the screenplay (*Diamond Lil* script sequences, November 8, 1932, B-35, West Collection, box 2). Emily Leider notes that the identities of Serge and Rita were changed from South American to Russian for fear of alienating the Latin American film market. Along similar lines, earlier references to Rio de Janeiro as the destination of Gus Jordan's white slavery captives were changed to the Barbary Coast (*Becoming Mae West*, 247).

21. Bruce Redfern Buckley, "Frankie and Her Men: A Study of the Interrelationships of Popular and Folk Traditions" (PhD diss., Indiana Univ., 1961), 40; Curry, *Too Much*, 6–8.

22. West, *Diamond Lil*, full script, n.d., 2.10, West Collection, box 2.

23. Mae West and John Bright, treatment of *Diamond Lady* for Paramount production staff meeting, October 18, 1932, 16, West Collection, box 2.

24. Douglas, *Terrible Honesty*, 6–9, 217–253.

25. Hamilton, *"When I'm Bad,"* 108–125.

26. *Chicago Evening American*, February 10, 1929, quoted in Louvish, *Mae West: Ain't No Sin*, 162–163.

27. Leider, *Becoming Mae West*, 15, 256–257.

28. As Leider notes, even in West's youth, "for her amateur outings, Mae never chose to sing the flowery sentimental storytelling sob ballads like 'After the Ball' or 'The Fatal Wedding', which were still popular in the first years of the new century" (*Becoming Mae West*, 40).

29. Reprinted in Louvish, *Mae West: Ain't No Sin*, xi; see also Mae West, "Me and My Past," *Delaware Star*, September 9, 1934.

30. Gus Jordan's establishment was known as "Suicide Hall" in the play *Diamond Lil*, but West eventually dropped this moniker from the film out of censorship concerns; see West and Bright, treatment of *Diamond Lady* for Paramount production staff meeting, October 18, 1932, 2, West Collection, box 2.

31. Jacobs, *Wages of Sin*, 5–9; Deborah Anna Logan, *Fallenness in Victorian Women's Writing: Marry, Stitch, Die, or Do Worse* (Columbia: Univ. of Missouri Press, 1998), 1–26.

32. West, *Diamond Lil*, full script, n.d., 1.17, West Collection, box 2.

33. Sandra Lieb, *Mother of the Blues: A Study of Ma Rainey* (Amherst: Univ. of Massachusetts Press, 1981), 126. In a similar vein, Angela Davis writes of Bessie Smith's "Easy Come, Easy Go Blues": "This song is about a woman who refuses to allow the mistreatment she has suffered at the hands of a man to plunge her into depression. She refuses to take love so seriously that its loss threatens her very essence" (Davis, *Blues Legacies and Black Feminism: Gertrude "Ma" Rainey, Bessie Smith, and Billie Holiday* [New York: Vintage, 1998], 39).

34. David A. Jasen and Gene Jones, *Spreadin' Rhythm Around: Black Popular Songwriters, 1890–1930* (New York: Schirmer, 1998), 145–151; Peter C. Muir, *Long Lost Blues: Popular Blues in America, 1850–1920* (Urbana: Univ. of Illinois Press, 2010), 123–124.

35. West's snappy delivery of lines and lyrics in *She Done Him Wrong* contrasted with her stage performance in *Diamond Lil*, which critics singled out for her *slower* pace relative to the other actors'. The reviewer Charles Brackett, for example, noted West's manner of "pushing hip after hip with defiant languor," in *Diamond Lil* ("Charles Brackett Reviews Diamond Lil," *New Yorker*, April 21, 1928, reprinted in George Oppenheimer, ed., *The Passionate Playgoer: A Personal Scrapbook* [New York: Viking, 1958], 597). For a discussion of the importance of West's up-tempo pace to her successful turn in the film *Night After Night*, see Hamilton, *"When I'm Bad,"* 176, and West, *Goodness*, 133.

36. Douglas, *Terrible Honesty*, 165, 356–357.

37. Watts, *Mae West: Icon*, 194; Curry, *Too Much*, 12–13.

38. Chris Albertson, *Bessie*, rev. ed. (New Haven, Conn.: Yale Univ. Press, 2003), 233–234.

39. Barry Singer, *Black and Blue: The Life and Lyrics of Andy Razaf* (New York: Schirmer, 1992), 257–258.

40. Watts, *Mae West: Icon*, v, 67–68; Leider, *Becoming Mae West*, 128, 220; Louvish, *Mae West: Ain't No Sin*, 173–174.

41. Hamilton, *"When I'm Bad,"* 94; Louvish, *Mae West: Ain't No Sin*, 107.

42. See, for example, West and Bright, *Ruby Red*, revised final script, November 22, 1932, A-19–A-21, West Collection, box 2. On West's connections to burlesque, see Hamilton, *"When I'm Bad,"* 47–48, 52–55.

43. Davis, *Blues Legacies*, 38–39.

44. Only these two verses of Rainger and Robin's composition remain, because alarmed Hollywood censors insisted that Paramount recall all prints of the film and delete the rest of the song (Hamilton, *"When I'm Bad,"* 187; Curry, *Too Much*, 33.). Among the lyrics left on the cutting room floor were the following: "A hasty job really spoils a master's touch / I don't like a big commotion / I'm a demon for slow motion or such."

45. Albertson, *Bessie*, 66–73, 102–106; Paige A. McGinley, *Staging the Blues: From Tent Shows to Tourism* (Durham, NC: Duke Univ. Press, 2014), 31, 54–56.

46. Robert Hayden, "Homage to the Empress of the Blues," in *Robert Hayden: Collected Poems* (New York: Liveright, 1985), 32.

47. Leider, *Becoming Mae West*, 248–251.

48. Emily Rutter, "The Blues Tribute Poem and the Legacies of Gertrude 'Ma' Rainey and Bessie Smith," *MELUS* 39, no. 4 (Winter 2014): 65–79.

49. In the stage play *Diamond Lil* and early screenplay drafts, set pieces of dialogue involving the saloon's patrons insightfully captured the simultaneous impulses of fear and attraction that drew "society" audiences in substantial numbers to working-class venues such as Bowery saloons in the 1890s—and by implication, to cabarets in the late 1920s and early 1930s. West referred to such audiences as "blue-stocking slummers seeking thrills" in one undated *Diamond Lil* script (West Collection, box 5); see also "Dialog for Tables" ("Society Tables"), in ibid.

50. Davis, *Blues Legacies*, 38.

51. Albertson, *Bessie*, 83–85, 196–200; McGinley, *Staging the Blues*, 51.

52. Lieb, *Mother of the Blues*, 17, 124–125; Albertson, *Bessie*, 78–85, 112–116, 133–138; McGinley, *Staging the Blues*, 63–66.

53. Leider, *Becoming Mae West*, 123, 220–221; Watts, *Mae West: Icon*, 207–208; Curry, *Too Much*, 17–18. Although clearly intrigued by homosexuality, West seems to have embraced the prevailing medical diagnosis of the day, which described it as a mental illness that might be "corrected" through treatment (Hamilton, *"When I'm Bad,"* 55–66; Leider, *Becoming Mae West*, 156–157).

54. Lieb, *Mother of the Blues*, 25.

55. Leider, *Becoming Mae West*, 277–279; Hamilton, *"When I'm Bad,"* 190.

56. *I'm No Angel* pressbook, Margaret Herrick Library, Academy of Motion Picture Arts and Sciences, quoted in Watts, *Mae West: Icon*, 164.

57. Max Wilk, *The Wit and Wisdom of Hollywood* (New York: Atheneum, 1971), 34.

58. Hilary Lynn, "Has Mae West a Dual Personality?," *Modern Screen* 12, no. 5 (April 1936): 41; Dana Rush, "Back of the West Front," *Photoplay* 45, no. 3 (February 1934), 109; Mae West, "Notes for Opening Speech," n.d., West Collection, box 5.

59. Lynn, "Has Mae West," 98. In an earlier article, Lynn aptly commented on West's approach to making love on screen: "Sex is no tragedy. Nor should there be any sense of guilt attached to it. Sex is something to enjoy, something to laugh about. Certainly not a harmful thing, a sinful thing" (Lynn, "How 12 Stars Make Love," *Photoplay* 44, no. 3 [August 1933], 31).

60. McGinley, *Staging the Blues*, 57.

61. Patricia Keats, "The Four Big Shots of Hollywood," *Silver Screen* 4, no. 4 (February 1934): 14–15, 57.

62. Douglas Fairbanks Jr., interview by Kathlyn Hayden, "Why I Quit Hollywood," *Photoplay* 45, no. 3 (February 1934): 54.

63. Jill Watts observes that an earlier draft of the *She Done Him Wrong* screenplay granted Lou's maid (at that point named Maizie) a more cutting line. When Lou quips of a controlling man, "I thought Lincoln put an end to slavery," Maizie remarks, "Ah ain't heard tell of it." When Lou then says, "Well, that guy never heard of it either," it seems to mark a clear linking of racial and gender oppression. Unfortunately, this scene did not make it into the final film; see West and Bright, *Ruby Red*, first script, November 8, 1932, A-32, West Collection, box 2, quoted in Watts, *Mae West: Icon*, 160.

64. Watts, *Mae West: Icon*, 159; see also Donald Bogle, *Toms, Coons, Mulattoes, Mammies, and Bucks: An Interpretive History of Blacks in American Films* (New York: Continuum, 1990), 45–46. West's play *The Wicked Age* (1927) and her novel *The Constant Sinner* (1930) include maids that balance stereotypical dialect with more well-rounded personas, offering advice to West's protagonists and at least hinting at independent lives of their own (Watts, *Mae West: Icon*, 97–98, 128).

65. Leider, *Becoming Mae West*, 266, 293, 306; Louvish, *Mae West: Ain't No Sin*, 233–234. Watts, however, describes West's earlier relationship with the maid Bea Jackson as closer than the one with Taylor (*Mae West: Icon*, 69).

66. One of West's screenplay drafts calls for Lou's dress to be "a stunning glitter of flame and sparkle" (West, Diamond Lil Sequence "B" outline, October 31, 1932, 3, West Collection, box 2). In the initial run of *Diamond Lil*, West's dress for the performance of "Frankie and Johnny" was "flaming red" (Watts, *Mae West: Icon*, 101).

67. In an appearance on Rudy Vallée's radio program to promote *She Done Him Wrong*, West concluded with the stock verse: "The moral has no story / This story has no end / Story only goes to show / There ain't no good in men" (Watts, *Mae West: Icon*, 158–159).

68. West sought to craft her public image through witty, spontaneous performance, but her biographers describe a more prosaic reality that involved "long days and nights spent alone, painstakingly writing the notes, treatments, and ideas" that became her plays and screenplays (Louvish, *Mae West: Ain't No Sin*, 117).

69. West and Bright, *Ruby Red* script, November 8, 1932, C-7, West Collection, box 2.

70. West and Bright, *Ruby Red*, revised final script, November 22, 1932, C-36–C-37, West Collection, box 2.

71. *Diamond Lil* script, n.d., C-9, West Collection, box 5; *Ruby Red* script, November 8, 1932, C-8, West Collection, box 2.

72. West and Bright, *Ruby Red*, first script, November 8, 1932, C-13–C-14, West Collection, box 2.

73. As one reviewer noted of the film: "Another virtue is that Mae . . . remains likable and humorous in all her outrageousness. She makes you feel that she doesn't take herself too seriously and that she won't make a bid for your tears by attempting repentance and refinement in the end" (unidentified review, Mae West Scrapbook #2 compiled by Dolly Dempsey, West Collection, box 13).

74. Hamilton, *"When I'm Bad,"* 207–213; Jacobs, *Wages of Sin*, 106–116; Mick LaSalle, *Complicated Women: Sex and Power in Pre-Code Hollywood* (New York: Dunne, 2000), 200–201; Curry, *Too Much*, 34–35.

75. Jacobs, *Wages of Sin*, 5–9.

76. Other variants that refer to Frankie's acquittal in court appear, for example, in Ethel Park Richardson, *American Mountain Songs* (New York: Greenberg, 1927), 38–39; John Huston, *Frankie and Johnny* (New York: Boni, 1930), 131–135; H. M. Belden, "Ballads and Songs Collected by the Missouri Folk-Lore Society," *University of Missouri Studies* 15, no. 1 (January 1940): 330–333; Alan Lomax, *The Folk Songs of North America in the English Lan-*

guage (Garden City, N.Y.: Doubleday, 1960), 569–570; and Buckley, "Frankie and Her Men," 96–99.

CHAPTER 6. THE LYNCHING OF JOHNNY:
STERLING BROWN'S SOCIAL REALIST CRITIQUE

1. Alain Locke, "Sterling Brown: The New Negro Folk-Poet," in *Negro: An Anthology*, ed. Nancy Cunard (New York: Continuum, 1996 [1934]), 88.

2. Joanne Gabbin, *Sterling A. Brown: Building the Black Aesthetic Tradition* (Charlottes-ville: Univ. Press of Virginia, 1985), 139–140.

3. See, for example, Brown's essays "The Blues as Folk Poetry," in *Folk-Say: A Regional Miscellany*, vol. 1, ed. Benjamin A. Botkin (Norman: Univ. of Oklahoma Press, 1930), 324–339, and "Negro Folk Expression: Spirituals, Seculars, Ballads and Work Songs," *Phylon* 14, no. 1 (Winter 1953): 45–61.

4. *The Collected Poems of Sterling A. Brown*, ed. Michael S. Harper (Chicago: TriQuarterly Books, 1989), 44. All subsequent quotations from the poem are from this edition, which is identical to the original.

5. Adam Gussow, *Seems like Murder Here: Southern Violence and the Blues Tradition* (Chicago: Univ. of Chicago Press, 2002), 4.

6. Hurd to Brown, May 25, 1932, box 6, H folder, Sterling A. Brown Papers, Moorland-Spingarn Research Center, Howard University (hereafter cited as Brown Papers).

7. Brown to Walter White, May 21, 1937, box 51, WPA folder, Brown Papers. Correspon-dence in the Brown Papers indicates that the primary factor that led Scott, Foresman and Company to reject his second poetry manuscript, *No Hiding Place*, in 1937 was their fear that "most of the selections from Brown would be dynamite throughout the Southern area." Thus, the manuscript did not see publication until its inclusion in *The Collected Poems of Ster-ling A. Brown* in 1980; see W. E. Gobble to Eda Lou Walton, Damon, and Anderson, June 29, 1939, and Walton to W. E. Gobble, July 4, 1939, box 7, 1930s Correspondence, W folder, Brown Papers.

8. Sterling Brown, "Cabaret," *Collected Poems*, 111–113.

9. Sterling Brown, *The Negro in American Fiction* (New York: Atheneum, 1969 [1937]), 51–53, 93–95.

10. Gabbin, *Sterling A. Brown*, 24–29, 32; Sterling Brown, "A Son's Return: 'Oh, Didn't He Ramble'" (1973), in *A Son's Return: Selected Essays of Sterling A. Brown*, ed. Mark Sanders (Boston: Northeastern Univ. Press, 1996), 15, 19–21.

11. See, for example, Botkin to Brown, May 22, 1932, box 7, 1930s Correspondence, B folder, Brown Papers; Steven B. Shively, "No 'Urbanized Fake Folk Thing': Benjamin Botkin, Sterling Brown, and 'Ma Rainey,'" in *America's Folklorist: B. A. Botkin and American Culture*, ed. Lawrence Rodgers and Jerrold Hirsch (Norman: Univ. of Oklahoma Press, 2010), 149–167; John Edgar Tidwell, "Reading Sterling A. Brown through the Alembic of Benjamin A. Botkin and *Folk-Say*," in Rodgers and Hirsch, *America's Folklorist*, 168–183. Brown published an additional six poems in the 1932 edition of *Folk-Say*, which became part of his *No Hiding Place* manuscript.

12. S. Brown, "Blues as Folk Poetry," 325.

13. Brown to Mr. Jones of the Urban League, January 14, 1939, box 51, WPA folder, Brown Papers. The Federal Writers' Project's collection of oral histories from ex-slaves, which Brown helped guide, subsequently served as the basis for Benjamin Botkin's edited collection *Lay My Burden Down: A Folk History of Slavery* (1945).

14. Brown to Newsom, March 1, 1940, box 51, WPA folder, Brown Papers. For a concise sampling of Brown's conflicts with various state offices of the FWP, see Tidwell, "Reading Sterling A. Brown," in Rodgers and Hirsch, *America's Folklorist*, 174–177.

15. Brown to Gene [Eugene Holmes], July 17, 1936, box 51, WPA folder, Brown Papers.

16. Sterling Brown, *Negro Poetry and Drama* (New York: Atheneum, 1969 [1937]), 29. On Gellert's complicated legacy, see chapter 2, note 132.

17. Sterling Brown, "The Social Song," from "Freedom: A Concert in Celebration of the 75th Anniversary of the Thirteenth Amendment to the Constitution of the United States," held at the Library of Congress, December 20, 1940. A recording of the concert was released on the CD *Freedom*, Bridge Records 9114 (2002). This "Program of Negro Folk Songs" featured music by the Golden Gate Quartet and Josh White, and was divided into three parts. Alain Locke served as introducer for the opening section, "Negro Spirituals," followed by "Ballads and Blues," with remarks from Brown. A third section, "Reels and Work Songs," featured commentary by Alan Lomax. These same speakers and performers participated in a nearly identical program in commemoration of Fisk University's seventy-fifth anniversary the following year; see Fisk University Seventy-Fifth Anniversary Celebration program booklet, box 6, Documents folder, Brown Papers.

18. Sterling Brown, "Old Time Tales," *New Masses*, February 25, 1936, 25 (emphasis in the original).

19. Sterling Brown, "The Literary Scene," *Opportunity* 16 (April 1938): 120.

20. *Sterling A. Brown's A Negro Looks at the South*, ed. John Edgar Tidwell and Mark A. Sanders (Oxford: Oxford Univ. Press, 2007), 37–39. McCorkle served as the inspiration for Brown's poem "Revelations."

21. Lewis W. Jones, "Sterling A. Brown: The Fisk Year—1928–29," in Black History Museum Committee, ed., *Sterling A. Brown: A UMUM Tribute* (Philadelphia: Black History Museum UMUM Publishers, 1976), 50–54.

22. Brown to Davis, January 23, 1939, box 7, 1930s Correspondence, B folder; Davis to Brown, January 23, 1939, box 7, 1930s Correspondence, D folder, Brown Papers; see also Gabbin, *Sterling A. Brown*, 33–36, 91–93.

23. Brown to J.H. [possibly J. H. Harmon], October 27, 1936, box 51, WPA folder, Brown Papers.

24. Sterling Brown, "The Approach of the Creative Artist," *Journal of American Folklore* 59, no. 234 (October–December 1946): 506. Although the conference at which Brown delivered these remarks was held in 1942, the proceedings were not published until 1946; see Tidwell, "Reading Sterling A. Brown," 182.

25. S. Brown, "Spirituals, Seculars, Ballads," 52–53.

26. Gabbin, *Sterling A. Brown*, 89–90.

27. Hughes to Brown, September 14, 1931, box 6, H folder, Brown Papers.

28. Gabbin, *Sterling A. Brown*, 30–31; Sanders, *Afro-Modernist Aesthetics and the Poetry of Sterling A. Brown* (Athens: Univ. of Georgia Press, 1999), 61.

29. Bond to Brown, December 25, 1931, box 7, Correspondence 1930s, B folder, Brown Papers; S. Brown, "Blues as Folk Poetry," 324. "TOBA" refers to the Theater Owners Booking Association performance circuit, which catered to African American vaudeville performers.

30. S. Brown, "A Son's Return," 14; see also Gabbin, *Sterling A. Brown*, 23–24; Sanders, *Afro-Modernist Aesthetics*, 97.

31. Sterling Brown, "Negro Folk Expression," *Phylon* 11, no. 4 (Autumn 1950): 318.

32. Brown to Gunner Myrdal, "Descriptive Catalog of Forty-one Records," October 10, 1942, box 54, Untitled Folders, Brown Papers.

33. Brown to editor of Viking Press, September 2, 1929, box 6, Correspondence 1920s-1930s, unsigned folder, Brown Papers.

34. Sterling Brown, "Odyssey of Big Boy," *Collected Poems*, 20–21; Sanders, *Afro-Modernist Aesthetics*, 44–45.

35. Gabbin, *Sterling A. Brown*, 122–123.

36. Sterling Brown, "Southern Road," *Collected Poems*, 52–53.

37. Gabbin, *Sterling A. Brown*, 132.

38. Sterling Brown, "Ruminations of Luke Johnson," *Collected Poems*, 36–37.

39. Sterling Brown, "Southern Road," *Collected Poems*, 53.

40. Sanders, *Afro-Modernist Aesthetics*, 152. For more on the badman archetype in African American folklore, see John W. Roberts, *From Trickster to Badman: The Black Folk Hero in Slavery and Freedom* (Philadelphia: Univ. of Pennsylvania Press, 1989), chap. 5.

41. Sterling Brown, "Virginia Portrait," *Collected Poems*, 38–39.

42. Sterling Brown, Arthur P. Davis, and Ulysses Lee, eds., *The Negro Caravan: Writings by American Negroes* (New York: Arno Press/New York Times, 1970 [1941]), 461–462; Brown to Myrdal, "Descriptive Catalog of Forty-one Records," October 10, 1942, box 54, Untitled Folders, Brown Papers.

43. Gerald V. O'Brien, *Framing the Moron: The Social Construction of Feeble-Mindedness in the American Eugenic Era* (Manchester, UK: Manchester Univ. Press, 2013), 58–70.

44. Edward J. Larson, *Sex, Race, and Science: Eugenics in the Deep South* (Baltimore: Johns Hopkins Univ. Press, 1995), esp. chap. 6; James B. Meriwether and Michael Millgate, eds., *Lion in the Garden: Interviews with William Faulkner, 1926–1962* (New York: Random House, 1968), 222. For a concise discussion of intellectual disability in Faulkner's fiction, see Gerald Schmidt, "Fictional Voices and Viewpoints for the Mentally Deficient, 1929–1939," in *Mental Retardation in America: A Historical Reader*, ed. Steven Noll and James W. Trent Jr. (New York: New York Univ. Press, 2004), 193–201.

45. Sanders, *Afro-Modernist Aesthetics*, 55.

46. Another artwork in a similar vein is Philip Evergood's drawing *Lynching Party* (1935), which features a grim-visaged, bejeweled blonde woman pointing an accusing finger at a young black male whose head is already encircled by a noose; see Dora Apel, *Imagery of Lynching: Black Men, White Women, and the Mob* (New Brunswick, NJ: Rutgers Univ. Press, 2004), 122–125.

47. Gwendolyn Brooks, "The Ballad of Pearl May Lee," *A Street in Bronzeville* (New York: Harper and Brothers, 1945), 42–45.

48. Sterling Brown, "Negro Character as Seen By White Authors," *Journal of Negro Education* 2, no. 2 (April 1933): 202.

49. Roy Flannagan, *Amber Satyr* (Garden City, N.Y.: Doubleday, Doran, 1932).

50. S. Brown, *A Negro Looks at the South*, 105–108.

51. Ibid., 170.

52. Popel's poem appeared in the *Crisis* in August 1934 and several times thereafter. For an analysis of her poem, see Jon Woodson, "Anti-Lynching Poems in the 1930s," *FlashPøint* 17 (Spring 2015), www.flashpointmag.com/Woodson_Anti_Lynching_Poems_in_the_1930s .htm. For details of the 1933 lynching case that inspired Popel's poem, see Anne P. Rice, ed., *Witnessing Lynching: American Writers Respond* (New Brunswick, NJ: Rutgers Univ. Press, 2003), 282–283.

53. Edith Segal, "Directing the New Dance," *New Theatre* (May 1935), 22, quoted in Ellen Graff, *Stepping Left: Dance and Politics in New York City, 1928–1942* (Durham, NC: Duke Univ. Press, 1997), 43–44.

54. Karen Keely, "Sexuality and Storytelling: Literary Representations of the 'Feeble-minded' in the Age of Sterilization," in Noll and Trent, *Mental Retardation in America*, 207–209; O'Brien, *Framing the Moron*, 65–68; Larson, *Sex, Race, and Science*, 1–4.

55. Sanders, *Afro-Modernist Aesthetics*, 38–39, 55.

56. Sterling Brown, "Strong Men," *Collected Poems*, 56–58.

57. Robin D. G. Kelley, *Hammer and Hoe: Alabama Communists during the Great Depression* (Chapel Hill: Univ. of North Carolina Press, 1990), 164; Elizabeth Davey, "The Souths of Sterling Brown," *Southern Cultures* 5, no. 2 (Summer 1999): 34. For more on the Southern Tenant Farmers' Union and Sharecroppers' Union from the vantage of their participants, see Howard Kester, *Revolt among the Sharecroppers* (Knoxville: Univ. of Tennessee Press, 1997 [1936]); H. L. Mitchell, *Roll the Union On: A Pictorial History of the Southern Tenant Farmers' Union* (Chicago: Kerr, 1987); Theodore Rosengarten, *All God's Dangers: The Life of Nate Shaw* (New York: Vintage, 1984 [1974]); Michael K. Honey, *Sharecropper's Troubadour: John L. Handcox, the Southern Tenant Farmers' Union, and the African American Song Tradition* (New York: Palgrave Macmillan, 2013).

58. Sterling Brown, "Old Lem," *Collected Poems*, 180–181. This poem first appeared in the lone issue of *New Challenge* (1937), edited by Dorothy West and featuring Richard Wright's important essay "Blueprint for Negro Writing."

59. Sanders, *Afro-Modernist Aesthetics*, 97.

60. Sterling Brown, "Johnny Thomas," *Collected Poems*, 42–43.

61. Sterling Brown, "Sam Smiley," *Collected Poems*, 45–46.

62. Gabbin, *Sterling A. Brown*, 131.

63. Gussow, *Seems like Murder Here*, 32–36, 159–194. "Crazy Blues" was composed by the African American songwriter Perry Bradford.

64. S. Brown, "Blues as Folk Poetry," 326, 329, 338.

65. S. Brown, "Negro Folk Expression," 326–327.

66. Ibid., 319.

67. S. Brown, "Spirituals, Seculars, Ballads," 52.

68. Langston Hughes, "Christ in Alabama," in *The Collected Poems of Langston Hughes*, ed. Arnold Rampersad (New York: Vintage, 1994), 143.

69. Cary Nelson, *Repression and Recovery: Modern American Poetry and the Politics of Cultural Memory, 1910–1945* (Madison: Univ. of Wisconsin Press, 1989), 200–203. *Contempo* (1931–1934) was a radical publication based in Chapel Hill, North Carolina. For more on the Scottsboro Boys, see Dan T. Carter, *Scottsboro: A Tragedy of the American South* (Baton Rouge, Louisiana State Univ. Press, 1969).

70. Wright's poem first appeared in the July–August 1935 issue of *Partisan Review* and was soon thereafter anthologized in Joseph Freeman's edited collection *Proletarian Literature in the United States* (New York: International Publishers, 1935), 202–203.

71. Sterling A. Brown, interview by Steven Jones and Stephen Henderson, Howard University, May 10, 1973, quoted in Gabbin, *Sterling A. Brown*, 38.

72. Correspondence in the Brown Papers includes numerous details of these publications and activities. See, for example, Dorothy West to Brown, June 5, 1937, box 6, Correspondence 1920s–1930s, W folder; Richard Wright to Brown, May 20, 1937, box 6, Correspondence 1920s–1930s, W folder; Brown to Granville Hicks, January 3, 1939, box 51, WPA folder; Brown to Cecile H. Biondo [League of American Writers], June 30, 1939, box 51, WPA folder; Brown to Ted Poston, December 12, 1936, box 7, 1930s Correspondence, B folder; Nan Golden [executive secretary of the League of American Writers] to Brown, October 6, 1938, box 7, 1930s Correspondence, G folder; Brown to Nan Golden, October 8,

1938, box 7, 1930s Correspondence, B folder; Brown to Richard Wright, January 23, 1939, box 51, WPA folder; Martha Millet [president, Labor Poets of America] to Brown, January 9, 1939, box 7, 1930s Correspondence, M folder; Brown to Mr. Jones [Urban League], January 14, 1939, box 51, WPA folder.

73. For more on these two exhibitions, including analysis of many of the featured artworks, see Marlene Park, "Lynching and Antilynching: Art and Politics in the 1930s," *Prospects* 18 (1993): 311–365; Margaret Rose Vendryes, "Hanging on Their Walls: *An Art Commentary on Lynching*, the Forgotten 1935 Art Exhibition," in *Race Consciousness: African-American Studies for the New Century*, ed. Judith Jackson Fossett and Jeffrey A. Tucker (New York: New York Univ. Press, 1997), 153–176; Apel, *Imagery of Lynching*, 83–131.

74. For more on Turner's case and its subsequent interpretation in works of art and literature, see Julie Buckner Armstrong, *Mary Turner and the Memory of Lynching* (Athens: Univ. of Georgia Press, 2011).

75. Apel, *Imagery of Lynching*, 87.

76. Vendryes, "Hanging on Their Walls," 166.

77. Brown referred to this practice as part of a much more graphically rendered lynching scene in the later poem "Call for Barnum" from his *No Hiding Place* manuscript.

78. Biddle to Walter White, January 13, 1935, quoted in Apel, *Imagery of Lynching*, 117. Biddle submitted this work for the NAACP's *Art Commentary on Lynching* exhibition, but White omitted the work from the show because he worried that its relationship to the theme of lynching might not be direct enough for viewers to grasp.

79. Frances K. Pohl, *In the Eye of the Storm: An Art of Conscience, 1930–1970* (San Francisco: Pomegranate Artbooks, 1995), 49; Apel, *Imagery of Lynching*, 116–117.

80. Apel, *Imagery of Lynching*, 102.

81. Walter White to Brown, December 28, 1937, box 51, WPA folder, Brown Papers.

82. Sterling Brown, "The Problems of the Negro Writer," in *Official Proceedings of the Second National Negro Congress, October 15–17, 1937* (Philadelphia: Metropolitan Opera House, 1937), n.p.

83. Joe Klein, *Woody Guthrie: A Life* (New York: Delta, 1980), 144–145. For their part, the Carter Family used the melody as the basis for their song "Little Darling, Pal of Mine."

84. Charles Wolfe and Kip Lornell, *The Life and Legend of Leadbelly* (New York: Harper-Collins, 1992), 209.

85. Gibbs M. Smith, *Joe Hill* (Salt Lake City: Univ. of Utah Press, 1969), 20–21; C. Nelson, *Repression and Recovery*, 58–61.

86. S. Brown, "Spirituals, Seculars, Ballads," 55.

87. Sanders, *Afro-Modernist Aesthetics*, 32.

EPILOGUE. AFRICAN AMERICAN WOMEN'S VOICES AND THE TIGHTROPE OF RESPECTABILITY

1. Adam Gussow, *Seems like Murder Here: Southern Violence and the Blues Tradition* (Chicago: Univ. of Chicago Press, 2002), 225.

2. Walker, "Kissie Lee," in *For My People* (New York: Arno, 1969 [1942]), 38–39.

3. Zora Neale Hurston, *Mules and Men* (Bloomington: Indiana Univ. Press, 1978 [1935]), 65–66.

4. Robert E. Hemenway, *Zora Neale Hurston: A Literary Biography* (Urbana: Univ. of Illinois Press, 1980 [1977]), 115, 202–203.

5. For a biographical account of Dunham's academic and dance training, as well as her

time with the New Deal programs, see Joyce Aschenbrenner, *Katherine Dunham: Dancing a Life* (Urbana: Univ. of Illinois Press, 2002), esp. chaps. 2–7. For Dunham's own accounts of her research travels in the Caribbean, see *Journey to Accompong* (New York: Holt, 1946), and *Island Possessed* (New York: Doubleday, 1969).

6. John Martin, *Ruth Page: An Intimate Biography* (New York: Dekker, 1977), 105–108.

7. "Backwater Blues" is most often associated with Bessie Smith, who composed it in 1926 with the assistance of the pianist James P. Johnson; "Grievin' Hearted Blues" is most closely linked with Gertrude "Ma" Rainey, who recorded it in 1927. For more on Piper's paintings, see Graham Lock, "Blues on the Brush: Rose Piper's *Blues and Negro Folk Songs* Paintings of the 1940s," *International Review of African American Art*, 22, no. 1 (2008): 18–29. For a detailed description of both the actual circumstances of Bessie Smith's death and its subsequent mythologization, see Chris Albertson, *Bessie*, rev. ed. (New Haven, Conn.: Yale Univ. Press, 2003), 255–267.

8. Evelyn Brooks Higginbotham, "African-American Women's History and the Metalanguages of Race," *Signs* 17, no. 2 (Winter 1992): 271–272; see also Kevin K. Gaines, *Uplifting the Race: Black Leadership, Politics, and Culture in the Twentieth Century*, 2nd ed. (Chapel Hill: Univ. of North Carolina Press, 1996).

9. Abby Arthur Johnson and Ronald Mayberry Johnson, *Propaganda and Aesthetics: The Literary Politics of African-American Magazines in the Twentieth Century* (Amherst: Univ. of Massachusetts Press, 1979), 32–63.

10. Eustace Gay, *Philadelphia Tribune*, February 12, 1927, quoted in Arnold Rampersad, *The Life of Langston Hughes*, vol. 1, *1902–1941: I, Too, Sing America* (New York: Oxford Univ. Press, 2002), 140.

11. For more on Baker's early career in New York and Paris, see Phyllis Rose, *Jazz Cleopatra: Josephine Baker in Her Time* (New York: Vintage, 1989), 56–64, 81–83, 97–101, 105–113.

12. Arthur Palmer Hudson, *Folksongs of Mississippi and Their Background* (Chapel Hill: Univ. of North Carolina Press, 1936), 189.

13. Ethel Waters, *His Eye Is on the Sparrow: An Autobiography*, with Charles Samuels (Garden City, N.Y.: Doubleday, 1951), chaps. 1–5; Donald Bogle, *Heat Wave: The Life and Career of Ethel Waters* (New York: HarperCollins, 2011), 3–21; James F. Wilson, *Bulldaggers, Pansies, and Chocolate Babies: Performance, Race, and the Sexuality in the Harlem Renaissance* (Ann Arbor: Univ. of Michigan Press, 2011), 132–135; David Krasner, *A Beautiful Pageant: African American Theatre, Drama, and Performance in the Harlem Renaissance, 1910–1927* (New York: Palgrave Macmillan, 2002), 70–71.

14. William Gardner Smith, "*Phylon* Profile, XXI: Ethel Waters," *Phylon* 11, no. 2 (1950): 115–116.

15. Randall Cherry, "Ethel Waters: 'Long, Lean, Lanky Mama,'" in *Nobody Knows Where the Blues Come From: Lyrics and History*, ed. Robert Springer (Jackson: Univ. of Mississippi Press, 2006), 266–268; Bogle, *Heat Wave*, 30–38; Wilson, *Bulldaggers, Pansies, and Chocolate Babies*, 135–138, 145–146; Waters, *Eye on the Sparrow*, 91–92.

16. Cherry, "Ethel Waters," 274.

17. Smith, "*Phylon* Profile," 116.

18. Krasner, *Beautiful Pageant*, 57, 72–77; Wilson, *Bulldaggers, Pansies, and Chocolate Babies*, 136–138, 145–148; Bogle, *Heat Wave*, 35–37.

19. Bogle, *Heat Wave*, 303–304.

20. Cherry, "Ethel Waters," 266–277. For a concise account of the crooning aesthetic, see Allison McCracken, *Real Men Don't Sing: Crooning in American Culture* (Durham, NC:

Duke Univ. Press, 2015), 75–78. On Carr as a blues crooner, see Elijah Wald, *Escaping the Delta: Robert Johnson and the Invention of the Blues* (New York: HarperCollins, 2004), 36–37.

21. Dudley McClure, "The Real Story of Frankie and Johnny," *Daring Detective Tabloid*, June 1935, 64, quoted in John R. David, "Frankie and Johnnie: The Trial of Frankie Baker," *Missouri Folklore Society Journal* 6 (1984): 8.

22. "Frankie Could Stand Song, but That Movie 'Done' Her Wrong," *St. Louis Globe Democrat*, February 13, 1942.

23. David, "Frankie and Johnnie," 5, 9.

24. McClure, "Real Story," 64, quoted in David, "Frankie and Johnnie," 8–9.

25. Edwin M. Bradley, *Unsung Hollywood Musicals of the Golden Era: 50 Overlooked Films and Their Stars, 1929–1939* (Jefferson, NC: McFarland, 2016), 186–190. The film was based on a play of the same title by John Kirkland, which was itself shut down by New York authorities shortly after its debut in 1930; see chapter 4, note 75.

26. *Frankie Baker v. Republic Pictures Corporation*, "Amended Petition for Damages," St. Louis Circuit Court, Civil Division Case No. 24125 (May 1939), 1–8, quoted in David, "Frankie and Johnnie," 9.

27. *St. Louis Globe Democrat*, February 20, 1942, quoted in David, "Frankie and Johnnie," 15.

28. "Frankie Baker Loses in Suit For $200,000," *St. Louis Star Times*, February 24, 1942.

29. McClure, "Real Story," 32, quoted in David, "Frankie and Johnnie," 5–6.

30. David, "Frankie and Johnnie," 6.

31. "Amid the Suffering," *St. Louis Post-Dispatch*, October 19, 1899, 16; Belden Kittredge [Vance Randolph], *The Truth about Frankie and Johnny, and Other Legendary Lovers Who Stalked across the American Scene* (Girard, Kans.: Halderman-Julius, 1945), 13–14; David, "Frankie and Johnnie," 7.

32. McClure, "Real Story," 33, quoted in David, "Frankie and Johnnie," 7; David, "Frankie and Johnnie," 10–12; Kittredge, *Truth about Frankie and Johnny*, 19–20.

33. McClure, "Real Story," 64, quoted in David, "Frankie and Johnnie," 7–8.

34. David, "Frankie and Johnnie," 10–12.

35. Lyrics reprinted in Angela Davis, *Blues Legacies and Black Feminism: Gertrude "Ma" Rainey, Bessie Smith, and Billie Holiday* (New York: Vintage, 1998), 204. "Black Eye Blues" was written by the legendary Thomas Dorsey.

36. Lyrics reprinted in Davis, *Blues Legacies*, 210. "Cell Bound Blues" was written by Rainey.

37. Paige A. McGinley, *Staging the Blues: From Tent Shows to Tourism* (Durham, NC: Duke Univ. Press, 2014), 44–45.

38. Danielle L. McGuire, *At the Dark End of the Street: Black Women, Rape, and Resistance; A New History of the Civil Rights Movement from Rosa Parks to the Rise of Black Power* (New York: Vintage, 2010).

39. "Frankie Loses Again," *St. Louis Post-Dispatch*, February 25, 1942.

40. One of the most significant works of scholarship on the movement of culture across categories remains Lawrence W. Levine, *Highbrow/Lowbrow: The Emergence of Cultural Hierarchy in America* (Cambridge, Mass.: Harvard Univ. Press, 1988).